Single People and Mass Housing in Germany, 1850–1930

Visual Cultures and German Contexts

Series Editors

Deborah Ascher Barnstone (University of Technology Sydney, Australia)
Thomas O. Haakenson (California College of the Arts, USA)

Visual Cultures and German Contexts publishes innovative research into visual culture in Germany, Switzerland and Austria, as well as in diasporic linguistic and cultural communities outside of these geographic, historical, and political borders.

The series invites scholarship by academics, curators, architects, artists, and designers across all media forms and time periods. It engages with traditional methods in visual culture analysis as well as inventive interdisciplinary approaches. It seeks to encourage a dialogue amongst scholars in traditional disciplines with those pursuing innovative interdisciplinary and intermedial research. Of particular interest are provocative perspectives on archival materials, original scholarship on emerging and established creative visual fields, investigations into time-based forms of aesthetic expression, and new readings of history through the lens of visual culture. The series offers a much-needed venue for expanding how we engage with the field of Visual Culture in general.

Proposals for monographs, edited volumes, and outstanding research studies are welcome, by established as well as emerging writers from a wide range of comparative, theoretical and methodological perspectives.

Advisory Board

Donna West Brett, University of Sydney, Australia
Charlotte Klonk, Humboldt Universität Berlin, Germany
Nina Lübbren, Anglia Ruskin University, UK
Maria Makela, California College of the Arts, USA
Patrizia C. McBride, Cornell University, USA
Rick McCormick, University of Minnesota, USA
Elizabeth Otto, University at Buffalo SUNY, USA
Kathryn Starkey, Stanford University, USA
Annette F. Timm, University of Calgary, Canada
James A. van Dyke, University of Missouri, USA

Titles in the Series

Bauhaus Bodies: Gender, Sexuality, and Body Culture in Modernism's Legendary Art School, edited by Elizabeth Otto and Patrick Rössler
Berlin Contemporary: Architecture and Politics after 1990, by Julia Walker
German Colonialism in Africa and its Legacies: Architecture, Art, Urbanism, and Visual Culture, edited by Itohan Osayimwese
Jeanne Mammen: Art Between Resistance and Conformity in Modern Germany, 1916–1950, by Camilla Smith
Material Modernity, edited by Deborah Ascher Barnstone and Maria Makela
Photofascism: Photography, Film, and Exhibition Culture in 1930s Germany and Italy, by Vanessa Rocco

Single People and Mass Housing in Germany, 1850–1930

(No)Home Away from Home

Erin Eckhold Sassin

BLOOMSBURY VISUAL ARTS
LONDON • NEW YORK • OXFORD • NEW DELHI • SYDNEY

BLOOMSBURY VISUAL ARTS
Bloomsbury Publishing Plc
50 Bedford Square, London, WC1B 3DP, UK
1385 Broadway, New York, NY 10018, USA
29 Earlsfort Terrace, Dublin 2, Ireland

BLOOMSBURY, BLOOMSBURY VISUAL ARTS and the Diana logo are trademarks of Bloomsbury Publishing Plc

First published in Great Britain 2020
Reprinted 2021
This paperback edition published 2023

Copyright © Erin Eckhold Sassin, 2023

Erin Eckhold Sassin has asserted her right under the Copyright, Designs and Patents Act, 1988, to be identified as Author of this work.

For legal purposes the Acknowledgments on p. xi constitute an extension of this copyright page.

Cover design by Maria Rajka
Cover image © John Heartfield, (detail) *Alle Fäuste zu einer geballt* (*All Fists Clenched as One*), Oct. 4, 1934; photomontage, rotogravure. © The Heartfield Community of Heirs / Artists Rights Society (ARS), New York / VG Bild-Kunst, Bonn 2018

All rights reserved. No part of this publication may be reproduced or transmitted in any form or by any means, electronic or mechanical, including photocopying, recording, or any information storage or retrieval system, without prior permission in writing from the publishers.

Bloomsbury Publishing Plc does not have any control over, or responsibility for, any third-party websites referred to or in this book. All internet addresses given in this book were correct at the time of going to press. The author and publisher regret any inconvenience caused if addresses have changed or sites have ceased to exist, but can accept no responsibility for any such changes.

Graham Foundation

This publication supported by a grant from the Graham Foundation for Advanced Studies in the Fine Arts.

A catalogue record for this book is available from the British Library.

Library of Congress Cataloging-in-Publication Data
Names: Sassin, Erin Eckhold, author.
Title: Single people and mass housing in Germany, 1850-1930: (No)home away from home / Erin Eckhold Sassin.
Description: New York: Bloomsbury Visual Arts, [2020] | Includes bibliographical references and index.
Identifiers: LCCN 2020035943 (print) | LCCN 2020035944 (ebook) | ISBN 9781501342745 (pdf) | ISBN 9781501342738 (epub) | ISBN 9781501342721 (hardback)
Subjects: LCSH: Housing policy–Germany–History–19th century. | Housing policy–Germany–History–20th century. | Single people–Housing–Germany–History–19th century. | Single people–Housing–Germany–History–20th century.
Classification: LCC HD7339.A3 (ebook) | LCC HD7339.A3 S265 2020 (print) | DDC 363.5/9652094309034–dc23
LC record available at https://lccn.loc.gov/2020035943

ISBN: HB: 978-1-5013-4272-1
PB: 978-1-3502-8278-0
ePDF: 978-1-5013-4274-5
eBook: 978-1-5013-4273-8

Series: Visual Cultures and German Contexts

Typeset by Deanta Global Publishing Services, Chennai, India
Printed and bound in Great Britain

To find out more about our authors and books visit www.bloomsbury.com and sign up for our newsletters.

Contents

List of Illustrations	vi
Acknowledgments	xi
Introduction: The Lodger Problem and the Crisis of the Modern Age	1
1 Adolph Kolping's Revolution: Catholicism, the Artisan Question, and Housing "Wild" Youth	23
2 Beyond the Company Town: Industrialists House the Roving Male	81
3 Making the Municipality a Home: Appropriate Luxury for All	127
4 The Woman Question and the Housing Question	201
Conclusion: Weimar Twilight and Continued Relevance	247
Bibliography	263
Index	287

Illustrations

Plates

1 Jacob Pallenberg's Arbeiterheim/Settlement, Cologne-Nippes (1905)
2 Jacob Pallenberg's Arbeiterheim/Settlement, Cologne-Nippes (1905)
3 Jacob Pallenberg's Arbeiterheim/Settlement, Cologne-Nippes (1905)
4 Jacob Pallenberg's Arbeiterheim/Settlement, Cologne-Nippes (1905)
5 Jacob Pallenberg's Arbeiterheim/Settlement, Cologne-Nippes (1905)
6 Jacob Pallenberg's Arbeiterheim/Settlement, Cologne-Nippes (1905)
7 Dankelmannstrasse 46–47 Ledigenheim, Berlin-Charlottenburg (1908)
8 Dankelmannstrasse 46–47 Ledigenheim, Berlin-Charlottenburg (1908)
9 Dankelmannstrasse 46–47 Ledigenheim (for men), Berlin-Charlottenburg (1908)
10 Alt Moabit 38 Ledigenheim, Berlin (1908)
11 Dankelmannstrasse 46–47 Ledigenheim (for men), Berlin-Charlottenburg (1908)
12 Alt Moabit 38 Ledigenheim, Berlin (1908)
13 Bergmannstrasse Ledigenheim, Munich (1927)
14 Hedwig Rüdiger Häuser, Berlin-Charlottenburg (1924–5)

Figures

1.1	Catholic Ledigenheim (also Gesellenhaus), Neuss am Rhein (1910)	35
1.2	Blücherstrasse 4–8 Catholic Ledigenheim (also Kolpinghaus), Düsseldorf (1909)	37
1.3	Blücherstrasse 4–8 Catholic Ledigenheim (also Kolpinghaus), Düsseldorf (1909)	38
1.4	St. Antoniushaus Catholic Ledigenheim, Dagobertstrasse 32, Cologne (1903/4)	40
1.5	Catholic Gesellenhaus/Ledigenheim, Neuss am Rhein (1910)	41

Illustrations vii

1.6	Catholic Ledigenheim (also Gesellenhospiz) on the Breitestrasse, Cologne (1852, expanded 1865)	42
1.7	St. Antoniushaus Catholic Ledigenheim, Dagobertstrasse 32, Cologne (1903/4)	43
1.8 (also 3.8)	Dankelmannstrasse 46–47 Ledigenheim, Berlin-Charlottenburg (1908)	44
1.9	Blücherstrasse 4–8 Catholic Ledigenheim (also Kolpinghaus), Düsseldorf (1909)	46
1.10	Catholic Ledigenheim, Marxloh-Bruchhausen (*c.* 1900)	47
1.11	Blücherstrasse 4–8 Catholic Ledigenheim (also Kolpinghaus), Düsseldorf (1909)	49
1.12	Ledigenheim (also Gesellenhospiz) on the Bitscherstrasse, Strasbourg (*c.* 1900)	51
1.13	Catholic Ledigenheim (also Gesellenhospiz) on the Breitestrasse, Cologne (1852, expanded 1865)	55
1.14	New Catholic Ledigenheim (also Gesellenhospiz) on the Breitestrasse, Cologne (1910)	58
1.15	Catholic Gesellenhaus/Ledigenheim, Neuss am Rhein (1910)	61
1.16	Blücherstrasse 4–8 Catholic Ledigenheim (also Kolpinghaus), Düsseldorf (1909)	62
1.17	St. Antoniushaus Catholic Ledigenheim, Dagobertstrasse 32, Cologne (1903/4)	63
1.18a–d	Suggested room arrangement and types of furnishings	66
1.19	Catholic Ledigenheim on the Spree, Berlin. View from the Spree River	70
2.1	*Schlafhaus* for unmarried miners of Royal Coal Mine von der Heydt near Saarbrücken (*c.* 1865)	85
2.2	Ledigenheim of the Bochumer Verein, Stahlhausen Settlement, Bochum (1872–4)	87
2.3	Ledigenheim of the Bochumer Verein, Stahlhausen Settlement, Bochum (1872–4)	89
2.4	Four-in-block family housing, Stahlhausen Settlement, Bochum (1872–4)	92
2.5	Plan of the Stahlhausen Settlement, Bochum (1872–4)	93
2.6	Plan of Krupp's Kronenberg Settlement, Essen (1872)	94
2.7a, b	Ledigenheim of the Bochumer Verein, Stahlhausen Settlement, Bochum (1872–4)	96

2.8	Plan of Krupp's Altenhof Settlement, Essen (1892)	100
2.9a–c	Jacob Pallenberg's Arbeiterheim/Settlement, Cologne-Nippes (1905)	105
2.10	Jacob Pallenberg's Arbeiterheim/Settlement, Cologne-Nippes (1905)	107
2.11a, b	Jacob Pallenberg's Arbeiterheim/Settlement, Cologne-Nippes (1905)	108
2.12	Jacob Pallenberg's Arbeiterheim/Settlement, Cologne-Nippes (1905)	109
2.13	Fürstengrube Settlement, Fürstengrube, Upper Silesia (1917)	111
2.14	Fürstengrube Schalfhaus/Ledigenheim, Fürstengrube, Upper Silesia (1917)	112
2.15	Fürstengrube Schalfhaus/Ledigenheim, Fürstengrube, Upper Silesia (1917)	113
3.1	Dankelmannstrasse 46–47 Ledigenheim, Berlin-Charlottenburg (1908)	140
3.2	Heusteigstrasse 45 Ledigenheim, Stuttgart (1890)	143
3.3	Eisenstrasse Ledigenheim, Düsseldorf (1910)	144
3.4a, b	Dankelmannstrasse 46–47 Ledigenheim, Berlin-Charlottenburg (1908)	146
3.5	Dankelmannstrasse 46–47 Ledigenheim, Berlin-Charlottenburg (1908)	147
3.6	Villa Strasse Ledigenheim, Stuttgart (1910)	148
3.7	Neue Schönhauserstrasse 13 Volkskaffeehaus und Speisegesellschaft, Berlin (1895)	151
3.8	Dankelmannstrasse 46–47 Ledigenheim, Berlin-Charlottenburg (1908)	154
3.9	Galluswarte Ledigenheim, Frankfurt am Main (1894)	158
3.10a, b	Dankelmannstrasse 46–47 Ledigenheim, Berlin-Charlottenburg (1908)	159
3.11	Kaiser Wilhelm Ledigenheim on the Weberplatz, Essen (1912–13)	160
3.12a, b	Rowton House in Newington Butts, London (1890s)	164
3.13	"Albergo Popolare," Milan (*c.* 1900)	165
3.14a, b	Villa Strasse Ledigenheim, Stuttgart (1910)	166
3.15	Dankelmannstrasse 46–47 Ledigenheim, Berlin-Charlottenburg (1908)	167

3.16a, b	Model bedroom and living room for a single person, exhibited at the *Ausstellung bemalter Wohnräme*, Würzburg (1911)	169
3.17	Waldenserstrasse 31 Ledigenheim, Berlin (1914)	173
3.18	Dankelmannstrasse 46–47 Ledigenheim, Berlin-Charlottenburg (1908)	174
3.19	Eisenstrasse Ledigenheim, Düsseldorf (1910/11)	175
3.20a–c	Rehoffstrasse and Herrengraben Ledigenheim, Hamburg (1910)	179
3.21	Dankelmannstrasse 46–47 Ledigenheim (for men), Berlin-Charlottenburg (1908)	181
3.22a–c	Kommunalen Zentrum Ledigenheim, Berlin-Weissensee (1911–14)	182
3.23	Siedlung Lindenhof Ledigenheim, Berlin-Schöneberg (1919)	185
3.24	Siedlung Lindenhof Ledigenheim, Berlin-Schöneberg (1919)	185
4.1	Alt Moabit 38 Ledigenheim, Berlin (1908)	203
4.2a, b	Dankelmannstrasse 46–47 Ledigenheim (for men), Berlin-Charlottenburg (1908)	208
4.3a, b	Lehrerinnenheim, Berlin-Pankow (1909)	211
4.4a, b	Alt Moabit 38 Ledigenheim, Berlin (1908)	212
4.5	Herberge für Fabrikarbeiterinnen, Ludwigstrasse 15, Stuttgart (1874)	214
4.6	Herberge für Fabrikarbeiterinnen, Ludwigstrasse 15, Stuttgart (1874)	215
4.7	Alt Moabit 38 Ledigenheim, Berlin (1908)	218
4.8a, b	Alt Moabit 38 Ledigenheim, Berlin (1908)	220
4.9 (also 3.4)	Dankelmannstrasse 46–47 Ledigenheim (for men), Berlin-Charlottenburg (1908)	221
4.10	Alt Moabit 38 Ledigenheim, Berlin (1908)	223
4.11	Alt Moabit 38 Ledigenheim, Berlin (1908)	224
4.12 (also 3.1)	Dankelmannstrasse 46–47 Ledigenheim (for men), Berlin-Charlottenburg (1908)	226
4.13a (also 3.11) and 4.13b	Kaiser Wilhelm Ledigenheim on the Weberplatz, Essen (1912–13) and the Ledigenheim for Women, Ulm (1907)	228

4.14	Arbeiterinnheim, Mannheim-Walddorf (*c.* 1905)	231
4.15	Lehrerinnenheim, Berlin-Pankow (1909)	233
5.1a, b	Bergmannstrasse Ledigenheim, Munich (1927)	249
5.2	Ledigenheim of the Werkbund Exhibition "Wohnung und Werkraum", Breslau (1929)	250
5.3	Hedwig Rüdiger Häuser, Berlin-Charlottenburg (1924–5)	251
5.4	Adikesallee, Frankfurt am Main (1928)	251
5.5	Ledigenwohnungen, Heimstatt Siedlung, Berlin-Mariendorf (1929/30)	252
5.6a, b	Ledigenwohnungen, Heimstatt Siedlung, Berlin-Mariendorf (1929/30)	253
5.7	Ledigenwohnung with vestibule, living room, and bath. Designed by Lily Reich for the exhibition, "Die Wohnung unserer Zeit" (Berlin, 1931)	256

Acknowledgments

This book could not have happened without the support and help of so many friends and colleagues along the way, dating back to my days as a doctoral candidate in the history of art and architecture in Providence, Rhode Island. Special thanks are due not only to the financial support of Brown University, the guidance of my adviser Dietrich Neumann and second reader Carol Poore but also (and especially) to the wonderful friends I made at Brown: Caitlin Bass, Divya Rao Heffley, and Emily Chase Morash—there is no way I could have managed graduate school and the academic job market without you.

I would also like to thank the German Department at Brown University for facilitating my research in the form of a generous fellowship at Humboldt Universität in Berlin, as well as the many librarians and archivists at numerous institutions who procured the most obscure German titles and images for me—from Brown to UMass Dartmouth, Connecticut College to Middlebury College, the Staatsarchiv in Berlin to the RWWA in Cologne, and the Essen Stadtsarchiv to the Canadian Centre for Architecture in Montreal. Feedback from countless colleagues at numerous institutions, conferences, and symposia have also greatly informed and improved my book.

I would be hugely remiss if I failed to mention the colleagues and friends who have made Middlebury, Vermont, a wonderful home from the moment I arrived on campus, not to mention their support of my book project. Eliza Garrison, Eddie Vazquez, Cynthia Packert, and Kirsten Hoving were incredibly generous in sharing their own book prospectuses, advising me on how to find and contact an editor, and even fielding questions on responding to reader reports—I owe you all a debt of gratitude. For sound advice and encouragement, I am also deeply thankful to Glenn Andres, Richard Saunders, Katy Smith Abbott, Sarah Rogers, Emmie Donadio, Pieter Broucke, Michaela Davico, and Carrie Anderson. Additionally, special thanks are due to Middlebury's wonderful German Department and my many students in art history and architectural studies—almost all of whom have been subjected to my fascination with housing, social reform, and Wilhelmine Germany.

This book was immeasurably improved by inclusion in the inaugural year of Middlebury College's Spotlight Program. A program supporting junior faculty working on their first books, my Spotlight event in April of 2017, which brought together Middlebury colleagues and scholars from outside institutions to provide substantive in-person feedback on my draft, was incredibly helpful in helping me recast and reframe my manuscript. Although I could not take every great suggestion on board, I know my book is vastly improved due to the diligence, thoughtfulness, and generosity of the many colleagues who took part: Abigail van Slyck, Esra Akcan, John Maciuika, Eliza Garrison, Katy Smith Abbott, Roman Graf, Florence Feiereisen, Sujata Moorti, Tamar Mayer, Charlotte Tate, and the Spotlight Program Steering Committee. Additionally, I want to thank my anonymous Bloomsbury reviewers and the trustees of the Graham Foundation for Advanced Studies in the Fine Arts, who found the value in my work and were generous in their feedback and support.

Abigail van Slyck and Despina Stratigakos have been indefatigable champions of my scholarship, and I am so grateful for the many letters of support they have written on my behalf—as well as their well-timed and always thoughtful advice. I would also like to thank Anne Donahue for her guidance on navigating the world of academic publishing at a critical time. Heartfelt thanks are due to my initial editor at Bloomsbury Academic, Margaret Michniewicz, who saw the potential in my project from our first meeting and helped place my book in Deborah Ascher Barnstone and Thomas Haakenson's excellent Visual Cultures and German Contexts series. For shepherding the book through the production process, I also owe a debt of gratitude to Bloomsbury's Barbara Cohen Bastos, Mohammed Raffi, April Peake, and Anita Iannacchione. A publication and presentation grant from the Graham Foundation for Advanced Studies in the Fine Arts and Middlebury College's generous subvention fund have further enabled my book to reflect the vision I had for it.

My sabbatical buddy Florence deserves her own paragraph—from checking my German footnotes to helping me come up with a title, not to mention encouraging me at every turn—she is a fantastic friend, who also happens to be a colleague and collaborator. How lucky I am to have someone I can talk about Berlin tenements with, while also drinking (lots of) coffee and chatting about kindergarten soccer.

Finally, my deepest thanks go to my family. My parents, John and Peggy Eckhold, have only ever encouraged me to do what I loved and have never made a secret of how proud they are of me. To my German family: Karin, Robert, Ben and Julia Schüller, Liesel and the late Herbert Stephan, thank you for four generations of family friendship. Your warm welcome makes every research trip a joy. I also want to thank Patrick and Jamie Eckhold, as well as Scott, Carrie,

Reed, and Duncan Eckhold, for wandering around Cologne and Berlin with me. I am so fortunate that my husband Mike signed up for life with an academic—delaying adulthood as long as we could (and eating Döner Kebab along with way) has been a blast. As a colleague and friend noted, this book is my third baby—and far longer in incubation than my two children. Cecilia and Jack, you make my life more fun than I thought possible. And lastly, but most importantly, I would like to thank my brother John—you were always my biggest cheerleader and a beautiful person. I miss you terribly.

Introduction

The Lodger Problem and the Crisis of the Modern Age

In the spring of 1900, a "festive play" authored by noted dramatist, stage designer, and critic Georg Fuchs appeared in the German arts and culture publication *Deutsche Kunst und Dekoration*.[1] Written in honor of the consecration of the Darmstadt Artists' Colony on the Mathildenhöhe, the ultimate aim of which was nothing less than the aesthetic and cultural renewal of German society, Fuchs's "Zur Weihe des Grundsteins," or "Consecration of the House," paid homage to the foundations of German society—enumerated as various social types, ranging from the builder to the great lord, the student to the artisan. In total, Fuchs's work featured ten representative societal types, one of whom was simply entitled *der Geselle*, translatable to *both* apprentice and single person.[2] Yet, as with the carefully constructed world of the Darmstadt colony—the brainchild of the Grand Duke of Hesse—Fuchs's society bore little relationship to the realities of life in the industrializing and urbanizing German Empire. His harmonious and integrated society was a preindustrial idyll featuring an artisan and a count, not an industrialist nor a laborer; beyond the borders of the colony on the Mathildenhöhe neither apprentices nor single people were cause for celebration. Far from the "foundations" of society, single people of both genders (and single apprentices in particular) were dangerously cast adrift.

In an echo of the early twenty-first century, when single men and women fill hastily built company towns in China, German authorities struggle with how to house single refugees, and even educated single people in established economies are priced out of founding their own households, the effects of industrialization and urbanization left their mark on their nineteenth- and early twentieth-century counterparts. Upon leaving (or being forced from) their childhood homes, only the most affluent single people in the young German Empire could afford to live on their own, and older models, such as an apprentice residing with his master, were often no longer available. Single people literally and figuratively did not fit into the new world that had been wrought, and it was not simply their single status that was troubling, but where and with whom they would live. Then, as now, they were the "canaries in the coalmine," bellwethers of a society dangerously in flux.

Early industry had relied upon a local workforce, but the Franco-Prussian War of 1870 and the founding of the German Empire under the auspices of Prussia in 1871 helped to spur intense industrialization, changing old traditions forever. Those seeking employment were forced to move to specific locations connected to the growth of industry, and where the existing housing stock could rarely accommodate them. Workers flocked to large urban centers, from transportation hubs (Berlin) to regions that were rich in natural resources (Upper Silesia, Saxony, the Saar, and the Ruhr). Population density increased in cities throughout the Reich, and Berlin—a city of approximately two million by 1900—grew to one of the largest and most densely populated cities in Europe.[3] The constant influx of workers and their families into rapidly industrializing areas resulted in unregulated, usually speculative, building in new industrial districts both within and on the outskirts of existing towns.[4] Typically, this housing stock was unhygienic, severely overcrowded, and, in the most extreme of cases, consisted only of "das Gewölbe unter dem Zinkofen" (the vault under the zinc oven) in a factory.[5]

This mass movement of the working class and resultant overcrowding not only made the suffering of the working poor more visible to the middle classes but also signified something more ominous, that industrialization was creating a permanent working class. Those who, even decades earlier, might have aspired to social and economic advancement saw their prospects dwindle as the nineteenth century closed. For many, being poor was no longer a stage of life, but had become a lifelong condition as the boundaries between social classes hardened. Even those on the fringes of the middle class—shopkeepers and master craftsmen, or old members of the preindustrial "middle estate" or *Mittelstand*—were newly in peril, far from immune from the dangers of economic degradation.[6] In particular, one financial or social miscalculation might cast a once-proud member of the Mittelstand into the working class with its attendant moral and physical dangers. Positioned as early as the 1870s as the inverse of middle-class conceptions of society, working-class life was purportedly beset by "overcrowding, violence, poverty, sickness, excessive drinking and untrammeled sexuality."[7] Working-class life had to be remade, or at the very least *controlled*, lest all of German society—and the newly formed German Empire—be contaminated.

Bourgeois observers quickly identified one practice associated with working-class life that they found greatly troubling, the taking in of overnight lodgers—

usually young men and sometimes women between eighteen and twenty-five years of age—by working-class families. As 20 percent of German households in 1905 took in lodgers, the majority of whom were households with children,[8] this was a matter that affected millions of families, as well as the single people with whom they lodged.[9] Prohibitively high rents meant that most members of the working class were largely tied to this practice, even though the margins were decidedly small and subletting further congested crowded apartments in the slum tenements colloquially referred to as "rental barracks" (*Mietskasernen*).[10] For example, a 1903 study found that *only* 17 percent of Berlin families could afford to rent lodgings of two rooms and a kitchen *without* taking in a lodger.[11] Lodgers exacerbated the already overcrowded conditions of working-class homes, but the moral danger these (mostly) young men posed to the German family was more troubling. Middle-class critics categorically dismissed lodgers as foreign objects in family life, classing them as "terrible dangers."[12]

Lodgers were blamed for—among other crimes—the spendthrift ways of working-class mothers, for the more cramped the apartment was, the more difficult it was for the housewife to economize in her household tasks, such as canning food and doing the washing at home.[13] Critics claimed that lodgers forced the housewife to purchase goods and services she could have produced or conducted at home, stretching her already meager resources. Lodgers were even cited as the reason working-class families lost their housing in difficult economic times, as the young men who made up the majority of lodgers were usually the first to lose their positions and thus could not pay their subletting landlords, who were dependent on this source of extra income to pay their own rent.[14] Finally, as "non-family elements," lodgers were not only a danger to the closeness of the family unit but also threatened the virtue of its daughters and the relationship between husband and wife.[15] In overcrowded housing where family members—even members of the opposite sex—were often forced to share a bedroom and even a bed, the specter of sexual impropriety loomed large. Contemporaries feared that unregulated lodging "contaminated" working-class girls as young as eleven or twelve,[16] and as related by John Kulczycki in his work on the mining communities of the Ruhr region, the mixture of tired husbands, younger wives, and even younger lodgers in a small apartment or even a single room—was a recipe for marital disaster.[17] Even if such instances were rare (and it is nearly impossible to ascertain how frequently abuse or infidelity occurred), the addition of an unrelated and unmarried individual served to heighten middle-class angst regarding the sexual proclivities and practices of the working class.

Looking more closely though, the concern about lodgers as a group, as well as their supposed threat to the family, was a smokescreen. Older forms of familial life, such as existed in urban and rural contexts and often accommodated lodgers—from the taking in of apprentices by a master artisan, or the housing of farm workers with the families for whom they worked—were rarely cause for concern. Only the improvised families typical of the urban working class under industrial capitalism were deeply problematic. The existence of a "lodger problem" thus indicated a deep unease with a rapidly shifting world—a discomfort with the modern age that sharpened and intensified as the nineteenth century came to a close. In a society already suspicious of the effects of industrialization and urbanization, the institution of marriage and the shelter of the familial home stood for permanence. Unmarried lodgers were doubly dangerous in that they both stood outside of the family and threatened it from within.

The plight of the unmarried individual in Germany had become a lightning rod—the illustration of the problems and possibilities of the modern age—in a society that held marriage and the familial home as "natural" and desirable,[18] a defense against pauperism and radicalism alike.[19] Even before the emergence of the German nation-state, nineteenth-century cultural critic Wilhelm Riehl positioned the German family as a replacement for one's *Heimat* (imprecisely translatable to hometown/land, with its powerful emotional ties and sense of belonging), such as might have been known in an earlier age.[20] To stand outside of the family fold was to be without a *home*, and possibly without a *homeland*—belonging to no one and nowhere. Unmoored from family and home, not quite adults, but certainly not children, single people were a danger to the stability of society and to the viability of the new German nation. If one could solve the "lodger problem," it was argued, one could save the German family and by extension, stabilize a nation marked by religious, regional, economic, political, and social divisions. Ultimately, the lodger crisis would be resolved by institutionalizing it, making the unintelligible legible to the middle classes.

My book combines a close reading of specific buildings with their architectural and symbolic relationship to the larger community, culture, and nation, tracing the evolution and larger meaning of Ledigenheime—purpose-built class- and gender-specific homes for unmarried people. Largely constructed from the middle of the nineteenth century through the first decades of the twentieth in what became the German Empire and then the Weimar Republic, the Ledigenheim building type was more than a transitional housing model mitigating the detrimental effects of rapid industrialization and urbanization on families and lodgers. What began as a capitalist and nationalist building type promulgating an enticing vision of self-determination within an increasingly stratified society had an impact that stretched well beyond the physical and temporal borders of the German Empire—ranging from municipal housekeeping efforts in the Atlantic world at the turn of the twentieth century to Soviet cooperative dwellings, from accommodations for guest workers in the Federal Republic of Germany during the 1950s–70s to the housing of single refugees in Germany today.

So, what was a Ledigenheim precisely, and why was it so important? It was quite literally a home (*Heim*) for single people (*Ledigen*), and yet a Ledigenheim was not a home in the conventional sense. Specifically developed to fight unregimented lodging in already overcrowded, working-class dwellings, and built in the hundreds,[21] Ledigenheime (plural) offered a hygienic and affordable housing option for unmarried men and women. Born of necessity, and primarily designed to serve residents for several months to several years (with the notable exception of middle-class single women, who were expected to remain more permanently), it became a recognizable architectural type, albeit one full of variety extending well beyond its original program. Loosely related to existing and new forms of mass housing in German-speaking Central Europe, as well as in the rest of Europe and the United States—from lodging and boarding houses, monasteries and convents to the YMCA, reformed tenements to Salvation Army hostels, and single occupancy hotels to Socialist People's Homes (*Volkshäuser*)—Ledigenheime were distinct in serving individuals en masse, rather than housing single people alongside families, and in being neither a form of charity nor overtly religious in nature. Supporters positioned the Ledigenheim as different from other mass-housing experiments: *the* antidote to general societal unrest *and* a bulwark against economic decline. They laid the foundation for the construction of a *new* form of mass housing by mounting a sophisticated public argument for engagement with the "social question," to which the Ledigenheim was proposed as a compelling solution—a progressive and reactionary manifestation of a divisive and disquieted age.

With the potential to be freeing and coercive, elevating and oppressive, a Ledigenheim functioned as a space between the public and private realms—approximating the warmth and amenities of the familial home while including public educational and cultural spaces. Although supporters were never under the illusion that a Ledigenheim was equivalent to the familial home, they all believed that they could come close to recreating the "natural" order through the construction of specialized housing for unmarried individuals. The typical Ledigenheim functioned as a third space, combining and existing between the public world and the private realm of the family, and typically housing upward of fifty residents. While a resident might possibly have a single or shared bedroom, the rest of the space was communal, generally including (but not usually limited to) a dining room, library, reception hall, and classrooms or studio workspaces. As the housing type was further developed in the first years of the twentieth century, many Ledigenheime came to play a role as a center of public life for the larger community—as contemporaneous British and American settlement houses did—for they increasingly housed public libraries and kitchens (*Volksbibliotheken* and *Volksküchen*), which partially offset the costs of their construction, but more importantly, bridged the gap between the private home and public sphere, decades before noted Modernist social housing experiments in the 1920s.

Although designers, architects, and theoreticians of the Modern Movement as it emerged in Europe in the 1920s were keen to draw a line between their efforts and those of nineteenth- and early twentieth-century aesthetic reformers, efforts they characterized as primitive and retrograde, the engagement of governmental and nongovernmental groups around the project of the Ledigenheim helped to set the stage for later Modernist efforts, particularly those related to the design of mass social housing in the Weimar Republic. Ledigenheime, however, were certainly not built on the physical or symbolic scale of these later efforts: disparate Ledigenheime were constructed by myriad interrelated and yet separate groups of aesthetic and social reformers—a far cry from the expansive housing settlements designed and overseen by identifiable players in postwar German architectural culture like Martin Wagner, Ernst May, or Walter Gropius.[22] evertheless, prewar design reformers shared with interwar designers, architects, planners, and critics the belief that the primary means to societal change was through the redesign of everyday life, and that a broad network of interrelated institutions and organizations, both governmental and private, was necessary to support the advancement of civil society. The intense organization, research, and design efforts enabling Weimar-era housing projects were presaged by the organizational and architectural intelligence devoted to Ledigenheime. Of course, the distinction here is that Modernist efforts in the Weimar Republic were at least publicly positioned as helping to advance a Socialist agenda, where prewar Ledigenheime were a means to *manage* capitalism by better supporting the physical and moral health of both residents and local families.

With a suspicion of the profane and boisterous, the benefactors of *most* Ledigenheime sought not only to physically remove residents from overcrowded and unhealthy dwellings but also to cleanse them of working-class practices and tastes. Reflecting the fears and priorities of their bourgeois supporters, these homes inculcated middle-class habits by introducing residents to *healthy* habits of consumption and by providing a *proper* education both formal and aesthetic, including exposure to "good" books, elevating programming, as well as simple, functional, and well-designed and furnished spaces.[23] That is, such Ledigenheime contributed to a seductive vision of *Bildung*, or as Susan Henderson has concisely defined, to the bourgeois "ideal of personal growth and self-fulfillment in the eventual service of societal development."[24] Ledigenheime were intended to be transformative places—akin to the museum in the nineteenth-century bourgeois imagination and housing settlements in the Weimar era—providing access to that which was both appropriate and aspirational, and standing in stark opposition to traditional (and typical) working-class habits and dwellings. The modernized neoclassical style chosen for the exterior of a typical Ledigenheim reflected the culture and taste of the educated middle classes (*Bildungsbürgertum*), even as proponents positioned it as universally applicable and desirable.[25]

However, the aspirational messaging of these homes appears to have been dangerously out of step with the reality facing most lower-middle-class or skilled working-class Ledigenheim residents. Ledigenheime typically included spaces and programming that concretely served residents' contemporary needs, from libraries to formal lectures, classrooms to instructional workshops, and yet the larger message was one that relied heavily on an outdated ideal of self-determination and social advancement dating to a nostalgia laden age of old-fashioned "estates" rather than social "classes," the era of thinkers and poets like Goethe and Schiller, rather than industrialists such as Krupp and Siemens. Much like the American myth of meritocracy, the overall project of the Ledigenheim was a form of inadvertent misdirection, leading residents and supporters alike to believe that upward mobility was still more possible than it was, and laying the blame for one's failure to rise not on the systemic inequities but firmly on the individual. Ledigenheime actually contributed to the cultural project of the hardening of class lines by cloaking the control of single men and women in the language of empowerment and drawing a sharp line around those who were deserving of help, and who were not.

The delusion of a Ledigenheim resident's agency had to be maintained, for he or she had an important role to play in the ultimate success of German capitalism and empire building. Quality housing for lower-middle-class or skilled working-class individuals, and artisans in particular, was positioned by supporters not only as a means to educate and elevate a resident's individual taste but also as a way to improve the overall quality of German design work. *Bildung* was never simply personal work, it was national work. Quality products resultant from a quality education (formal and aesthetic) would not only elevate the public taste, no small feat in itself, but ultimately enable German export goods to better compete with those from other industrialized nations—decades before architects, designers, bureaucrats, and industrialists formed the famed *Werkbund* with a nearly identical goal, and similarly sought to balance individuality with standardization (of products *and* men).[26] The project of the Ledigenheim was thus always intrinsically linked to the requirements of a globally competitive nation, the stakes of which only intensified as the twentieth century dawned.

Yet, in spite of its origins in and importance for what became the German Empire, the Ledigenheim should not—in fact, cannot—be uncoupled from numerous transnational social and architectural debates and movements of the nineteenth and early twentieth century—the subject of scholarly inquiry for decades. The relationship between the Ledigenheim and other attempts to come to terms with the detritus of the Industrial Revolution by supporting those members of society most vulnerable are explored throughout my book, moving from the last decades of the nineteenth century through the 1920s, from the Atlantic world to Eastern Europe, and from company towns to what Daphne Spain and Marta Gutman have termed "redemptive spaces" (such as settlement houses, public kitchens, and the YMCA).[27]

Dating from the 1870s, the discourse surrounding the provision of improved mass housing, proper nutrition, and healthy habits—of which the Ledigenheim was a central component—clarifies the close (and sometimes personal) connections between bourgeois reformers on both sides of the Atlantic. These reformers believed that their efforts on behalf of working people could help to close the chasm between the lower and middle classes, and even heal social divisions. While the specific methods differed by organization and individual, transatlantic reformers often sought to combat the "fateful, unsettled present" by sharing (upper) middle-class culture and values with the "poor,"[28] or to use the words of Henrietta Barrett, doyenne of London's famed settlement house, Toynbee Hall, to bring "the best to the lowest" in the true spirit of neighborliness.[29] Nearly all bourgeois reformers, including the supporters of Ledigenheime, were keen to position their activities not as charity but as philanthropy with the distinction that charity was a donation of money or resources ultimately disempowering to the recipient's sense of self, whereas philanthropy (purportedly) worked "for the benefit of (both) parties involved."[30] Reformers did not believe that they were buttressing undesirable lifestyles, but, instead, were helping those on the margins help themselves.

Stabilizing their relationship with the working classes, and perhaps turning them into allies, not only was a means to prevent massive social upheaval, even revolution but also might be a means to social reintegration that lay safely outside of the realm of politics. Again and again, supporters of both Ledigenheime and other reformist initiatives claimed that they and their projects were forging a middle way in a contentious and highly politicized age. As the German land and social reformer Adolf Damaschke proclaimed, the reformer did not stand for "Mammonism [nor] Communism, but instead social justice and personal freedom!"[31]

Related to how Ledigenheime and similar reformist efforts structured the narrative around social class, these homes conditioned the formation of gender identities and attempted to control—or at least give the appearance of control over—dangerous sexualities. This was pressing considering how social class, particularly exposure to working-class cultures and habits, was a threat to the middle-class conception of the proper way one's gender ought to be performed. Working-class men were typically seen by middle-class observers as dangerously hypermasculine, and working-class women seemed profoundly unfeminine, even exhibiting male traits and behaviors.[32] Just as one's class status is constantly exhibited through the consumption of goods and services, and through habits and behaviors, nineteenth and early twentieth-century observers realized, as Judith Butler and Gail Bederman have theorized, that an individual's gender identity is not fixed but has to be continually performed.[33] That is to say, lower-class German men and women with aspirations to a higher socioeconomic status had to be given the opportunity, even a physical place, to practice their gender in a way that was acceptable to the middle classes far from the nefarious influence of overnight lodgings in working-class homes.

And yet, a Ledigenheim could never be counted as a real home, simply by virtue of combining the public realm with the private realm.[34] According to nineteenth-century domestic ideology, a stark divide existed between the public world of business and civic life, and the private or domestic sphere, the supposed guardian of privacy, morality, and identity (although in practice this divide was hardly absolute, and Ledigenheime for working women actively challenged this notion). This division between public and private was also a gendered divide, one that German sociologist Ferdinand Tönnies used in his 1887 book *Gemeinschaft und Gesellschaft* to position what he termed community (*Gemeinschaft*) in opposition to society (*Gesellschaft*). This is to say, Tönnies associated community, or the preservation of "naturalness, feeling, intimacy and tradition," with local churches and the home—the domains of women.[35]

By contrast, Tönnies identified society as the public world that valued "abstract rationality" over "feeling"—a world dominated by men.[36] The middle-class and gendered construct Tönnies relied upon, the so-called ideology of separate spheres, problematized working-class homes for precisely this blending of the private and public, the threatening of natural community by unnatural society. Working-class families were destroying their homes by treating them as factories, bringing work (piecework or others' laundry) into a domain that was to be free of the taint of commerce, and more troubling, they were threatening the sanctity of their homes by housing overnight lodgers. Yet, even if it was headed by a morally suspect working-class woman, a working-class home still was a "home" worth defending.

By contrast, even while positioned as a means to save the working-class home and family by their defenders, Ledigenheime for men were doubly problematic. They not only included libraries and reading rooms that made them far more *public* than any working-class home but could also never be homes because the domestic realm itself was gendered female—even the notion of domesticity was strongly associated with women.[37] As a Ledigenheim was a primarily male homosocial space outside of the family fold, the buildings themselves *had* to be positioned by their supporters as substitutes for a wife or mother. Ultimately, Ledigenheime not only were charged with the task of domesticating social dissent by helping residents identify with the aesthetic and educational culture of their social betters but also with domesticating heterosexuality.

Ledigenheim supporters sought to smooth the rough edges of working-class and lower-middle-class manhood into something more palatable to bourgeois sensibilities by controlling and softening it. Ledigenheime were disciplinary apparatuses for the creation of what Michel Foucault termed "docile bodies," places where no detail was overlooked in the interest of moral, physical, and educational improvement, where the "smallest fragment of life" was subject to control that did not *necessarily* look or feel like discipline.[38] As Ledigenheime provided most of what a young man needed in house (with the key exception of work), there was no need for him to roam the streets in his free hours, "fill(ing) the streets with noise and disorder."[39] Tempted by what were certainly luxuries for an overnight lodger, from clean sheets to flush toilets, a resident could then frequent the Ledigenheim's reading room to educate or entertain himself, ply his trade in a drafting room, drink lemonade with his healthy but hearty dinner, and even rest and relax in his (ideally single) bedroom. In fact, everything that men or boys received in the marital or familial home for "free," from food and drink to tailoring, laundry, and cleaning services, was provided by the Ledigenheim, though at a cost. He need not run the risk of physical and moral corruption from threats as varied as loose women and Socialist agitators. A Ledigenheim resident would happily return "home" after the working day—just like a good bourgeois son or husband returning to the (supposedly) protective embrace of the domestic fold.

Ledigenheime certainly drew men in by providing many of the services associated with wives and mothers, though they were also charged with providing something less tangible—they were to domesticate the residents. Instead of only encountering women and children on the street or other public spaces, or worse yet, as an overnight lodger in a working-class apartment, at least some of a Ledigenheim resident's exposure to and interactions with women and children could be carefully calibrated and monitored, primarily through the inclusion of public kitchens and libraries that served not only residents but also the local community. Through this exposure, the resident was trained as to how he should behave, prepared for his future life as a sober and steady husband and father. As a further indication that Ledigenheime were intended to soften the rough edges of the residents, nearly every image circulated in support of the construction of these buildings show residents pursuing pastimes that were decidedly genteel, even "feminine." In stark contrast to popular imagery of male working-class life, residents were never depicted loafing around or engaged in acts requiring physical exertion (even as gymnasia and bowling alleys are clearly indicated on many building plans and appeared in written reports). By contrast, residents were nearly always photographed quietly reading or drawing, and occasionally in quiet conversation with one another.[40]

Lest one worry that this feminization might have negative consequences for a residents' assumed heterosexual status—that they might become *too* feminine—the Ledigenheim was also a means of managing sexual angst around nonnormative behaviors. The overt emphasis the supporters of every Ledigenheim variant placed on providing single bedrooms, and barring this, triple rooms, betrays their fear that male (and female) single-sex housing could easily encourage dangerous sexualities, particularly among those who— simply by being single—were already not performing their expected societal role.[41] Homosocial spaces might encourage homosexuality, but not if adequate oversight was maintained. A resident could be alone, but two residents could never be alone together. Ultimately, Ledigenheime for men were an apparatus of moral and social training, respectable spaces for the performance of a particular version of heterosexuality by men who had a role to play in success or failure of German society and the German nation.

Although the majority of Ledigenheime were constructed for men, a significant number were also built for women, generally in cities where potential residents were unable to reside with relatives. *(No) Home Away From Home* contends that Ledigenheime constructed for women working outside of the home were the most radical of all variants. They served as agents of change, and a symbol of the shifting social and economic landscape of German women at the turn of the century, one which would have been visible to all urbanities, not just potential residents.

The unmarried German woman (*alleinstehende Frau*) was a signifier of modernity—at once a victim, a threat, and a heroine—and the subject of nonfiction works by Karl Marx, Lily Braun, and August Bebel, and (even later) of fiction written by Arthur Schnitzer, Stefan Zwieg, and Irmgard Keun (among others).[42] She literally "stood alone" (*alleinstehend* translates both to "single" and to "standing alone"), as Catherine Dollard's "The Surplus Woman" and Patricia Mazon's work on German university women have explored.[43] The Ledigenheim helped to mitigate the difficult situation of an unmarried woman in the late nineteenth and early twentieth century by providing both community and a morally uncompromised housing option—one specifically tailored to a resident's social class. The highly differentiated and integrated spaces of the buildings—from semipublic dining rooms to semiprivate parlors—allowed unmarried women a safe and secure space within which they could learn to navigate the public world while retaining their respectability. These homes challenged traditional gender roles by (largely) mirroring the style and internal organization of buildings for men, forever breaking from the restrictive model of the convent or cloister, and most importantly, freeing residents from the burden of housework through the removal of the private kitchen. Even though they were not constructed to *directly* support nascent feminist advances, and certainly not radical feminism, these buildings were a drastic intervention in the urban fabric. They provided appropriate housing to those who could not otherwise afford housing commensurate with their social station, and enabled residents to lead lives that were far more open than most women, not only because of their employment outside of the home but also because of the socially progressive public-private nature of the building type.

In considering the relationship between housing, women, and agency at the turn of the century, *(No) Home* joins an expanding body of feminist scholarship problematizing traditional conceptions that middle-class women had little engagement with public life in the nineteenth and early twentieth century.[44] However, in challenging conventional thinking on the rigidity of "separate spheres" for men and women, scholars have often focused on the spaces of *middle class* or *elite* women. When scholarship has turned to working-class women, it has largely considered *married* women's encounters with tenements and public housing, rather than existing housing types that had long encouraged the cultivation of an unmarried life.[45] My work extends these discussions to examine the form and impact of class- and gender-specific housing on the agency of both unmarried working- *and* middle-class women.

Designed by both unknown craftsmen and renowned architects (including, among many others, Peter Behrens, Theodor Fischer, Bruno Taut, Hannes Meyer, and Hans Scharoun), Ledigenheime were constructed by nearly every powerful interest group in Germany from the middle of the nineteenth century to the third decade of the twentieth century, uniting secular and Catholic reformers, aesthetic reformers and civil servants, intellectuals and industrialists. Constructed for both unmarried men and women, few building types featured so prominently in the architectural discourse *and* the popular press for so long.

In order to uncover the greater meaning of the Ledigenheim, this book considers four key variants—those built by the Catholic Church, industrialists, secular reform organizations often allied with municipalities, and women's groups—over four main chapters, treating the decline of the building type in the 1920s and its extensive afterlife in an extended conclusion. As these variants emerged at different historical moments in reaction to different circumstances and even served different social classes and genders, Chapters 1 through 4 treat them separately, though the chapters remain tightly bound together in attending to the shared concerns of all Ledigenheim supporters. The main chapters proceed roughly chronologically, beginning with the emergence of Catholic Ledigenheime in the 1850s and ending with the rise of Ledigenheim for women at the turn of the twentieth century. In each case, *(No) Home* traces the development of each variant and the spatial experience of the residents, coupling the visual analysis of specific buildings and localities with intertextual analysis linking these buildings to larger German and transnational culture. This is to say, my book will explore numerous Ledigenheime, examining their relationship to the urban fabric and surrounding community, the style and massing employed by their designers, and the organization and types of spaces within—with individual chapters centered on those best representing the institutional and architectural values of their supporters. While the arrangement, scale, and decoration of residents' bedrooms remained a leitmotif in every subset of Ledigenheim, other spaces (or their lack) helped to confirm the particular aims (and biases) of their varied supporters. For example, the Catholic supporters of Ledigenheime privileged communal studio spaces though (rather surprisingly) not chapels, as befitting their emphasis on educating a community of young artisans. Alternately, employers typically designed buildings with up-to-date bathroom facilities, but few exterior or interior places for residents to gather in relative privacy or pursue further education, indicating that while curtailing the spread of disease was a concern, creating community was not. Reform Ledigenheime for men almost always included public kitchens, though not semiprivate kitchenettes, while contemporaneous Ledigenheime for women usually included public kitchens *and* semiprivate kitchenettes (alongside private or semiprivate parlors). The inclusion and positioning of certain spaces in buildings serving clientele of a near-identical social status—but different genders—underscore the continued importance of retaining *certain* gender-specific markers of domesticity, even in buildings that otherwise subverted gendered expectations.

Despite their differing architectural and institutional agendas, advocates of this building type—whether a coal baron in the Ruhr or a Liberal civil servant—were decidedly fluid and flexible in their thinking, constantly negotiating between progressive and conservative positions (provided socialism was held off and capitalism enabled). As mentioned in the previous paragraph, in Catholic Ledigenheime chapels were often omitted in favor of studio spaces, but also gymnasia, bowling alleys, and auditoria. While this should be read as acquiescence to the quotidian needs of young artisans in the face of dwindling social and economic prospects, it was not necessarily a bow to the pressures of secularization. Catholic Ledigenheime may have sometimes excluded chapels and always welcomed apprentices and journeymen craftsmen regardless of religious background, but the activities surrounding the construction and maintenance of this housing type also allowed supporters to nurture their identity as active and engaged Catholics in an age characterized by government-sanctioned anti-Catholic sentiment. Similarly, maintaining the future of the artisan estate through an ethical and applied education in a space perfectly geared to residents' needs did not mean that supporters wanted to turn their back on the industrial age. Instead, Catholic Ledigenheime sought to prepare residents for life within the modern national economy, but with a deep respect for local craft traditions and social structures.

The Ledigenheim as an architectural and social project was thus always a question of balance, a means not only to forge a middle way but also to pivot between positions often sharply opposed to each other. It was an attempt to reconcile tradition with modernity, the local with the national, the working classes with bourgeois reformers, and the needs of communities and families with unmarried lodgers. More improbably, supporters sought to standardize residents, situating them as rationalized *types*—the single apprentice, the single woman, the single man who makes less money, or more—all while putting the freethinking man (or woman) on a pedestal. Unfortunately, rationalized solutions and the rational individual do not necessarily coexist happily, a quandary that continues to bedevil the practice of architecture and the success of social housing in particular—leading us to the conclusion of *(No) Home*.

The final chapter of my work considers the decline of the Ledigenheim in the waning years of the 1920s, both as a recognizable architectural type and as a social cause linked to the discourse around mass housing, as well as the ultimate legacy of these homes. Occasionally constructed in the Weimar era by prominent figures on German architectural culture as integral components of mass housing Siedlungen (such as Bruno Taut's Lindenhof settlement [Berlin, 1918–21]), and model housing exhibitions supported by the Werkbund (e.g., Hans Scharoun's work for the *Wohnung und Werkraum* exhibition [Breslau, 1929]), Ledigenheime began to fade from the built environment and public consciousness, largely replaced by the rise of the studio apartment. Precisely as their early supporters foresaw, many existing Ledigenheim buildings also gained a new lease on life as hotels and student dormitories during the interwar years and (to a lesser degree) following the Second World War.

Yet, the building type also served as a precedent for far more radical critiques of societal norms. While the radical left at the turn of the century disavowed Ledigenheime as distinctly bourgeois in form and conception, the Ledigenheim building typology deeply informed numerous housing experiments in Czechoslovakia and Soviet Russia in the 1920s—designs challenging traditional conceptions of family life. While the German Ledigenheim was largely intended to strengthen the family—protecting the nuclear family from the dangers of unregulated lodging and creating a safe and secure substitute for the patriarchal home for residents—these experiments employed elements derived from the Ledigenheim to loosen familial bonds, creating a citizen whose family was the state.

After the Second World War, what began as a capitalist and nationalist type remained an apparatus of moral control, though now as an immigrant space positioned central to the reinvigoration of the West German economy—the so-called economic miracle, or *Wirtschaftswunder*. Like the nineteenth- and early twentieth-century Germans who were forced to travel far from home for work, Italian, Turkish, Yugoslav, and other "guestworkers" (*Gastarbeiter*) of the 1950s through the 1970s left their families to take jobs that German workers could or would not fill. As was the case a century before, they found themselves faced with overcrowded and substandard housing, a situation (partially) rectified by the erection of purpose-built mass housing and the occasional repurposing of prewar buildings. By 1962, nearly two-thirds of these guestworkers, 90 percent of whom were between eighteen and forty-five years of age, were living in single-sex communal hostels—Ledigenheime.[46]

Then, as now, housing is a way of imagining a nation, of distinguishing between who is *in*, and who is *out*, who deserves a place in an emerging economy, and who does not. So, is the model of the Ledigenheim appropriate now, given (re)current housing crises? How might the architectural and organizational intelligence devoted to the design and maintenance of Ledigenheime be leveraged in the interests of the general public, and single people in particular? What are the roles and limits of governmental activity, and where does this intersect with the maintenance, reconfiguration, or expansion of both civil society and the welfare state? In short, does a class- and gender-specific form of mass housing from the nineteenth century still have a place in the lives of individuals as varied as an American college graduate and a single refugee in Germany? What about the housing of an individual worker in a Chinese company town? While my work does not attempt to answer all these questions, I hope that the reader will bear them in mind as we consider a building type that was an architectural and social phenomenon in an age marked by innovation and reform—and in doing so, help to challenge the long established focus of housing and social reform scholarship, as well as public policy and discourse around housing, by broadening it to better consider the needs of *unmarried* men and women.[47]

Notes

1 Georg Fuchs, "Zur Weihe des Grundsteins: ein Festliches Spiel," *Deutsche Kunst und Dekoration* VI (April–September 1900): 357–65.
2 Fuchs, 363.
3 Between 1870 and 1910 the average population density of German cities rose exponentially (Anthony McElligott, *The German Urban Experience, 1900–1945* (London: Routledge, 2001), 68).
4 Walter Kuhn, *Siedlungsgeschichte Oberschlesiens* (Würzburg: Oberschlesischer Heimatverlag, 1954), 76 (Abbildung).
5 Kuhn, *Siedlungsgeschichte Oberschlesiens*, 246.
6 Carole Elizabeth Adams, *Women Clerks in Wilhelmine Germany: Issues of Class and Gender* (Cambridge: Cambridge University Press, 1988), 3.

Similarly, in her examination of the YMCA in the postbellum United States, Paula Lupkin reports that the boundary (in status and prospects) between employers and their lower-middle-class or middle-class clerks was hardening while the distinction between clerks and factory workers was diminishing (*Manhood Factories: The Making of Modern Urban Culture* (Minneapolis: University of Minnesota Press, 2010), 19).

7 McElligott, 66.
8 In 1890, of the Berlin households that took in overnight lodgers, 71.6 percent were households with children. The percentages for Essen and Frankfurt am Main in 1900 are even higher, with 73.5 percent for Essen and 85.8 percent for Frankfurt am Main (Lutz Niethammer, "Wie Wohnten die Arbeiter im Kaiserreich?" *Archiv für Sozialgeschichte* 16 (1979): 118).
9 *Allgemeine Rundschau* (1911): 263.
10 Margins were small to begin with, but factoring in increased household labor for the housewife (cleaning, use of utensils, simple washing) and expenses (providing coffee and rolls), margins grew even smaller (British Board of Trade, *Cost of Living in German Towns* (London: H.M. Stationary Office, 1910), 30).
11 British Board of Trade, 30.
12 *Reichsarbeitsblatt* (1913): 440.
13 R. Wiedfeldt, "Versammlungsbericht," in *Schlafstellenwesen und Ledigenheime: Vorbericht und Verhandlungen der 13. Konferenz der Zentralstelle für Arbeiter-Wohlfahrtseinrichtungen am 9. und 10. Mai in Leipzig* (Berlin: Schriften der Zentralstelle für Arbeiter-Wohlfahrtseinrichtungen, 1904), 122.
14 Wiedfeldt, 127.
15 "Non-family elements" does not quite capture the negative meaning of the original term used, "familienfremde Elemente" (Johannes Altenrath, *Das Schlafgängerwesen und seine Reform*, Diss. Halle 1907, 1–3, 28, in *Wohnalltag in Deutschland*, ed. Hans Teuteberg and Clemens Wischermann (Münster: F. Coppenrath Verlag, 1985), 317).
16 Otto von Leixner, *Soziale Briefe aus Berlin* (Berlin: F. Pfeilstücker, 1894), 124.
17 Georg Werner, *Ein Kumpel* (Berlin: Die Knappshaft, 1930), 67–8, quoted in John Kulczycki, *The Foreign Worker and the German Labor Movement* (Oxford: Berg, 1994), 32.
18 *Schlafstellenwesen und Ledigenheime: Vorbericht und Verhandlungen der 13. Konferenz der Zentralstelle für Arbeiter-Wohlfahrtseinrichtungen am 9. und 10. Mai in Leipzig* (Berlin: Schriften der Zentralstelle für Arbeiter-Wohlfahrtseinrichtungen, 1904), 156.
19 Mid-nineteenth-century German cultural critics Wilhelm Riehl and Constantin Franz claimed that the pauperization and revolutionary tendencies of factory workers could be combated by strengthening family ties (Ute Frevert, "The Civilizing Tendency of Hygiene: Working Class Women under Medical Control in Imperial Germany," in *German Women in the Nineteenth Century: A Social History*, ed. John C. Fout (New York: Holmes and Meier, 1984), 325).

20 Frevert, 325.

21 Records indicate that employers built 82 buildings between 1870 and 1918, and that by 1909 there existed 249 Ledigenheime built by Catholic authorities (Msgr. Dr. Schweitzer, *Hospize und Ledigenheime der kath. Gesellenvereine* (M. Gladbach: Volksvereins Verlag, 1911), 15). Regarding "free," or denominationally independent Ledigenheime, I was able to find published records from 1870 to 1918 that dealt in detail with and provided exact dates for only twenty-two buildings, though actual numbers were certainly higher. Similarly, records for Ledigenheime built for women were scarce, with only thirty-five built precisely datable within the period of 1870–1918, though certainly they were built in larger numbers.

22 Of course, not all social housing in the Weimar Republic was constructed by those identified with the Modern Movement, and the *Neues Bauen* specifically. Settlements were also built utilizing a more traditional architectural vocabulary, as advocated for by many members of the Stuttgart School and (later) the Block.

23 This was certainly not a tactic specific to German reformers, for as Lizabeth Cohen has revealed, turn-of-the-century American reformers similarly sought to redecorate the tenement apartments of recent immigrants to reflect middle-class tastes (Lizabeth A. Cohen, "Embellishing a Life of Labor: An Interpretation of the Material Culture of American Working Class Homes, 1885–1915," in *Common Places: Readings in American Vernacular Architecture*, ed. Dell Upton and John Michael Vlach (Athens, GA: University of Georgia Press, 1986), 261–80.

24 Susan R. Henderson, *Building Culture: Ernst May and the New Frankfurt Initiative, 1926–1931* (New York: Peter Lang, 2013), xvii–iii.

25 As Pierre Bourdieu formulated, an individual's aesthetic dispositions are tightly bound his social position, though the dominating class positions its tastes as most desirable and natural (*Distinction: A Social Critique of the Judgement of Taste* (Cambridge: Harvard University Press, 1979).

26 An extensive body of scholarly work deals with the cultural and national project of the *Deutscher Werkbund*, founded in Munich in 1907 by leading artists, architects, designers, and industrialists. Significant works that have aided my understanding of this organization and its far-reaching influence include John V. Maciuika, *Before the Bauhaus: Architecture, Politics, and the German State, 1890–1920* (Cambridge: Cambridge University Press, 2005); Frederic Schwartz, *The Werkbund: Design Theory and Mass Culture before the First World War* (New Haven: Yale University Press, 1996); Joan Campbell, *The German Werkbund: The Politics of Reform in the Applied Arts* (Princeton: Princeton University Press, 1978); Mark Jarzombek, "The Discourses of a Bourgeois Utopia, 1904–1908, and the Founding of the Werkbund," in *Imagining Modern German Culture, 1889–1910*, ed. Francoise Forster-Hahn (Washington: National Gallery of Art, 1996); Mark Jarzombek, "The Kunstgewerbe, the Werkbund, and the Aesthetics of Culture in the Wilhelmine Period," *The Journal of the Society of Architectural Historians* 53, no. 1 (March 1994): 7–19.

27 Daphne Spain, *How Women Saved the City* (Minneapolis: University of Minnesota Press, 2001); Marta Gutman, *A City for Children: Women, Architecture, and the Charitable Landscapes of Oakland, 1850–1950* (Chicago: University of Chicago Press, 2014).

28 Brett Fairbairn, "Self-Help and Philanthropy: The Emergence of Cooperatives in Britain, German, the United States, and Canada from the Mid-Nineteenth to Mid-Twentieth Century," in *Philanthropy, Patronage, and Civil Society: Experiences from Germany, Great Britain, and North America*, ed. Thomas Adam (Bloomington: Indiana University Press, 2004), 61.

29 Henrietta Barnett, *Canon Barnett: His Life, Work, and Friends*, Vol. 2 (London: John Murray, 1918), 51.

30 Susannah Morris, "Philanthropy in the Voluntary Housing Field in Nineteenth- and Early-Twentieth-Century London," in *Philanthropy, Patronage, and Civil Society: Experiences from Germany, Great Britain, and North America*, ed. Thomas Adam (Bloomington: Indiana University Press, 2004), 151.

31 Kevin Repp, *Reformers, Critics, and the Paths of German Modernity: Anti-Politics and the Search for Alternatives, 1890–1914* (Cambridge: Harvard University Press, 2000), 100.

32 Judith Walkowitz, *City of Dreadful Delight* (Chicago: University of Chicago Press, 1992), 34.

33 Judith Butler, *Gender Trouble: Feminism and the Subversion of Identity* (New York: Routledge, 1990); Gail Bederman, *Manliness and Civilization: A Cultural History of Gender and Race in the United States, 1880–1917* (Chicago: University of Chicago, 1995).

34 Elizabeth Collins Cromley's work on the rise of the New York apartment building in the nineteenth and early twentieth century and Paul Groth's book on the architectural arrangement and (male) residents of American single occupancy hotels similarly address the problematic status of mass housing in relationship to middle-class notions of privacy. In the American context, apartments, apartment hotels, and single occupancy hotels were too public to constitute a "real" home (Elizabeth Collins Cromley, *Alone Together: A History of New York's Early Apartments* (Ithaca: Cornell University Press, 1990); Paul Groth, *Living Downtown: The History of Residential Hotels in the United States* (Berkeley: University of California Press, 1994)).

35 Kenneth T. Barkin, "The Crisis of Modernity," in *Imagining German Culture, 1889–1910*, ed. Francoise Forster-Hahn (Washington: National Gallery of Art), 28.

36 Barkin, 28.

37 Numerous scholars have written on the nineteenth-century ideology of separate spheres and the related "cult of true womanhood," an ideal promoted in popular and proscriptive literature in both America and Europe that positioned (middle-class) married women (and mothers in particular) as domestic, secular saints who

bore physical and moral responsibility for the arrangement and running of the familial home.

A *very brief* survey of relevant literature is as follows: Barbara Welter, "The Cult of True Womanhood: 1820–1860," *American Quarterly* 18, no. 2 (Summer 1966): 151–74; Caroll Smith-Rosenberg, "The Female World of Love and Ritual," in *Disorderly Conduct: Visions of Gender in Nineteenth-Century America* (New York: Oxford, 1985); Gwendolyn Wright, "Victorian Suburbs and the Cult of Domesticity," in *Building the Dream: A Social History of Housing* (Cambridge: MIT Press, 1981); Dolores Hayden, "Catherine Beecher and the Politics of Housework," in *Women in American Architecture: A Historic and Contemporary Perspective*, ed. Susana Torre (New York: Whitney Library of Design, 1977), 40–9.

38 Michel Foucault, *Discipline and Punish*, trans. Alan Sheridan (New York: Vintage Books, 1995), 136–40, 215.

39 (Father) Adolf Kolping, *Der Gesellenverein: zur Beherzigung für Alle, die es mit dem wahren Volkswohl gut meinen* (Köln/Neuss: Schwann, 1849), 4.

40 Paula Lupkin's recent examination of the form and meaning of YMCA buildings for American manhood has shown that American masculinity was similarly dynamic and fluid, particularly from the mid-nineteenth century to early twentieth century, with YMCA boosters keen to show patrons engaged in both (masculine) physical activities (swimming, gymnastics) and (feminine) quiet and genteel pastimes (reading and chatting) (Paula Lupkin, *Manhood Factories: YMCA Architecture and the Making of Modern Urban Culture* (Minneapolis: University of Minnesota Press, 2010).

41 Judith Walkowitz has argued that concern over dangerous sexualities in the late nineteenth and early twentieth century had more to do with nonnormative gendered behaviors, "work, lifestyle, self-display, non-familial attachments," than actual sexual activity (Walkowitz, 6).

42 Translated titles are as follows: Marx, *Capital* (1867); Braun, *The Woman Question* (1901); Bebel, *Woman Under Socialism* (1904); Schnitzler, *Fräulein Else* (1924); Zweig, *Transformative Trance* (written 1931, posthumously published, 1982); Keun, *The Artificial Silk Girl* (1932).

43 Catherine Leota Dollard, *The Surplus Woman: Unmarried in Imperial Germany* (New York: Berghahn Books, 2009); Patricia Mazon, *Gender and the Modern Research University: The Admission of Women to German Higher Education, 1865–1914* (Palo Alto: Stanford University Press, 2003).

44 Dolores Hayden, *The Grand Domestic Revolution* (Cambridge, MA: MIT Press, 1982); Despina Stratigakos, *A Woman's Berlin: Building the Modern City* (Minneapolis: University of Minnesota Press, 2008);

Temma Balducci and Heather Belnap Jensen, eds., *Women, Femininity and Public Space in European Visual Culture, 1789–1914* (Burlington: Ashgate, 2014).

45 In particular, the social housing settlements of Frankfurt am Main and Berlin in the 1920s have been of great interest to feminist scholars. Mary Nolan, "'Housework

Made Easy': The Taylorized Housewife in Weimar Germany's Rationalized Economy," *Feminist Studies* 16, no. 3 (Autumn, 1990): 549–77; Susan R. Henderson, "Housing the Single Woman: The Frankfurt Experiment," *Journal of the Society of Architectural Historians* 68, no. 3 (2009): 358–77.

46 Ulrich Herbert, *A History of Foreign Labor in Germany, 1880–1980*, trans. William Templer (Ann Arbor: University of Michigan Press, 1990), 212, 218.

47 Key works include Barbara Miller Lane, *Architecture and Politics in Germany, 1918–1945* (Cambridge: Harvard University Press, 1968); Andrew Lees, *Cities, Sin, and Social Reform in Imperial Germany* (Ann Arbor: University of Michigan Press, 2002); Lynn F. Pearson, *The Architectural and Social History of Cooperative Living* (New York: St. Martin's Press, 1988); Daniel T. Rodgers, *Atlantic Crossings: Social Politics in a Progressive Age* (Cambridge: Harvard University Press, 1998); Nicolas Bullock and James Read, *The Movement for Housing Reform in Germany and France, 1840–1914* (Cambridge: Cambridge University Press, 1985); Eve Blau, *The Architecture of Red Vienna 1919–1934* (Cambridge: MIT Press, 1999).

1

Adolph Kolping's Revolution
Catholicism, the Artisan Question, and Housing "Wild" Youth

Located on the corner of Cologne's St. Apern Strasse and Helenenstrasse the *Kolping Jugendwohnen Köln-Mitte*, or Kolping Youth Home of Central Cologne, appears to be a typical mid-priced hotel, complete with single and double occupancy rooms ranging over six floors, a fitness center, and WiFi access. Instead, it offers residents not only a place to sleep and socialize but also "socio-educational support" and (a Catholic) community far from home—and stands on the exact site of the very first purpose-built Catholic residence for youth, the home of a movement that over 160 years before similarly promised the young men of Cologne "rooms with a future."[1] Predating and deeply informing later experiments by municipalities and secular groups,[2] as well as less ambitious efforts by other religious groups, the homes (alternately termed Gesellenheime, Kolpinghäuser, and Ledigenheime) built by the Verband katholischer Gesellenvereine (Organization of Catholic Journeymen's Associations) for a largely, though not exclusively, Catholic residency number among the earliest interventions in housing for single people,[3] and the first for apprentices and journeymen.[4]

The founding of this movement can be traced to a single figure and very specific set of circumstances. In 1851 the Catholic priest Adolph Kolping (1813, Kerpen-1865, Cologne) founded the Verband katholischer Gesellenvereine, or the Association of Catholic Organizations for Single People, "the oldest German social reform organization concerned with the working class."[5] He did so in response to concerns that artisans were losing both social and economic standing in industrializing Germany, (purportedly) leading to a decline in the quality of goods produced.[6] While the latter would have problematic economic ramifications for allied German design industries and their global competitiveness—a concern that sharpened in the last decade of the nineteenth century, spurring the creation and redesign of governmentally supported applied arts schools and eventually the formation of the German *Werkbund*—it was the dislocation of a previously important social group that was profoundly troubling to Kolping. Much as leading figures of the British Arts and Crafts movement, such as John Ruskin and William Morris, blamed the decline of working conditions, the quality of products, and the moral and physical poverty of individual workers on the alienating effects of industrial labor under capitalism, the decline of the German artisan as a group was shorthand for a larger issue, a profound discomfort with capitalist modernity and its effects.

Long before the consecration of the Darmstadt Artists' Colony and Georg Fuchs's celebration of his foundational role, the German artisan had played a significant and symbolic role in the public consciousness. Even in the eighteenth century he represented the ideal of Germanic self-sufficiency and hard work, leading Johann Wolfgang von Goethe to recommend state support for the education of arts, crafts, and trades practitioners as early as 1776.[7] In the middle of the nineteenth century, and in a society rapidly becoming unrecognizable, the artisan, as "producer, educator, *and* the head of a family," stood as the model for a fully integrated and healthy society.[8] By the beginning of the twentieth century, following the influence of the Arts and Crafts movement, the German economist Werner Sombart positioned the artisan, who united both technical and artistic skill, as a "model of the fully-developed, well-rounded personality," something increasingly rare in the industrial age.[9]

Yet, despite his symbolic appeal, the artisan was in dire peril from the beginning of industrialization, not least because the entire preindustrial artisan estate (*Handwerkerstand*), which had traditionally encompassed "small and large master artisans together with their journeymen and apprentices," was increasingly fractured.[10] As the numbers of journeymen and apprentices increased in comparison to master artisans over the first decades of the nineteenth century, opportunities for the formers' economic independence decreased, and more problematically, this overabundance absolved masters of the role they had traditionally played in the training, education, and housing of these young men.[11] This is to say, masters increasingly looked to their own needs, rather than those of their dependents, leading to a breakdown in solidarity among segments of the skilled crafts population.[12]

In addition, as early as the 1840s, Prussian politicians began to position the entire (albeit internally fractured) preindustrial artisan estate (*Handwerkerstand*) as endangered and increasingly susceptible to socialism and revolution.[13] This was particularly troubling, as the artisan estate was a key component of the middle estate (*Mittelstand*)—ultimately part of the emerging lower middle class or petit-bourgeoisie, at least according to Marx—and a means to hold both the bourgeoisie and the working class in check.[14] By the turn of the twentieth century, the decline of the previously proud, independent, and self-sufficient craftsman served as both symbol and warning. He was heralded as the exemplifying traditional German practices and values, while illustrating their failure to flourish in the modern age. While simultaneously providing a bulwark between the social classes in increasingly unstable times, he posed a threat to society and nation.[15]

Yet, the capacity of the artisan estate to "strengthen *or* break" society had been identified a half century before, and a potential—or at least partial—solution had been found.[16] In the 1840s, Roman Catholic Priest Adolph Kolping—who had himself been an apprentice in his youth—wrote that the main cause of the declining craft tradition, and relatedly, the status of the artisan, was directly attributable to the increasingly dire living conditions of the journeyman or apprentice.[17] Traditionally, a master artisan not only provided his journeymen and apprentices with a place of vocational training but also housed them and provided an education in the social and moral values of the artisan estate.[18] By the middle of the nineteenth century, these domestic habits were changing. As Donald Olsen has written, "masters no longer ate at the same kitchen table with their journeyman, and their children no longer shared a bed with their apprentices."[19] Social lines—symbolized by increasing physical distance—were beginning to harden, with dangerous consequences.

Without the direct and day-to-day oversight and guidance of their masters, Kolping feared the future of the artisan estate was becoming unmanageable, disrespectful, and irreligious.[20] In particular, Kolping identified one practice that both deeply troubled him and served as a potential site of intervention, the unregulated lodging of young artisans with working-class families (termed *Schlafstellenwesen*), and what he termed "wild" lodging in common lodging houses.[21] A description of the latter—from as late as 1908—is as follows:

> The subhuman lodgings were located in the basement near the bake house and served four individuals. The [room] is 3 meters high, 3 meters wide, and 5 meters long . . . there is one [very small] window in the room leading to the courtyard . . . the walls of the room are wet. There is no source of heat, nor is the room lit. The toilets are not located inside the building, but in the courtyard, and are in an unclean condition. The room is not lockable from either inside, nor outside . . . and many mice disturb the residents' sleep.[22]

Unfortunately, unregulated lodgings like those described above were a nearly unavoidable fact of life for the German apprentice or journeyman in the nineteenth and early twentieth centuries. Instead of the respectable surroundings of the master's home and the gentle guidance of his master in matters both professional and personal,[23] the future of the artisan estate was forced into a housing situation and social milieu far from respectable and home-like. The unregulated lodging house, or even worse, unregulated lodging with families, held the young man accountable to and cared for by no one, besides perhaps the barkeeper at his local pub (*Kneipe*) or tavern (*Wirtshaus*).[24]

Kolping posited that the miserable external circumstances of his life drove the young artisan to the pub and the street, exposing him to dangerous elements in society, with detrimental effects on his inner character.[25] Foreshadowing turn of the century cultural critics who blamed societal discord on the "rootless" nature of modern life (and the modern city in particular), Kolping claimed that artisans were "flit(ting) from one city to another," not simply in search of work but also because they had formed no lasting and significant attachments—neither to place, friends, master, nor larger social estate.[26] Like Otto von Bismarck in his 1849 speech to the Prussian Diet,[27] Kolping did not shy away from stating what he saw as the gravest threat to these young men, referring to the young artisan as a Proletarian in the making.[28] Both Bismarck and Kolping's fears were certainly not unfounded, as many journeymen had taken to referring to themselves as "workers" as opposed to "artisans."[29] While misdirected youth might well "fill(ing) the streets with noise and disorder" today,[30] the danger to society would only increase as they became men—unless they could be carefully redirected.[31]

A Safe Harbor

Decades before the creation of other "youth saving" movements, from German *Wandervogel* to American Boy Scouts, Kolping sought to rescue the most endangered members of the artisan estate by housing them in a building geared to their needs. A Ledigenheim not only offered a safe harbor to its youthful residents but also provided an ethical and applied education. While contemporaries commonly laid the blame for the "wildness" of apprentices and journeyman at the feet of their absentee masters,[32] Kolping recognized that this negligence stemmed from the impoverishment and diminishing prospects of the masters themselves and the increasing alienation of work life from home life under industrial capitalism—in German-speaking lands as elsewhere. As Josh

Tosh has written regarding the British context, even where the total separation of home and work was impossible, "traditional" households headed by farmers and artisans increasingly "dispensed with live-in laborers, replacing them with day laborers who boarded elsewhere. [Over the course of the nineteenth century] the home became a place for family only, with servants (when there) accommodated as discreetly as possible."[33]

By contrast, Kolping sought to reclaim a preindustrial unity of life, education, and community through the vehicle of the Ledigenheim—a modernized version of what a master artisans' home would have traditionally modeled. Unlike elite undertakings like the famed Darmstadt Artists' Colony, which sought to both facilitate a community of artists and forge "harmonious connections between art and life,"[34] Kolping's work did not reflect the short-lived and imagined world of a Grand Duke. Instead, his homes—built over three-quarters of a century—were an early and lasting solution to the profound alienation of artisans under advancing industrial capitalism. Kolping and his followers believed that Catholic Ledigenheime could loosely approximate the "natural" order in the modern "socioeconomic" realm,[35] providing both a place of education (writ large) and a "home" for those outside of the family circle.[36] Preparing residents for Catholic family values through *strictly* homosocial spaces—Ledigenheime were a means to manage the future of the artisan estate. As an apparatus of moral control positioned as a new version of tradition, they are also related to contemporaneous denominational efforts elsewhere, such as the American YMCA, which similarly sought to counteract the alienating effects of the modern age by serving the needs of young men.

Additionally, in the face of rising anti-clericalism and anti-Catholic sentiment in government circles, prejudices culminating in the Bismarkian *Kulturkampf*, Catholic Ledigenheime were a means by which this denominational group could support and gather with other Catholics, albeit under the auspices of social reform, without drawing the ire of the government. Although not so exclusive as to reject members of other Christian groups, even housing August Bebel, the future leader of German Social Democracy, in his youth,[37] Catholic Ledigenheime were specifically geared to the needs of Catholic artisans, and as such, the construction and continued support of these buildings were acceptable forms of activism for this minority population in the nineteenth and early twentieth centuries. Ultimately, Catholic Ledigenheime were simultaneously an integrated community of apprentices and journeymen addressing the destruction of networks of extended- and extra-familial support, from guilds to master-apprentice relationships, and an attempt to address a crisis of Catholicism that was, in the case of the Rhineland, a central component of Rhenish identity.

The pressing need for social and economic support among single men of the artisan estate, underscored by a religious and hierarchical framework ensuring economic success, resulted in the dramatic growth of Catholic Ledigenheime. What began in the late 1840s with the creation of "friendly and spacious" social spaces in rented rooms[38] continued with the purchase of the Lendersche Haus in Cologne and its conversion into a home for single artisans in 1852,[39] growing to 367 buildings housing 4,890 permanent residents by 1909, and a resource for over 90,348 members by 1911.[40]

The Development and Organization of the Verband katholischer Gesellenvereine

Kolping did not immediately undertake to found Ledigenheime, but instead realized that he would have to garner support from numerous Catholic groups and create an organizational framework for the project at hand. He founded the first *Gesellenverein*, an association composed of and serving the needs of young artisans, in Elberfeld in 1846/7, which was quickly followed by the Cologne Gesellenverein in May of 1849.[41] Soon after, Kolping purchased the "Lendersche Haus" on the Breite Strasse in Cologne—the site of the current *Kolping Jugendwohnen Köln-Mitte*—with a view to converting the building into a Ledigenheim.[42] While each Gesellenverein served, and was primarily composed of, apprentices and journeymen, it was headed by established community leaders—local clergy, master craftsmen, and interested notables, all of whom served on a guardian executive committee.[43] These men served as the public face of the association—attending regional meetings in Düsseldorf, Cologne, and Mainz,[44] and drawing upon their connections within the community to gain support for the construction of Ledigenheime.[45]

While one can note a significant local component, this was balanced by a larger organizational model—the centralized and hierarchical Roman Catholic Church. While local associations functioned at the level of the parish, these were oriented toward Diocesan seats,[46] and after 1858 all local associations were required to report to the larger "mother" organization (Verband katholischer Gesellenverein), centered under Kolping in Cologne.[47] This "mother" Gesellenverein served a quality-control function, ensuring that all Catholic Ledigenheime built retained some local autonomy, but also reflected the ultimate goals of the founder of the movement.

This was a necessity, for by the late 1850s the total number of Gesellenvereine had grown to 191, with 63,000 individual members (not necessarily residents).[48]

Most were located in urban areas, as it was expected that most young artisans would be drawn to the educational and training opportunities more readily available there.[49] While the cities and large towns of the Rhineland—the birthplace of the movement—and the neighboring Ruhr valley remained centers of Catholic Ledigenheim construction, building efforts quickly spread to other regions undergoing both rapid urbanization and industrialization, as well as where Catholicism had long been the dominant belief system and the Catholic clergy had historically wielded the greatest power, primarily the western and the southern regions of what would become the German Reich,[50] as well as neighboring Austro-Hungary.[51]

Strict rules, put in place by Kolping, and codified by his successors, governed the creation of these local Catholic organizations and their associated Ledigenheime, for as a later proponent put it, from the beginning, such a home "must support itself through the rents it collects."[52] For example, if one was to gain the official support of the Kolpinghaus organization for a construction project, local supporters had to prove the worthiness of their plans to an administrator higher placed in the administration, namely at the level of the diocese, rather than the parish. Supplicants were required to answer a number of questions regarding the future building, ranging from what would be provided to the residents to the financing and practicality of the building, even the availability and cost of the land upon which the Ledigenheim was to be built.[53] This questionnaire would then be submitted to the diocese-based leader of the organization, who either approved or rejected the project.[54] These regulations helped to determine if a building would be supported, and if so, where it was most feasible to position it.

The mother organization in Cologne also ensured that the clergy, or *Präsis* (lay-leader), retained a prominent position at every level within the organization. For example, the *Generalpräsis* in Cologne served as the head of all local organizations, the *Dioezesanpräsis* was responsible for leadership at the level of the diocese, and a *Präsis* was in charge of each individual Ledigenheim.[55] Clergymen were carefully positioned within the larger organization not only as a way to ensure unity in a rapidly expanding organization but also because Kolping saw them as "the right doctors to apply the right medicine."[56] Kolping believed that the clergy—and the local clergy in particular—already understood the proclivities and needs of the people they were to serve, and yet remained "more independent than anyone else in any other social station,"[57] something that I will revisit when considering rising tensions between the government in Berlin and the Catholic Church.

Above all, one cannot view Gesellenvereine and their resultant Ledigenheime in isolation, but as one element in a reimagining of the role of the Catholic Church (and the Catholic clergy) in the lives of the faithful. Kolping was able to gather his colleagues and garner a large level of support for his project relatively quickly because the 1850s and 1860s saw a reinvigoration of both monasticism and Catholic lay organizations, the majority of whose members were trying to find their way in a world stripped of old networks of organization and support.[58] Ledigenheime were part of a larger reinvigoration of Catholic life and a symbol of activism in the face of massive social changes, as well as rising tensions between Protestants and Catholics.

Decades before Otto von Bismarck's Kulturkampf of the 1870s and 1880s, which targeted "un-German" clerical and Polish influence in education, expelled mendicant monastic orders, and placed the state in charge of the appointment and education of Catholic priests, the Prussian government began to put pressure on their Catholic subjects, concentrating on the heavily Catholic Rhineland.[59] What came to be termed the Cologne Troubles (*Kölner Wirren*) was a heavy-handed attempt by the government in Berlin to undermine Catholic doctrine on marriages between Catholics and Protestants and the religious upbringing of any children resultant of such unions. Resulting in the imprisonment of the Archbishop of Cologne in 1837, the Cologne Troubles were taken as an attack by the state on Rhenish Catholic culture and institutions, and ultimately marked the beginning of a popularly driven religious revival.[60] This is to say, this revival—which united the clergy with laymen in a common cause—was both a form of protest and a means to affirm local and religious identities.

Rather than "counsel(ing) only prayer, forbearance and obedience,"[61] the supporters of what scholars have termed Popular Catholicism sought to cultivate a specifically Catholic identity while reforming lower-class popular culture, replacing what they perceived to be an ethos of "alcohol consumption and tavern life, dancing, playing cards, gambling, reading novels, foul language and sexual license" with one that valued sobriety, piety, and thrift.[62] In practice, this often took the form of reimagining and reconstituting older forms of (local) Catholic associational life, many of which had been dissolved or secularized during the Napoleonic period.[63] This is to say, the 1840s saw the revival or refounding of local associations marked by a decidedly cooperative spirit, none of which dealt exclusively with religious matters, but instead sought to support their members in numerous ways and to counteract, or at least curb, the excesses of both emerging industrialization and an overreaching and increasingly authoritarian state.

The most visible fruit of this rebirth of communal and fraternal organizations was the Cologne Cathedral, the completion of which was spearheaded by both a main civic organization (the *Zentral-Dombauverein*, founded in 1842) and numerous branch organizations. Supported by figures like the romantic German nationalist Joseph Görres and the Brothers Reichensperger, these *Dombauvereine* were not "narrowly based antiquarian societies," but a means to mobilize widespread (local) public support.[64] The cathedral and the organizations supporting its completion were thus the site of community and symbol of Catholic identity—on both a local and regional level—just as Kolping intended for his Gesellenvereine and associated Ledigenheime.[65]

More specifically, the sodality, a parish-based organization of lay Catholics born of the Counter-Reformation fervor of the sixteenth century,[66] was a direct precedent for Catholic Ledigenheime. Not only was the sodality revived in the decades before the birth of Kolping's organization (the 1850s–70s),[67] but the clergy also led sodalities in order to assure continuity and oversight.[68] Most significantly, sodalities sought to work with, rather than against, the social and demographic changes of mid-nineteenth-century Germany, advocating for regular meetings on Sunday afternoons or weekends, encouraging education, sobriety, and frugality,[69] and even maintaining meeting rooms and small private libraries.[70] Both before and after the construction of residential buildings, Catholic Gesellenvereine acted much like sodalities, from the prominent role of the local priest to an emphasis on sober behavior and educational access.[71] In fact, the Catholic clergy viewed membership in a Gesellenverein as an acceptable option for young men who did not want to join a sodality, or as a supplement to membership in one.[72]

Thus, the emergence of Catholic Ledigenheime in the middle of the nineteenth century is evidence of a reinvigoration of Catholic religious and associational life and an engagement with the "social question" well before the papal encyclicals of 1884 (*Humanum Genus*) and 1891 (*Rerum Novarum*).[73] While what would come to be known as Social Catholicism emphasized the inherent dignity of working people, making the case that all were worthy of dignified work and fair treatment, the construction of Catholic Ledigenheime was a concrete means to elevate and protect the future of the artisan estate while also maintaining local religious and cultural identities.

Ideal Residents, the Church, and the State

It was made perfectly clear by Catholic reformers that the Ledigenheime they supported were not intended for what Marx termed the *Lumpenproletariet* but for those who aspired to rise beyond their social station. As such, Catholic

Ledigenheime were "not only facilities for basic accommodation, but also homes for the community that support the professional ideals and aspirations of the residents."[74] As late as 1913, as it had been in the 1860s, the "cultural, spiritual, and professional education of their members" remained central to the Catholic Ledigenheim project.[75] Importantly, these three aspects of education were not and could not be easily divided from one another, as Kolping believed that supporting young men culturally, spiritually, and professionally during the "storm and stress period" of life was central to the maintenance of traditional practices and beliefs,[76] as well as a key component of maintaining social stability—a fact that was particularly important in the face of the perceived growth of "cultural *and* religious wildness" among youth.[77]

Despite the proliferation of Catholic associations in the 1840s and 1850s, Catholicism, and organized religion on the whole, was beginning to lose its grip on many lower-middle- and working-class men by the middle of the nineteenth century. Church attendance by both lower-class Catholic and Protestant men declined sharply from the 1850s, diving even more precipitously in the early years of empire, a trend that would intensify through the turn of the century.[78] In a survey of both skilled and unskilled working-class men in 1912, over 51 percent of respondents stated that they did not believe in God and no longer attended services. Only 12 percent stated that they did believe in God, even though the majority of respondents did not *officially* leave the Catholic Church, their Protestant denomination, or another religious community for a variety of reasons.[79]

In the case of artisans, this estrangement from religious practice not only indicated a perceived decline in piety but was more worrisome in that it also served as further illustration of the breakdown of the traditional relationship between masters and apprentices—a dereliction of duty by artisan masters, who had previously been responsible for at least modeling devout behavior, if not some formal religious instruction in addition to vocational training.[80] Most dangerous of all, at least in the eyes of Kolping and his followers, was the fact that secularization was strongly correlated with Social Democracy, a movement that the leadership of the Kolpingsverein termed "deceptive" and "egotistical" in 1870.[81] This was particularly pressing as the very group Kolping sought to aid, young artisans forced to travel from their hometowns for their training, had become a "vital source for the Social Democrats" in the latter half of the nineteenth century.[82] Thus, Catholic Ledigenheime were to counter secularization and its attendant evils by protecting apprentices from the "seduction" of "negative elements," and Socialist agitation in particular.[83] Kolpingsvereine even applied to tax breaks on the basis that their homes served as bulwarks against Social Democracy.[84] Ultimately, the supporters of Catholic Ledigenheime saw one of their most important goals as the conversion of Socialist elements in the artisan estate to serve both church and state.

This emphasis on serving both church and state is significant, as it indicates the delicacy of the position of the Kolpingsverein in the mid-nineteenth-century political landscape. Although the specific threat of the *Kulturkampf*, the anti-Catholic policies enacted by the prime minister of Prussia, Otto von Bismarck, only arose in the 1870s, twenty years after the Catholic Ledigenheim movement had begun, the government in Berlin had long been distrustful of all forms of Popular Catholicism, and after the Cologne Troubles, the sociopolitical activities of the Catholic clergy in particular. Not only were the Jesuits, who took their orders from Rome, problematic, with Protestant historian and government minister Heinrich von Sybel claiming Catholics constituted "a militarily organized corporation, which in Germany contains more than 30,000 agents sworn to absolute obedience,"[85] many government officials also believed "the (local Catholic) clergy had made common cause with the Democratic party" in the turmoil of 1848,[86] and lacked a "truly honest and warm devotion to the Prussian monarchy."[87] In particular, National Liberal member of parliament and noted political historian Heinrich Treitschke worried that universal suffrage would further mobilize Catholic dissent, "grant[ing] the powers of custom and stupidity to such an unfair superiority . . . [and constituting] . . . an invaluable weapon of the Jesuits."[88] Catholics were untrustworthy at best, traitorous at worst.

How then did the supporters of Catholic Ledigenheime mediate these commonly held (though perhaps unfounded) fears of political Catholicism and divided loyalties, all while helping to solve the "artisan question"?[89] First, seeking to calm fears of ultramontane influence, Ledigenheime were run with close ties to the parish within which they were constructed. Accordingly, the leader of each particular Ledigenheim was the local priest, a far less threatening and worrisome figure to Berlin than a member of a mendicant or missionary order,[90] and the "mother" Gesellenverein was based in the Rhineland, not in Rome.

Second, in opposition to the strict religiousness of Protestant homes for youth, religious duties in Catholic Ledigenheime were few, and a decidedly tolerant, even interconfessional, emphasis was the norm, not the exception.[91] Given their broader appeal, Kolping was exceedingly successful in obtaining support outside of Catholic circles, and the local Protestant community was commonly involved in both the construction and administration of Catholic Ledigenheime. This ranged from the signing of an 1854 petition to incorporate a Gesellenverein and Ledigenheim in Cologne by the "distinctly non-Catholic ... representatives of the Schaafhausen and Oppenheim banking houses,"[92] to Protestant notables serving on the board of directors of their local Catholic Ledigenheime.[93] Kolping's active courting of leading Rhineland Protestants even won over the provincial governor of the Rhineland, Hans von Kleist-Retzow, an arch-conservative Pietistic Protestant, generally distrustful of Rhineland Catholics.[94] This relationship-building between Catholics and Protestants for the benefit of the youthful artisan predated calls for interconfessional understanding and coalition building by Christian Socialists in order to counter the forces of Social Democracy and facilitate "the moral and material improvement of the working class by all legal means" by nearly half a century.[95]

Kolping also carefully positioned his project as very much in line with official government attitudes to democratic programs and ideals, terming the secular and democratic press the "bad press," characterizing it as both "irreligious" and, "in the end, revolutionary."[96] While this active animosity to both socialism and democracy was largely based on fears of its impact on the piety and cultural identity of the artisan estate, it also placed the *Verband* as an enemy of the enemies of the state, and thus the friend of the government in Berlin. As Kolping's organization sought to find a place in the contentious political ground of nineteenth- and early twentieth-century Germany, its leadership continually and actively professed its disinterest in politics with statements such as "the Association of Gesellenvereine avoids politics and all that goes along with politics"[97] and "all things brashly political must be shut out."[98]

However, a lack of (political) party affiliation certainly did not mean that Kolping's organization was apolitical. Public claims by the organization's leadership that they sought to "serve both church and state in our own way" can certainly be construed as a political statement,[99] even if this was not engagement in party politics. This is also telling as it indicates that the organization's members felt that their allegiances needed to be made clear, something that would not have been necessary had there been no question of Catholic loyalty to the state. Certainly, the rising threat of and lasting wounds inflicted by the Bismarckian *Kulturkampf* on Catholicism in Germany cannot be discounted when considering the remarks of the Kolpingsverein's leadership—statements that remained remarkably unchanged over nearly three-quarters of a century.

From the passage of a school inspection law targeting the Catholic clergy to the expulsion of Jesuits, Redeptorists, and Laraists from the German Empire in 1872 alone, the Kulturkampf sought to curb the power of the Catholic Church—to nullify what the government in Berlin saw as an existential threat to the new empire.[100] Although no legislation was passed that explicitly targeted Kolping's successors or Catholic Ledigenheime during the Kulturkampf,[101] there was nevertheless a *relative* lull in the active building of Ledigenheime.[102] Had the leadership of the Kolpingsverein not tread as carefully around the subject of political loyalties and continually emphasized local and regional lay participation, the organization would not have been allowed to exist. In fact, not only did it emerge from the 1870s and 1880s but the 1890s and early 1900s saw a sharp uptick in construction efforts marked by the hiring of increasingly high-profile architects—in 1907 no less than Theodor Fischer, Richard Reimerschmid, Paul Schultze-Naumburg, and Peter Behrens, all leading figures in German architectural culture, participated in the open competition to design a new Ledigenheim for the Rhineland city of Neuss (Figure 1.1).[103] While such growth and increasing visibility in the architectural community corresponds to the emergence of a new source of competition, secular municipally backed Ledigenheime (the subject of Chapter 3), as well as increasing governmental interest in the plight of artisans and involvement in their education, it also fits with the resurgence of numerous Catholic organizations in the wake of the Kulturkampf.

As Helmut Walser-Smith put it, "the experience of persecution and resistance created the conditions for the formation of a Catholic community that transcended, at least in part, differences of class and status."[104] Catholic Ledigenheime had always been vehicles to facilitate closer relationships between local notables, master artisans, journeymen, and apprentices. In the years following the Kulturkampf, when the other ties that bound these groups

Figure 1.1 Catholic Ledigenheim (also Gesellenhaus), Neuss am Rhein (1910). Street Façade, oriented toward the southeast.

Source: Msgr. Schweitzer, *Hospize und Ledigenheime der kath. Gesellenvereine* (M. Gladbach: Volksvereins Verlag, 1911), 75.

together were becoming increasingly frayed, Catholicism continued to be employed and referred to as the "binding material" of a Ledigenheim.[105] In fact, Catholic reformers took care to distinguish their creations from all other Ledigenheim variants by stressing their use of religion as a means to bring disparate demographic groups together. They explicitly stated that secular homes could never function as "second family home[s],"[106] for they were missing a key component—they had no "larger [social and religious] goals."[107]

Yet, despite this positioning of Catholic homes as superior to secular variants, supporting and encouraging an individual's *personal* piety was always less important than facilitating his identification as a Catholic member of the artisan estate—a resident's religious identity was *always* a secondary consideration to his status as an artisan. Adolph Kolping's proclamation that "religion and work is the golden foundation of the people"[108] is not a terribly inaccurate representation of his views, but his word order is faulty. In Catholic Ledigenheime, emphasis was placed on the encouragement of meaningful work (and the formal and cultural education this entailed), rather than the practice of religion per se. (Even more confusingly, Kolping's quote was emblazoned on the wall of Cologne's St. Antoniushaus's billiard room, a place of neither work nor piety.) In fact, the supporters of Catholic Ledigenheime had a difficult time formulating what would help to create a "Catholic-Christian" home, and what specifically constituted a Christian "tone," beyond "protecting and car[ing] for everything that strengthens the bond to the church, the holy community of belief."[109]

Instead, moral danger lurked *outside* a Catholic Ledigenheim. For example, Ledigenheim apologist and Stuttgart civil servant *Oberregierungsrat* Falch wrote in 1904, "a Christian home . . . must provide protection from everything that is alien to the church . . . those who think and believe differently, if not *avoided and shut out*, can endanger it."[110] Yet, Falch did not explain how—with the exception of restricting access and house rules—to keep un-Christian forces at bay, and who these forces actually were. Considering the Kolping organization's long-standing and vocal antipathy toward Social Democracy, Falch was almost certainly referring to this avowed enemy of both the Catholic Church and the state, and an easily grasped symbol of the unmooring of sociocultural traditions—the dangers of modernity writ large.

The provision of physical spaces for religious practice—or their lack—*inside* Catholic homes reflects this lack of clarity and indicates that supporting the spiritual growth of their members was not the central priority. Considering that some chapels were constructed (Cologne Breitestrasse, Cologne St. Antoniushaus, Düsseldorf, Strasbourg), this was not a decision taken in reaction to anti-Catholic sentiment, but rather an acknowledgment that community and education—broadly construed—took precedence over more narrow conceptions of what Catholic religious practice entailed. As such, rooms reserved for religious services or prayer were *never* lavished with the same amount of attention or given as much physical space as other aids to social and cultural elevation. Across the board, drafting rooms, libraries, and even gymnasia or bowling alleys took precedence over chapels. For example, the plans of the Kolpinghaus Düsseldorf (1909) show that while a chapel (Kapelle) was located on the second floor in close proximity to residents' bedrooms and across from the larger of two primary stairwells, it and the attached sacristy were only slightly larger than the triple bedroom it directly abutted, and were lit by only four small windows (Figure 1.2). By contrast, the third floor drafting room (Zeichensaal)—used by painters and for day courses—was 143 square meters, about six times the size of a triple room, and at least five times as large as the chapel and sacristy (Figure 1.3). Not only was the space larger, but its placement was also more carefully considered to maximize both quiet and natural light. The rectangular

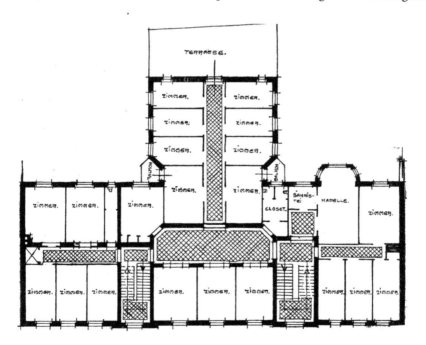

Figure 1.2 Blücherstrasse 4–8 Catholic Ledigenheim (also Kolpinghaus), Düsseldorf (1909). Plan of the first upper floor. Note the location of the chapel (Kapelle) and attached sacristy.

Source: Msgr. Schweitzer, *Hospize und Ledigenheime der kath. Gesellenvereine* (M. Gladbach: Volksvereins Verlag, 1911), 71.

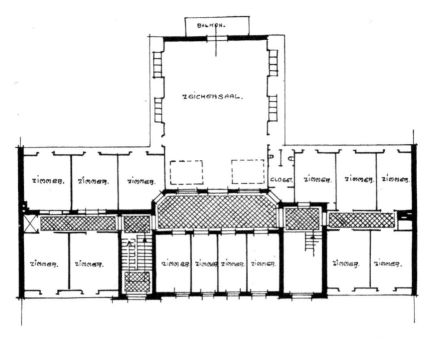

Figure 1.3 Blücherstrasse 4–8 Catholic Ledigenheim (also Kolpinghaus), Düsseldorf (1909). Plan of the third floor. Note the location of the drafting room, labeled Zeichensaal.
Source: Msgr. Schweitzer, *Hospize und Ledigenheime der kath. Gesellenvereine* (M. Gladbach: Volksvereins Verlag, 1911), 72.

room was extruded out from the mass of the building so that only one of its four walls ran the entire length of the widest section of the main hallway connecting both stairwells. This meant that as access was only provided from this hallway and party walls were minimized, quiet was maximized, and also that two of the walls could be ringed with windows and a balcony placed on the wall opposite the entrance. As if this did not provide enough natural light and ventilation, two skylights were situated above what would have been the darkest corners of the room—those penetrating the body of the building near the entrances.[111] Yet, as the Düsseldorf building included a chapel (even if it was less than optimally positioned), the home was still better appointed than many Ledigenheime, for often a dining hall or gathering space (sometimes referred to as a club room) was simply modified to accommodate religious services.[112]

Unsurprisingly, Catholic Ledigenheime failed to stem the tide of secularism among their residents. After all, the support of personal piety and religious devotion had never been the ultimate aim. Instead, organized religion *complemented* a resident's greater cultural education—it was a part of the larger "educational method" employed to counteract the dangers of modern life, those capable of "destroying the life of the soul."[113] More to the point, the creation of a greater Catholic family home—modeled on that of a devout and benevolent master artisan—rather than the observation of Catholic ritual was central.

Yet, while emulating the idealized master artisan's home, one marked by "devoutness, obedience, self-discipline, honesty, frugality,"[114] the proponents of Catholic Ledigenheime added another reference point, one which is reflected in the programmatic, aesthetic, and stylistic choices they made. This was the bourgeois ideal of *Bildung*, or self-cultivation and advancement. An indicator of an individual's "social and cultural maturity,"[115] Bildung could be cultivated by both formal education and activity in public voluntary associations.[116] Its pursuit suggested the specific class values of the rising middle classes, and in particular, the dominant value system of Liberalism.[117] Catholic Ledigenheime attempted to marry what was most appealing of these two completing value systems—the traditional belief structures and community of the master artisan and the individualistic values of the middle classes were cast as the residents' salvation, not God.

A Multitude of Spaces

What then were the spaces and programming that would aid the resident in developing his mental abilities and cultural awareness, confirming his identity as a member of the artisan estate, and marking him as different from the average worker?[118] The typical Catholic Ledigenheim, beginning in the 1860s and continuing through to the outbreak of the First World War, contained a multitude of spaces intended to aid the residents' physical, moral, and mental well-being, ultimately molding them into sober and respectable members of society, and ultimately, junior partners in the revival of German craftwork. To this end, the Catholic journal *Concordia* noted that three types of rooms were necessary in a Catholic Ledigenheim: "Clubrooms for education and socializing [including dining rooms], guest room accommodations for those travelling through and rooms for permanent accommodation."[119]

As previously mentioned, spaces dedicated to the express practice of religion were not listed as necessary components on their own, but rather were folded into the category of "clubroom," of which the most important was the Ledigenheim dining hall. Doubling as chapels and lecture halls in smaller buildings, dining halls were generally the largest spaces in these homes and the most easily accessible from the street. For example, after entering the vestibule of Cologne's St. Antonius house, the visitor was funneled into the dining hall, which also served as the primary circulation space on the ground floor, and was not only the largest room but the only means to access other recreational spaces—the courtyard, billiard room, and reading room (Figure 1.4). While the Neuss Ledigenheim included a small dining room tucked into the northeastern corner of the building, close to both the stairwell and entrance vestibule, the small and great halls—the latter of which performed triple duty as gathering hall, dining hall, and theater—were both on axis with the primary street entrance (Figure 1.5). In fact, even before he opened the door, the visitor could see through the building, from the vestibule to the open courtyard through to the small hall, and finally to the great hall.

Above all, dining halls were the primary place where reformers sought to foster a respectable and 'sober'—in both senses of the word—community. Hard liquor was prohibited and alcohol consumption was strictly limited. Nearly six-sevenths of all beverages consumed in 1900 were nonalcoholic, with beer

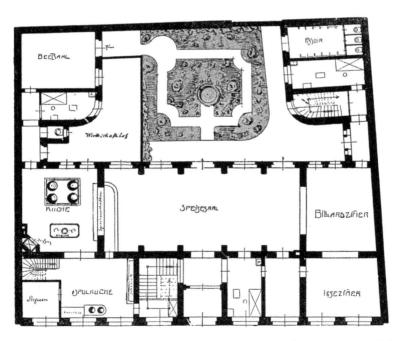

Figure 1.4 St. Antoniushaus Catholic Ledigenheim, Dagobertstrasse 32, Cologne (1903/4). Plan of the ground floor. Note the locations of the dining hall (Speisesaal), billiard room (Billiardzimmer), and reading room (Lesezimmer).

Source: Msgr. Schweitzer, *Hospize und Ledigenheime der kath. Gesellenvereine* (M. Gladbach: Volksvereins Verlag, 1911), 55.

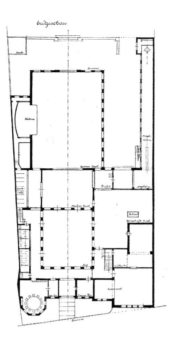

Figure 1.5 Catholic Gesellenhaus/Ledigenheim, Neuss am Rhein (1910). Plan of the ground floor. Note the locations of the courtyard (Hof), small hall (kleiner Saal) and great hall (grosser Saal).
Source: Msgr. Schweitzer, *Hospize und Ledigenheime der kath. Gesellenvereine* (M. Gladbach: Volksvereins Verlag, 1911), 78.

consumption constituting the remainder.[120] Sobriety, or at least moderation, was further encouraged by the fact that *nonresident members* of the Verband Katholischer Gesellenvereine, including master artisans and local notables (Protestant and Catholic alike), frequented Ledigenheim dining halls, either as fellow diners or to attend lectures—even as the general public was excluded.[121]

In a nod to the requirements of these esteemed visitors, the decoration of these large spaces was decidedly lavish. The dining hall of the first Cologne Ledigenheim on the Breitestrasse (1865) was a dramatic double-height space that not only featured stained-glass lancet windows and a hammer-beamed ceiling but was also ringed on three sides by a wooden gallery—medievalizing treatment consistent with the home's gothic-revival exterior (Figure 1.6). Nearly four decades later, the dining hall of the St. Antoniushaus of Cologne (1900), which could accommodate up to 120 men, was similarly marked by materials, detailing, and surface treatments that bespoke wealth—at least according to its proponents, who proudly boasted of its beautiful imitation mahogany wainscoting and elegant blue mosaic tilework (Figure 1.7).[122] Additionally, the

Figure 1.6 Catholic Ledigenheim (also Gesellenhospiz) on the Breitestrasse, Cologne (1852, expanded 1865). View of the gathering/dining hall.
Source: Msgr. Schweitzer, *Hospize und Ledigenheime der kath. Gesellenvereine* (M. Gladbach: Volksvereins Verlag, 1911), 16.

dining room featured three busts positioned along the walls (only two of which are visible in the photograph): the Kaiser; the (current) head of the *Verband*, Professor Cauer; and the pope.[123] Beyond serving as a not-so-subtle assertion that in such homes Catholic identity was balanced by patriotism and loyalty to the state, such decorative details also served as a reminder of the importance of the traditional artisanal crafts in creating pleasant and elevating surroundings. Constructed ten years later, the Neuss Ledigenheim's large gathering hall/dining room employed an even more formal language to enliven and lend structure to the room, from the columns that divided the space from the smaller hall to the elegant articulation of the walls through rectilinear geometric patterning, even a recessed ceiling featuring a two-dimensional approximation of ceiling coffers including an innovative integrated lighting system that provided even and diffuse light.[124]

Such attention to detail stands in contrast to the aesthetic treatment of the typical municipal Ledigenheim's dining hall, which similarly served the needs of its residents *and* those of the larger community. Conceived of as "public

Figure 1.7 St. Antoniushaus Catholic Ledigenheim, Dagobertstrasse 32, Cologne (1903/4). View of the dining hall.
Source: Msgr. Schweitzer, *Hospize und Ledigenheime der kath. Gesellenvereine* (M. Gladbach: Volksvereins Verlag, 1911), 33.

kitchens," or *Volksküchen*, these dining halls never received such decorative attention, and certainly not coffered ceilings. In the case of the dining hall of the municipal Dankelmannstrasse building, the only decoration consisted of a clock mounted on the wall and shoulder-height wainscoting that gave it the appearance of a pub, even as—similar to Neuss—direct access was provided to an outside terrace and garden (Figure 1.8 [also 3.8]).

What can account for such different treatment, particularly considering that the residents of municipal homes were generally drawn from the *Mittelstand*, as were the residents of a Catholic Ledigenheim? Both were open to nonresidents in the hopes that these visitors would prove a positive influence on the residents, and yet, while welcoming other *Gesellenverein* members, Catholic Ledigenheime were inaccessible to the *general* public.[125] Secular Ledigenheime constructed by municipalities and their allies opened their dining halls to the general public, in part of offset running costs, but also to educate the larger community as to healthy eating habits and expose the residents of the home to the "softening" presence of local women and children. This is to say, secular buildings served

Figure 1.8 (also 3.8) Dankelmannstrasse 46–47 Ledigenheim, Berlin-Charlottenburg (1908). View of the people's kitchen or *Volksküche*.
Source: 50 Jahre Volkswohnheim Gemeinnützige Aktien-Gesellschaft Berlin-Charlottenburg (Basel: Länderdienst Verlag, 1955), 41.

a broader and less-affluent clientele, whereas Catholic homes were explicitly homosocial spaces excluding the larger working-class community. From the outset, the former had a dual purpose, while the aim of a Catholic dining hall was singular. Encouraging young artisans to dine and socialize with *only* each other and *local men of standing* in a tightly controlled social setting was a means to forge connections in the service of the residents' economic and social advancement. In the face of the increasing alienation of masters and their subordinates, as well as growing divisions between artisans and the middle classes,[126] the facilitation of what amounted to a less elite version of a members-only club took precedence over any tangible benefits to the larger community. It is in this context that the lavish appointment of Catholic Ledigenheim dining halls makes sense. Handcrafted detailing and furnishings would have felt familiar to a local notable and appealed to the occupational pride of a master artisan, but as proponents believed that one's surroundings—respectable people and an elegantly appointed space alike—encouraged certain desired behaviors in the residents, the dining halls of Catholic Ledigenheime also drew residents further and further away from proclivities of the Proletarian class and toward the values of the middle classes.

A Catholic Ledigenheim's libraries and reading rooms similarly formed the components of what Adolf Kolping termed a "bürgerlichen Leben," or a bourgeois life.[127] From the beginning, Kolping had called for the inclusion of libraries in his Ledigenheime, indicating that they were to avoid the publications of the "wicked" democratic press,[128] and contain "good" books, pamphlets, and newspapers.[129] In particular, Kolping directed that his libraries be devoid of "filth" (*Schmutz*), meaning works with sexual content, and "trash" (*Schund*), silly, and insipid works such as spaghetti westerns or detective stories.[130] While Kolping was decidedly worried about growing consumerist tendencies in general, and the dangers the modern publishing industry—emerging contemporaneously with the first Catholic Ledigenheime—posed to morality specifically,[131] he specifically used the vehicle of the Ledigenheim library to counter the Liberal Protestant charge that Catholics were akin to women—emotional, undereducated, and superstitious—and that artisans were both undereducated and disinterested in education.[132] Basically, Liberal Protestant critics believed that neither group was interested in cultivating that which they held was a key to sociocultural advancement and made one deserving of full membership in the nation, *Bildung*. As mentioned earlier, Catholic Ledigenheime were able to confront these misconceptions directly, by not only supporting Bildung through one's membership in a public voluntary association, the Gesellenverein, but more importantly, through a Ledigenheim's well-appointed library, free of *Schmutz-* and *Schundliteratur*. The library, usually a single room (Düsseldorf, Neuss, St. Antoniushaus) and occasionally a suite of rooms (Marxloh-Bruchhausen), was almost always placed on the ground floor or first floor of a Ledigenheim, ideally in close proximity to other semiprivate spaces, such as dining rooms (Figure 1.9, see also Figure 1.4).

In addition to dining halls, which facilitated face-to-face interactions between the local bourgeoisie, elites, master artisans, and residents in the hope of elevating the latter, and libraries, which facilitated Bildung, drafting rooms and studio spaces—as in the Düsseldorf building—were rarely omitted from Catholic Ledigenheime. Of all spaces in a Catholic Ledigenheim, the inclusion of the latter directly spoke to the quotidian and practical needs of its residents—a pendant to the ideal of Bildung and a supplement to varied outside training and occupational facilities, ranging from the traditional master's workshop to burgeoning applied arts schools, even apprenticeship programs in small factory shops. Underscoring their importance, it was common to position these spaces in areas easily accessible

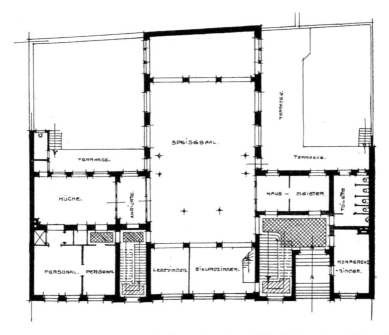

Figure 1.9 Blücherstrasse 4–8 Catholic Ledigenheim (also Kolpinghaus), Düsseldorf (1909). Plan of the ground floor.
Source: Msgr. Schweitzer, *Hospize und Ledigenheime der kath. Gesellenvereine* (M. Gladbach: Volksvereins Verlag, 1911), 69.

to the residents, with larger rooms for instruction located on the ground or first floor, while smaller practice spaces (drafting rooms and studios) were typically located on the upper floors (Figure 1.10, see also Figure 1.3).

Relatedly, the need to supplement the offerings of a Ledigenheim by facilitating professional connections and educational access beyond its walls greatly impacted a building's placement within the urban fabric. Often, Catholic Ledigenheime were located in the historic inner city, or *Altstadt*, commonly near a central cathedral square. This is a testament to the extensive landholdings of the Catholic Church and its various organizations, which allowed large Ledigenheime to be constructed in the central city on land that would have proven prohibitively expensive if purchased on the open market. This positioning also made the use of the building by local notables highly convenient. If a central location was not available, which was common for a second or third Ledigenheim in a large city, special care was taken to position the new building along routes of greatest circulation and near streetcar lines in particular, providing easy access to numerous urban and suburban workshops and applied arts schools.

Figure 1.10 Catholic Ledigenheim, Marxloh-Bruchhausen (c. 1900). Plan of attic story.
Source: Msgr. Schweitzer, *Hospize und Ledigenheime der kath. Gesellenvereine* (M. Gladbach: Volksvereins Verlag, 1911), 90.

For example, the first Catholic Ledigenheim built in Cologne (1865) was located in the historic city center, well within the ring roads encircling the growing city.[133] The building was located at Breitestrasse 108, only 100 meters to the north of the *Neumarkt*, one of the busiest market squares in Cologne, from which nearly all of Cologne was accessible by streetcar.[134] In contrast to the central location of the aforementioned Breitestrasse Ledigenheim, the St. Antoniushaus at Dagobertstrasse 32 (1900) was positioned to the north of the ancient heart of the city, though still within the ring roads and ring parks that skirted the city's edge. Located less than a block from a number of streetcar lines, all of which would allow one to easily commute to both the center city only half a kilometer to the south, it was also close to the northern suburbs of Nippes, Merheim, and Niehl, with their growing industrial districts. However, despite providing ready access to industrial areas or small shops, it is worth stressing again that Catholic Ledigenheime were rarely placed within the industrial outskirts of burgeoning cities. Instead, the more expensive and pleasant surroundings of the central city or first ring of suburbs were typically chosen, as befitted a resident on the fringes of the *Mittelstand*.[135]

As an added inducement to potential residents, and to encourage current residents to remain, Catholic Ledigenheime coupled socio-educational opportunities and convenient locations with another tactic—fun. Like the YMCA, which, as the nineteenth century wore on, increasingly abjured its Protestant revivalist roots (in the form of the hall) for decidedly more secular attractions like swimming pools, gymnasia, and billiard rooms in order to attract men to Christianity,[136] as well as municipal Ledigenheime (the subject of Chapter 3), Catholic Ledigenheime—particularly those built after the end of the Kulturkampf—nearly always featured spaces focused on "healthy" pastimes. Above all, they provided an alternative to the frequenting of outside pool halls, billiard rooms, pubs, bowling alleys, theaters, dancehalls, and by the early twentieth century, cinemas. All of these spaces were not negative in and of themselves, but were problematic because they were commonly linked to immorality, from the relatively safe (tobacco use to the use of profanity) to the ruinous (gambling, excessive drinking, and interactions with women [and men] of dubious moral character—that is, socialist activity to sex).

If one could uncouple some of these problematic spaces from the negative aspects that often accompanied them, safely housing them within the confines of the Ledigenheim, they became acceptable. Accordingly, billiards, increasingly associated with upper-class leisure—though not pool, a game associated gamblers and other dissolute types[137]—were often included in Catholic Ledigenheime from the 1890s, as were bowling alleys. The former were usually positioned either on the ground floor, commonly off a relaxation room (Marxloh-Bruchhausen, Cologne Breitestrasse, Cologne St. Antoniushaus [see Figure 1.4]), and sometimes even off dining halls (Düsseldorf) (see Figure 1.9). Though occasionally linked to other recreational spaces on the ground floor (Neuss) (Figure 1.5), (relatively noisy) bowling alleys generally were located in the basement (Altenessen, Münster, Marxloh-Bruchhausen, Cologne Breitestasse, Düsseldorf) (Figure 1.11).

Gymnasia were also common features of Catholic Ledigenheime, as in the case of the Cologne Breitestrasse building, where (like the bowling alley) the *Turnhalle* was located in the basement. More than any other space ostensibly devoted to fun, a gymnasium was also an elevating space—strongly linked to the burgeoning life reform movement of the Second Reich. Physical culture, and gymnastic activity in particular, had a relatively long history in what became the German Empire, dating back to 1811, when German teacher and patriot Friedrich Ludwig Jahn (*Turnvater* Jahn) founded his association of gymnasts in Berlin to cultivate health, strength, and patriotism in the face of Napoleonic

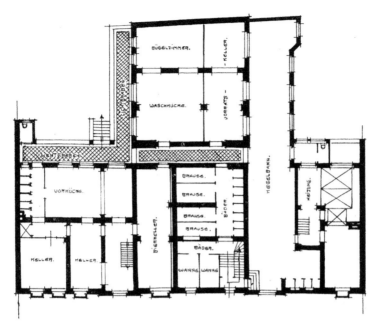

Figure 1.11 Blücherstrasse 4–8 Catholic Ledigenheim (also Kolpinghaus), Düsseldorf (1909). Plan of the basement.
Source: Msgr. Schweitzer, *Hospize und Ledigenheime der kath. Gesellenvereine* (M. Gladbach: Volksvereins Verlag, 1911), 70.

France. Always strongly linked to German nationalism, Jahn's movement became increasingly identified with democratic agitation in the 1840s and, as the century wore on, was also a way to combat fears that urban life and the division of labor resultant of industrial capitalism were detrimental to not only the mental and moral development of young men but also their physical development. German Turners, alongside their counterparts in Sweden and the United States,[138] held that gymnastic activity—alongside proper diet and hygiene—aided socio-emotional development and supported the performance of a moral life. While this emphasis on the development of the whole individual fits neatly with the outlook of the Verband Katholischen Gesellenvereine, there is an additional reason why gymnasia featured in Catholic homes toward the turn of the century—competition. Catholic homes sought to draw young artisans away not only from overtly morally problematic spaces like pool halls but from other gymnasia and gymnastic clubs, many of which were aligned with workers' organizations and democratic clubs, and all of whom actively courted young artisans.[139]

The simplest way to consider the wide-ranging recreational options available to the residents of a typical Catholic Ledigenheim in the 1890s is through a brief description of what was offered to the residents of the St. Josephshaus of Cologne. In this case, not only was a library with 900 volumes included but further rooms were set aside for socializing, and a gymnasium was included.[140] As far as religious instruction and professional education was concerned, drawing, reading, and writing classes were offered, as were regular lectures on local History, (Catholic) Church History and Natural Science.[141] The Ledigenheim even convened its own choral group, and its twenty-five men performed for the Kaiser on the nearby *Neumarkt* in May of 1891.[142]

Thus, as proponents of Catholic Ledigenheime like the St. Josephshaus wrote that they were attempting to replicate, at least in part, the sociocultural benefits of an idealized master craftsman's home, the physical spaces created were markedly different from what an apprentice would have encountered under his master's roof. Most tellingly, *each* type of room in a Catholic Ledigenheim was carefully included in light of its particular benefits to the individual. When one considers that room taxonomy was an indicator of class, the number of spaces dedicated to a single activity in a Catholic Ledigenheim—from a library to an art studio—more closely approximates the home of a prosperous member of the middle class, rather than that of the middling master artisan, whose dwelling in the latter part of the nineteenth century commonly consisted of a workshop, combined living room/kitchen, "good" room (*gute Stube*), a bedroom (or two), and possibly an attic.[143] Despite such discrepancies, however, their proponents still positioned Catholic Ledigenheime simply as larger and more formalized versions of an artisan's home—places to work, to learn, and to socialize, all under one roof—and one where the guiding hand of the master was gentle, yet omnipresent.

Freedom and Control: Circulation and Bedrooms

While residents' behavior was largely conditioned through positive measures, namely pleasant company and surroundings, healthful leisure activities, and educational opportunities, Catholic reformers realized that programming as protection could only go so far. In a physically large and programmatically complex building, and in lieu of the moderating presence of a master artisan or his wife, the supporters of Catholic Ledigenheime actively sought to restrict certain behaviors by instituting house rules, as well as controlling access to and

Figure 1.12 Ledigenheim (also Gesellenhospiz) on the Bitscherstrasse, Strasbourg (*c.* 1900). Plan of the ground floor.
Source: Msgr. Schweitzer, *Hospize und Ledigenheime der kath. Gesellenvereine* (M. Gladbach: Volksvereins Verlag, 1911), 92.

circulation within the building. This was a careful balancing act, for Catholic Ledigenheime housed young men who increasingly saw themselves as mature and independent.[144] Thus, the administration—though the person of the *Präsis*, who resided in the building—instituted and enforced regulations they considered "neither too strict, nor too lenient,"[145] and that respected the residents' right to a minimum level of "individuality, self-sufficiency, and freedom."[146]

In regard to access and circulation, nearly all Catholic Ledigenheime had one primary entrance for the use of residents, and never more than two, which meant that the movements of residents and visitors into and out of the building were readily observable, either by the Präsis or by the porter, and sometimes both. For example, the two entrances to the Strasbourg Ledigenheim—from the street and a courtyard—were positioned so that both could be easily and simultaneously observed from the porter's office and his lodgings (Figure 1.12). Additionally, the hallways leading from these entrances intersected on the main hall of the ground floor near stairwells leading to the bedrooms, and were but a short distance from all administrative offices, including that of the Präsis. If one assumes that this was coincidental, a statement by Schweitzer noting that the single entrance or careful position of two entrances "has the purpose of serving to make it easy to watch those who leave and enter the building"[147] should disabuse one of such a notion. Nonresidents and nonmembers could be easily rooted out through a constant observation of transitional spaces, if they were allowed to enter the building at all. Such Ledigenheime were closed communities intended to protect the morality and customs of the future of the German artisan estate, lest it be polluted by outsiders.

Those standing most outside, notwithstanding the social subversives Kolping feared, were those typically held up as the guardians of German customs, piety, and morality—women. As briefly mentioned in relationship to dining halls, unlike municipal Ledigenheime (the subject of Chapter 3), whose public kitchens and libraries were carefully arranged to serve both residents and the women and children who frequented them, and even (largely homosocial) institutions like the YMCA, where women were encouraged to attend lectures in the assembly hall or converse with residents in carefully appointed parlors,[148] Catholic Ledigenheime neither facilitated carefully calibrated interactions between the sexes nor included gender-integrated programming. Even accidental interactions of service personnel with residents were sharply curtailed by the careful placement of service quarters. For example, Cologne's St. Josephshaus employed not only a Präsis and porter but also a house inspector and a night porter, all of whom ensured that residents never came in contact with female staff (nuns and lay personnel), who were housed in a separate wing of the building, complete with their own dining room, rather than in the basement of the main building with male staff.[149] In the case of the St. Antoniushaus of Cologne, separate entrances for female personnel were even provided.[150]

Thus, the positioning of these homes as a close approximation of a master artisan's home is not *quite* apt, as most such homes would have featured women and children. Instead, these homes were entirely homosocial spaces that recreated the master-apprentice dynamic in somewhat domesticated institutional setting—a setting modeled on the patriarchal Catholic Church, where women held a secondary position and were largely relegated to their own organizations, as well as male-oriented artisans' guilds—the creation of which ran different risks.

These unintended risks explain the extreme concern the organization evidenced regarding the format of a Ledigenheim's bedrooms, which the administration discussed in even greater depth than entrances, exits, and other transitional spaces. While the Kolpinghaus organization advised that Catholic

Ledigenheime contain a variety of bedrooms, or "guestrooms," serving both transient guests and long-term residents,[151] single rooms were held up as the ideal room formulation from the beginning of the construction of Catholic Ledigenheime, although due to their relative expense remained relatively rare until the turn of the century. For example, it was nearly twice as costly to rent a single room in the Cologne Breitestrasse building (of 1864) (2 marks/week) than it was to lodge in a room with four beds (1.25 marks/week).[152] If a single room was not feasible, a room for three or four residents was acceptable, and—deviating sharply from the organization of space in all other Ledigenheim variants—even a dormitory was preferable to a double room. While this could read as a nod to the precedent of monastic living, Catholic reformers were direct in stating why double rooms were to be avoided at all costs. They were problematic for "cultural reasons"—code for homosexuality.[153]

While much of the bourgeois discourse on lower-middle- and working-class men cast them as dangerously hypermasculine, the potential corrupters of women and girls,[154] as evidenced by a sensationalized reports of the illicit liaisons and illegitimate births resultant of unregulated lodging, the press in mid- to late nineteenth-century Germany began to exhibit an increasing concern with supposedly "unnatural" sexualities, culminating with the media circus around the suicide of Friedrich Alfred Krupp in 1902 and a series of sex scandals in the highest circles of the imperial government, most notably the Harden-Eulenburg affair.[155] While the common saying, "[the Schlafstelle] is rarely without a bit of love,"[156] generally referred to sexual relations between men and women, or men and girls, it was no longer beyond the pale that this also referred to homosexual acts between men. Despite the fact that Paragraph 175 in the German Empire's penal code still criminalized such acts, the nineteenth century saw the development of new vocabularies associated with same-sex attraction, from urning and invert to homosexual, the latter coined in 1868 by Austrian-born Karl Maria Kertbeny.[157] Fertile ground began to be laid for the emergence of active homosexual subcultures, as evidenced by the founding of homosexual emancipation's first organization, Magnus Hirschfeld's "Scientific Humanitarian Committee" (WhK) in 1897, and beginning in 1894, the publication of Adolf Brand's *Der Eigene*, a periodical devoted to "masculine culture."[158]

While the corrupting effect of a particular individual (usually positioned as older and morally unsalvageable) on another was most commonly positioned as the cause of same-sex attraction, such proclivities were also increasingly linked to extreme *homosociality* during young adulthood,[159] an age when contemporaries believed an individual's sexual orientation could most easily be influenced.[160] On the opposite side of the Atlantic, the leadership of the YMCA also began to blame sex-segregated social activities, and resultant "intense friendships," for a series of sex scandals that rocked the organization. They argued that extreme homosocial programming, rather than any innate proclivity, was preventing young men from forming relationships with the opposite sex, writing that "whenever any normal outlets of life are denied, abnormal ones are likely to be substituted."[161]

While the leadership of Catholic Ledigenheime remained mute on homosexuality except obliquely, they could also hardly admit to the (purported) dangers of extreme homosociality. The creation of a community of men—young and old, master and apprentice—standing strong against the vicissitudes of the modern age was always central to Kolping's project, and unlike the YMCA, which rarely included dormitories until the beginning of the twentieth century,[162] the leadership had somewhere they could redirect any concern regarding illicit sexualities. As opposed to the home as a whole, blame was entirely placed on the double bedroom—an "unnatural" living situation encouraging morally compromising behavior among those still developing a "strong sense of honor" and "strength of will."[163] Single rooms provided the perfect—if not always available—cover, allowing the administration to both champion the (developing) moral fiber of their residents and shield them from temptation.

The Symbolism of Style

In keeping with the careful messaging of discipline and control evidenced in Catholic Ledigenheime, buildings featured recognizable architectural styles intended to connote both the power of the church *and* the elevated (or rising) status of their residents, abjuring anything that could be construed as coldly functional, institutional, or barrack-like in massing, style, or decoration.[164] More specifically, most nineteenth-century buildings used a visual vocabulary that overtly referenced interwoven local, professional, and Catholic identities. This was particularly pronounced in the Rhineland, the birthplace of the movement and backdrop of its greatest expansion—a heavily Catholic region marked by rapid industrialization and urbanization, a historically strong artisan estate, and recent religious strife.

The very first purpose-built Ledigenheim, which also served as the seat of the organization, was located on the Breitestrasse in Cologne (1852, expanded 1865), and recalled the commercial buildings typical of many late medieval "republican" *Hansastädte*, of which Cologne was one, replete with elaborate brickwork, stone,

Figure 1.13 Catholic Ledigenheim (also Gesellenhospiz) on the Breitestrasse, Cologne (1852, expanded 1865). Primary facade.
Source: Msgr. Schweitzer, *Hospize und Ledigenheime der kath. Gesellenvereine* (M. Gladbach: Volksvereins Verlag, 1911), 16.

and molded brick segmental arches framing first floor windows, and modified stepped gables (Figure 1.13).[165] It also referenced details drawn from medieval ecclesiastical architecture, from the construction polychromy so favored by John Ruskin, to Gothic finials surmounting numerous projecting niches and attic-level dormer windows, to the portal-like central entrance within a slightly projecting bay also featuring a traceried pointed-arch window. This medievalizing language was replicated in the dining hall, which as mentioned earlier, featured stained-glass lancet windows and wooden hammer-beamed ceilings.

Such references to the late medieval period in general, and Gothic architecture in particular, were certainly not accidental. In the years between the Cologne Troubles and the Kulturkampf, Catholic historians began to position the late fifteenth century as the golden age of German history, an age of faith and unity before the destructive and divisive powers of the Reformation.[166] While they were not alone in doing so, with Catholics in other countries under Protestant rule making similar claims—most notably architect, designer, and Gothic revivalist Augustus Welby Northmore Pugin in *Contrasts* (1836)—Rhenish Catholics purposefully employed the Gothic revival to draw a connection between a difficult present and the glorious distant past, when the Rhineland was one of the most powerful commercial and ecclesiastical centers of the German-speaking world. Helpfully, the style was sufficiently flexible in meaning, as not to alarm the authorities. Buildings in this style *should* be read as documents of Catholicism, indicating the role that the church had long played and would continue to play in the lives of the faithful, but were also read as symbolic evidence of—following Kolping's "balancing act between church and state"—a period that saw the supposed coexistence of state, church, and private institutions, a "harmonious and stable balance of authority," such as *might* be recovered in the present.[167]

For artisans, including the artisans of Cologne, the late medieval period also had particular resonance, as this Catholic "golden age" was synonymous with the medieval "guild age," or at least nineteenth-century artisans' collective memory of it.[168] Works such as Richard Wagner's *die Meistersinger von Nürnberg* (1868) popularized the image of the medieval handicraftsman as "prosperous, respectable, talented, and skilled,"[169] a vision that was increasingly attractive in an age that saw the artisan estate's fortunes precipitously decline. Yet, while the Gothic served as a symbol of a more harmonious age, it was also positioned by its proponents as a key to the revival of the artisan estate. As the essence of the Gothic, according to leading theoretician August Reichensperger, was not "what" but "how" to build, the building process of Gothic buildings provided a model to the present.[170]

The lessons of the Gothic were thus: one need not be a trained architect coming from Berlin's *Bauakademie* to create monumental works of art, training should occur on-site and at the side of a master craftsman; in fact, art arising from the collective life of people rather than trickling down from the elites was a sign of health;[171] as a total work of art, or *Gesamtkunstwerk*, a Gothic building required every craftsman to exercise his skill, expertise, and creativity; art need not be a "luxury good . . . like oysters and caviar," only available to the elite, but instead should be a central experience in the lives of all;[172] architecture should always be based on local building traditions, customs, and materials.

While there is no indication that the young artisans housed in Kolping's Ledigenheime actually helped to construct the buildings that housed them, the amount of labor involved in their construction, including their incredibly detailed decorative programs (as discussed in relationship to dining halls), all point to the prominent presence of master craftsmen. On a deeper level, Catholic Ledigenheime reflected the greater values of the German Gothic revival, at least as espoused by the circle around Reichensperger—who was both known to and friendly with

Kolping[173]—that access to beauty and culture not only is the domain of the elite but also belongs to those on the margins, and that to ensure its success, the centralized authority of the *Verband* was balanced by self-determining regional organizations with direct knowledge of local conditions and customs.

However, such attempts to recall the pre-Reformation world while maintaining regional specificity were largely jettisoned in the final decade of the nineteenth century. Although nothing in the literature indicates that this was a choice *officially* decided upon by the leadership of Kolping's organization, the ecclesiastical and civic precedents of the Gothic revival—which had fallen out of style and lost much of its moral force—gave way to an altogether more domestic reference point. As the turn of the century neared, most new (or newly renovated) Catholic Ledigenheime adopted a style recalling the vernacular building traditions of late eighteenth- and early nineteenth-century German-speaking lands, the *Biedermeier revival*, and the modest home of an urban burgher in particular.

A building constructed in this style, as it was popularized at the turn of the twentieth century, was one marked by a number of features: overall symmetry (or balanced asymmetry), a light color, a hipped roof (complete with eyebrow windows and gables), and delicate decorative details contributing to an overall impression of elegance and lightness. Illustrative of this shift from the Gothic to the Biedermeier revival is none less than the flagship home and headquarters of Kolping's movement, Cologne's central Gesellenheim on the Breitestrasse, which after repeated expansions (1864, 1885) was finally rebuilt in 1910 in the Biedermeier revival style (Figure 1.14).

Celebrated by architects such as Paul Mebes in his celebratory tome *um 1800: Architektur und Handwerk im Letzten Jahrhundert ihrer Traditionellen Entwicklung*, or *circa 1800: Architecture and Craftwork in the last Century of their Traditional Development* (1908), the Biedermeier revival retained many of the Gothic revival's symbolic benefits, while appearing even more suited to the modern age. As relayed by publisher Eugen Diederichs, the times of Dürer *and* Goethe served as the Blütezeiten, or "springs" of German civilization, "nourishing the flowering of culture in which the integration of life and art [would] find its origin."[174] Like the Gothic of the late fifteenth century, the employment of the Biedermeier recalled an era that was both culturally rich and within which social divisions were (supposedly) not felt as strongly. Particularly compelling to artisans, the Biedermeier referenced a time where art and life (purportedly) still formed an organic whole, and when the artisan estate and their work was still of value. Of course, in visually recalling a "simpler" age German aesthetic reformers were purposefully partaking in an established practice at the turn of

Figure 1.14 New Catholic Ledigenheim (also Gesellenhospiz) on the Breitestrasse, Cologne (1910). Primary facade.
Source: Msgr. Schweitzer, *Hospize und Ledigenheime der kath. Gesellenvereine* (M. Gladbach: Volksvereins Verlag, 1911), 101.

the century, for "wrapping philanthropic buildings in styles which conjured up historical associations with [specific preindustrial] periods believed to have been more harmonious and caring."[175] This effort to shape the present was not only a German phenomenon but also common in the United States and England, as well as in the Nordic countries. If Germans favored the Gothic and afterward the Biedermeier, their reform-minded peers in England tended toward the use of a simplified Gothic recalling "olde England,"[176] and Scandinavians often drew from Norse prehistory and wooden (often log) farm buildings.[177] Activist Americans favored the Queen Anne style (courtesy of Britain),[178] which not only recalled an earlier age, but—like the Biedermeier revival—was suitably "refined and delicate,"[179] turning to "native" styles like the Prairie Style slightly later.[180]

Yet, in referencing a time within living memory, the Biedermeier revival felt more familiar—it was the age of one's "grandfathers," rather than a distant golden age. Additionally, if art and architecture of the (late) middle ages was associated with the church, the baroque era with royalty, the Biedermeier era belonged to the middle classes—and the domestic realm. Of course, a Ledigenheim neither was a private dwelling, nor did it replicate the layout of an early nineteenth-century home (it replicated only the symbolism of its facade and interior appointments). Yet, this discrepancy hardly mattered to those who believed that the cultural and societal regeneration of the German Empire was to be pursued through the redesign of the domestic realm and who saw the plight of the artisan as increasingly entwined with that of the new nation-state. By the last decade of the nineteenth century, the education of young artisans—long a regional and denominational concern—had found a national audience and was now a matter of state policy. This was evidenced by the massive redesign and expansion of applied arts schools operating under the auspices of the Prussian commerce ministry, which jumped from 715 schools in 1885 to 1,774 in 1900,[181] the fuller ramifications of which I will return to shortly.

Put more bluntly, to remain competitive with residents and local supporters, even the growing number of German officials newly invested in the "artisan question," Catholic Ledigenheime needed to seem relevant—socially and stylistically. The choice of the Biedermeier Revival also visually allied Catholic Ledigenheime with contemporaneous efforts by secular reform organizations and municipalities, their new competitors (and the subject of Chapter 3). In short, proponents held that a Catholic Ledigenheim serving artisans and constructed using the "proper" style could be a "step forward for [German national] culture," not remain merely a narrow and local concern.[182]

Positioned in a central location, and at the forefront of architectural design efforts, as well as utilizing the most expensive of materials, Catholic Ledigenheime bespoke permanence *and* timeliness, a statement of power highly visible to the surrounding community. Befitting their status as deep investments in the Catholic community and heightened profile in the urban fabric, such buildings were by the turn of the century also designed by the most notable of architects—such as Architect and Professor Peter Behrens.

Behrens not only was the teacher of a number of pivotal figures in the Modern Movement, from Mies van der Rohe and Le Corbusier to Walter Gropius, but also served as artistic consultant to the Allgemeines Electricität Gesellschaft (General Electric Company) of Berlin, arguably creating the first unified corporate identity for his client. He was also a leading member of the *Deutscher Werkbund*, founded by artists, cultural critics, and industrialists in 1907 to develop new directions in design and forge a more fruitful relationship between art and industry.[183] Additionally, Behrens served as director of the reorganized Düsseldorf School of Arts and Crafts (*Kunstgewerbeschule*) between 1903 and 1907. Even earlier, he was an artist in residence at the Darmstadt Artists' Colony, designing not only his own home on the Mathildenhöhe but also—in concert with Georg Fuchs—the colony's opening ceremony (*Das Zeichen*) on May 15, 1901.[184] If the new German nation had a "yearning for culture," Behrens believed that design reform was the primary means to effect change.[185]

Behrens's Catholic Ledigenheim in the Rhineland city of Neuss (designed in 1907 and opened to residents in 1910) is a fitting monument to Behrens's ethos (see Figure 1.1). It was the winner of an open competition featuring leading architects Theodor Fischer, Richard Riemerschmid, and Paul Schultze-Naumburg, and

Behrens's contemporaries considered it a model building on every level, particularly as regards its silhouette, style, and functionality.[186] The three-story Ledigenheim, complete with moderated mansard roof, was both traditional and modern—a somewhat stripped and sharply geometric version of the early nineteenth-century Biedermeier house so popular in aesthetic reform circles at the turn of the twentieth century, though the massing, flexible arrangement of space, and rectilinear detailing of the interiors reflected Behrens's particular aesthetic proclivities.

If Behrens's monumental architecture, from his AEG turbine factory in Berlin (1908–9) to the offices he designed for Mannesmann in Düsseldorf (1910–12), often relied on "cubic compactness and the creation of large forms,"[187] his work for the Catholic Gesellenverein of Neuss was carefully formulated to present an elegant appearance, while still reading as appropriately domestic. While the subdued ornamentation, planar surfaces, and lapidary lettering above the entrance to the home recall both the Biedermeier and Behrens's AEG turbine factory, the massiveness of the Ledigenheim was moderated by a number of devices—from the consideration of each corner of the site in relationship to the urban landscape, to a balanced asymmetry of interlocking volumes, which saw vertical elements placed alongside a low and welcoming entrance, to the inclusion of a variety of roofscapes and window groupings that not only were specific to the height of a particular section of the building but also indicated a change in use.

Beyond its arresting formal appearance, Behrens's flexible composition provided programmatic benefits (Figure 1.15, see also Figures 1.1 and 1.5). In particular, the types, grouping, and placement of windows allowed for the ample provision of both natural light and the interweaving of exterior and interior space—these ranged from eyebrow windows to dormers, and groupings of three or four tall and slender windows to a courtyard featuring a spare open and glazed round-arched arcade. Behrens was also exceedingly prescient in his attention to solar orientation, a fact that did not fail to escape the notice of Schweitzer, who happily noted that bedrooms nearly all had southern exposure, while the northern side of the building primarily housed service spaces.[188]

Most importantly, Behrens saw the Neuss Ledigenheim as a leading example of the "old/new style" he sought to popularize, stressing both its timelessness and contemporaneity, writing:

> Just herein, i.e. in the breakdown, the tradition lies—this is the means through which ancient architectural creations have retained their beauty, though this is also useful for our time and worth pursuing. Undoubtedly each time has its own forms, but the overall arrangements of old buildings can be used as guides or laws, the examination of which connects the past to the present.[189]

Figure 1.15 Catholic Gesellenhaus/Ledigenheim, Neuss am Rhein (1910). View of courtyard.
Source: Msgr. Schweitzer, *Hospize und Ledigenheime der kath. Gesellenvereine* (M. Gladbach: Volksvereins Verlag, 1911), 76.

For a project that sought to make a home in the modern age for the displaced remnants of the preindustrial world, the use of old forms, adapted and reconstituted for new ends, seems particularly well suited. Like the architecture housing them, artisans would be remade, and at the same time, even more tightly bound to old belief systems and traditional practices.

Aesthetics and Bedrooms

While Dr. Schweitzer, leader of the Verband katholischer Gesellenvereine and author of *Hospize und Ledigenheime der kath. Gesellenvereine* (1911), devoted most of his coverage of Catholic Ledigenheime to the appointment of communal spaces, the circulation of space within, and the exterior style of the representative buildings he chose, he did not fail to mention the (contentious) bedroom as a site of aesthetic and cultural renewal. In his codification of the acceptable standards of Catholic Ledigenheime,[190] he established what supporters saw as essential to every bedroom, particularly in regard to the lauded single occupancy room or "acceptable" triple bedroom.[191] Namely, he advised that each resident be provided with a wardrobe, a bed of at least 1.95 by .90 meters, and a chair, as well as one table per room, and a wash basin with stand.[192]

Such specifications were met by the majority of Catholic Ledigenheime, particularly those constructed or updated after 1890. For example, residents of the Gesellenheim on the Blücherstrasse in central Düsseldorf, built in 1909, were provided with a wardrobe, a bedstead with blankets and pillows, a chair, and even a built-in bookshelf doubling as storage space (Figure 1.16). Similarly, a single room in Cologne's St. Antoniushaus contained an iron bedstead, complete with footboard and springs, as well as a three-part sea-grass mattress. Additionally, bed linens, a feather pillow, a feather comforter, and two woolen blankets were provided to each St. Antoniushaus resident, as was a solid wooden table with chair (Figure 1.17). Specially appointed locations within Catholic Ledigenheime for the storage of bulky personal items, such as bicycles and luggage, also reduced clutter and maximized square footage.

Figure 1.16 Blücherstrasse 4–8 Catholic Ledigenheim (also Kolpinghaus), Düsseldorf (1909). Single bedroom.
Source: Msgr. Schweitzer, *Hospize und Ledigenheime der kath. Gesellenvereine* (M. Gladbach: Volksvereins Verlag, 1911), 74.

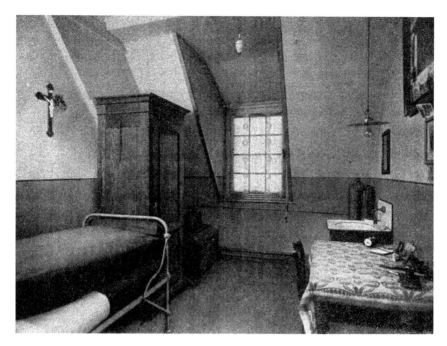

Figure 1.17 St. Antoniushaus Catholic Ledigenheim, Dagobertstrasse 32, Cologne (1903/4). Single bedroom.
Source: Msgr. Schweitzer, *Hospize und Ledigenheime der kath. Gesellenvereine* (M. Gladbach: Volksvereins Verlag, 1911), 58.

However, while everything necessary for resting, relaxing, and sleeping in hygienic and (relatively) spacious surroundings was provided to residents, the relative sparseness of these spaces stood in contrast to the average home of a master artisan. Even when Schweitzer was writing in 1911, such homes would have typically been marked by heavy pieces of furniture and a good deal of fabric, from wall hangings to decorative tablecloths.[193] Why create spaces significantly different from the homes that the residents would have been accustomed to? While sanitary reasons and spatial constraints were cited by Catholic reformers,[194] and apprentices and journeymen generally would not have owned substantial pieces of furniture, the role that changing bourgeois tastes played cannot be discounted. Certainly, anything recalling the interior of a *Mietskaserne*—the working-class tenement building characteristic of late nineteenth-century German cities—was studiously avoided. Descriptions of these unacceptable lodgings usually mentioned filth, but also that they were disorderly, as well as overcrowded with furnishings and decorations.[195] This meant that a Ledigenheim bedroom needed to be clean, neat, and uncrowded, all of which were markers of respectability and moral rectitude.

Yet, it was not simply filth and overcrowding that were the enemy. While American observer William Harbutt Dawson noted that domestic decorations and furnishings, even if poor quality, still "belonged to the primary comforts of a [German] home,"[196] German aesthetic reformers (and their counterparts elsewhere) took a different view. As technical changes in reproduction widened the sphere of cultural consumers,[197] these reformers, most prominently members and allies of the Werkbund, began to fight against what they characterized as kitsch and trash—decorations and furniture of bad design and/or quality. They feared that German design culture was falling behind that of other industrial nations and that the taste of the German public was being "corrupted." Aesthetic want and nouveau riche vulgarity were both dangers, not only to the individual but to the nation.[198] Although it cannot be considered a monolithic entity, members of the Werkbund generally sought to replace "cheap and nasty" goods with well-designed quality products,[199] which would then elevate German taste and increase national competitiveness. What precisely made an object "cheap and nasty"? Members of the organization largely felt that the manner of production was often problematic, but also that the original models were themselves derivative and of poor quality.[200] Instead, new and healthy directions in design were to be based on "timeless" models, the "building blocks of (German) culture," of which the aforementioned Biedermeier revival (as employed by Behrens's Neuss Ledigenheim) was an exemplar.[201]

As Jennifer Jenkins writes, it was not enough to simply encourage consumers to either throw them away or refrain from purchasing them in the first place, they had to be replaced with "improved" domestic goods, which were carefully "sold" to the masses through a variety of wide-ranging educational programs.[202] Indeed, the stakes were high, and ultimately the Werkbund sought nothing less than the "re-conquest of a harmonious culture," as invoked at the founding meeting of the organization in 1907.[203]

In a Ledigenheim, this task was far easier than in a private home. Not only did the residents have little purchasing power, their transient status made certain that they would not amass much in the way of material possessions, and mandating certain designs in small spaces built en masse seemed both reasonable and responsible. Though as vulnerable as the rest of society to the seductive charms of bad design (from "dishonest" materials to superficial ornamentation), reformers believed that just as a lack of clutter and easy-to-clean surfaces encouraged cleanliness, providing a model of what residents should consume *and* produce could (gently) (re)form the residents' tastes and proclivities.

What then was the "right" sort of furniture and its arrangement? Again, here it is useful to turn to Schweitzer. In his report on the history of his organization, the acting head of all Gesellenvereine proposed furnishing the bedrooms of *all* current and future Ledigenheime with specific furniture exactingly designed (Figures 1.18a, b, c, d). Beyond providing plans indicating their precise placement to maximize all 9.5 square feet of a single room, the furnishings were carefully designed to be multifunctional if possible—the chair seat lifts up to provide additional storage and the wash table can be closed and its inclined top pulled forward to form a writing desk. Solidly constructed of "German" oak, with planar detailing and rectilinear proportions that recall the Biedermeier era but remain contemporary, these everyday furnishings are not one-of-a-kind art objects but neither are they "cheap and nasty."

In fact, the designs Schweitzer mandated bear great similarity to what was being proposed by design reformers for the use of the general public, as featured in publications such as the Bruckmann publishing house's *Wohunung und Hausrat: Beispiele Neuzeitlicher Wohnräume und ihrer Ausstattung* (1908), and as exemplified by the products of the Dresden Workshops for Handcrafted Art (later the German Workshops, or *Deutsche Werkstätten*), founded by Karl Schmidt in 1898 and later housed in the "garden city" of Hellerau. Of particular interest, Schmidt's workshops produced quality objects of the sort that had been tied to the traditional crafts—fabrics, jewelry, silverware, books, and most notably furniture—but with a twist.[204] His products were not only well-designed but also more affordable than what an independent artisan could produce. By minimizing middle-men, selling through catalogs, and emphasizing the quality, affordability, and timelessness of his wares, Schmidt aimed directly at Germany's *Mittelstand*, an estate to which artisans as a group, and the typical Ledigenheim resident in particular, belonged.[205]

Yet, Schmidt did not merely seek to make his fortune by selling quality goods to those whose earlier options had largely consisted of cheap and shabby items. Like other members of the Werkbund, he sought to educate their buying habits, thus elevating the aesthetic taste of the general public. In employing leading designers like Richard Riemerschmid, Bruno Paul, and Heinrich Tessenow alongside artisans, and training apprentices through an in-house mentorship program, Schmidt also sought to "overcome the alienation of the designer from the producer ... by [restoring] joy in work, which would [have the added benefit of] improve[ing] quality."[206] In short, the German Workshops created both

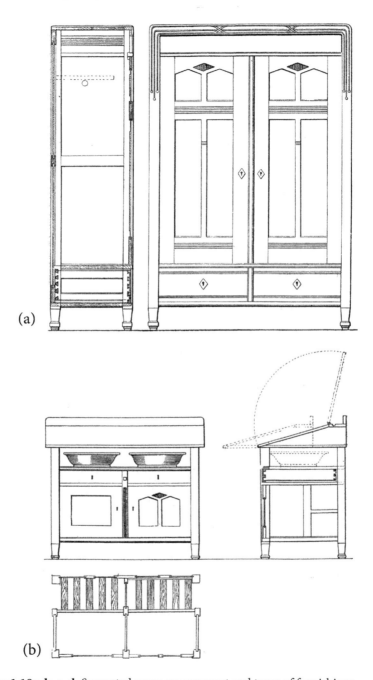

Figure 1.18a, b, c, d Suggested room arrangement and types of furnishings.
Source: Msgr. Schweitzer, *Hospize und Ledigenheime der kath. Gesellenvereine* (M. Gladbach: Volksvereins Verlag, 1911), 109–12.

Adolph Kolping's Revolution

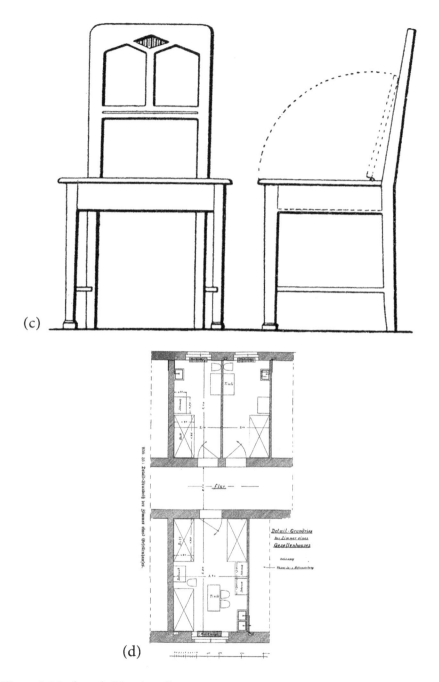

Figure 1.18a, b, c, d (Continued)

high-quality "modern" goods that remained rooted in tradition and supported the "modernized" artisan—a set of concerns that certainly allied it with Kolping's organization.

Yet, the German Workshops and other Werkbund associated industries tended to think in rather narrow terms—they sought to reeducate and position artisans in a mutually beneficial relationship with industry, but on their terms and those of the state, not on the terms of the artisan estate, or the individual artisan.[207] Basically, in order to save him, the artisan had to be allied with a designer, which could occur through a "modern" apprenticeship program like that of the German Workshops or, to an even greater extent, through the numerous reorganized applied arts schools operating under the auspices of the Prussian commerce ministry and other governmental entities.[208] As John Maciuika has explicated, these schools ranged from *Kunstgewerbeschulen* (as headed by Behrens in Düsseldorf), which were intended for the most promising art and design students, and encouraged independent design work, to *Handwerker-* and *Gewerbe- Schulen*, which were charged with training "accomplished craftsmen" to "execute previously prepared designs."[209] Such a system left little place for the typical Ledigenheim resident, who, had he attended one of these schools, would have been placed in a *Handwerker-* or *Gewerbe-Schule*, and discouraged from pursuing independent design work. The latter was the purview of the academically trained "artist" alone, who was to "remold the arts and crafts through [his] expertise."[210] While the German Workshops were less rigidly hierarchical than these schools, and paid lip service to the conventions of the artisan estate by using the terminology of "apprentice," even its master artisans stood below "artists," and all were ultimately employees, company men.

Thus, while the traditional artisan was repeatedly discussed as the model of the well-rounded and complete individual, and his well-being was held as an indicator of the overall health of society, the very institutions ostensibly developed to help him positioned him not as a partner in the revival of German design culture but forever as a subordinate.

Whereas the dream of eventually becoming a master artisan may have been fading, it still remained a possibility under the old system. Under the new order, the artisan could never hope to be able to work freely—to execute his own designs, or to own his own workshop. To young men of the artisan estate searching for a means to self-determination, the vanishing of the old artisan estate—hastened by efforts made by others on its behalf—would have chafed.

By contrast, Catholic Ledigenheime provided a gentler *and* more totalizing solution than the efforts of the state or allied organizations. Instead of considering education in the narrowest of ways, Catholic Ledigenheime held out the promise of developing the whole person. The education in good taste demanded by organizations such as the Werkbund was not only conducted on the job site, and possibly within a redesigned and expanded system of applied arts schools, but augmented by the form and style of the building, as well as considered programming that encouraged his personal *and* professional development. The practical skills needed by an artisan and the cultural literacy demanded of men sitting on the edges of the bourgeoisie were addressed through the inclusion of drafting rooms and dining halls, libraries and gymnasia, even well-designed bedroom furnishings. Most importantly, this aesthetic, formal, and cultural training was not instituted from outsiders, but was a gentle intervention undertaken by those who knew them best—fellow Catholics and local artisans. While officials in Berlin increasingly held that even "modernized" artisanal craftwork was unsalvageable,[211] Kolping's organization believed that the *artisan* was.

Conclusion

In leveraging the plight of young artisans and their substandard housing to renew a declining craft tradition and restore the artisan to his rightful place in German society, Kolping addressed one of the most contentious issues of the day. To move German society away from its present corrupted state, he did not reimagine the artisan either as a transcendent artist or as a factory operative. Instead, he sought to harness an artisan's measured independence, something that proved highly successful in appealing to the young men he sought to serve. In the case of the St. Antoniushaus of Cologne, the popularity of the building with potential residents was highlighted not only by its being fully booked by its opening (1900) but also by the fact that by the following summer, twenty men were being turned away daily and the building remained fully occupied.[212] Unfortunately, this last sentence indicates that there were never enough Catholic Ledigenheime to effectively house all those in need, and as the century wore on, the problems of the disenfranchised artisan estate only intensified.

While the German artisan remained a touchpoint in the decades that followed—including, but not limited to, the Bauhaus's use of "apprentice" and "master" to designate students and professors and Lyonel Feininger's woodcuts evoking medieval mason's guilds—his fate always was entwined with the unstoppable forces of industrialization and empire building, powers that Kolping's organization did not have the resources to combat. By the late 1920s, as the artisan estate continued to slip in socioeconomic status and into the arms of the far right,[213] the Catholic authorities in Berlin were forced to open a Ledigenheim—not in a leafy borough, in the central city, nor by a prominent architect, but in a disused factory on the Spree (Figure 1.19).[214]

Yet, even with the realization that there was no future for the German artisan and with the subsequent destruction of many Catholic Ledigenheime during the Second World War, something of Kolping's project remains. The Verband Katholischen Gesellenvereine, officially renamed *Kolpingwerk* in 1935, survives to the present—though it largely shifted its attention from the well-being of apprentices to humanitarian projects in the third world, aid to the elderly, and the health of the family. Yet, what was old is new again and 2009 saw the (re) founding of *Kolping Jugendwohnen GmbH* in Cologne, an initiative to build *new* homes (in Berlin-Prenzlauerberg, Frankfurt am Main, Hamburg, Cologne Ehrenfeld and Mitte, Trier, Ulm, and Wuppertal) for young men *and* women

Figure 1.19 Catholic Ledigenheim on the Spree, Berlin. View from the Spree River. *Source:* "Heime in ehemaligen Fabriken," *Bauwelt* 45 (1928): 1073.

seeking community, or "more than a roof over the head," during what Kolping termed "the storm and stress period of life."[215] A combination of realistic expectations founded on firm economic ground, a tacit acknowledgment of and adaptation to the realities of a rapidly industrializing and urbanizing nation, the Catholic Ledigenheim movement was ultimately a dream heavily reliant upon the idealization of a Catholic Germany, past mores, and a dying community—but one within which there may still be life.

Notes

1 Kolpingwerk Deutschland, "Jugendwohnen in Köln-Mitte," 2018, accessed May 20, 2018, https://www.kolping-jugendwohnen.de/koeln-mitte
2 Derek S. Linton, *Who Has the Youth, Has the Future: The Campaign to Save Young Workers in Imperial Germany* (Cambridge: Cambridge University Press, 1991), 72.
3 Dr. Msgr. Schweitzer, *Hospize und Ledigenheime der kath. Gesellenvereine* (M. Gladbach: Volksvereins Verlag, 1911), 3; Heinrich Festing, *Adolph Kolping und sein Werk* (Freiburg: Herder, 1981), 45, 63.
4 Simon Hyde, "Roman Catholicism and the Prussian State," *Central European History* 24, no. 2 (1991): 107; *Concordia* (1911): 431. Historically, journeymen were not allowed to be married and conversely, guild regulations precluded awarding mastership to bachelors. Consequently, marriage and mastership often coincided (Mack Walker, *German Home Towns: Community, State, and General Estate: 1648–1871* (Ithaca: Cornell University Press, 1971), 84).
5 Schweitzer, 3.
6 *Concordia* (1911): 431.
7 John V. Maciuika, *Before the Bauhaus: Architecture, Politics, and the German State, 1890-1920* (Cambridge: Cambridge University Press, 2005), 59.
8 Shulamit Volkov, *The Rise of Popular Antimodernism in Germany: The Urban Master Artisans* (Princeton: Princeton University Press, 1978), 27. Emphasis mine.
9 Kevin Repp, *Reformers, Critics, and the Paths of German Modernity: Anti-Politics and the Search for Alternatives, 1890-1914* (Cambridge: Harvard University Press, 2000), 184, from Sombart, Kapitalismus (1902), vol. 1, pp. 84–6.
10 Volkov, 18.
11 Jonathan Sperber, *Popular Catholicism in Nineteenth Century Germany* (Princeton: Princeton University Press, 1984), 87.
12 Volkov, 101.
13 Maciuika, 15.
14 Maciuika, 15; Volkov, 61, 125.

15 Volkov, 9.
16 Adolph Kolping, *Der Gesellenverein: zur Beherzigung für Alle, die es mit dem wahren Volkswohl gut meinen* (Cöln/Neuss: Schwann, 1849), 6.
17 Festing, 25.
18 Volkov, 26, see also page 110. Although this could vary by location and trade, a master artisan typically took on one apprentice, who was then obliged to train under him for between three and four years, and no more than two journeymen (Walker, 82, 87).
19 Donald J. Olsen, "Inside the Dwelling: The Viennese Wohnung," in *Housing and Dwelling*, ed. Barbara Miller Lane (London: Routledge, 2007), 118.
20 Kolping, 13.
21 *Concordia* (1911): 431. Before the nineteenth century, guild statutes mandated that apprentices and journeymen reside only in the home of a master artisan or in a registered hostel. If he did not, or if he remained in town without guild-approved work, he was "treated as a vagrant" (Walker, 83).
22 Richard Calwer, *Das Kost- und Logiswesen im Handwerk* (Berlin: Verlag der Generalkommission den Gewerkschaften Deutschlands, 1908), 84; Wilhelm Keil, *Erlebnisse eines Sozialdemokraten* (Stuttgart, 1947), 30.
23 Kolping, 19.
24 Kolping, 5,18.
25 Kolping, 7–8.
26 Kolping, 5.
27 Maciuika, 15.
28 Kolping, 8.
29 Volkov, 104.
30 Kolping, 4.
31 Kolping, 6.
32 Ernst Cahn, *Das Schlafstellenwesen und seine Reform* (Stuttgart, 1908), 44.
33 Josh Tosh, "New Men? The Bourgeois Cult of Home," *History Today* 46, no. 12 (December 1996): 2.
34 Maciuika, 35–7; Stanford Anderson, "Peter Behrens, Friedrich Naumann, and the Werkbund," in *The Architecture of Politics: 1910–1940* (Miami Beach: Wolfsonian, 1995), 11–12.
35 Charitas-Sekretär Salzgeber, *Schlafstellenwesen und Ledigenheime, Vorbericht und Verhandlungen der 13. Konferenz der Zentralstelle fuer Arbeiter-Wohlfahrtseinrichtungen am 9. Und 10. Mai in Leipzig* (Schriften der Zentralstelle für Arbeiter-Wohlfahrtseinrichtungen (no. 26)) (Berlin: Carl Henmanns Verlag, 1904), 156.
36 Schweitzer, 11; Salzgeber, 43.
37 Festing, 65.

38 Festing, 19.
39 Festing, 63. The Lendersche Haus was purchased for 14, 200 Taler (Michael Schmolke, *Adolph Kolping als Publizist: ein Beitrag zur Publizistik und zur Verandsgeschichte des deutschen Katholizismus im 19. Jahrhundert* (Münster: Verlag Regensburg, 1966), 67). This building in turn was renovated and expanded in 1865, again in 1884, and finally in 1910.
40 Schweitzer, 3, 15, 18.
41 Schmolke, 63.
42 Festing, 63.
43 Jonathan Sperber, "The Transformation of Catholic Associations in the Northern Rhineland and Westphalia 1830–1870," *Journal of Social History* 15, no. 2 (Winter, 1981): 258.
44 Though accounts conflict somewhat, it appears that the first conference took place in Düsseldorf, with the second and third held in Cologne (on November 9, 1851) and Mainz (on October 7–10, 1851) respectively (Schmolke, 63). It was at the "Generalversammlung" held in Mainz in 1851 where the organization decided to purchase the "Lendersche Haus" on the Breite Strasse in Cologne, with a view to converting the building into a Ledigenheim (63).
45 Kolping, 19.
46 Schmolke, 64.
47 Ibid., 68–9.
48 This statistic was drawn from Kolping's reports to *Rheinische Volksblätter* in 1858 (Ibid.).
49 Schweitzer, 8.
50 By way of illustration, of the nineteen Catholic Ledigenheime built in the German Reich between 1905 and1910, fifteen were located in the Rhineland or the neighboring Ruhr valley. The four exceptions were located in Catholic Bavaria (Bamberg and Würzburg), as well as Hildesheim (Saxony) and Lübeck (Schleiswig-Holstein) (Schweitzer, 19–20).
51 Schweitzer, 64.
52 Schweitzer, 20.
53 Schweitzer, 29–30.
54 Schweitzer, 27.
55 Schweitzer, 27.
56 Kolping, 24.
57 Kolping, 24.
58 Michael B. Gross, *The War against Catholicism: Liberalism and the Anti-Catholic Imagination in Nineteenth-Century Germany* (Ann Arbor: University of Michigan Press, 2005), 128–9. See also: Jonathan Sperber, "The Shaping of Political Catholicism in the Ruhr Basin, 1848–1881," *Central European History* 16, no. 4 (December, 1983): 354.

59　Lewis, 40–1.
60　Lewis, 21–2.
61　Gross, 221.
62　Gross, 42.
63　Sperber, *Popular Catholicism*, 32.
64　Lewis, 38.
65　Lewis, 22–3, 37.
66　Sperber, "The Transformation of Catholic Associations," 257.
67　Sperber, "The Transformation of Catholic Associations," 258.
68　Sperber, "The Transformation of Catholic Associations," 256, 258.
69　Sperber, "The Transformation of Catholic Associations," 256.
70　Sperber, *Popular Catholicism*, 77.
71　Sperber, *Popular Catholicism*, 86.
72　Sperber, *Popular Catholicism*, 86.
73　Leo XIII's papal encyclical of 1884, *Humanum Genus*, insisted the wealthy and powerful had an obligation to assist working men, and that this was not charity or almsgiving, but a "performance of a duty in justice" (Joseph Fichter, *Roots of Change* (New York: Appleton, 1939), 238).
　　The related encyclical of 1891, *Rerum Novarum*, insisted that workers were not chattel, but individuals deserving of dignity and dignified work (Fichter, 225, 228).
74　*Concordia* (1911): 432.
75　*Reichsarbeitsblatt* (1913): 440.
76　Schweitzer, 157. The transition to adulthood, or period of "Sturm und Drang," was a literary reference to the Romantics of the early nineteenth century.
77　*Das Arbeiterwohl* (1892): 116. Emphasis mine.
78　Helmut Walser-Smith, *German Nationalism and Religious Conflict* (Princeton: Princeton University Press, 1995), 87–8.
79　Only 6.2 percent left officially (Adolph Levenstein, *Die Arbeiterfrage: mit besonderer beruecksichtigung der sozialpsychologischen seite des modernen grossbetriebes und der psycho-physischen einwirkung auf der arbeiter* (München: Ernst Reinhardt, 1912), 353).
80　Volkov, 29, 114.
81　Sperber, *Popular Catholicism*, 180.
82　Richard J. Evans, *Proletarians and Politics: Socialism, Protest and the Working Class in Germany before the First World War* (New York: St. Martin's Press, 1990), 11.
83　Schweitzer, 52. Concerning the direct Socialist threat, see Schweitzer, 17; *Das Arbeiterwohl* (1893): 55; Linton, 5, 17.
84　Schweitzer, 52.
85　Walser-Smith, 38.
86　Hyde, 116.

87　Hyde, 117.
88　Walser-Smith, 38.
89　Sperber, *Popular Catholicism*, 180.
90　Gross, 350.
91　Schmolke, 66.
92　Sperber, *Popular Catholicism*, 90.
93　Hans Joachim Kracht, "Adolph Kolping und die Gründung der ersten Gesellenvereine in Westfalen," in *Studia Westfalica* (Münster: Verlag Aschendorff, 1973), 199–200, 204–5.
94　Sperber, *Popular Catholicism*, 90; Schmolke, 69.
95　Sperber, "The Shaping of Political Catholicism," 365.
96　Schmolke, 29.
97　Schweitzer, 13; Salzgeber, 153.
98　Salzgeber, 154.
99　Schweitzer, 13.
100　Lewis, 40–1.
101　Sperber, *Popular Catholicism*, 223.
102　Festing, 79.
103　Gisela Moeller, *Peter Behrens in Düsseldorf: die Jahre von 1903–1907* (Weinheim: VCH, 1991), 500.
104　Walser-Smith, 44.
105　Schweitzer, 14.
106　Schweitzer, 13.
107　Schweitzer, 13.
108　Schweitzer, 54.
109　Salzgeber, 153.
110　Salzgeber, 153. Emphasis mine.
111　Schweitzer, 69–72.
112　Salzgeber, 38–40.
113　Salzgeber, 157.
114　Volkov, 29.
115　Gross, 191.
116　Gross, 205.
117　Walser-Smith, 21.
118　Schweitzer, 12.
119　*Concordia* (1911): 431.
120　Schweitzer, 22.
121　For example, the Aschaffenburg Ledigenheim had eighty members, though only ten of these members resided in the Ledigenheim. However, twenty men, both residents and nonresidents, were served lunch and dinner daily in the dining hall (Schweitzer, 19).

122 Schweitzer, 54.
123 Schweitzer, 54.
124 Stanford Anderson, *Peter Behrens and a New Architecture for the Twentieth Century* (Cambridge: MIT Press, 2000), 198.
125 Schweitzer, 23.
126 Volkov, 101.
127 Kolping, 20.
128 Sperber, *Popular Catholicism*, 221; Schmolke, 29.
129 Kolping, 20.
130 Laurie Marhoffer, *Sex and the Weimar Republic: German Homosexual Emancipation* (Toronto: University of Toronto, 2015), 31.
131 Peter U. Hohendahl, "The Origins of Mass Culture: The Case of Imperial Germany 1871–1918," *New German Critique* 29 (1983): 5.
132 On the coding of Catholic men as women, see Gross, 191; Walser-Smith, 35. On the poor formal education of artisans, see Volkov, 145.
133 By 1884 this home had expanded into a neighboring building, also on the Breitestrasse. Yet, even this expansion did not provide enough space, and in 1910 the building was further expanded through the city block to the Helenenstrasse running parallel behind the Breitestrasse, fully renovated, and given an entirely new facade.
134 As of 1910, eight different streetcar lines converged on the Neumarkt, which was a major transfer location (*Pharus Plan von Köln* (Berlin: Pharus Verlag, 1904)).
135 Schweitzer, 60.
136 Paula Lupkin, *Manhood Factories: YMCA Architecture and the Making of Modern Urban Culture* (Minneapolis: University of Minnesota Press, 2010), 112; John Donald Gustav-Wrathall, *Take the Young Stranger by the Hand* (Chicago: University of Chicago, 1998), 26.
137 Lupkin, 132.
138 Lupkin, 45; Gustav-Wrathall, 5.
139 Dieter Langewiesche, "Für Volk und Vaterland," in *Kulturgut oder Körperkult?*, ed. Ommo Gruppe (Tübingen: Attempto, 1990), 22–61.
140 *Das Arbeiterwohl* 12 (1892): 117.
141 *Das Arbeiterwohl* 12 (1892): 118.
142 *Das Arbeiterwohl* 12 (1892): 118.
143 British Board of Trade, xi–xii.
144 Volkov, 117.
145 Salzgeber, 153.
146 Salzgeber, 153; Schweitzer, 48, 59.
147 Schweitzer, 77.
148 Gustav-Wrathall, 12, 21; Lupkin, 63, 75, 79–80, 115.
149 Schweitzer, 106.

150 Schweitzer, 59.
151 *Concordia* (1911): 431.
152 Schweitzer, 98; *Schlafstellenwesen und Ledigenheime*, 38.
153 Irina Winter, *Georg Benjamin: Arzt und Kommunist* (Berlin: Verlag Volk und Gesundheit, 1962), 34.
154 Judith Walkowitz, *City of Dreadful Delight* (Chicago: University of Chicago Press, 1992), 34.
155 Marhoffer, 24.
156 Winter, 31.
157 Robert Tobin, *Peripheral Desires: The German Discovery of Sex* (Philadelphia: UPenn, 2015), 4.
158 Tobin, 2.
159 Marhoffer, 44–5.
160 Marhoffer, 122.
161 Gustav-Wrathall, 66.
162 Lupkin, 112.
163 Marhoffer, 45.
164 Schweitzer, 53.
165 Lewis, 80. Hansastädte were free cities that formed an economic alliance in the medieval period in order to support trade and member cities' merchant guilds. These cities, stretching from the Baltic to the North Sea, were as varied as Danzig (Gdansk), Bremen, Bruges, Lübeck, Cologne, Hamburg, Riga, and Tallin.
166 Lewis, 65.
167 Lewis, 151.
168 Volkov, 23, 305.
169 Volkov, 24.
170 Lewis, 56.
171 Lewis, 65, 153, 160.
172 Lewis, 161.
173 Lewis, 54.
174 Anderson, *Peter Behrens*, 65.
175 Deborah E. B. Weiner, "Hull House and the Production of Women's Space in the Late Victorian City," *Critical Matrix* 11, no. 2 (June 1999): 87.
176 H. F. Wilson, "Toynbee Hall," *Cambridge Review* (February 18, 1885): 214.
177 Barbara Miller Lane, *National Romanticism and Modern Architecture in Germany and the Scandinavian Countries* (Cambridge: Cambridge University Press, 2000), 36–9, 82–95.
178 Helen Lefkowitz Horowitz, "Hull House as Women's Space," *Chicago History* 12, no. 4 (Winter 1983): 45.
179 Cynthia Rock, "Building the Women's Club in Nineteenth Century America," *Heresies* 3, no. 3 (1981): 89.

180 Horowitz, 47.
181 Maciuika, 115.
182 Spiegel, "Ledigenheime," 425.
183 For a fuller discussion of the genesis of the Werkbund and its implications for German design culture, see footnote 27 of the Introduction.
184 Anderson, *Peter Behrens*, 50.
185 Maciuika, 103.
186 Schweitzer, 75.
187 Anderson, *Peter Behrens*, 194.
188 Schweitzer, 75.
189 Behrens, quoted in Schweitzer, 75.
190 Schweitzer.
191 In Schweitzer's ideal formulation, a room for a single resident measured 2.10 by 4.50 meters, and that for three men sharing 3.30 by 5.20 meters (109–112).
192 Ibid., 109–12.
193 Lizabeth Cohen, "Embellishing a Life of Labor," in *Common Places* (Athens, GA: University of Georgia, 1986), 261–80.
194 Schweitzer, 109–12.
195 Cahn, 22.
196 Dawson, *Municipal Life and Government in Germany* (New York: Longmans, Green and Co., 1914), 309.
197 Eric Hobsbawm, *Age of Empire* (New York: Pantheon, 1987), 221–2.
198 Ellen Gates Starr, "Art and Labor," in *Hull House Maps and Papers* (New York: Thomas Y. Crowell and Co., 1895), 176; See also, Cohen, 263.
199 "Cheap and nasty" was the verdict on the German objects on view at the 1876 Philadelphia world's fair (Frederic Schwartz, *The Werkbund: Design Theory and Mass Culture before the First World War* (New Haven: Yale, 1996), 27).
200 Ferdinand Avenarius, "Hausgruel," *Dürerbund. Flugschrift zur Ausdruckskultur* 44, no. 1 (November 1908), quoted in Jennifer Jenkins, "The Kitsch Collections and the Spirit in the Furniture: Cultural Reform and National Culture in Germany," *Social History* 21, no. 2 (May 1996): 125.
201 Kai Gutschow, "Schultze-Naumburg's Heimatstil: A Nationalist Conflict of Tradition and Modernity," in *Traditional Dwellings and Settlements* 36, ed. Nezer Alsayyad (Berkeley, CA: Center for Environmental Design Research, 1992), 6.
Similarly, Hermann Muthesius, a leading member of the Werkbund, called for a "modern medium of expression" drawn from "vernacular building traditions" at the turn of the previous century ("Wo stehen Wir?" *Jahrbuch des deutschen Werkbundes* (Jena, 1912): 35).
202 Jenkins, 131.

203 Fritz Schumacher, "Die Wiedereroberung harmonischer Kultur," address at the founding meeting of the Werkbund, Munich, October 5, 1907, published in *Der Kunstwart* 21, no. 8 (1908): 138, quoted in Schwartz, *The Werkbund*, 13.
204 Anderson, "Peter Behrens," 9.
205 Jenkins, 140; Maciuika, 66.
206 Anderson, "Peter Behrens," 18; Maciuika, 66.
207 Anderson, *Peter Behrens*, 110.
208 Maciuika, 115.
209 Maciuika, 109, 117.
210 Maciuika, 125.
211 Hermann Muthesius criticized Theodor Fischer for holding "the unjustified assumption that the schools should rescue the failing crafts [Handwerk] and bring them back to a golden existence . . . one cannot expect this from even the best school" (Maciuika, 232).
212 Schweitzer, 99.
213 Volkov, 6.
214 "Heime in ehemaligen Fabriken," *Bauwelt* 45 (1928): 1073.
215 Kolpingwerk Deutschland.

2

Beyond the Company Town
Industrialists House the Roving Male

In February 1967 the German economic journal *Handelsblatt* published the following expose on the living conditions of guestworkers (*Gastarbeiter*) in Düsseldorf:

> Six Turkish and Greek guestworkers are housed in a space of not more than 15 square meters. The beds are pushed close together, and even though it is only half past eight, the men are already lying in them. What else is there to do in this hole in the ground? Not enough chairs are available. Under a slanting bare lightbulb in the middle of the room stands a small table covered by a "tablecloth" of newspaper. The floor is bare and dirty, as are the walls. A picture, a curtain, is sought in vain.[1]

Unfortunately, for guestworkers in postwar (West) Germany such living conditions were far from uncommon.[2] As thousands, then millions, of Italians, Spaniards, Greeks, Yugoslavs, Moroccans, Tunisians, and Turks arrived in the Federal Republic of Germany beginning in the 1950s, employers and society grappled with how to house this much needed migrant labor force—largely young men of marginal socioeconomic and ethnic status living far from home and (at least early on) without their families.[3] To curb their maltreatment at the hands of unscrupulous landlords and curtail the sociocultural "wildness" of these economically useful men, large industrial firms in the 1950s and 1960s turned to a solution their predecessors had devised over one hundred years before—the Ledigenheim.[4]

The roots of the Ledigenheim building type as built by employers for their workforce first developed in the 1850s–70s in regions where industrial labor—catastrophically for Kolping's residents—was replacing artisanal and agricultural labor. This new factory work was significantly different from the specialized work of the old crafts or the agricultural economy in many ways but, like the journeyman or apprentice before him, often required laborers to relocate to find work, and often in places where little infrastructure or housing existed.[5] When factories and mines were located in areas where no, or no acceptable, living options were available, employers quickly realized that it was in their business interests to provide more than a wage to their growing workforce, and began to reconsider their obligations. Housing—for families and singles alike—had to be constructed, lest they lose their workforce to a competitor providing decent (or any) accommodations, but also because they believed what groups such as the Verein zur Verbesserung der Arbeiterwohnungen (Organization for the Betterment of Workers' Housing) had recognized as early as 1846 that the primary means to "improve of the moral conditions of the poorer classes" and preserve them from "misleading and incendiary tendencies" lay in providing "improved" housing.[6]

By the 1860s, private employers like Villeroy and Bosch in Mettlach and Krupp in Essen began to build permanent detached and semidetached brick cottages for skilled and semiskilled workers and their families within easy walking distance of the factory complex—the beginnings of extensive company towns.[7] As with their predecessors and contemporaries in New Lanark, Scotland, Lawrence, Massachusetts, and Saltaire, England, company towns in what would become the German Empire were built not only in locations undergoing rapid industrialization and urbanization, such as Berlin, the Rhineland/Ruhr, Upper Silesia, and areas of Hessen and Saxony, but also in rural and remote places where there were no other boarding opportunities, such as the vast eastern reaches of the Reich, including Brandenburg and East and West Prussia.[8] Regardless of the location and scale of the enterprise, nearly all *forbade* unrelated individuals—lodgers—in housing meant for families (even as this dictate was sometimes ignored).[9]

While the New England farm girls turned factory workers in early northern mill towns like Lowell and Laurence, Massachusetts were lauded in the press as fresh-faced, virtuous, and innocent—and housed in (privately run and company overseen) dormitories that preserved these qualities[10]—most *single male* workers on both sides of the Atlantic lodged with families, sometimes illicitly in (new) company housing, or more commonly, outside a company complex, creating what historian Franz-Josef Brüggemeier referred to as a "half-open" family structure.[11] Though apprentice and journeymen artisans *and* agricultural workers traditionally lodged with or in the near vicinity of their masters and employers, contemporaries noted that this was different. Not only were these men young, unmarried, largely unskilled, and transient[12]—all signifiers of marginal status—

they also were rarely local and increasingly drawn from the eastern reaches of what would become the German Empire, often from East Prussia and the Polish provinces, which had troubling ethnic and religious implications.[13]

Their marginality meant that they easily became—as with Italian, Yugoslav, or Turkish guestworkers a century later, and migrant workers in Europe and the United States now—the locus of numerous (largely misplaced) fears, from their potential use as strikebreakers (feared by other workers) *and* their supposed propensity to go on strike (a concern of employers and government officials),[14] to their supposed sexual immorality in particular. As John Kulczycki has reported in his work on the Ruhr region, a dearth of potential brides in burgeoning industrial regions,[15] alongside typically older husbands, younger wives, and even younger lodgers was seized upon as proof that lodgers, "[working] a different shift than the husband, [did] the same thing that his landlord was not above doing before his marriage."[16] They were *the* source of illicit liaisons, unwanted pregnancies, venereal disease, and marital breakdown.

Although *all* male lodgers—be they Catholic apprentices in the Rhineland, unskilled workers from Posen, or clerks in Berlin—were tarred with a similar brush, employers took particular note. While Adolph Kolping worried about young artisans as a group and the future state of the artisan estate as a whole, employers were much less concerned about the moral well-being of their single workers, and more about what this supposed abandonment of sexual norms meant for the subversion of others. The sexual immorality of their workers may have offended employers *personally*, but more importantly, it also posed a danger to their power. Most German industrialists—particularly those engaged in heavy industry—ascribed to the notion of *Herr-im-Haus*, or "master in my own house," meaning that they saw their factories and mines as their exclusive domain, one in which neither the government nor even the king (and later, emperor) had any right to meddle.[17] Like feudal lords before them, they positioned themselves as father figures who alone understood the needs of and could control their workers. If patriarchal norms were already being subverted through problematic lodging practices, who was to say that this would not have a trickle-down effect and that *all* employees—single and married, unskilled and skilled, German and foreign—would begin to challenge the "natural" authority of their employers?

Disquieted by what they saw as the emergence of a dangerous class of men, neither rooted to place nor bound to family, and feared as the most uncontrollable and easily radicalized members of the workforce,[18] industrialists began to segregate their single employees from the rest of their workforce in specialized housing—in what I am terming an *industrial* Ledigenheim. From the earliest variants to the last iterations, their goal was not the transformation of men into good husbands and fathers, nor softening of the rough edges of working-class masculinity with an eye to sociocultural elevation. A decidedly less idealistic undertaking than Adolph Kolping's contemporaneous project, such employers *always* conceived of industrial Ledigenheime as a means by which a company could regulate and retain a large group (often upward of one hundred residents) of solid and virtuous single workers in the midst of a constantly shifting working population by policing residents' bodies within and outside of the home.[19] Through a complex and interrelated system of overt rules, spatial controls, and visual cues they took a robust population (including non-German elements) under control—culling undesirable employees from the home while protecting more reliable and compliant residents.[20] Echoing this "protection" at a larger scale, and *unlike* other Ledigenheim variants, which were often well integrated into the larger community and actively sought to facilitate connections between residents and others, industrial Ledigenheime nearly always segregated residents from the surrounding community of workers. Ledigenheime and their residents were rarely placed at the center of these settlements, but were instead purposefully placed on the periphery, even as the spare and architecturally unremarkable barracks of the nineteenth century gave way to more aesthetically sophisticated creations, and gridded and monotonous company towns were transformed into idyllic "garden cities." While industrial Ledigenheime and their immediate surroundings increasingly allowed employers to position themselves as progressive, modern, and profitable, they *remained* a means to discipline labor through a sliding scale of privilege.

The Roots of the Early Industrial (Proto-)Ledigenheim

It is difficult to consider the majority of the buildings constructed by employers for their single employees before the 1870s to be "true" Ledigenheime. A more apt label is proto-Ledigenheim, though these buildings were generally termed *Schlafhäuser* (literally, houses for sleeping) or *Schlafbaracken* (sleeping barracks), and occasionally *Logierhäuser* (lodging houses), *Arbeiterkaserne* (military barracks for workers), or *Menagen* (reassemblies of the household) by their builders. Certainly, the companies supporting the construction of these early Ledigenheime—Bibiella near Tarnowitz and Maxgrube near Laurahütte in Upper Silesia, Grube von der Heydt near Saarbrücken, as well as Krupp's Rheinhausen Menage on the Freistattestrasse in Essen (1856),[21] among others—never claimed that their creations were "architecture" in any sense of the word, rarely employing architects to design them (Figure 2.1). Typically, these buildings—largely undifferentiated in form from army barracks or homeless shelters—did not employ a recognizable architectural style, and were laid out very simply, with several large rooms arranged along a central corridor running the length of the building.[22] In lieu of a complex organization of space or architectural detailing, early employers privileged advanced ventilation systems and utilized modern "hygienic" materials. Walls and floors were typically constructed of cement and then plastered, and the easily dirtied high-use spaces—kitchens, bathrooms, and corridors—were fitted out with tiles to facilitate easy cleaning.[23]

As proto-Ledigenheime were often used to test out new building materials and technologies, this new building type was heavily covered by building trade journals—*Deutsche Bauhütte*, *Die Bauwelt*, *Moderne Bauformen*, and *Süddeutsche Bauzeitung*—featured alongside articles celebrating advances in ventilation and heating, as well as exciting new materials like linoleum. The artistic merit of these early buildings was never a topic of discussion, and it was rare that coverage dealt with the larger societal implications of these buildings, the exception being publications not geared to the architectural profession,

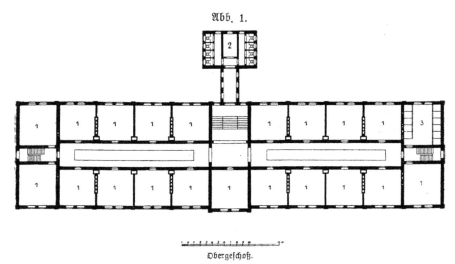

Figure 2.1 *Schlafhaus* for unmarried miners of Royal Coal Mine von der Heydt near Saarbrücken (*c*. 1865). Plan of first and second upper floors.
Source: Weyls Handbuch der Hygiene (Leipzig: Barth, 1918), 342.

such as the *Arbeiterwohl*, published by the *Verband katholischer Industriellen und Arbeiterfreunde*, an organization of Catholic industrialists who felt that a Catholic employer had a duty to his employees, and the *Arbeiterfreund*, the "voice of reforming liberalism."[24]

Although older models continued to be used (and constructed) by employers, this began to change in the early 1870s with the development of buildings that can more precisely be termed Ledigenheime. Far more than sanitary housing, even employers continued to use language (*Logierhaus, Schlafhaus, Arbeiterkaserne,* or *Menage*) that had been devised to describe their predecessors; Ledigenheime—as with the (new) company towns they were nearly always placed within—had come to serve as examples of precisely the sort of thing a forward-thinking employer *should* provide to his workers. In a *modern* industrial Ledigenheim, paternalism stood in perfect alignment with capitalist rationality.

Breaking with Convention: The Bochumer Verein's *Stahlhausen*

Built by the mining and steel fabricating company Bochumer Verien in 1872 to house 1,200 to 1,500 of its single workers, the *Kost- und Logierhaus Stahlhausen* (lodging and boarding house Stahlhausen—Stahlhausen translates directly to "house of steel") of the Ruhr city of Bochum serves as a preeminent example of this shift from hygienic barracks to more permanent and aesthetically sophisticated structures (Figure 2.2). Bochum was typical for the Ruhr in that the housing situation began to decline in the late 1840s, driven by a population imbalance in favor of young, single men and a chronic housing shortage.[25] As early as 1858 the average number of residents per household numbered thirteen, most of whom were crammed into one- or two-room dwellings, many as unregulated overnight lodgers or *Schlafgänger*.[26] This extreme overcrowding not only had negative consequences for family life but also was a contributing factor to reoccurring epidemics plaguing the area from the 1850s.[27] For employers in the area—including the administration of the Bochumer Verein—these conditions were particularly troubling. Instability in Bochum was beginning to negatively affect their profitability, with those individuals already on the margins—semiskilled and unskilled single workers—looking to better living conditions in neighboring towns.[28] Additionally, if an employee was over twenty-one years of age, there was little that an employer could do to regulate his behavior when he was not at

Figure 2.2 Ledigenheim of the Bochumer Verein, Stahlhausen Settlement, Bochum (1872–4). Photograph.
Source: *Schlafstellenwesen und Ledigenheime* (Berlin: Carl Henmanns Verlag, 1904), 10.

work—even though the average working week for an unskilled German laborer was seventy-two hours in 1871, which left precious little for anything else.[29]

To battle both high worker turnover and a perceived lack of control over social mores, the administration of the Bochumer Verien decided to integrate significant portions of its overwhelmingly nonlocal, unskilled, and single workforce into its "more disciplined and productive" permanent body of workers,[30] though the provision of "good and inexpensive accommodation" owned by the company—in short, a Ledigenheim in a company town.[31] Great claims were made for the potential of this building and those of its ilk—an expansion of the rhetoric surrounding the creation of company towns in general—that ranged from "stabilizing" the larger community of workers,[32] the city of Bochum, and the greater Ruhr,[33] to "destroying the roots" of Social Democracy (a particular bugbear of German industrialists, akin to the labor movement in the United States).[34] All would supposedly contribute to the financial success of company, and even further the expansion of heavy industry in the area—particularly exciting with the founding of the German Empire the year before.[35]

While the impetus behind (and lofty claims regarding) the construction of the Stahlhausen Ledigenheim was typical for the 1870s, in other ways the building was remarkable. Dr. Spetzler, acting *Baumeister* or chief building designer of the Bochumer Verein, abjured the construction of numerous small-scale temporary barracks and designed a massive, permanent, well-built, and self-contained building providing residents with *all* their needs, one that remained in use until it was destroyed in a 1943 Allied bombing raid.[36] Even as late as 1904 the building was still considered to be well priced and modern, with the amenities it provided to residents outstripping those of contemporaneous buildings by other employers,[37] including the Ledigenheime of the nearby Krupp works, the primary competition of the Bochumer Verein.[38]

Company apologists aside, although Stahlhausen and similar Ledigenheime provided residents with housing of significantly better quality and more amenities than they would have obtained either as an overnight lodger or in a pro-Ledigenheim, this does not necessarily indicate that they were viewed differently than they had been in the preceding decades—merely that more *permanent* measures were needed to control and house a growing workforce that increasingly consisted of migrants from the eastern reaches of the German Empire.[39] Young, unattached men were still the largest group among all migrants to industrial areas,[40] and they remained the most vulnerable and peripheral of employees. Unlike the residents of other Ledigenheim variants, they subject to a rule-based, paternalistic attitude that saw them as potential criminals, rather than individuals to be elevated.

Controlling Single Men

To control the formerly uncontrollable—young, unattached, migratory men—the Bochumer Verein had two interconnected means at its disposal: namely, beneficial programs and pleasant surroundings encouraging hard work, self-control, and allegiance to the company, which were coupled with both covert and overt systems of surveillance and control. In an industrial Ledigenheim, as with other variants, supporters hoped that "official" festivals, balls, and concerts, as well as the provision of food and drink, would pull workers away from the places and habits employers deemed problematic and keep them "at home" under watchful eye.[41] Like earlier proto-Ledigenheime, Stahlhausen's hygienic and technological advantages, from advanced ventilation systems to steam heating and gas lighting, provided another draw.[42] Unlike earlier barracks, however, Spetzler coupled this with a greater emphasis on aesthetics. While hardly elegant in relationship to the interior of one of Kolping's Ledigenheime, the architectural press deemed the interior of Stahlhausen to be "pleasant, light and bright."[43] Large evenly spaced windows let ample light into every room, and Spetzler married functionality with decorative detailing in carefully chosen locations. For example, while the staircases were treated with basalt lava to prevent both wear and tear, as well as accidents,[44] the dining rooms featured wooden floors laid in a herringbone pattern, and a dado surmounted by trim ringed the room.[45] In a move that seemed to pull Stahlhausen closer to other Ledigenheim variants housing residents of greater means and social standing, cavernous sleeping halls were replaced by bedrooms generally housing eight men (though rooms for two, four, eight, ten, or twelve men also existed), all of which contained a table and benches, lockable wardrobes, and cast-iron bedsteads (each with a straw mattress, sea grass filled pillow, linen bedcover, with woolen blankets available upon request) (Figure 2.3).[46]

This shift from large dormitories to what contemporaries deemed bedrooms (though at eight men to a room, most really were smaller sleeping halls) had several purposes. Smaller numbers of men per room made it easier to house workers on the same shift together, meaning that a resident who worked a day shift was less likely to be disturbed by a roommate returning from a night shift, ostensibly leading to better rested workers less prone to jobsite accidents (at least not for reasons of exhaustion). More importantly, under this system one's roommates remained the same from day to day and week to week, if not longer.[47] Commensurate with the supporters of other Ledigenheim variants, Spetzler believed that a stable roommate situation would ultimately foster longer tenancies *and* camaraderie, what he saw as key components in the creation of a community of contented workers.[48]

Yet, the healthful surroundings of a modern industrial Ledigenheim like Stahlhausen were only part of the equation in maintaining stability and order. Even as contemporaries consistently wrote that overtly controlling tactics were doomed to fail,[49] in Stahlhausen residents' bodies were policed as though they remained on the shop floor or in the mine, and to a far greater degree than any

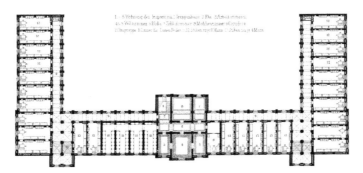

Figure 2.3 Ledigenheim of the Bochumer Verein, Stahlhausen Settlement, Bochum (1872–4). Plan of the second floor.
Source: Zeitschrift für Baukunde 2, no. 4 (1879): 537–50.

other company employee on his "own" time. While it is possible that friendships organically developed between roommates, Spetzler had purposefully devised a system that actively discouraged total anonymity and gave the administration eyes into what might have been the most private of spaces, the bedroom. Closely replicating a system that was already in place in the mines of the Ruhr, Spetzler placed one "trustworthy" individual, or *Stubenälteste*, in each group of roommates.[50] This person, chosen from a pool of long-term residents who had proven themselves loyal, played the *official* role of interpersonal intermediary, meeting with the management to air residents' grievances. Yet, considering that he was *not* elected by his peers, but chosen by the management, most contemporaries viewed a Stubenälteste as a creature of the management at best. At worst, he was a spy, hired to report on his fellow workers in matters ranging from illegally cleaning boots in a bedroom to planning a strike.[51] For Spetzler's system to work well, it was necessary that bedrooms contain reasonably small numbers of residents, which not only made the observational job of the Stubenälteste easier but also facilitated the placement of more spies throughout the Ledigenheim.[52]

Lest one think that this is painting the administration with too dark a brush, under this "comradely" (*Kameradisch*) system residents were not even allowed to visit each other's bedrooms, nor were they to enter their own bedrooms during the daytime (unless they worked a night shift).[53] Most significantly, in sharp distinction from other Ledigenheim variants that often saw the inclusion of semiprivate spaces such as relaxation and drafting rooms on the upper floors, Stahlhausen provided its residents with neither. In fact, the observational powers of the administration were increased by not only the omission of such spaces and the presence of the Stubenältesten but also the placement of bedrooms within the Ledigenheim. In a building housing 850 men, only 3 stairwells led to all the bedrooms, and the primary stairwell directly abutted the house inspector's second-floor apartment (see Figure 2.3).[54] This placement not only provided him visual and auditory access to residents' movements but further curtailed their movements as it effectively cut off one wing of the building from the other. To protect the Bochumer Verein from real or imagined subversive activity, a resident was always in a semipublic space where anything could be seen or overheard at any time.[55] In the manner of Jeremy Bentham's Panopticon, the power of the Bochumer Verein was made even more manifest by its omnipresence and its un-verifiability, as well as its ability to arrange individuals as if they were objects.[56]

If this was not enough to maintain order, the disciplinary power of the company was further underscored by an extensive set of house rules. Such regulations were not only the most stringent of any Ledigenheim variant but also remarkably static over three-quarters of a century, rarely varying from company to company.[57] Considering their near universality, the rules of Krupp's contemporaneous Ledigenheim (termed *Menage*) are as useful as those of the Bochumer Verein in indicating the types of infractions punishable by a (heavy) fine, as well as what constituted more pronounced and serious misdeeds.[58] The former included, but were not limited to, the requirement that one make one's bed daily and attend meals with washed hands and without a hat, that "haircutting and shaving must only be done in the corridors and cleaned up promptly," and a prohibition on throwing things out of windows and smoking in bedrooms.[59] Though Krupp stressed that these rules were largely meant to ensure the health and safety of the residents, requiring men to take off their hats and to help keep the building tidy indicate that the company was interested in defining how one should *reside* in a domestic space, not simply sleep for the night.[60] They also connect to the notion—as popularized by the social insurance schemes inaugurated by Otto von Bismarck—that both employers and employees had to have a hand in schemes supporting workers in order for the latter to be fully invested in the reforms undertaken on their behalf.[61]

Of course, not all residents could be redomesticated, and in an exercise in total authority (and little forgiveness) incomparable to any other variant of Ledigenheim, residents who did not easily conform—particularly as this concerned the systems of control and surveillance put in place by the administration—were severely punished. Simply bringing a nonresident into the home without permission, or changing one's bedroom, bed, or dining hall seat, resulted in immediate dismissal.[62] While this level of control without benevolence was quickly dismissed by the management, who attributed any resistance to dwelling in the company Ledigenheim to a dislike of "punctual and orderly behavior,"[63] and "complainers who are never happy and are not used to order and cleanliness,"[64] it had several precedents. Mimicking the paternalistic and unforgiving stance *within* the factories and mines of the Ruhr, as well as "closed mining towns" elsewhere,[65] the rules and regulations of an industrial Ledigenheim like Stahlhausen can also be compared to those of British Rowton Houses, which required their residents to vacate their bedrooms mid-morning,[66] and perhaps more troublingly, homeless shelters, which required (and still often require) overnight guests to leave not only the dormitory but also the building during the working day.[67] Such undesirable reference points, coupled with an omnipresent system of surveillance and lack of semiprivate spaces within which to socialize, placed the residents of an industrial Ledigenheim in the same position as groups German industrialists considered with disdain and mistrust—the lowest class of British worker and destitute Germans reliant on the charity of others.

However, an industrial Ledigenheim was never intended to be the medicine that would heal a fractured society, what the industrialists of Bochum branded "humanitarian nonsense."[68] Instead, visual cues, overt rules, and a careful organization of space providing residents with a paucity of spaces to be alone *or* together ensured that the residents of industrial Ledigenheime remained guests—not partners as with Catholic Ledigenheim residents, nor potential *Zimmerherrn* as in municipal homes—in what was not a home, but a camp.

The Ledigenheim and the Company Town

Ironically, at the same time the Bochumer Verein began enacting increasingly sophisticated systems of surveillance over its single residents through the vehicle of the Ledigenheim, it was constructing family housing that increasingly privileged privacy, or at least its appearance. While earlier family housing had taken the form of "barracks," where numerous families shared the same door

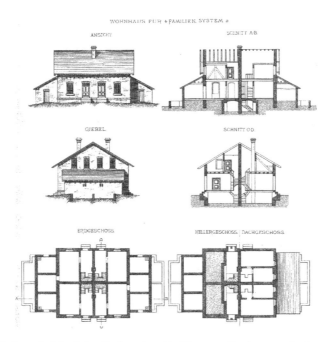

Figure 2.4 Four-in-block family housing, Stahlhausen Settlement, Bochum (1872–4). Plans, sections, and elevations.
Source: Zeitschrift für Baukunde 2, no. 4 (1879): 537–50.

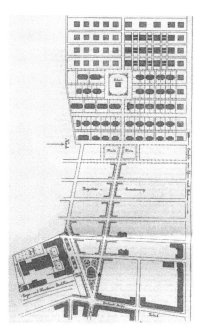

Figure 2.5 Plan of the Stahlhausen Settlement, Bochum (1872–4). Note the location of the Ledigenheim to the south-east of the gridded family housing.
Source: *Zeitschrift für Baukunde* 2, no. 4 (1879): 537–50.

and stairwell—essentially a *Mietskaserne*—this new housing employed the four-in-block system, meaning that a small two-story building resembling a single-family home housed four families in total, or two families per floor, none of which shared a door to the outside with more than one other family (Figure 2.4).[69] Spetzler also took care to place this housing within a well-ordered and hygienic settlement—the first company town serving the employees of the Bochumer Verein (Figure 2.5).

As with the construction of Ledigenheime, the building of company towns commonly developed with other employer-supported initiatives for the general health and well-being of their employees—"welfare work" in the English-speaking world and *Fürsorge* programs *or Wohlfahrtseinrichtungen* in German—ranging from the construction of playgrounds and other green spaces to the creation of social aid programs and bathing facilities, all of which were carefully positioned by their supporters as grounded in economic necessity and of direct benefit to business, rather than "a frill or vehicle for the fulfillment of philanthropic impulses."[70] As George Pullman of the Pullman Palace Car Company put it, the ill-fated and self-named model town he constructed for his workers to the South of Chicago beginning in 1880 was "a strictly business proposition."[71]

Though it was by no means certain that an employer, even a large and prosperous one, would construct housing settlements, nor a Ledigenheime within such a complex, leading German firms began to do so, including the most famous contemporary and competitor of the Bochumer Verein, Fried. Krupp of Essen.[72] Under the leadership of Alfred Krupp, the firm of Krupp continued to build proto-Ledigenheim barracks housing over 2,500 men in the Segeroth area in the early 1870s, but also began to construct what Alfred Krupp termed "more hotel-like lodgings for his workers," such as his Kronenberg "colony" (1872–3).[73] This complex not only contained 233 family residences but also a gymnasium, a low-cost grocery, kindergarten, bath house, a sewing school, and a Ledigenheim (Figure 2.6).[74]

Yet, like the welfare programs that accompanied their creation, full access to the amenities of such a complex was applied selectively. As in company towns in Germany and elsewhere, various residential zones for different groups of residents served as markers of one's place within the hierarchy of workers. For example, in the town of Pullman, Illinois, "neat rows of brick houses" housed skilled workers, while management lived in detached villas on a wide

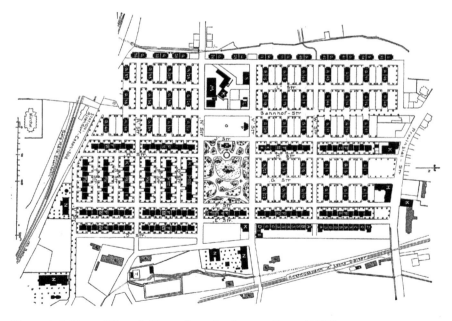

Figure 2.6 Plan of Krupp's Kronenberg Settlement, Essen (1872).
Source: Richard Klapheck, *Siedlungswerk Krupp* (Berlin: Ernst Wasmuth, 1930), 29.

boulevard, and unskilled, mostly foreign-born laborers resided in unregulated speculative housing outside of the town proper.[75] By contrast, the management of Stahlhausen primarily lived off-site and nearly identical family housing—access to green space and the size and location of apartments in family dwellings were remarkably consistent—revealed little of their residents' socioeconomic status (see Figure 2.4). This meant that the Ledigenheim played, at least in part, the role that unregulated speculative housing did in other contexts.

The visual and spatial distinctiveness of a Ledigenheim was thus a constant reminder of the low status of its residents, a means of defining their "otherness" within the larger community of workers. It was not enough to remove lodgers from family apartments and house them in a Ledigenheim. The placement of this "home" for single workers—on the southeastern edge of the settlement, one block west of the factory complex and over six blocks southeast of the nearest housing for families—underscored their separateness (see Figure 2.5).[76] The Ledigenheim was not even positioned on the same *axis* as the rest of the housing. Where single-family homes were oriented precisely north-south/east-west, the rigid grid of nearly identical buildings set within small yards a tacit promise of a uniform standard of living and relative equality, the Ledigenheim was positioned on a diagonal, not even fronting the primary road leading from the settlement to the factory. Though the Bochumer Verein planned an expansion of the settlement to fill in the six blocks between the factory and extant family housing, nothing was planned that would have encouraged residents to spend any time outside, nor facilitated interactions between residents and families. Unlike the settlement proper, where a centrally located school and a market place on the eastern edge interrupted the geometry of the grid, no projections, setbacks, irregular street widths, or parks were featured near the Ledigenheim—the only exception being a small manicured plaza directly abutting the main facade of the building and around a bathhouse across the street. The Stahlhausen Ledigenheim might as well have been part of a city block or directly on the factory grounds as set within the larger settlement.

Beyond its positioning on the edge of the larger company town, the visual language and scale of the Stahlhausen Ledigenheim also marked it as distinct. While two variants of family homes featured harmonizing and homogenizing elements such as door frames, windows, and other detailing, even replicating the pitch of their roofs and the alignment of rooflines throughout the settlement, nothing beyond materials—red industrially produced bricks and roof tiles—bound it and the Ledigenheim together. At five stories (excluding a basement partially above grade), the height of the latter did not reference two-story family homes, but the nearby winding towers of the mines, and its massiveness was underscored by the unrelenting horizontality of the facade, nearly five times as wide as it was high (Figure 2.7a, b). Scale was further emphasized by a decorative program, which, while more extensive than that employed for nearby four-in-block housing, would never be softened by lush greenery as the latter were. Instead, the Ledigenheim rose from the ground like a vision from an earlier age, with details like paired lancet windows, an entrance approximating a Gothic portal, turret-like towers, and a stepped gable all failing to enliven the facade. The unrelenting repetition of medieval architectural details actually underscored the solidity and severity of the building. The feudal castle was the reference point, not the cathedral, nor the free city of the late middle ages, as had been the case with Kolping's contemporaneous homes.

Lest anyone forget that it was not the Middle Ages, but the industrial age, details from the distant past were always married to those referencing the present

Figure 2.7a, b Ledigenheim of the Bochumer Verein, Stahlhausen Settlement, Bochum (1872–4). Elevation of Primary Façade. Detail of Primary Façade.
Source: Zeitschrift für Baukunde 2, no. 4 (1879): 537–50.

and unabashed *presence* of the Bochumer Verein. While critics at the turn of the century would increasingly take exception to the industrial materials used and lack of vernacular precedent for such buildings, seeing this as visual evidence of a rootlessness industry had wrought,[77] the Stahlhausen Ledigenheim wore its place in the emerging industrial order with pride. The terminus of the central stepped gable was appointed with two symbols of the factory order, a clock and a bell, and a series of small shields running horizontally between the windows of the fourth floor did not feature the heraldic device and motto of a feudal lord, but the hammer and chisel, interlocking gears, and drafting equipment of his nineteenth-century equivalent— at least in terms of the near absolute power he wielded over his employees—the great industrialist of the Ruhr.[78] As with the fortresses anchoring the lands of a great lord, the Ledigenheim of the Bochumer Verein was a bulwark against external and internal foes alike, and not simply in a symbolic sense. While residents were certainly subject to the omnipresent gaze of the management while inside, the building's close mass, height, association with management, and positioning one block from the works proper ensured that it not only was a proxy for the power of the Bochumer Verein but maintained a panoptic function. Anyone passing by—especially the residents of family housing—was dwarfed and a made subject of, as Michel Foucault wrote in relation to the house of the director within Ledoux's Saline Royale at Arc-et-Senans (1775), "the policing functions of surveillance, the economic functions of control and checking, the religious functions of encouraging obedience and work."[79] Essentially, the presence of the Ledigenheim allowed for the creation of the larger settlement. Yet, if living in an industrial settlement placed all residents—regardless of their place within the hierarchy of workers—under the thumb of the management, a single man was more constantly aware of the restrictions under which he lived and labored.[80] Unlike his more skilled and affluent married counterparts, who might have momentarily forgotten the ties that bound them, he was never allowed to think that he had control over his living arrangements. An industrial Ledigenheim was never a home, but a civilizing tool.[81]

The Ledigenheim as Corporate Advertising

And a home has grown here for thousands
Who remain loyal to the Bochumer Verein
For this thank this gallant pair
—Stanza of a song sung by Bochumer Verein workers during a celebration to honor the general director and company founder in 1894.[82]

While Ledigenheime in the manner of Stahlhausen continued to be built and remained typical, the early years of the twentieth century saw the construction of small numbers of *increasingly* sophisticated buildings by employers. The reason for the emergence of these modifications to an existing and well-established typology can *partially* be attributed to an intensifying level of concern that "young working males [still] constituted a pressing and distressing social problem that demanded remedial welfare measures," including, but not limited to, purpose-built housing for single people.[83] In light of an even more fraught relationship between labor and capital,[84] the first national conference devoted to addressing the problem of *Schlafstellenwesen* (located in Leipzig in 1904, and a subject of Chapter 3), featured not only municipal officials and the administration of Kolping's Association of Catholic Gesellenvereine but also the representatives of heavy industrialists, including *Baumeister* Berndt (Spetzler's successor) of the Bochumer Verein, who forcefully advocated for the construction of greater numbers of and higher quality Ledigenheime.[85]

Yet, while industrialists might look to outside social welfare organizations for applicable advancements and innovations related to the Ledigenheim building type, and increasingly, the planning of their company towns, they continued to view the efforts of secular and denominational reformers with consternation, if not disdain.[86] As a journal supported by Rhine-Ruhr industrialists put it, reformers commonly approached individual workers and employers with an off-putting and patronizing attitude, "I am doing welfare work, stay still, I will guide you, I will conduct welfare work."[87] Not only were reformers resented when they provided unsolicited and patronizing help, but also when they applied pressure to owners and management without a clear understanding of how a particular business operated.[88] In short, while industrialists increasingly connected themselves to bourgeois social and aesthetic reforms through in-house social welfare initiatives, including the construction of model housing, they maintained a patriarchal mindset that saw others as interlopers in a world they failed to understand and had no right to be involved with in the first place. Rather than the saving of souls or the transformation of the working class into middle-class burghers in the interests of societal health, industrial Ledigenheime continued to aid what had always been their ultimate aim—increasing productivity—by reducing turnover and supporting the *physical* health of a significant portion of the workforce,[89] as well as forestalling the much feared Socialist leanings of unskilled workers.[90]

What was new, or new to a greater degree, was the *expectation* that *every* large industrial firm would build a Ledigenheim, and not simply because it was needed, but as a form of corporate advertising.[91] What had long been true of companies like Krupp and the Bochumer Verein, which coupled their building programs with self-published and lavishly illustrated celebratory tomes,[92] was broadening to include the other "great industrialists" of the Rhine-Ruhr region. Spending considerable sums of money on a project that was useful, but perhaps not necessary in such costly form, was one of the most public ways to show that business was profitable—or give the *impression* that it was, for in the cutthroat business atmosphere of Wilhelmine Germany they were constructed in times of economic plenty as well as want.[93] With seventy-five Ledigenheime constructed or under construction by 1900, any mining, metallurgy, textile, or chemical company aspiring to "greatness" could hardly sit idly by.[94]

If the appearance of prosperity mattered, so did the physical appearance of a Ledigenheim building in underscoring one's place in the business hierarchy. Where in the 1870s, spare and barrack-like Ledigenheime with no pretensions to "architecture" had sufficed for most industrialists (if they were built at all), and the way by which a company showed its creditworthiness was through the lavish decoration of functional industrial architecture (such as the winding towers positioned above the entrance to the mines), an industrial Ledigenheim constructed at the turn of the century had to appear "similar but better" than the competition.[95] Even in an architecturally conservative sphere like heavy industry, this meant that an industrialist needed to (at minimum) build a Ledigenheim in a *style* that compared favorably with contemporaneous examples constructed by municipalities and reform organizations. While representative of many Ledigenheime built by employers at the turn of the century, and still held up for emulation as regarded its hygienic and technological innovations,[96] the construction of a building like the Stahlhausen Ledigenheim no longer functioned as an advertisement of a company's modernity in the way it previously had. While clearly a step above building a barrack, it would position a company as rather unexceptional.

Additionally, a Ledigenheim needed to complement the aesthetically pleasing surroundings of the model housing estates they were often placed within. The latter—ranging from BASF to Farbwerk Meister, Lucius and Bruning, Fried. Krupp to Villeroy and Bosch—increasingly reflected an idealized version of preindustrial village life, complete with curvilinear streets, landscaped greenspace, and an appealing variety of pseudo-vernacular house types, rather than a repetitive grid of near-identical "four-in-block" homes on plots of land abutting factory grounds.[97]

Where and how did this shift occur? While the planning of English (and, to a lesser extent, American) company towns had long been a touchpoint for

German industrialists and their designers,[98] the clean and orderly, but gridded and architecturally uninspired, model provided by settlements like Titus Salt's Saltaire (1851) was beginning to give way to new complexes that seemed to have risen organically from the English soil. Following a long tradition of English manufactured villages, such as Blaise Hamlet by John Nash (1811), chocolate manufacturer George Cadbury's Bournville (1893), and soap manufacturer William Lever's Port Sunlight (1899) were near-instant (if not entirely accurate) recreations of the traditional rural English village, complete with winding lanes and visually rich low-density housing set in verdant surroundings.[99] Such efforts did not fail to impress German industrialists like Friedrich Alfred Krupp, who coupled with his interest in the work of Swedish author and illustrator Carl Larsson, charged Robert Schmohl, the newly appointed lead architect of his company towns, with designing a settlement along the same lines.[100] Begun in 1892, Krupp and Schmohl's Altenhof estate was the first of many Krupp settlements that took the form of cottage-like detached or semidetached houses placed along picturesque streets that were not laid out rigidly, but meandered freely (Figure 2.8).[101]

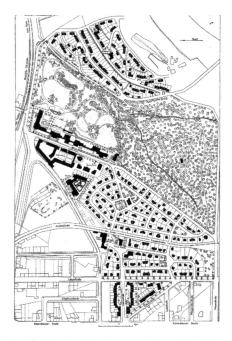

Figure 2.8 Plan of Krupp's Altenhof Settlement, Essen (1892).
Source: Richard Klapheck, *Siedlungswerk Krupp* (Berlin: Ernst Wasmuth, 1930), 41.

Further inspiration came from England, this time in the figure of Ebenezer Howard and his publication of 1898, *To-morrow: A Path to Real Reform* (reissued in 1902 as *Garden Cities of Tomorrow*). While Howard may have been influenced by figures as varied as the writers Edward Bellamy and Henry George, the Russian anarchist Peter Kropotkin, communitarian experiments like Oneida in upstate New York, designers like James Silk Buckingham and Frederick Law Olmstead, and (as with Krupp) the English industrialists William Lever, George Cadbury, and (earlier) Titus Salt and George Pullman, his particular genius lay in synthesizing numerous threads of housing and land reform to prescribe something he called a garden city. This was a self-sufficient new town marrying the sociocultural advantages of the city with the quiet and low land prices of the countryside, to be capped at 30,000 residents. While Howard did not draw up detailed plans for the design of any particular garden city, leaving this to be determined by both the site and its architects and planners, his diagrams placed an emphasis on centrally located cultural institutions, extensive parklands, including a green belt ringing the city, and zoned housing. Land was also to be held in common, meaning that land speculation was impossible.[102]

Appealing because he proposed a middle way between philanthropy and large-scale state intervention, Howard's ideas quickly gained ground in English and German reformist circles—largely composed of middle- and upper-class artists, intellectuals, and philanthropically oriented businesspeople—resulting in the founding of the (English) Garden City Association, founded in 1899, and the German Garden City Association (Deutsche Gardenstadt Gesellschaft, hereafter abbreviated DGG) in the Berlin suburb of Friedrichshagen in 1902.[103] However, even as Howard's social reformist garden city vision was quickly and enthusiastically embraced, the radical aspects of his proposal—communal ownership of land, self-sufficiency—were lost along the way, and if what was built in England (most notably, Letchworth and Welywn) deviated significantly from his original idea, in Germany Howard's ideas were even more freely interpreted. This meant that what was often called a Garden City (*Gartenstadt*) could be a garden suburb, a garden residential settlement, or even a garden factory town or village, so long as it was well-laid out and picturesque, with ample green space and hygienic vernacular-inspired housing and other facilities.[104]

Yet, while more prominent and decidedly more international in outlook, the DGG was not alone in advocating for the traditional rural village or small town as a meaningful model for the design of new housing and garden cities in particular.[105] This model also proved enticing to reformers interested in not only new construction but also the preservation of traditional forms of German architecture and site planning, as well as the natural environment—most notably, the *Bund Heimatschutz*. This organization, founded two years after the DGG in 1904, was responsible for the propagation of the so-called *Heimatstil*, or "style of the homeland" through its members' courting of tastemakers and educational institutions, as well as widely published literature, including Paul Schultze-Naumburg's pamphlet *The Disfigurement of Our Land*, which sold 20,000 copies between April and October of 1908.[106] Like the DGG, the Bund Heimatschutz was also effective at popularizing the idea that the national landscape (including quality housing) belonged to all *German* people, including workers. As an anonymous Heimatschutz author wrote in 1913, the common people should be given the beautiful surroundings that their forefathers had enjoyed, though sadly, "only a minority is so lucky that it can recuperate body and soul in a yearly trip to the beach . . . the majority of our citizens stand day in and day out in the noise and exhaust of factories . . . they therefore have a special right to beauty in the world that surrounds them."[107] To Heimatschutzer, this beauty lay in traditional, small town Germany, not in the industrial city, and while the Bund Heimatschutz sought to conserve "picturesque" small towns and villages, they also—alongside the DGG—advocated for new settlements that took these "organically derived" forms as models, which they saw as attuned to the local German landscape and to a sense of local German history.[108]

If the German village or small town provided a model for the overall organization of such a settlement, the buildings were to be based on two "timeless" building types. Both the simplified neoclassicism of the *Biedermeier revival* villa of "circa 1800" and the German farmhouse were singled out for praise by members of the Bund Heimatschutz, though the latter model was far more widely employed in the construction of worker's (and other) settlements. As mentioned in Chapter 1, a Biedermeier revival villa was simply defined as a stuccoed and whitewashed two-story building consisting of simple cubic volumes with a symmetrically arranged facade.[109] The German farmhouse, idealized for its purported rootedness to the German soil, was described as a "rural, free-standing, post and beam structure with brick infill, little to no extraneous ornament, and a large pitched roof . . . covered in clay tile and had eyebrow windows."[110] While these variants ran the risk of becoming an overly nostalgic pastiche, a "degeneration" of the German vernacular into a "cottage style,"[111] apologists contended that this was a risk worth taking—that any style could be taken up by philistines (the *Spiessbürgertum*) without understanding its application and implications, and that a profusion of derivative forms did not mean that the original was without merit.[112] In its ideal form, according to

Schultze-Naumburg, both the farmhouse and Biedermeier villa represented a timeless, honest, solid, and serious way of building that could tie the present to the heritage of the German people.[113]

Drawing on extant factory towns, as well as the influence of Howard filtered through the DGG and the Bund Heimatschutz, German industrialists quickly embraced this new/old form of planning and architecture, and began to construct garden factory towns using vernacular precedents as models—from Krupp's Margarethenhöhe (Essen, from 1906) and Dahlhauser Heide (Bochum, from 1906), to Gmindersdorf (Reutlingen, from 1903) and the German Workshop's Hellerau (Dresden, 1909)—that they and others erroneously referred to as Garden Cities (*Gartenstädte*).

Yet, why would an industrialist be interested in visually referencing the preindustrial past in the site planning and style chosen for his settlements beyond the fact that his competition was likely doing so? Though seemingly nostalgic and at odds with a company engaged in technologically advanced pursuits, such designs remained a means to discipline labor in the service of productivity, albeit a modern (and gentler) one.

If the fifteenth century was the ideal time to be a Catholic artisan, at least to the proponents of Kolping's Ledigenheime, the largely rural preindustrial world was appealing to industrialists because it provided a model of an "organic community" where everyone knew and was satisfied with their place in society. In an era where considerable interest was devoted to the working classes' position as neither "urban nor rural," including the nascent *Schrebergärten* (small garden) movement, settlements with ample green space—the roots of which lay in the kitchen gardens surrounding four-in-block housing, such as at Stahlhausen— held out the promise that workers could be brought back to their formerly landed roots while remaining *satisfied* members of the industrial workforce. As Wilhelmine cultural critic Gustav Schmoller wrote in 1886, it was not *necessarily* the ownership of property that bound a worker to society, but the "'cultivation of (a) garden and (a) home that *binds* mankind firmly to a *settled* way of life.'"[114]

According to the Bund Heimatschutz and the DGG, styles of architecture and types of urban planning could even—along with historical and mythological ethnic traditions—"revitalize German culture and with it a German nation."[115] If this strengthening of the German people as a group did lead directly to a "German future, German ascendance" (in the words of land reformer and DGG supporter Adolf Damaschke), at the very least it would strengthen the Volk against foes at home and abroad, from Social Democracy to the industrial might of Great Britain.[116] As German observers proudly noted in relation to the latter, the provision of model industrial Ledigenheime and settlements indicated that the *German* industrialist was more knowledgeable of, and active in, combating the ills that had accompanied the growth of industry than his *British* competitor.[117] A German industrialist need only apply his "typical hard work, knowledge and intelligence" to reap advantages which were "threefold: industrial, economic, and societal."[118]

Perhaps most significantly, the construction of a Ledigenheim in a *Heimatstil* variant within a garden city allowed industrialists to compete not only with their direct competitors (German and foreign alike) but also with those the middle- and upper-class do-gooders interloping on what industrialists saw as their land *and* their workers. What this meant in respect to the *Bildungsbürgertum* (educated upper middle class) was that an industrialist's wealth and power were not enough. Instead, as Thomas Adam has written, an individual had to behave in certain ways and pursue particular activities to secure one's place within existing elite social structures—philanthropy in general, and the patronage of cultural institutions or undertakings specifically, were popular choices.[119] While industrialists remained suspicious of the motives and tactics of many reformers, and were loath to call their building projects charity, or even philanthropy, they *could* attend conferences and utilize a visual aesthetic highly favored by the educated upper middle classes, and they could do so at a scale even an aristocrat would be hard pressed to undertake. In doing so, they carefully repositioned themselves, not as the parvenus and philistines so many Bildungsbürger thought them, but as individuals who could speak the language of the old urban elites. Purposefully aligning themselves with the interests *and* tastes of the Bildungsbürgertum allowed an industrialist to do what he was used to doing in relationship to the competition—in both the works proper and in social welfare initiatives—outmaneuver them to be "similar, but better," and on their own terms.[120]

The alienation accompanying modernity and industrialization need not be tackled with political legislation, as many reformers were calling for, nor with revolution, as demanded by those on the left. Instead, as Adolf Kolping had formulated in relationship to the artisan estate specifically, physically, economically, and culturally, unhealthy developments in German society could be combated by improving the everyday environment of working-class Germans, including single men, while industrialists remained firmly *Herrn-im-Haus*.[121] Yet, despite a discourse that increasingly preached the use of architecture and planning as a means to societal healing, and while most buildings constructed after the turn of the century utilized a visual language that bespoke reform, this was always mediated. Not all industrial Ledigenheime were available in their ideal form, and *never* to all single residents. The sort of men who had resided (and still resided) in buildings like Stahlhausen would continue to be marked out from the rest of the working population, further alienating the most peripheral of residents.

The Pallenberg Ledigenheime

In 1905, the Cologne-based furniture manufacturer Jacob Pallenberg built two Ledigenheime as part of a model housing complex within the village of Merheim just north of Cologne-Nippes (Figures 2.9a, b, c). These homes—termed Pallenbergheime (Pallenberg's homes), as with the small settlement they were positioned within—provided their *thirteen* residents with surroundings unheard of in the typical industrial Ledigenheim, and rare even in contemporaneous Catholic and municipal homes.[122] In stark contrast to the appearance and positioning of Stahlhausen and similar buildings, these homes—for men and women respectively—did not further segregate their residents from the larger

Figure 2.9a, b, c Jacob Pallenberg's Arbeiterheim/Settlement, Cologne-Nippes (1905). View of the entrance to the Pallenberg settlement.
Source: Author's photographs.

106 *Single People and Mass Housing in Germany, 1850–1930*

Figure 2.9a, b, c (Continued)

community of Pallenbergheim residents. While the Ledigenheime were both located on the western edge of the small settlement, that which could have read as peripheral placement was decidedly not (Figure 2.10). Instead, the buildings loosely approximated a medieval gatehouse by bracketing the primary entrance to the complex, a function further underscored by the archway linking the buildings upon which "Pallenbergheime" was emblazoned. Directly opening into a dirt path ringing communal green space, all housing—including the Ledigenheime, as well as the terraced family housing running along the northern and southern boundaries of the complex and a community center on the western edge—was designed in the Biedermeier vernacular beloved of Heimatschutzer and the DGG, presenting a harmonious and unified appearance that papered over the minimal differences in class while still hinting at individuality (Figures 2.11a, b). Varied rooflines, different window types, sizes, and decorative details, as well as slight projections and setbacks, were balanced by consistent scale, repeatable component parts, shared materials, and a restrained color palette. This meant that the buildings were either half-timbered or stuccoed and were painted in muted cream or white, with dark green and brown trim and accents. All stood between

Figure 2.10 Jacob Pallenberg's Arbeiterheim/Settlement, Cologne-Nippes (1905). Plan of the settlement.
Source: "Pallenbergheime" *Zeitschrift für Wohnungswesen* 4, no. 1 (1905): 2–3.

Figure 2.11a, b Jacob Pallenberg's Arbeiterheim/Settlement, Cologne-Nippes (1905). View of gatehouse and two Ledigenheime from the east; detail of Ledigenheim.
Source: Author's photographs.

two and three stories,[123] and were capped with brown roof tiles (Figure 2.12). The only meaningful difference between the exterior treatment of the Ledigenheime and the rest of the housing was that the former exhibited a slightly more formal variant of the Heimatstil—akin to a Biedermeier villa than a farmer's cottage of the same era—largely resultant of its positioning as a gatehouse at the entrance to the complex, rather than its function as housing for single people. Within the Ledigenheime proper and without, both privacy and community were accounted

Figure 2.12 Jacob Pallenberg's Arbeiterheim/Settlement, Cologne-Nippes (1905). View of family housing along the south side of the settlement.
Source: Author's photograph.

for, all without the housemaster or system of informants marking Stahlhausen and its ilk. Every resident was appointed a single room or a suite of two rooms supplemented by communal living space, as well as access to a large semiprivate covered veranda and garden supplementing the public green and the social spaces, including a library, of the community center.[124]

What accounts for the integrative approach taken by Pallenberg, the owner of a large "art-furniture" factory (*Kunstmöbelfabrik*) in Cologne and a man affluent enough to finance the purchase of model furniture designs (*mustergultiger Möbel*) for the Cologne Museum of Applied Arts (*Kunstgewerbemuseum*)? Certainly, Pallenberg's business placed him at the center of the design reform movement in Cologne, one that required remaining current in all matters concerning aesthetic *and* social reform.[125] This is to say, Pallenberg's interests and purview lay far closer to those of Schmidt and his German Workshops in Dresden (later Dresden-Hellerau), than those of Krupp in Essen. The Pallenbergheim complex, complete with *Heimatstil* dwellings and community center surrounding a central green, may look—at first glance—like a preindustrial village in which near-feudal authority was exercised in the manner of Krupp, the village square and church updated to modern forms supporting civic life and Jacob Pallenberg a contemporary version of Lord Bountiful. Yet, while playing the benevolent village squire might have been the expected role for Pallenberg, the complex was not directly constructed by its benefactor, who had no interest in remaining *Herr-im-Haus*. Instead, Pallenberg relinquished control by willing the land and the complex's funding to the city of Cologne.[126]

Why did Pallenberg not retain control? One answer is that like Schmidt and other socially and aesthetically progressive Werkbund members, he saw himself *and* his residents as partners in the renewal of German taste. Additionally, vernacular-inspired settlements such as his were not only used by industrialists to placate their workers and underscore their power but also increasingly employed by municipalities, whose officials saw the embrace of the *Heimatstil* and the use of vernacular idioms in housing as a way to align the middle classes (to which they and Pallenberg belonged) with the working classes (Pallenberg's employees) against the power of the Junkers and other Conservative forces (including heavy industry).[127]

Finally, and most significantly, Pallenberg did need to retain control of his Ledigenheime because the buildings were intended to house the most privileged members of his current *and* former workforce, long-term *and* retired employees of the Pallenberg furniture factory.[128] A carrot without a stick (to twist the words of Otto von Bismarck), these homes were a reward for loyal service (such as was purportedly in short supply elsewhere, and heavy industry in particular). Pallenbergheim residents were thus doubly removed from the single men housed by the Bochumer Verein, for not only were they middle-aged, even elderly, they were also skilled workers. The loyal men (and women) served by Pallenberg's generosity formed the apex of the working class in a world that trusted age over youth, and privileged skilled workers over their unskilled brethren. Even after the turn of the century such an ideal housing situation was *never* made available by employers to their unskilled or even semiskilled single workers, as evidenced by the Ledigenheim within the Upper Silesian "colony" of Fürstengrube (1917). Like Pallenberg's settlement, all buildings within Fürstengrube employed a variant of the *Heimatstil* and the site planning attempted to approximate a traditional German village, but unlike the integrative model utilized by Joseph Pallenberg in Cologne, the traditional heavy-handed approach of industry was coupled with the nationalistic, even xenophobic, implications of DGG and Bund Heimatschutz rhetoric. During wartime, and on the fringes of the faltering German Empire, such Ledigenheime served the most peripheral of all industrial workers in the most oppressive of ways.

Fürstengrube

In 1917, the Fürstliche Plessische Bergwerkdirektion—a mining company based in Upper Silesia—began to build four model settlements, or "colonies," on the land it owned south of what was then called Kattowitz, now Katowice. Designed by *Bauinspektor* Alfred Malpricht of Kattowiz, the colonies of Emmanuelssegen, Ober-Lazisk, Böerschächte, and Fürstengrube were the ultimate inheritance of a truly feudal system—the last in a long line of company towns first begun under the direction of both Friedrich the Great and *Plesser Standesherren* (local nobles) in 1754.[129] While the coal barons of the Ruhr might have imagined themselves to be *Herr-im-Haus*, the Upper Silesian nobles who controlled, and continue to control, these settlements had long enjoyed special rights under the Prussian government allowing them to function without interference.[130] Although they could no longer require local peasants to work for them in *any* capacity that they required, the *Fürstliche Plessische Bergwerkdirection* had other means of control at its disposal, as exemplified by the site planning and visual language of its Fürstengrube colony.[131]

Largely composed of four-in-block and six-in-block housing often attached to small barns for livestock and surrounded by kitchen gardens, as well as single villas or duplexes for company officials, the settlement presented a unified vision that easily married the visual aesthetics preferred by the DGG with those of the Bund Heimatschutz (and Pallenberg) (Figure 2.13). Placed along well-shaded curvilinear lanes, the buildings recalled a variant of the traditional German farmhouse in form and materials, from steeply pitched hipped tile roofs to

Figure 2.13 Fürstengrube Settlement, Fürstengrube, Upper Silesia (1917). View of four-in-block family housing and gardens with the Schlafhaus/Ledigenheim in the background.
Source: Bau-Rundschau no. 31–4 (1918): 127.

stucco walls, wooden shutters, and eyebrow windows. Yet, not all residents of the complex were afforded such homey treatment. In contrast to the domestic scale and detailing of the surrounding housing, the Ledigenheim of Fürstengrube employed the most restrained and formal visual language. It's verticality and mass unmitigated by the decorative elements marking neighboring buildings, the "home" presented a severe and authoritative appearance—for the model here was not the comfortable surroundings of the Pallenberg Ledigenheime. Instead, it drew upon the visual language developed by heavy industry to house single men forty to fifty years earlier (Figure 2.14).

Just as the large clock on its steeply pitched roof was a clear nod to Ledigenheime like Stahlhausen, the interior arrangements of Fürstengrube also recalled earlier industrial precedents. However, at Fürstengrube, the bedrooms were not intended for individuals, or even "comradely" groups of four to six men (as sometimes was the case in Stahlhausen), but for groups of ten to twelve men (though the small size of the bedrooms was buttressed by an attached "conversation room")[132] (Figure 2.15). Additionally, where even the Bochumer Verein had provided the residents of the Stahlhausen Ledigenheim their choice of three dining halls, one of which was open to all (male) employees, the men

Figure 2.14 Fürstengrube Schalfhaus/Ledigenheim, Fürstengrube, Upper Silesia (1917).
Source: *Moderne Bauformen* 16 (1917): 79.

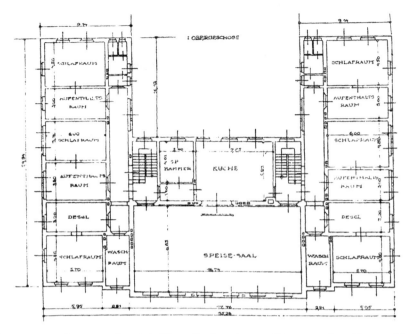

Figure 2.15 Fürstengrube Schalfhaus/Ledigenheim, Fürstengrube, Upper Silesia (1917). Plan of the first upper floor.
Source: *Bau-Rundschau* no. 31–4 (1918): 127.

living in the Fürstengrube Ledigenheim had no access to any other dining hall beyond a second-floor room included for their sole use.[133] Largely sequestered within the walls of the Ledigenheim, residents were also given little to no direct *or* mediated access to green space. There was no shared lawn (much less a community center with a library) binding the different buildings of the settlement together in the manner of the Pallenbergheime, and although residents looked out over numerous cottage gardens belonging to family housing, they were not even provided with a porch, terrace, or veranda, much less a garden plot. In stark contradistinction to DGG and Heimatschutz discourse, and despite its positioning within a garden-colony, a noble facade took precedent over access to the positive effects of nature, and certainly one's own parcel of land.

The Fürstengrube Ledigenheim was thus nothing more than updated cladding on an older model, one that had been in existence from the 1870s. Yet, while industrial Ledigenheime and other forms of company housing had long consolidated divisions among the workers along not only class but also ethnic and regional origin,[134] the overly formal architectural language, segregated spaces, and little direct access to green space created by the Ledigenheim at

Fürstengrube must be read as an illustration of *more* than had been typical in the past. This is because Fürstengrube was located in a district east of the Oder River in Upper Silesia, where ethnic Poles constituted 73 percent of the population—a population that was growing.[135] Even before the outbreak of the First World War, the supposed "Polonization" of Upper Silesia was a source of great fear to nationalist groups like the Pan-German League (*Alldeutscher Verband*) and the Eastern Marches Society (*Ostmarkverein*), who urged an escalation of Germanization policies in the east. Specifically, they called for "Germanizing the (eastern) soil" with "a rooted German peasant and worker population,"[136] despite the fact that the government in Berlin kept the eastern frontier open to seasonal Polish laborers from Russian and Austrian controlled Poland.[137] Fürstengrube would have been far from immune to such outside pressure and attendant ethnic tension,[138] compounded by the fact that *all* the administrative and upper level positions at Fürstengrube were held by ethnic Germans (many of whom would not have been born in Upper Silesia), while the single workers housed in the Ledigenheim were *exclusively* ethnic Poles from Upper Silesia or Congress Poland.

The use of the *Heimatstil*—in both its farmhouse and villa variants—therefore had even greater meaning in Upper Silesia than elsewhere, and it was not the conciliatory and community-creating meaning it held in the Rhineland or Ruhr. Considering that a proponent of the vernacular "German" styles such as Paul Schultze-Naumburg "equated a ravaged physical landscape" (including the application of improper or "foreign" architectural forms) "with a weak national character and a failed national destiny,"[139] the reiteration of German presence through traditionally and identifiably *German* architectural forms were intended to strengthen Upper Silesia against the Polish "threat." Certainly, neither the vernacular German farmhouse nor the Biedermeier home had anything to do with building traditions in Upper Silesia, which not only employed different forms but favored construction in wood.[140] Additionally, the site planning of Fürstengrube did not draw from traditional (Polish) Upper Silesian village models, where dwellings were arranged on both sides of a single long and straight street with no discernable center (termed a *Lineindörf*), nor even from the layout of eighteenth-century designs in the service of Frederick the Great, which also followed this Polish precedent, but favored the central square and meandering lanes of a typical German "garden city."[141]

The intentional *German-ness* of Fürstengrube as a whole, coupled with the overly formal architectural language of a building used to house the most marginal of its residents, helped to reassert the control of German owners over their ethnically Polish workers. While "foreign" Polish workers were needed, they were certainly not to be afforded equal housing. In Upper Silesia, reformist architecture and site planning was only available in its *ideal* form to skilled, married, and ethnic German workers. After all, following DGG and Heimatschutz logic that vernacular German architecture and urban forms were central to the formation of the Volk's identity and the support of its physical and economic health (particularly important during wartime), there would be no such impact on non-Germans. As a leaning toward privacy was supposedly a German trait regardless of class, but apparently unimportant to Polish workers,[142] so too only Germans were able to fully appreciate the beauty of and access the larger meaning of the Heimatstil and traditional forms of site planning. Additionally, since the connection to and cultivation of land—even a very small individual plot—was positioned as key to the creation of "a child-rich and future-rich country,"[143] Poles should be given no encouragement to reconnect to land which was not theirs, but the inheritance of the German people.

Even more ominously, the sequestration of Polish Ledigenheim residents reveals deeper concerns about racial degeneration. While the proponents of industrial Ledigenheime always referred to sexual impropriety in privately owned rental barracks and company housing as a reason for the construction of such buildings, they were traditionally concerned about what this meant for the breakdown of the social order and its managerial implications. With the increasing popularity of eugenic discourse in the first decades of the twentieth century—not only in Germany but in other western nations—it was feared that the children borne of extramarital affairs not only were socially undesirable but might also be of genetically inferior stock.[144] While Poles and Germans certainly lived in close proximity in the Ruhr and other German industrial regions, on the fringes of empire in Upper Silesia the undesirable mixing of Polish and German blood had greater implications.

Fürstengrube was ultimately intended to support the project of German cultural and political hegemony in Upper Silesia. After all, as Scott Spector writes, "throughout the long fin de siècle, German cultural 'work' (in the borderlands) was identified as national and therefore political."[145] Likewise, Edward Said's work indicates that culture (including architecture) is inseparable from national fantasies of identity, where identity is linked to not only the defense of one's culture but also where it can function as both a symbol and instrument of power by the "dominant" culture over the others within its orbit.[146] Fürstengrube was cultural work *and* national work—central to the (temporary) reiteration of social and economic hierarchies in Central Europe, and the German Reich in particular—where control was certainly slipping by 1917, and where in November of 1919, 73 percent of the population voted to join the new country of Poland, not the shadow of an empire that was.[147]

An Immigrant Type

In the end, the ultimate legacy of the industrial Ledigenheim as building type was not exemplified by the pleasant surroundings of the Pallenberg Ledigenheime, but by the segregation, control, and xenophobia of Fürstengrube—a problematic, but certainly not unforeseen, inheritance, and one with continued ramifications. While Dr. Wiedfeldt, a representative of Ruhr industrialists and leading participant at the *Schlafstellenwesen und Ledigenheim* conference of 1904, provided three reasons as to why employers might build an industrial Ledigenheim—business interests, humanitarian inclinations, or religious concerns—the latter two had *always* been made subject to the first.[148] The degree to which residents *personally* benefited from or even enjoyed living in a Ledigenheim was of little concern to an employer. At the same time, industrialists believed that they alone understood the habits and particularities of the industrial working classes. However, this "special relationship" was not one of equals. Instead, it was one within which an employer was able to play the benevolent patriarch, though *only to the point* where this would raise the productive capacity of the company. When employers claimed that such interventions would spare "their" workers from the "*Jammer*" (misery) of the private *Schlafstelle* they were not being disingenuous, it is simply that they were not particularly interested in the plight of any particular worker, nor his elevation—but always the bottom line.[149]

When necessity dictated during the First World War, most industrialists—the *Fürstliche Plessische Bergwerkdirektion* excepted—turned back to the cheapest and fastest models available, barracks that were near replicas of the proto-Ledigenheime developed in the middle of the nineteenth century.[150] These buildings, which would have felt outmoded even in the 1870s, were simply a means to warehouse a massive (and temporary) influx of war workers. They are also the best indication of how shallow most employers' efforts at *reform* truly were, and remained—particularly when residents were already on the margins in terms of marital status, education, and class.

As it had been in Fürstengrube, this superficiality was even more pronounced when residents' marginality was multiplied by the complicating factors of nationality, ethnicity, and race. In postwar (West) Germany, when the great industrialists of the Rhineland and Ruhr summoned the Ledigenheim back to life, they did not position it as central to their social welfare programs, nor use it as a means of self-promotion. Instead, the Ledigenheim was a means to warehouse foreign migrants, the Italians, Spaniards, Greeks, Yugoslavs, Moroccans, Tunisians, and Turks who, as William Manchester wrote in 1964, "formed the base of the [Ruhr's] economic pyramid."[151] If, as Manfredo Tafuri claims, capitalism made the entire working class the "other" of architecture—their needs, rather than the interests of the upper classes, remaining largely underserved—the living situation facing single, working-class, (largely) male, foreign nationals in postwar Germany was far more dire than even their bombed-out German counterparts.[152] A means to protect an industrialist's "investment" (in training and associated travel costs) from abuse by unscrupulous private market landlords, the postwar Ledigenheim remained a way to protect the German family from the dangerous sexuality of young men—in the 1960s, 90 percent of guestworkers were between eighteen and forty-five years of age.[153] To a greater degree than before in the Rhineland or Ruhr it was also a means to protect the *general public* from unhelpful foreign cultural influences that might undermine efforts to forge a specifically German identity in the wake of the Nazi era.[154]

By 1962 two-thirds of guestworkers were living in sex-segregated communal hostels—Ledigenheime—that fully cemented their marginal status in German society.[155] Whereas their nineteenth-century counterparts *could* move out (though the hygienic surroundings of a Ledigenheim were supposed to provide an inducement to remain), postwar guestworkers remained tied to employer and to place if they wanted to remain in Germany.[156] At the same time, residents were often denied that which had been the eventual means of their predecessors' integration into the industrial community of workers, the possibility of marriage and the establishment of a household. Though such restrictions lifted as the decades wore on,[157] guestworkers were usually disallowed from sending for girlfriends or fiancées, and if they were already married—which some were—their families were required to remain behind. To employers and policymakers, single status in a foreign worker, coupled with the fact that he was required to return home after a number of years, meant that neither the employer nor the state would be required to provide housing, schooling, medical care, or associated social services for a family. If the guestworker left while still relatively young and healthy, neither would he require much in the way of health care, nor would he draw a pension.[158] Inexpensive and highly disposable, the single guestworker (and his housing) was an astute, if not an ethically unproblematic, choice.

What was born in the nineteenth century as a means to discipline labor and harken industrial success remains remarkably relevant—and not just in Germany. The legacy of the industrial Ledigenheim and the company town can be seen in "Foxconn City" (Shenzhen, China), as well as similar complexes in Taiwan, Indonesia, Vietnam, Mexico, Bangladesh, Cambodia, and Myanmar—even the barracks of migrant agricultural workers in the United States.[159] Yet, that which has long been associated with migratory unskilled labor is increasingly and ominously being used to contain and control even more marginalized individuals. An apparatus to separate refugee families from each other, not only in Germany's "generous" asylum program of the late 1990s and early 2000s,[160] but also in the United States,[161] the Ledigenheim—in slightly altered form—remains a building type central to the construction and maintenance of the nation-state.

Notes

1 "Fremd- statt Gastarbeiter," *Handelsblatt: Deutsche Wirtschaftszeitung* 34 (February 16, 1967): 20. The translation above is mine.
2 See also: "Ein Raum, in dem zehn Männer auf Strohsäcken liegen können," *Die Welt* (August 22, 1960).
3 Ulrich Herbert, *A History of Foreign Labor in Germany, 1880–1980* (Ann Arbor: University of Michigan, 1990), 206, 212; Rita Chin, *The Guestworker Question in Postwar Germany* (Cambridge: Cambridge University Press, 2007), 50.
4 Herbert, 206; Chin, 218–20; "Es geht nicht ohne Italiener," *Industriekurier unabhängige Zeitung für Politik, Wirtschaft u. Technik* (October 4, 1955), 3.
5 A. F. Weber, *The Growth of Cities in the Nineteenth Century: A Study in Statistics* (Ithaca: Cornell, 1899), 267.
6 Nicolas Bullock and James Read, *The Movement for Housing Reform in Germany and France, 1840–1914* (Cambridge: Cambridge University Press, 1985), 31.
7 Bullock and Read, 115–23; *Deutsche Bauzeitung* 45 (1892): 267. See also Margaret Crawford, *Building the Workingman's Paradise* (New York: Verso, 1995), and Joshua Freeman, *Behemoth: A History of the Factory and the Making of the Modern World* (New York: Norton, 2018).
8 Of eighty-two industrial settlements built between 1870 and 1918, forty were located in either the Ruhr or the Rhineland—Greater Essen alone contained eight. Of the remaining forty-two, the Saarland contained five, Saxony, four, Hessen, six, and Upper Silesia, sixteen (Weber, 80, 92). See also: *Der Arbeiterfreund* (1902): 377; *Zeitung des Vereins Deutscher Eisenbahnverwaltungen* 51, no. 27 (April 5, 1911): 3.

9 *Deutsche Bauzeitung* 45 (1892): 267; R. Wiedfeldt, "Einleitendes Referat/ Versammlungsbericht," in *Schlafstellenwesen und Ledigenheime* (Berlin: Carl Henmanns Verlag, 1904), 146.
10 Freeman, 58–64.
11 Franz-Josef Brüggemeier, "Bedürfnisse, gesellschaftliche Erfahrung und politisches Verhalten," *Sozialwissenschaftliche Informationen für Unterricht und Studium* 6, no. 44 (1977): 155–7; quoted in Kulczycki, 40.
12 *Das Arbeiterwohl* (1892): 116. See also: K. Bade, *Population, Labour and Migration in Nineteenth and Twentieth Century Germany* (Leamington: Berg, 1897), 98.
13 Kulczycki, 25, 29.
14 Kulczycki, 48, 56.
15 Kulczycki, 33; see also R. C. Murphy, *Guestworkers in the German Reich* (New York: Columbia University Press, 1983), 103.
16 Werner, 67–8; quoted in Kulczycki, 32.
17 Kulczycki, 16.
18 Murphy, 103.
19 Wiedfeldt, 134.
20 *Das Arbeiterwohl* (1892): 116.
21 *Deutsche Bauzeitung* 18 (May 1895): 250; Theodor Weyl and August Gärtner, *Weyls Handbuch er Hygiene* (Leipzig: Barth, 1912), 342/114; Essen Stadtarchiv Signatur 901 1017.
22 *Baugewerkszeitung* 30 (1898): 1664. For coverage of the army barracks in Saxony, see *Deutsche Vierteljarhsschrift für Öffentliche Gesundheitspflege* 11 (1879): 76–91. Regarding the Munich *Obdachlose* buildings, see Johannes Altenroth, *Staatswirtschaftliche Dissertation: Das Schlafstellenwesen und seine Reform: Statistik, Schlafstellenaufsicht, Ledigenheime* (Universität Halle, 1916), 112–15. For the Berlin *Obdachlose* buildings, see Weyl's, 79/307-81/309.
23 *Baugewerkszeitung* 30 (1898): 1664.
24 Bullock and Read, 210.
25 Murphy, 30.
26 L. Abrams, *Workers' Culture in Imperial Germany: Rheinland and Westphalia* (London: Routledge, 1992), 25; S. H. F. Hickey, *Workers in Imperial Germany: The Miners in the Ruhr* (Oxford: Clarendon, 1985), 42.
27 Hickey, 43, 46–7.
28 Crew, 148.
29 Gerhard Bry, *Wages in Germany, 1871–1945* (Princeton: Princeton University Press, 1960), 51; Linton, 44.
30 Crew, 148.
31 Hickey, 42.
32 Crew, 68.

33 Baumeister Berndt, "Das Ledigenheim vom Stadtpunkt des Arbeitgebers, insbesondere das Ledigenheim des Bochumer Vereins für Bergbau und Gusstahlfabrikation," in *Schlafstellenwesen und Ledigenheime* (Berlin: Carl Henmanns Verlag, 1904), 173.
34 Crew, 148; Berndt, 173; *Der Arbeiterfreund* 46 (1906): 8.
35 Berndt, 162, 173; *Zeitschrift für Baukunde* 2, no. 4 (1879): 548.
36 *Zeitschrift für Baukunde* 2, no. 4 (1879): 543.
37 Berndt, 164–6.
38 Spetzler, 543; Berndt, 161–74.
39 Bade, 62; Murphy, 28.
40 Bade, 94.
41 *Zeitschrift für Baukunde* 2, no. 4 (1879): 546–7.
42 *Zeitschrift für Baukunde* 2, no. 4 (1879): 544–5. In a nod to the control of disease, and trachoma in particular, a number of showers were included as opposed to baths (*Zeitschrift für Baukunde* 2, no. 4 (1879): 544), which were all swapped out for showers in the mines themselves several decades later (Hickey, 124).
43 *Zeitschrift für Baukunde* 2, no. 4 (1879): 543.
44 *Zeitschrift für Baukunde*, 545; Bry, 51.
45 *Soziale Arbeit* (Bochum: Bochumer Verein, 1942), 56.
46 *Zeitschrift für Baukunde* 2, no. 4 (1879): 546.
47 *Zeitschrift für Baukunde*, 544.
48 Berndt, 163.
49 Altenroth, 138.
50 Ministerialdirektor Dr. Thiel, *Schlafstellenwesen und Ledigenheime*, 191.
51 Thiel, 191. Alfred Krupp similarly favored "Gesinnungsschnüffelei" (snooping) in his Ledigenheime and works (William Manchester, *The Arms of Krupp* (New York: Little, Brown, and Co., 1968), 153).
52 Berndt, 163; J. Radomski, *Über Fürsorge für Ledige Arbeiter in Posen* (Posen: W. Decker and Co., 1911), 8.
53 Hickey, 67; *Zeitschrift für Baukunde*, 544.
54 *Zeitschrift für Baukunde*, 548.
55 Hickey, 67; *Zeitschrift für Baukunde*, 544.
56 Michel Foucault, *Discipline and Punish: The Birth of the Prison*, trans. Alan Sheridan (New York: Vintage Books, 1995), 173, 187, 200.
57 Hickey, 50.
58 "Hausordnung für die Menage der Gusstahlfabrik von Fried. Krupp in Essen," in *Schlafstellenwesen und Ledigenheime*, 7.
59 "Hausordnung," in *Schlafstellenwesen und Ledigenheime*, 7.
60 Standish Meacham, *Toynbee Hall and Social Reform: 1880–1014* (New Haven: Yale University Press, 1987), 56.

61 *Der Arbeiterfreund*, 1907: 420, 423.
62 "Hausordnung," 7.
63 Hickey, 50.
64 Berndt, 171.
65 Crew, 155; Crawford, 30.
66 Altenrath, 107.
67 *Concordia* (1911): 27.
68 David Crew, *A Town in the Ruhr: A Social History of Bochum, 1860–1914* (New York: Columbia University Press, 1979), 150.
69 *Zeitschrift für Baukunde* 2, no. 4 (1879): 543; Kastorff-Viemann, 97.
70 *Der Arbeiterfreund* (1911): 277 and (1907): 357. For the American context, see Crawford, 54 and Freeman, 131.
71 Stanley Buder, *Pullman: An Experiment in Industrial Order and Community Planning* (New York: Oxford, 1967), 44.
72 *Die Arbeiterwohl* 9 (1889): 132–46.
73 "Robert Schmohl: Krupp-Siedlungen," in Roland Günter, *Der Deutsche Werkbund und seine Mitglieder* (Essen: Klartext, 2009), 90; *Essen Stadtarchiv*, Signatur 901 1017; Richard Klapheck, *Siedlungswerk Krupp* (Berlin: Ernst Wasmuth Verlag, 1930), 15.
74 *Essen Stadtarchiv*, Signatur 901 1017; Klapheck, 15.
75 Crawford, 39, for other examples in the USA, see 52.
76 *Zeitschrift für Baukunde* 2, no. 4 (1879): 543–8.
77 Bullock and Read, 116.
78 *Zeitschrift für Baukunde* 2, no. 4 (1879): 545, 547.
79 Foucault, 173.
80 As regards the rules, regulations, and police inspections that even skilled workers living in family housing were made subject to, see *Wohnalltag in Deutschland*, 204; Manchester, 209, 261.
81 It was also a tool that seems to have worked, for despite their supposed volatility, the residents of Ledigenheime like Stahlhausen were almost never the source of ferment that employers feared, and it was extremely rare for them to become involved in any sort of sustained protest—Socialist or otherwise—against their employers or other authority figures. Instead, it was the lauded skilled worker who had ties to the Socialist boogeyman (Evans, 67–9, 86–7).
82 *Bericht über die Jubelfeier des Bochumer Vereins, 14. Oktober 1894* (Bochum, 1894), 8, quoted in: Crew, 155.
83 Linton, 2.
84 *Der Arbeiterfreund* (1907): 420; *Der Arbeiterfreund* (1907): 423.
85 *Schlafstellenwesen und Ledigenheim*, ii.
86 *Der Arbeiterfreund* (1907): 357.

87 *Der Arbeiterfreund* (1907): 425.
88 *Der Arbeiterfreund* (1907): 423.
89 Wiedfeldt, 134.
90 Crew, 64.
91 Berndt, 141.
92 Crawford, 55.
93 Bade, 61.
94 *Schlafstellenwesen und Ledigenheime*, 134; *Reichsarbeitsblatt* (1913): 440.
95 Matthew Jefferies, *Politics and Culture in Wilhelmine Germany: The Case of Industrial Architecture* (Oxford: Berg, 1995), 27, 31, 35.
96 *Schlafstellenwesen und Ledigenheime*, 164–6.
97 Bullock and Read, 211.
98 Bullock and Read, 73.
99 Crawford, 70–1.
100 Barbara Miller Lane, *National Romanticism and Modern Architecture in Germany and the Scandinavian Countries* (Cambridge: Cambridge University Press, 2000), 146.
101 Bullock and Read, 138.
102 Ebenezer Howard, *Garden Cities of To-Morrow* (Cambridge: MIT Press, 1965).
103 Dirk Schubert, "Theodor Fritsch and the German (völkische) version of the Garden City," *Planning Perspectives* 19, no. 1 (2004): 14.
104 Schubert, 38.
105 In the immediate postwar period, prominent architects Heinrich Tessenow and Hermann Muthesius (among many others) promoted small single-family homes set in verdant surroundings in their respective books, *Handwerk und Kleinstadt* (1919) and *Kleinhaus und Kleinsiedlung* (1920).
106 Jefferies, 89.
107 William H. Rollins, *A Greener Vision of Home: Cultural Politics and Environmental Reform in the German Heimatschutz Movement, 1904–1918* (Ann Arbor: University of Michigan Press, 1997), 170.
108 Paul Schultze-Naumburg, *Die Entstellung Unseres Landes* (Munich: Hofbuchdruckerei Raftner und Callwen, 1907), 11. The most famous extant example of a Heimatschutz style settlement is the "Garden City" of Hellerau (Dresden), designed by Richard Riemerschmid and others in 1904.
109 Kai Gutschow, "Schultze-Naumburg's Heimatstil: A Nationalist Conflict of Tradition and Modernity," in *Traditional Dwellings and Settlements Working Papers Series*, ed. Nezer Alsayyad (Berkeley, CA: Center for Environmental Design Research, 1992), 14.
110 Gutschow, 13. See also Schultze-Naumburg, 17, abb. 12.
111 Jose-Ignacio Linazasoro, "Ornament and Classical Order," *Architectural Design* 54, no. 5/6 (1984): 23.

112 Paul Schultze-Naumburg, "Biedermeierstil?" *Kunstwart* 19, no. 3 (1905): 131.
113 Gary D. Stark, *Entrepeneurs of Ideology: Neoconservative Publishers in Germany, 1890–1933* (Chapel Hill: UNC Press, 1981), 89). See also: Stanford Anderson, "The Legacy of German Neoclassicism and Biedermeier: Behrens, Tessenow, Loos and Mies," *Assemblage* 15 (August 1991): 76 and 77.
114 Nicolas Bullock and James Read, 78.
115 Gutschow, 6.
116 Repp, 81.
117 *Der Arbeiterfreund* (1907): 419.
118 Berndt, 173.
119 Thomas Adam, "Philanthropy and the Shaping of Social Distinctions in Nineteenth Century U.S., Canadian, and German Cities," in *Philanthropy, Patronage, and Civil Society: Experiences from Germany, Great Britain, and North America*, ed. Thomas Adam (Bloomington: Indiana University Press, 2004), 17–18.
120 *Arbeitersiedlungen im 19. Jahrhundert: Historische Entwicklung, Bedeutung und aktuelles Erhaltungsintresse* (Bochum: N. Brockmeyer, 1985), 45.
121 Bernhard Kampffmeyer, "Die Gartenstadtbewegung in England," *Die Tat, Monatsschrift für die Zukunft deutscher Kultur, Herausgegeben Eugen Diederichs Verlag* 8 (1916/17): 1144.
122 On Merheim and Nippes, see Hans Vogts, *Kölner Bauliche Entwicklung, 1888–1927* (Köln: Architekten- und Ingenieurverein für den Niederrhein und Westfalen und Köln mit Unterstützung der Stadt Köln. Festgabe zum Deutschen Architekten- und Ingenieurtag, 1927), 58, 65, 70, 102; Reinhold Kruse, *111 Jahre Köln-Nippes* (Köln: Emons Verlag, 1999), 17).
123 In accordance with the new zoning laws of Cologne's outer ring of suburbs, buildings of greater height were disallowed (Vogts, 68).
124 *Zeitschrift für Wohnungswesen* (1905): 3.
125 *Der Arbeiterfreund* 38 (1900): 201.
126 It remains the property of the city of Cologne-Nippes, and is kept in very good repair, complete with well-tended gardens.
127 Maiken Umbach, "The Vernacular International: Heimat, Modernism and the Global Market in Early Twentieth-Century Germany," *National Identities* 4, no. 1 (2002): 60.
128 *Zeitschift für Wohnungswesen* (1905): 3; *Der Arbeiterfreund* 38 (1900): 201.
129 Kuhn, *Siedlungsgeschichte Oberschlesiens* (Würzburg: Oberschlesischer Heimatverlag, 1954), 199, 235, 245.
130 Kuhn, 237.
131 For images and plans associated with these settlements, and the Fürstengrube colony in particular, see *Bau-Rundschau* 31-4 (1918): 121–33; *Moderne Bauformen* 16 (1917): 65–85; C. H. Baer, *Kleinbauten und Siedlungen* (Stuttgart: Julius Hoffmann, 1918), 103–18.

132 *Bau-Rundschau* 31–34 (1918): 126; *Moderne Bauformen* 16 (1917): 84.

133 *Bau-Rundschau* 31–34 (1918): 126.

134 Hickey, 65, 222; Richard J. Evans, *Proletarians and Politics: Socialism, Protest and the Working Class in Germany before the First World War* (New York: St. Martin's Press, 1990), 83.

135 Murphy, 173.

136 Richard W. Tims, *Germanizing Prussian Poland: The H-K-T Society and the Struggle for the Eastern Marches in the German Empire, 1894–1919* (New York: Columbia University Press, 1941), 109.
See also: Susan R. Henderson, "Ernst May and the Campaign to Resettle the Countryside: Rural Housing in Silesia, 1919–1925," *Journal of the Society of Architectural Historians* 61, no. 2 (June 2002): 191 and William W. Hagen, *Germans, Poles and Jews: The Nationality Conflict in the Prussian East, 1772–1914* (Chicago: University of Chicago Press, 1980), 202.

137 Hagen, 170.

138 Murphy, 174.

139 Gutschow, 9.

140 Ludwig Loewe, *Schlesische Holzbauten* (Düsseldorf: Werner-Verlag, 1969), 6.

141 Hans Joachim Helmigk, *Oberschlesische Landbaukunst um 1800* (Berlin: Verlag für Kunstwissenschaft, 1937), 192; Kuhn, 304, 326.

142 C. H. Baer, the editor of *Kleinbauten und Siedlungen* and the journal *Moderne Bauforme* wrote in 1918 that "[German] miners in the Rhineland and Westfalia prefer to live in single-family homes, while [Polish] Upper Silesian miners prefer multi-family dwellings" (Baer, 104).

143 Werner Hegemann, *Das steinerne Berlin* (Berlin: Ullstein, 1930), 469.

144 Wolfgang Voigt, "The Garden City as Eugenic Utopia," *Planning Perspectives* 4, no. 3 (1989): 295–312.

145 Scott Spector, *Prague Territories* (Berkeley: University of California Press, 2000), 14.

146 Said, as quoted in Spector, 173.

147 T. Hunt Tooley, *National Identity and Weimar Germany: Upper Silesia and the Eastern Border, 1918–1922* (Lincoln: University of Nebraska Press, 1997), 240.

148 *Der Arbeiterfreund* (1904): 215; Abrams, 141.

149 Wiedfeldt, 134.

150 Stadtarchiv Essen 143 2677, Rep. 124.

151 Manchester, 17.

152 Manfredo Tafuri, *Architecture and Utopia: Design and Capitalist Development* (Cambridge: MIT Press, 1976), cited in Esra Akcan, *Architecture in Translation: Germany, Turkey, and the Modern House* (Durham: Duke University Press, 2012), 196.

153 Herbert, 212; Chin, 43, 55.

154 Herbert, 223, 239; Chin, 42, 48.

155 Herbert, 218; Ulrike Marie Meinhof, "Kuli oder Kollege? Gastarbeiter in Deutschland," *Konkret* (November 1966): 24; "100 Mill. Für Ausländerwohnheime," *Industriekurier unabhängige Zeitung für Politik, Wirtschaft u. Technik* (October 6, 1960).
156 Herbert, 206, 231–2.
157 Jürgen Hoffmeyer-Zlotnik, "Community Change and Invasion: The Case of Turkish Guest Workers," in *Spatial Disparities and Social Behavior*, ed. Jürgen Friedrichs (Hamburg: Christians, 1982), 114–26; Chin, 50; Ackan, 288.
158 Herbert, 212.
159 Freeman, 270–313; Crawford, 211–12.
160 Chin, 27.
161 "PBS NewsHour for June 25, 2018," *PBS Newshour* (June 25, 2018). This is one of hundreds of news reports documenting the ongoing refugee and immigration crisis in the United States.

3

Making the Municipality a Home
Appropriate Luxury for All

On May 9 and 10, 1904, the thirteenth conference of Germany's Central Organization for Workers' Welfare (Der Zentralstelle für Arbeiterwohlfahrtseinrichtungen) was held in the Saxon city of Leipzig.[1] It was devoted to the question of *Schlafstellenwesen* and *Ledigenheime*. The term *Schlafstellenwesen* referred to the lodging of single people with working-class families, and the conference exposed the need for *Ledigenheime*, or purpose-built housing for single people. Although the *Zentralstelle* had been in existence since 1891, this was the *first* time that the annual conference had been focused upon this particular topic. Attending this national conference were representatives of nearly every powerful interest group from the entire German Reich, ranging from secular reformers, with strong links to municipalities, to the spokesmen of the leading industrialists, as well as the leaders of Catholic and Protestant religious organizations.[2]

The conference participants agreed that the unregulated lodging of single people with working-class families had grave consequences for society, ranging from moral and cultural ills to hygienic dangers.[3] In contrast to established and accepted subletting practices of the middle classes, where an unmarried middle-class man might rent a room or suite of rooms within a larger apartment from a social peer (most likely a respectable widow), and was termed a *Zimmerherr* or *Zimmermieter*, the unregulated lodger, or *Schlafgänger*, shared a room with the family from whom he rented, sometimes even sleeping in a family member's bed. Subletting was thus not problematic per se. Instead, the lack of privacy for both lodger and family—combined with working-class status—presented an issue. As a contemporary wrote in regard to the difference between a Zimmermieter and a Schlafgänger in terms of living arrangements, "the problem is largely solved with a Zimmermieter, as his room within the larger apartment can be closed-off. It is *his own domain* and can be arranged to suit his disposition. The situation with Schlafgänger is quite the opposite."[4]

In the eyes of middle-class reformers, without a space he could call his own, a Schlafgänger was unable to make a "home," and conversely, his presence prevented the family with whom he lodged from doing the same. In the worst case scenario, not only was the lodger precluded from making a home for himself but the familial apartment might also become one large *Schlafstelle*, a place that could never function as a proper home and setting for German family life.[5] Contemporary journal articles and books were filled with reports detailing the spread of contagious diseases, *Ungeziefer* (bed bugs and the like), out of wedlock pregnancies, and other indicators of the collapse of society supposedly all attributable to the dissolution of the family home through unregulated lodging.[6]

The attendees of the 1904 conference agreed that this problematic situation and its negative consequences needed to be swiftly addressed and that real change could only come about by the replacement of unregulated lodging by an entirely different system—one that did not rely on families to bear the burden of housing a significant portion of the working population, but rather, provided single people with a place, even a "home," of their own. Yet, what was truly remarkable about what happened in Leipzig in 1904 was not simply that the lodger problem was taken up and addressed in a logical manner, but that a rational solution was advocated for by a broad coalition of individuals at a national conference. Representatives of nearly every powerful interest group in the German Reich placed the Ledigenheim on the national stage as a topic of great importance.

While the 1904 conference represented a cross section of the key players in German society, making their presence most known were secular reformers and their new allies—municipalities. The heart of *(No) Home Away From Home*, Chapter 3 attends to the ways that Ledigenheime built by moderate bourgeois organizations—largely secular or nominally Protestant, and often with municipal backing—indicated a shift in thinking about public welfare that not only remade the German landscape of reform and heralded the birth of the modern welfare state but also closely bound German reformers to their British and American cousins.

Empowered by the changing dynamics around them, as well as transnational discourse centered on the reform of the urban lower classes—from improving mass housing to providing access to "proper" nutrition, culture, and beauty—German reformers and their allies in government began to argue that the construction of Ledigenheime was both logical and necessary, well within the parameters of what a *modern* municipality should do for the most vulnerable of its residents. Yet, these Ledigenheime went far beyond simply battling overcrowding in working-class tenements to keep disease in check—their ultimate goal was not simply the maintenance of physical health but also moral health. Building upon the traditions of Adolph Kolping's organization, which sought to aid young Catholic artisans, the local artisan estate, and the larger Catholic community, the supporters of reform Ledigenheime saw reformed housing for single people as a means to aid not only single young men in straitened circumstances but also the local community, and more significantly, the nation. Their aim was nothing less than the regeneration of German society and the young German nation—socially, culturally, and economically.

The Era of Reform

The broad-based interest in the Ledigenheim highlighted by the 1904 conference would have been unthinkable only a few decades before, and the reasons why the building type was the subject of a national conference was not merely due to a new and pressing need. The conference was the culmination of decades of work in the realm of social reform by a number of organizations often allied with municipalities, the end result of a series of campaigns concerning the amelioration of the dreadful conditions of the working classes in German cities and industrial areas.[7] Above all, it was a clear manifestation of the "era of reform" in German history, which ranged from 1890 to 1914 and is roughly contemporaneous with the American Progressive Era.

Largely enabled by the rise of powerful municipal governments and their engagement with nongovernmental advocates for social reform, the era of reform was marked by increased municipal involvement in all matters relating to public health and well-being, ranging from public ownership and oversight of gasworks, transit networks, and slaughterhouses to employment agencies, libraries, and museums.[8] A pendant to Otto von Bismarck's (often uneven and ineffectual) social insurance programs, and enabled by the increasing professionalization and specialization of both local government officials and private aid workers, this late nineteenth-century turn toward "municipal socialism" began to actively reshape the urban fabric.[9]

In this context, Ledigenheime quickly became a marker of and means by which the *government*, particularly at the municipal level, could actively support the provision of sound and hygienic housing, a role that would become enshrined in law under Social Democratic leadership in the 1920s. The organizational and architectural intelligence enabling Weimar-era social housing projects was thus presaged by decades of work devoted to Ledigenheime, work that encompassed, but was not limited to, architectural design, food management, liberal education, defining varying levels of privacy, and engineering an apparatus of moral and social control. Yet, while later projects attempted to (or at least purported to) create a new citizenry—a self-consciously modern *Volk*—the construction of Ledigenheime was not a revolutionary undertaking, but a negotiation of modernity encouraging those on the margins to think of themselves as potential members of the bourgeoisie, even as this was increasingly an impossibility.

The Reformist Impulse: Beginnings

The emergence of broad-based and significant public activism characterizing the 1890s to the First World War was a direct result of bourgeois concerns regarding the health of society aired as early as the 1870s. As addressed in the Introduction and previous chapters, the founding of the German Empire under the auspices of Prussia intensified trends in industrialization and urbanization that contemporaries found disconcerting, even bewildering. While early industry—as with the artisanal crafts—largely relied on a local workforce, this new phase of industrialization drew millions of people from small towns and villages to labor in rapidly growing urban centers and industrial districts. Of course, new workers needed to be housed, and quickly, with the result that the structures constructed were often of poor quality, which would have been less problematic if they had not been quickly filled, and then overfilled. Often, there was no housing to rent at all. Shoddily built and overcrowded housing was certainly detrimental to residents' physical health, and the possible spread of disease was troubling to middle-class observers, but what the state of this housing indicated about the moral health of residents was far more problematic.

As a visiting delegation from Great Britain noted, the prevalent working-class dwelling in Germany by the end of the nineteenth century was a flat typically consisting of three rooms (including a kitchen) in a building containing a minimum of 6 or 7 apartments,[10] though many tenement buildings, such as the infamous Meyershof of Berlin-Wedding (1873/4), which initially housed over 2,000 people in 257 apartments alongside businesses and factories separated by 6 poly-functional courtyards, were far larger.[11] Already suspect simply because popular and prescriptive literature extolled the freestanding house on its own plot of land as the physical and moral ideal, "a means to maintain privacy, security, and respectability in a dangerous world," a tenement was doubly problematic in that it was located in the morally dubious surroundings of a city, rather than in the restorative setting of countryside, village, or small town.[12] The ideal home was also set apart from the public sphere and the market, an impossibility in most working-class homes, where the division between waged work and family life rarely existed. In a tenement, only the family as emotional refuge and moral sanctuary remained, and even this was threatened by the presence of lodgers. As early as the 1870s, middle-class observers saw substandard, overcrowded, and unhygienic tenements as exacerbating characteristics of working-class life that they already feared and distained, from "unemployment, high job turnover, long hours, low wages, drudgery, child labor, crowded housing, alcoholism and sexual abuse, to illegitimacy."[13] Such housing could never be a "home" in the bourgeois imagination. Working-class life—seen through the filter of substandard working-class housing—was the inverse of the lived experience and values of the middle classes, and the bourgeois social reformer was born, charged with bringing things back into balance.

The first interventions in the lives of the urban public, and the urban poor in particular, took the form of conferences and publications aired in both public and professional forums, such as the 1874 and 1875 meetings of the Deutscher Verein für öffentliche Gesundheitspflege, an organization of public health reformers, and publications such as Reinhard Baumeister's *Stadt-Erweiterungen (City Expansions)* of 1876.[14] These were important steps in civic engagement in that they were attempts to develop the mechanisms by which city dwellers would be provided with better sanitation, specifically "light and air" through the construction of wider streets and new sewer systems. By systematically laying out the sanitary problems facing the growing cities of the new empire, these groups provided a platform for newly empowered city governments to act upon as municipalities planned for expansions into the suburbs and modernized old city centers.[15]

The Expansion of Reform in the 1890s

The interventions proposed by the early reformers of the 1870s and 1880s had largely left private housing stock alone, instead concentrating on issues related to more general public health. It was only in the 1890s that more radical interventions in the lives of the public, and the urban poor in particular, became possible. While 1890 saw the lapse of Chancellor Otto von Bismarck's anti-socialist law and some action on the part of Kaiser Wilhelm II to increase protections and rights for workers, including personally hosting an international conference on workers' protections, it also marked the rise of powerful municipal governments and the engagement of these governments with nongovernmental reform advocates in matters that went beyond the provision of wider city streets and sewer systems.

This greater level of civic engagement has often been credited to the expansion of local government in a more professional capacity—a professionalization deeply informed by the many social reformers advocating for change both outside of and within a governmental framework—even the deepening of links between municipalities and reform-minded religious groups.[16] This shift seems to have emboldened reform organizations already in existence, leading to the founding of further organizations, the alliance of existing organizations, and the sharing of resources.[17] More to the point, the last decade of the nineteenth century saw the birth of what has been termed "vigorous civic activism within the urban bourgeoisie,"[18] and the educated middle class in particular, primarily as it pertained to the elevation of the working class.[19] While life in Wilhelmine Germany was marked by what seems to have been a near obsession with reform in all its forms—temperance to natural health, nudism to gymnastics and sports, animal rights to vegetarianism—finding an answer to the Social Question, or the alienation of the lower social classes under the capitalist system, lay at the heart of middle-class organizations such as the Protestant Social Congress, the German Women's League, the Ethical Culture Society, and the National Social Association, all of which were founded in 1890.[20]

Distinct from the landed aristocracy, the clergy, the entrepreneurial middle class, and the industrial working class, members of the educated middle class, or *Bildungsbürgertum*, held fast to ideals of their own.[21] Deeply valuing academic qualification and placing their faith in "the unifying and rationalizing effects of bureaucratization," German *Bildungsbürger* had long played a fairly substantial role in municipal government[22]—even as they saw themselves as apolitical.[23] What this meant was that while the late nineteenth century saw the rise of a politicized public, from the rise of certain political parties, even workers' organizations (*Arbeitervereine*) and labor unions, most activism at the local level was not led by political parties per se, and certainly not nationally prominent politicians, but by civil servants, university professors (particularly social scientists), and doctors. As an example, the Deutscher Verein für öffentliche Gesundheitspflege (founded in 1899) drew its membership from the public and private sectors—from physicians (Georg Varrentrapp of Frankfurt and Eduard Lent of Cologne) to engineers (Arnold Bürkli of Zürich), and city planners (Josef Stübben of Cologne) to the mayors of Frankfurt (Wilhelm Becker) and Düsseldorf/later Cologne (Franz Adikes).[24] This did not mean that these individuals, despite their professions of impartiality, lacked a vested interest in politics (the mayors certainly did not), only that they were relatively free from the control of the Imperial Legislature.[25] Instead, local character colored their outlook,[26] and like their American and British counterparts, they tended not to be radicals of the right nor the left.[27]

Largely sidestepping the overtly political realm, Wilhelmine reformers also maintained a certain critical distance from those they sought to help, which, as feminist and Wilhelmine reformer Gertude Bäumer argued, "mirrored the social distance separating these privileged observers from the fate of the masses in industrial capitalism."[28] Unfortunately this elite stance also meant that the voices of laborers, and organized labor in particular—from Social Democrats to the artisans and skilled workers who were members of trade unions and social clubs—were conspicuously missing from most local, regional, and national conferences and publications (including that of 1904) devoted to the Social Question. Likewise, workers found little representation on town councils as they found it difficult to penetrate into executive bodies of government.[29] Instead, educated professionals took the lead in reform organizations and local government alike and the lower classes remained largely peripheral to the critical discourse that developed, despite the fact that they were supposedly the beneficiaries of such efforts.

The economist Werner Sombart saw opportunities to benefit the common good in a number of places, all of which neatly align with what Daphne Spain and Marta Gutman have termed "redemptive spaces" in the American context, ranging from nurseries and kindergartens to the construction of cooperatives and settlements, and from popular education clubs to organizations promoting land reform, animal rights, and the prevention of venereal disease.[30] As with Sombart, reform-minded individuals were typically interested in a constellation of intersecting activities. In fact, reformers on both sides of the Atlantic, whether or not they were associated primarily with one particular cause, were almost always concerned with others, even those related only tangentially to their own. Just as German attempts to rid working-class homes of lodgers ultimately led to the construction of Ledigenheime (with further implications for reform writ large—from aesthetic reform to the temperance movement), the initial *cause* was often one's first foray into a deeper and wider world of reformist activities, as the example of Dresden's Victor Boehmert—Liberal economist, professor of economics, director of the Royal Statistical Bureau of Saxony, and director or member of no less than *six* reform organizations—proves.[31]

By the 1890s, the acknowledgment that hygienic and sound housing could serve both the public and private spheres, coupled with an existing organizational and institutional framework of reform, began to bear fruit in numerous ways, ranging from local and national attempts to pass legislation, to the selling or leasing of land to housing organizations, and even to the direct construction of housing by municipalities. Aiding the cause of housing reform was the development of a sophisticated public argument supported by not only sensationalized stories as to the perilous state of working-class housing, all of which were intended to appeal to middle-class sensibilities, but also, and perhaps more importantly, logical arguments and scientifically conducted surveys providing "evidence" for much needed change.

Surveys, Sociological Reports, and Sensationalizing Poverty

At the 1904 conference, many medical professionals attributed the prevalence of scabies and tuberculosis in working-class dwellings to unregulated lodging. Some went further, arguing that unregulated lodging was also responsible for the high death rate among tuberculosis victims.[32] Rickets, infant cholera, and venereal diseases were also closely associated with unregulated lodging in the public mind, as were unwanted pregnancies and the physical dangers resultant from attempting to end such pregnancies.[33] On the economic front, reformers linked unregulated lodging to the "artificial" inflation of rents in districts where it was a prevalent practice, noting that in the districts of Berlin-Charlottenburg where unregulated lodging was tolerated, rent was often 20 percent higher than in other comparable districts,[34] and that the more crowded a dwelling was, the more profitable it was to those subletting the spaces.[35]

The turn of the century also saw a profusion of "scientifically" conducted surveys and sociological reports focusing on both the low quality and dearth of housing for single people, such as a 1905 report by a Dr. Calwer, which studied the provisions afforded to unregulated lodgers (*Schlafgänger*) in their lodgings (*Schafstelle[n]*).[36] This report provided reformers not only with an indication of the perilous state of housing for single people but also was useful in indicating what middle-class reformers considered to be the bare minimum, at least by the standards of 1905. Basing his minimum standards on building police regulations, Calwer determined that lodgings must have 20 cubic meters of air per sleeping person and 4 square meters of floor space in order to qualify as acceptable.[37] In agreement with nearly every advocate of reform housing, he advised that no bedrooms be located in a basement or directly under the roof.[38] Finally, Calwer proposed that each lodger have a modicum of privacy, including a vermin-free bed of his own.[39] Pointing to the great need for quality housing for single people—and Ledigenheime specifically—only 14.6 percent of the surveyed rooms used as *Schlafstelle* met Calwer's minimum standards.[40] Significantly, Calwer's survey indicates that substandard lodgings were common (over 75 percent were substandard by his estimation) and were occupied not just by the destitute, or even unskilled laborers, but by the class of skilled workers and clerks the reform Ledigenheim was devised to serve. Similar reports underscore how widespread the "lodging problem" was, cutting through the lower middle and lower classes.

From Consciousness Raising to Action

Sensationalized reportage and scientific studies revealed the housing conditions the typical single worker in Germany faced and provided ammunition for a wide variety of reform activities, particularly increased municipal action. Most importantly, these efforts increasingly were considered a logical, economically feasible solution to a contemporary problem, not charity. The reforms of the late 1880s and early 1890s began with a number of attempts by specific municipalities to pass legislation setting minimum housing standards. This regulatory approach varied sharply depending on municipality and region and largely relied on inspections and fines. Significantly for our purposes, it specifically targeted working-class dwellings, particularly those that would typically take in lodgers.[41] As was also the case in the company towns constructed in Germany, elsewhere in Europe, and across the Atlantic, Charlottenburg's special Housing Deputation required that they be allowed to inspect "all dwellings consisting of not more than two habitable rooms and a kitchen [i.e., a small working-class apartment], all dwellings in which *lodgers are taken*, and all dormitories for work-people and other employees who sleep in the houses of their employers . . . special attention is given to lodging houses and the lodger system generally."[42]

While it is hard to ascertain how even and effective the enforcement of local legislation was, even passing legislation at all was a small victory, particularly when one notes how difficult this was on a regional and, certainly, national scale. For example, a rigorous system of housing regulations and inspections was put in place in Baden as early as 1874, though not in Bavaria until 1901, and in Prussia there existed no compulsory system of house inspection even as late as March of 1914.[43] In fact, in 1903 Prussia, a proposed comprehensive dwellings bill—heralded as a huge step in the reform of housing—which would have, among other things, mandated that "lodgers may not be taken unless their rooms (were) separated from those of the tenants," failed to pass in spectacular fashion,[44] as did a subsequent bill the following year.[45] In contrast to regional or national action, more direct involvement by local government was required.[46]

Municipalities and reformers realized the reform of housing—and relatedly, lodging—could only be mounted through comprehensive local legislation, but also, and perhaps more effectively, by supporting building societies, so-called *gemeinnützige Baugesellschaften*,[47] through gifts of land, tax breaks, and other means.[48] Many of these municipalities already owned land helpfully located near growing industrial districts that had been created by destroying medieval walls and filling in the glacis. Municipalities were also already responsible for the employment of architects and other officials necessary for such projects.

Foreign visitors noticed this surge in cooperation enabled by government support, with Madge Jenison of *Harper's Monthly* noting that Berliners in particular were "making experiments in co-operation everywhere. She has societies for cooperative buying; cooperative tenements and apartment buildings for civil service officials. . . . There are cafés and libraries, assembly halls and kindergartens. The co-operative associations build on only one-half their land instead of two-thirds and the courts are full of trees, and sand piles, where the children play."[49] As Jenison noted, municipal support enabled building societies to construct relatively low-cost housing of a higher quality than what was commonly available to lower-middle-class families, and more importantly, it allowed them to restrict lodging in these properties. Contemporaneous American reformer and observer of the German style of municipal government William Harbutt Dawson reported in 1914 that the municipality of Mannheim imposed restrictions on taking in lodgers in homes on the land they leased to building societies, pointing out that article number five of such contracts between the building society and municipality stated that the municipality of Mannheim required building societies "to take steps to prevent sub-letting and the keeping of lodgers, and the use of the dwellings in a manner injurious to the health and morality of the inhabitants."[50] Contemporaneously, the town council of Düsseldorf also forbade subletting and the taking of lodgers in the leases of dwellings funded by the city.[51]

Yet, simply restricting subletting in properties directly linked to a municipality and building better quality housing for families were not enough to solve the "lodger problem." Where precisely were these undesirable lodgers supposed to go? By the 1890s, those involved in the reform of housing had realized that if the majority of working-class families were to be rid of their lodgers and boarders, then some form of housing had to be devised for those who did not fit into the middle-class conception of what a working-class dwelling should look like. This recognition resulted in Ledigenheime, particularly those constructed through the combined efforts of reformers and municipalities. Sophisticated arguments bolstered Ledigenheime supported by municipalities as not only rational and inevitable but also economically sound.[52]

The above (and competition among various municipalities) was underscored at a 1904 conference, where building Ledigenheime was compared to new policies enacted by numerous cities regarding *Milchversorgung*, or the oversight of the urban milk supply. Specifically, a Dr. Wiedfeldt cited the old system of bringing milk door to door and the related high risk of bacterial contamination, which was replaced and mitigated by citywide *Milchversorgung*, or the establishment of a large central processing depot (Wiedfeldt spoke specifically to *Milchversorgung* in the city of Essen). Wiedfeldt felt that the system of lodging should be treated in an analogous manner, that bad lodgings should be "replaced through a large and extensive agency that is technically up to date and will bring advances in the business, hygienic, social, and cultural realms over what is currently provided."[53] Wiedfeldt's argument reflects those of forward-thinking civil servants of the 1890s. Ledigenheime could be constructed on a mass scale and logical basis. In a similar vein, other proponents of municipally supported Ledigenheime argued that cities would be less impacted by economic crises than private companies or charitable organizations.[54]

As with the efforts of industrialists discussed in Chapter 2, the building of a Ledigenheim was also a means by which the local notables and officials of particular municipality could telegraph the modernity of their hometown to their colleagues elsewhere. Competition between municipalities was particularly overt in the western and southern regions of the Reich, where a clear pattern of municipal activism connected the cities of the Rhine-Ruhr region to those of Hessen, Baden-Württemberg, and Hamburg. Bavarian, Saxon, and Thuringian cities, as well as the city of Berlin, also exhibited a relatively high level of building activity. In fact, of reform Ledigenheime built (and published on) between 1890 and 1914, the greatest number (25) were in Berlin, followed by Frankfurt am Main (9), Hamburg (5), and finally Stuttgart, Munich, and Dresden (2 each). In all cases, the respective city governments were particularly active in making other provisions for the public, or *Wohlfahrtseinrichtungen*.[55] By contrast, West

Prussia and Posen in the east remained a backwater of inactivity in providing public services, including Ledigenheime.[56]

In fact, this fear of being considered a backwater led many local officials to advocate for the construction of Ledigenheime, such as a gentleman in Posen who was not above comparing local efforts (or the lack thereof) to those of numerous other cities including Stuttgart, Hamburg, Düsseldorf, Berlin, Charlottenburg, Ulm, Fürth, and Frankfurt am Main.[57] In Munich, local officials feared that they were falling behind their peers and used recently constructed municipal Ledigenheime in Mönchen-Gladbach, Stuttgart, Charlottenburg, Milan, and Vienna to bolster their case that Munich—with 31.5 percent of all homes hosting lodgers—was in dire need of a municipally supported Ledigenheim.[58]

Women's groups, including the Association of Progressive Women's Organizations (Verband fortschrittlicher Frauenvereine), founded in 1899 in Berlin,[59] also unequivocally held municipalities responsible for the problematic state of housing, laying the blame for the dearth of new and quality housing firmly at their door. This indicates that varied reform groups, not just organizations specifically focused on housing, increasingly favored greater involvement in the "lodger problem" and "housing question," particularly when these interventions were supported in part by municipalities.[60]

Building Ledigenheime thus rid cities of negative consequences resulting directly from the evils of unregulated lodging. An antidote to one particular "cancer" affecting the body politic,[61] it was a central component in improving life for every member of society.[62] While turn-of-the-century cultural critics claimed that German society was degenerating without offering a workable solution, the reform Ledigenheime's bourgeois supporters proposed this building type as the medicine that could *potentially* repair a fractured society.

Elevating Residents

The sophisticated and logical public arguments supporting the Ledigenheim's contributions to the economy and a municipality's prestige, backed by scientific studies and sensationalized stories, tend to obscure the primary goal of supporters of Ledigenheime—elevating residents. Although not explicitly used to justify reform Ledigenheim to the general public, the literature indicates that— like Adolph Kolping's Catholic Ledigenheime—the reform Ledigenheim was intended to bolster a declining but important group, one that had traditionally served as a buffer between the middle class and working class. While Kolping's efforts focused more explicitly on the housing and well-being of young artisans, the proponents of reform Ledigenheime broadened their appeal to include other members of the *Mittelstand*, such as skilled workers and clerks, all of whom were proud of their social position on the edges of bourgeois respectability.

Reform Ledigenheime were designed to reflect middle-class priorities, distancing residents from Proletarian habits and political inclinations. As members of Munich's housing commission snobbishly noted, a Ledigenheim would show the lower classes how they "should live, *if* they desire to live in a customary and healthy way."[63] Despite these admittedly problematic underpinnings, Ledigenheim supporters always emphasized the agency and potential of residents, stressing their individuality and taste for personal freedom—essentially, their ability to *rise*.[64]

Certainly, the provision of affordable housing via the Ledigenheime was never considered to be a charitable act. While it is easy to see reformers and the organizations they ran as coercive and paternalistic, they believed (or at least consistently stated) that they were empowering, rather than quashing, the individualism of those they sought to aid.[65] In fact, it was feared that if such housing even *felt* like charity to residents, this would hurt their larger cause.[66] Reformers did not want to endanger the self-esteem of a proud and independent man by allowing him to think that he was the recipient of unwanted and unneeded charity.[67] This view certainly connects with that of most social reformers in America and Britain, from Charles Loring Brace of the Children's Aid Society, who sought to "'break up [street urchins'] service in the army of vagrancy' without weakening their 'sturdy independence,'"[68] to Sylvan Barnett of East London's settlement house, Toynbee Hall, who favored artisans and despaired of the "unemployables . . . unrepentant and unregenerate paupers,"[69] as well as Reverend George W. Bethune of the New York YMCA, who saw his residents as forming a line of defense against the "lowest order."[70] Accordingly, the supporters of reform Ledigenheime were decidedly blunt in stating who they sought to serve, and who was not of interest. As Adolf Kolping and his followers had done, they abjured the lowest echelons of society in favor of those on the margins of respectability, stating that "the LUMPENPROLETARIAT is as good as excluded."[71]

The Ledigenheim, then, were distinct from such forms of poor relief as "public infirmaries, shelters for the homeless (the *Asyl*), labor houses for loafers and the like, and orphanages," for which the inhabitants paid no rent or were forced to perform a "work test."[72] Foreign observers of German social insurance trends under Bismarck and Wilhelm II, which also drew a sharp line around those who should be helped and those who did not qualify for such aid as accident, health, and old age insurance, noted that the Ledigenheim was clearly differentiated from "municipal shelters of various kinds."[73] The latter included the "warm kitchen," or the "public doss-house where a mattress is offered free for the night 'with no questions asked.'" Those who frequented them "rarely belong[ed] to the work seeking class."[74] While the supporters of *industrial* Ledigenheime repeatedly stressed that their creations were entirely unrelated to charitable institutions such as the homeless shelter, supporters of *reform* Ledigenheime not only spoke to difference in the architectural press but illustrated it, circulating images of well-dressed and genteel residents in settings that read as comfortably bourgeois (Figure 3.1). Some even proposed the reform Ledigenheim as an architectural and sociological solution to the *Studentenheimfrage*, or how one should best house university students, indicating that they did not see an unbridgeable sociocultural gulf between members of the *Bildungsbürgertum* and those on the fringes of the *Mittelstand*.[75]

Essentially, the supporters of reform Ledigenheime sought to remake the threatening specter of the *Schlafgänger* into a respectable *Zimmermieter*.

Figure 3.1 Dankelmannstrasse 46–47 Ledigenheim, Berlin-Charlottenburg (1908). Single room.
Source: *50 Jahre Volkswohnheim Gemeinnützige Aktien-Gesellschaft Berlin-Charlottenburg* (Basel: Länderdienst Verlag, 1955), 33.

While the onus was still on the individual to avail himself of what it offered, these homes—to the extent that was possible—carefully approximated a well-rounded middle-class education, much as Kolping's homes had facilitated the education of artisans. In its ideal formulation, a reform Ledigenheim introduced them to the classics of German literature as well as the softening effects of respectable company (including women and children), and even proper forms of consumption. This is to say, it played the roles of both father and mother, advancing the middle-class ideals of (male) *Bildung* and (female) domesticity.

Libraries

This bourgeois belief in the power of the individual to rise—coupled with reformers' faith in education as the primary means for social advancement and its centrality to bourgeois self-identification—underpinned the inclusion of private reading rooms or public libraries in *every* Ledigenheim constructed by a reform organization.[76] Yet, in speaking of education, reformers were not simply thinking of formal education—though that was certainly desired—but the remaking of a young man on the fringes of respectability into an educated person in the broadest sense. The reform Ledigenheim, with its supporters' focus on formal, social, and, to a lesser degree, aesthetic education, should be set against the backdrop of Kolping's efforts, as well as other popular education efforts at the turn of the century. The latter ranged from university extension classes to Socialist youth groups and night classes and youth groups, the latter of which abjured Marxist theory for "professional training" and "cultural literacy."[77]

The holdings of a Ledigenheim library or reading room were still important. A brief foray into the literary lives of Ledigenheim residents shows the libraries' books, newspapers, and journals were carefully vetted and controlled to fit middle-class conceptions of what constituted healthy and varied reading habits. A decided focus on literature and educational materials reflected the tastes of the middle classes, rather than a cross section of everything available. Examining what did *not* feature in a Ledigenheim library, rather than what did, is helpful. *Schundliteratur*, or penny dreadfuls and pulp fiction, were banned from Ledigenheim libraries, despite, or perhaps because of, their affordability and popularity with the reading public.[78] Additionally, although the sociologist Werner Sombart deemed suspect reading material to be decidedly less corrupting than other "luxuries" available to the working classes, such as spending time in cafés and drinking alcohol,[79] the presence of Schundliteratur indicated the rise of a consumer culture the bourgeoisie had helped to enable, but that they had little control over.[80] It was not only the corrupting subject matter of these works that was at odds with a Ledigenheim library's educational aims but also the fact that they could typically be purchased on installment, an affront to the middle-class ideal of frugality. Supporters of reform Ledigenheime were not alone in waging this battle against "trash-literature." They had a great deal of company, including Kolping's homes. As late as March 1916, the central command of the German army published a list "banning 135 individual titles or series of penny dreadfuls,"[81] and a few years earlier the South German Evangelical youth council held a meeting specifically concerned with the "fight against trash-literature, the cinema, and other *dangers* to youth."[82]

Political journals published by leftist groups, such as *Sozialistische Monatshefte*, *Die Gleichheit*, and *Die Neue Zeit*, the latter two edited by Clara Zetkin and Karl Kautsky, respectively, were perhaps even more dangerous than penny dreadfuls.[83] However, omitting them from Ledigenheim libraries was hardly necessary, as highly theoretical and radical journals were not widely read by workers. Instead, Socialists used daily party newspapers and speeches to communicate with the lower middle and working classes.[84]

A general breakdown of popular reading material in the typical Ledigenheim library clearly reflected an emphasis on educational materials—daily newspapers and some journals, the latter primarily of a scientific, business, or otherwise practical or applied nature—and literary classics. Works of classic literature and sociology included authors such as Nietzsche, Schiller, Goethe, Haeckel, Darwin, Kant, Emerson, Ibsen, Malthus, Heine, Schopenhauer, Byron, Grillparzer, Shakespeare, Dickens, Zola, Gorki, and Fichte. The Bible also featured regularly. Interestingly, lengthy works by major leftist figures from Bebel to Marx, Kropotkin to Lassalle were also regularly featured, despite their controversial nature. Such works were evidently so well known by the turn of the century that including them was considered relatively unproblematic—or at least unavoidable. Notably, no record exists of residents making initial selections or expanding the collection.

Seemingly at odds with the level of control exercised over reading materials (and perhaps accounting for the inclusion of some potentially problematic materials), reformers stressed the "feeling" of the library space was far more important than what was on offer, noting that the ultimate aim was to foster "a joyful tone, communal recuperation, (and) noble camaraderie."[85] In the case of an early reform Ledigenheim libraries, like that of the Stuttgart Ledigenheim (1890), this meant that three long wooden tables were arranged in perpendicular

Figure 3.2 Heusteigstrasse 45 Ledigenheim, Stuttgart (1890). Reading room/library.
Source: Schlafstellenwesen und Ledigenheime (Berlin: Karl Henmanns Verlag, 1904), 44.

rows, each of which could easily accommodate ten men in the wooden chairs ringing them (Figure 3.2). Two lamps suspended from the ceiling hung above each table, ample natural light also streamed in from four large windows on three of the five walls, and hooks near the door provided space for coats or hats. No wallpaper or painted decoration featured, though the bare expanse of plastered wall was interrupted by a number of framed pictures placed (oddly) high on the wall, billowing window valances, and a floor-length mirror on a windowless wall perpendicular to the entrance, which was itself flanked by several glass-fronted and wooden-doored bookcases. While certainly not elegantly appointed—with the exception of the valances the decor feels somewhat ad hoc—the room is neither overcrowded nor spare, and (admittedly staged) images show residents availing themselves of the pleasant and well-lit surroundings to play a game of chess and peruse one of the many journals scattered on the tables.

However, by the first decade of the twentieth century, few Ledigenheim libraries were lacking in style, as the Stuttgart building had been, with the library of the Düsseldorf Ledigenheim (1910/11)—located on the ground floor of the building next to a suite of rooms for relaxation—providing an example of an edifying and refined leisure experience (Figure 3.3). Both the arrangement of space and the decor are more purposeful. Each type of media has its own

Figure 3.3 Eisenstrasse Ledigenheim, Düsseldorf (1910). Reading room/library.
Source: *Weyls Handbuch der Hygiene* (Leipzig: Barth, 1918), 361.

space and means of presentation, from the hanging of newspapers to special display cases for magazines and journals, as well as built-in bookcases for leather-bound books, all of which were grouped by binding and type. Similarly, the decor was carefully coordinated and very much on trend, marrying dark wooden wainscoting of shoulder height with a creative use of wallpaper—narrow panels arranged vertically at regular intervals to form repeating modules of white space and placed along the gently curving terminus of the wall with the ceiling—recalling both the restrained rectilinearity favored by members of the Viennese Secession and the neoclassical forms of the *Biedermeier revival*, an aesthetic choice the ramifications of which were treated in Chapter 1, and will be discussed further shortly.

Despite the (supposed) greater social aspirations of reform Ledigenheim residents (or at least the hopes Ledigenheim supporters had for them), and the importance reformers placed on elevating surroundings, residents were still men of very limited economic means.[86] Reformers therefore had to carefully consider how they could fulfill their goal of creating an atmosphere with the right "tone," while still keeping the building economically competitive.[87] The proponents of reform Ledigenheime realized that in order to maintain affordable rental rates while also covering building and operational costs, they would need to find alternate ways to create the revenue needed.[88] Namely, they would work with municipalities to lower costs by including elements benefiting both residents and the wider public, ranging from the aforementioned libraries to public kitchens (*Volksküchen*), as well as (less commonly) public bathing facilities (*Volksbäder*),[89] and employment agencies (*Arbeitsämter*).[90] As a contemporary wrote, "a city can combine a public library, kitchen or open reading room with a lodging house and thereby lower the costs of both establishments."[91]

The inclusion of such facilities had far greater implications than simply lowering costs for residents while keeping reform Ledigenheime solvent. Without Ledigenheim libraries, from the elegant library of the aforementioned Düsseldorf Ledigenheim to the small public library (*Volksbücherei*) of the Frankfurt Ledigenheim (1894), which contained a modest selection of books and newspapers for the perusal of residents and the public,[92] neither residents nor the surrounding citizenry would have had such easy access to educational resources. Ledigenheim libraries were intended to supplement the offerings of city and state libraries, which focused on academic titles and were not necessarily charged with elevating the reading (and possibly aesthetic, as will be explored shortly) taste of the public.[93] Supporters also positioned them as a substitute for commercial lending libraries (*Leihbibliotheken*), which typically held works of lesser quality and far fewer works in general. As an example, the lending library of the city of Flensberg contained 3,700 works, while the public library held 12,700 works, 3,080 of which were literary "classics" and 9,620 were "scientific-instructive" works.[94] While a public library was a guide to edifying quality works, a commercial lending library was merely a neutral mediator of what might be problematic titles.[95]

As with the reading materials, access to and the use of a Ledigenheim library was carefully controlled. For example, the public library, or *Volksbibliothek*, of the Dankelmannstrasse Ledigenheim in Berlin-Charlottenburg (1906) could only be accessed through a passageway nearly 10 meters long, the entrance to which was nestled between several storefronts on the main facade of the Ledigenheim (Figure 3.4a, b). There was *no* direct access to the library from the interior of the Ledigenheim proper—a resident would actually have to exit the Ledigenheim, enter the street, turn to his right, and then enter a different passage leading to the courtyard fronting the library. While one might think that this was due to space constraints, or even different opening hours, the entrance to the Ledigenheim and the library were both accessed from the *same*

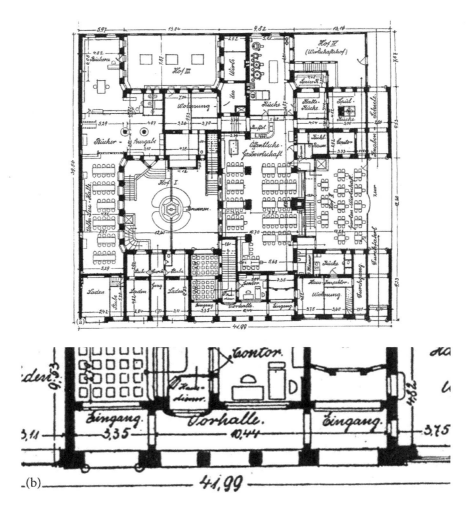

Figure 3.4a, b Dankelmannstrasse 46–47 Ledigenheim, Berlin-Charlottenburg (1908). Plan and detail of the ground floor. Note the vestibule labeled Vorhalle.
Source: *Weyls' Handbuch der Hygiene* (Leipzig: Barth, 1918), 354.

courtyard, complete with a shared fountain—all of which (fountain included) was neatly bisected by a brick and wrought iron fence of approximately 7 feet in height (Figure 3.5). Considering that a completely open courtyard would have felt larger and more pleasant—in keeping with the contemporaneous reformed tenement movement that saw potential in the expansion and reconfiguration of such spaces—why subdivide this space? Why preclude residents from directly accessing the library? And why use a combination of brick and wrought iron? While the literature on this particular building does not address the reasons

Plate 1 Jacob Pallenberg's Arbeiterheim/Settlement, Cologne-Nippes (1905). View of the entrance to the Pallenberg settlement.
Source: Author's photographs.

Plate 2 Jacob Pallenberg's Arbeiterheim/Settlement, Cologne-Nippes (1905). View of the entrance to the Pallenberg settlement from the west.

Source: Author's photographs.

Plate 3 Jacob Pallenberg's Arbeiterheim/Settlement, Cologne-Nippes (1905). Detail of the entrance to the Pallenberg settlement.
Source: Author's photographs.

Plate 4 Jacob Pallenberg's Arbeiterheim/Settlement, Cologne-Nippes (1905). View of gatehouse and two Ledigenheime from the east.
Source: Author's photographs.

Plate 5 Jacob Pallenberg's Arbeiterheim/Settlement, Cologne-Nippes (1905). View of the gatehouse and attached Ledigenheim from the east.
Source: Author's photographs.

Plate 6 Jacob Pallenberg's Arbeiterheim/Settlement, Cologne-Nippes (1905). View of family housing along the south side of the settlement.

Source: Author's photograph.

Plate 7 Dankelmannstrasse 46–47 Ledigenheim, Berlin-Charlottenburg (1908). Primary facade with "Abendsgäste" detail.

Source: Author's photograph.

Plate 8 Dankelmannstrasse 46–47 Ledigenheim, Berlin-Charlottenburg (1908). "Abendsgäste" detail.

Source: Author's photograph.

Plate 9 Dankelmannstrasse 46–47 Ledigenheim (for men), Berlin-Charlottenburg (1908). Passage through the Ledigenheim to the local school (*Gemeindeschule*).

Source: Author's photograph.

Plate 10 Alt Moabit 38 Ledigenheim, Berlin (1908), detail of primary facade in 2008. *Source:* Author's photograph.

Plate 11 Dankelmannstrasse 46–47 Ledigenheim (for men), Berlin-Charlottenburg (1908). Primary façade.

Source: Author's photograph.

Plate 12 Alt Moabit 38 Ledigenheim, Berlin (1908). Primary facade in 2008.
Source: Author's photograph.

Plate 13 Bergmannstrasse Ledigenheim, Munich (1927).
Source: Author's photograph.

Plate 14 Hedwig Rüdiger Häuser, Berlin-Charlottenburg (1924–5).
Source: Author's photograph.

Figure 3.5 Dankelmannstrasse 46–47 Ledigenheim, Berlin-Charlottenburg (1908). Bisected courtyard and fountain.
Source: *50 Jahre Volkswohnheim Gemeinnützige Aktien-Gesellschaft Berlin-Charlottenburg* (Basel: Länderdienst Verlag, 1955), 35.

behind this sharp and pointed division of exterior space, it seems to indicate a discomfort with the *relative* permeability of the building.[96] The wall was not only a physical barrier but also a visual one that partially obscured the gaze of all, and entirely blocked that of anyone under 5'2", including many women and all young children.[97] The extent to which the public and private realms collided had to be *controlled*, at least to an extent, though reformers were careful to couch this in quite different terms.

Spatial controls, rules, and regulations were reframed as simply a means to bring out the nascent qualities of the residents, particularly those demoralized by the moral and physical ills of unregulated lodging. Control did not need to be exercised in the heavy-handed manner of a cloister or military barrack,[98] or even, as discussed in Chapter 2, a Ledigenheim constructed by an industrialist. Residents were merely being offered the *opportunity* to *reacquaint* themselves with "a strict sense of order and discipline,"[99] a sentiment that would not have been entirely foreign to them, for as Richard Evans notes, comprehensive systems of "registration and documentation" were a part of everyday life during

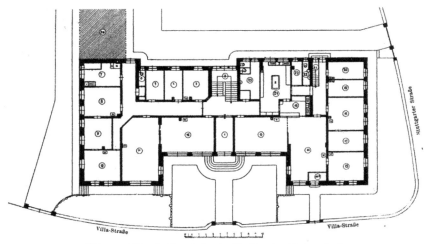

Abb. 77. Das Ledigenheim in Stuttgart. Erdgeschoß.

1 Hauseingang, *2* Aufgang zu den Wohnräumen, *3* Bureau des Verwalters, *4* u. *5* Schlafkammer für die Mägde, *6* Abort für den Verwalter, *7, 8, 9, 10* Wohnung des Verwalters, *11* Lesezimmer und Volksbibliothek, *12* Unterhaltungszimmer, *13, 14, 15* Kaffee- und Speisewirtschaft, *16* Büfett, *17–20* Wohnung des Wirts, *21* Zugang zu den Kellerräumen, *22* Abort des Wirts, *23* Speisekammer, *24* Wirtschaftsküche, *25* Abort, *26* Waschküchenanbau.

Figure 3.6 Villa Strasse Ledigenheim, Stuttgart (1910). Plan of the ground floor.
Source: *Weyls' Handbuch der Hygiene* (Leipzig: Barth, 1918), 352.

the *Kaiserreich*.[100] Like the governmental measures that ultimately served to "strengthen the official grip on the population,"[101] that which could be read as restrictive and controlling in a Ledigenheim was carefully recast. For example, the positioning of a housemaster's apartment near entrances and staircases leading to bedrooms—as with the home on the Dankelmannstrasse, the Kaiser Wilhelm Ledigenheim in Essen, the Ledigenheim on the Galluswarte in Frankfurt, and Stuttgart's Villastrasse Ledigenheim—to prohibitions on times that residents and visitors could enter and exit Ledigenheime were repositioned as aiding residents in comporting themselves as they were *naturally inclined* (Figure 3.6).[102] As such, critiques of house rules were not attributed to the residents themselves, but—like Catholic Ledigenheime—to "outsiders," specifically Social Democratic agitators.[103]

This repositioning of restrictions, including access to and use of libraries, as simply encouragement—an aid to the development or maintenance of good habits and customs—was buttressed by another supposedly beneficial aspect of a public library. Provided access was *controlled* spatially and supervision enabled in the person of the housemaster (or a librarian), its careful insertion into the fabric of a Ledigenheim mitigated what would have been an exclusively homosocial and youth-driven space. Unlike Catholic homes, which often included libraries, but restricted access to residents and association members, reform Ledigenheim libraries did not carve out the ladies' reading rooms and children's sections so typical of American libraries and not uncommon in other German library settings.[104] Men, women, and children shared the same reading space, thus exposing residents to the feminizing and domesticating effects of women and children with little risk to the moral rectitude of either party. The presence of women and children in an observable and controllable semiprivate space was thought to curb problematic behaviors, from spitting to swearing, thus smoothing and softening the rough edges of single lower-middle-class manhood into a form of masculinity more palatable to bourgeois sensibilities.[105] Most importantly, while their behavior might be positively informed by the presence of the "fairer sex," former lodgers were safely kept far from the sanctity of the familial home. While a supposed "advantage" of unregulated lodging was ample opportunity to conduct an illicit liaison,[106] the library of a Ledigenheim, with it its numerous rules and conditions of use, highly observable spaces, carefully planned access, and sharp division from the private spaces of the home, afforded little such chance.

With the danger of unmitigated interactions thus dissolved, what remained was the power of women and children—alongside carefully curated literature and aesthetically pleasing surroundings—to "improve" young men. Although a semipublic space, the library in a Ledigenheim was thus positioned as a variant of the nineteenth-century middle-class *home*, a space imbued with the power to soften "the deviant 'angles' and 'defects' of human character."[107] It was both a finishing school and a temporary substitute for the feminizing and domesticating hand of marriage and family, one that trained residents to their future calling as upstanding husbands and fathers. Yet, unlike the familial home, here there was no danger of over-feminization. While critics held that "sons who spent too much time in the company of their mothers and other female inmates of the [familial] home would grow up effeminate," residents of Ledigenheime faced no such danger.[108] Their interactions with women and children, as well as the rules and programming of the Ledigenheim, were enough to domesticate them, but never to the extent that their agency or independence was in jeopardy. The ideal Ledigenheim resident contained within himself both the beginnings of the family man and the virile and independent public man so valorized by the bourgeois cult of masculinity.[109]

Dietary Reform

The dining spaces (most often a *Volksküche*, or public kitchen) of reform Ledigenheime were yet another ambitious means for integrate residents with the surrounding community, and vice versa, further illustrating the increasing level of collaboration between disparate reform groups and municipalities. Even more than libraries and reading rooms, the Ledigenheim dining hall kept residents "at home," encouraging "healthy" habits far from the temptations of the tavern (*Wirtshaus*) and pub (*Kneipe*)—where drunkenness and its attendant physical and moral ills were thought to be rife.

As had Kolping, secular reformers saw the tavern and pub as an extension of the street, with its disordered spaces, cheap thrills, and morally suspect women. German-Austrian historian and publisher Otto von Leixner's *Soziale Briefe aus Berlin* (1891) positioned many pubs as "antechambers to prostitution" housing "white slaves,"[110] a corrupting effect multiplied by the luxurious decor of such spaces. As a consequence, even men still living at home, and certainly those whose only home was a *Schlafstelle*, had difficulty avoiding temptation.[111] Young men were particularly susceptible to the sway of such luxuries, with von Leixner identifying young boys of fifteen to sixteen years of age, high school students and students in their first semester of university, apprentices, trainee clerks, young artists, and even younger writers as particularly endangered.[112]

Beyond the pub, the Wiener Café, a Viennese import that had replaced the humble German *Konditerei* in many locations, posed still another danger to the moral rectitude of its young denizens. Von Leixner held that these richly appointed spaces—complete with billiard rooms, game rooms, and reading rooms featuring "hundreds of newspapers from every conceivable land"—were too opulent and too foreign to be healthful.[113] Instead of playing host to the (German) writer, artist, and actor, even the occasional politician, as had the Konditerei, the Wiener Café was populated by a different clientele—couples wearing ball gowns and tuxedoes, numerous foreigners, even the "spiritual Proletariat"—until 3 or 4 in the morning.[114] While von Leixner's reservations should be read as an abhorrence of aping one's social betters, his critique is also code for sexual impropriety. The extravagantly dressed couples, foreigners, and impoverished left-leaning intellectuals and academics are all dissolute types in reformist discourse. All were threats to the upstanding German family. While von Leixner does not directly term them prostitutes, at least some of the ladies wearing ball gowns should be understood as courtesans, or, at the very least, unchaperoned young women of dubious morals. The coupling of opulence with foreigners was meant to allude to, alternately, the "French disease," syphilis, or the "eastern vice," homosexuality. Similarly, mention of well-educated but impoverished Social Democratic sympathizers in such a

Making the Municipality a Home 151

Figure 3.7 Neue Schönhauserstrasse 13 Volkskaffeehaus und Speisegesellschaft, Berlin (1895). Primary facade.
Source: Architektonische Rundschau 11, no. 9 (1895).

context recalled a certain subset of Social Democrats who saw the patriarchal German family as oppressive and advocated both waged work for women and "free love."[115]

This is to say, social observers like Leixner linked the relatively luxurious atmosphere of many pubs and Wiener Cafés to the luxuries of the flesh, both of which held sway over impressionable youths. By contrast, although the supporters of denominational homes accused reform Ledigenheime as having the character of a *Gasthaus* (an inn with an attached tavern) and exhibiting a "multinational character" in the manner of a Wiener Café,[116] the supporters of Ledigenheim held that its appealing yet regimented spaces and programming could discipline impulses toward dissolute and corrupting "luxuries." In particular, the Ledigenheim dining hall contrasted with these less salubrious options. In fact, the reformist press paid most attention to the Ledigenheime's providing food, particularly the relationship of Ledigenheime to *Volksküchen*, or public kitchens (Figure 3.7).[117]

Adapted from Lina Morgenstern's noted Berliner *Volksküchen* (plural) dating to the 1860s, the overall goals reformers had for these dining spaces were similar to Morgenstern's: to improve the dining habits of the working classes, to curb the consumption of alcohol, and above all, to provide an alternative to the supposed unhealthiness of the tavern, pub, or Wiener Café.[118] As with its British cousin, the tea room, the Ledigenheim dining hall served "healthy" meals at very affordable rates, never required patrons to purchase beer or liquor with a meal (unlike many restaurants and pubs frequented by young men), and were often open to women and children, as well as men. As American journalist Frank Carpenter noted on his visit to Berlin in 1892,

> Here in Berlin meals are served to poor people at almost cost prices, and among the cellar institutions of the city are the "Volks Kitchens" or the people's kitchens. There are a number of these.... They have good cooks, and they feed hundreds of people every day. In them you can get a dinner for about 5 cents, and a bowl of soup or of rice costs you 3 cents, whiles you can get a first-class cup of coffee for a cent.... Everything was clean as could be, and the class of people appeared respectable.[119]

With the inclusion of Volksküchen, reformers had found a way to embrace the working-class habit of gathering in a pub (or frequenting a café), while curbing its most problematic aspects. Like the library, the dining hall of a reform Ledigenheim saw the controlled introduction of respectable men and women (and their children) into what would otherwise have been a homosocial space. Whereas Kolping's homes sought to facilitate connections between (male) residents and (male) association members, and similarly, the dining halls of Ledigenheime built by employers served their (male) employees, the dining spaces of reform Ledigenheime were always intended to serve the needs of the residents and larger local community—men, women, and children.

For example, the ground floor of the Ledigenheim on the Galluswarte in Frankfurt am Main (1894) contained a double-height dining hall with 270 seats— far more seats than there were residents—directly accessible from the street and also easily accessible from all three interior floors of the Ledigenheim proper. This building even contained an additional dining hall *explicitly* for the use of up to 120 local youths and children on a daily basis.[120] Similarly, the Kaiser Wilhelm Ledigenheim on the Weberplatz in Essen (1912/13) contained several dining spaces, including a *Speisesaal* (dining hall) serving the needs of residents,[121] as well as a Volksküche for the use of *both* the residents and the local community (this particular Volksküche was referred to as a *Wirtschaftlokal* in contemporary literature).[122]

While residents were sometimes provided with private dining spaces in addition to the public offerings of a Volksküche, and specific spaces for children and youth were occasionally craved out, the literature indicates that the Volksküchen of Ledigenheime were well integrated in terms of gender. They were even better integrated than many Volksküchen unaffiliated with Ledigenheime, as mentioned by Carpenter, and further illustrated by one of the buildings owned of the *Volkskaffee* and *Speisehallengesellschaft* of Berlin, which provided male guests with 300 seats in the main dining hall on the ground floor, while seating for 100 female guests was provided in an upper dining hall (*Speisesaal*) (see Figure 3.7).[123] Not only were the dining spaces of reform Ledigenheime welcoming to residents and nonresidents (regardless of gender), they were made affordable by the organizations governing the construction and operation of these buildings, which often stipulated that the meals provided in these spaces be available to the residents *and* the community at very reasonable rates—forty pfennig for the primary mid-day meal in the Dankelmannstrasse Volksküche.[124]

The dining spaces of a reform Ledigenheim also illustrate the increasingly close relationship between reform organizations and municipalities, an indicator that government was becoming more involved in matters concerning public health writ large. We saw this earlier with respect to milk, and the mass provision of food and drink could hardly be treated with less care and oversight. The extent to which the mass provision of food was regulated by the municipal authorities can be gleaned from a *Schankkonzession*—a contract given by the governing municipality to a Ledigenheim, which allowed the Ledigenheim organization to provide meals on a mass scale—to the administration of the *Evangelische Arbeiterverein*, which was responsible for both the construction and administration of the Kaiser Wilhelm Ledigenheim on the Weberplatz in Essen.[125] After the Ledigenheim had been constructed and inspected by the building police, the governing body of the Ledigenheim was required to apply for permission to serve food and alcohol from the municipal authorities.[126] Once it was granted, the governing body of the Ledigenheim could hire a manager to run the dining hall and public kitchen.[127]

This level of oversight underscores that the Volksküchen of reform Ledigenheime were thought of—at least by municipal authorities—as institutional spaces open to men, women, and children, not private homes, despite their supporters' emphasis on their "home-like" qualities. With distinct spaces for every associated activity—kitchen for warm meals, kitchen for cold meals, main kitchen, mess room, scullery, cold storage room, serving counter(s), buffet, dining hall, and outside terrace dining space in the case of Dankelmannstrasse—these Volksküchen were a far cry from the "dining room" of a typical lower-middle-class or working-class dwelling, which was rarely even a dining room at all, but

Figure 3.8 Dankelmannstrasse 46–47 Ledigenheim, Berlin-Charlottenburg (1908). Volksküche.
Source: *50 Jahre Volkswohnheim Gemeinnützige Aktien-Gesellschaft Berlin-Charlottenburg* (Basel: Länderdienst Verlag, 1955), 41.

a *Wohnküche*, a single room that served as living, dining, and kitchen space (Figure 3.8, see also Figure 3.4a, b).[128]

While room taxonomy was a marked aspect of middle-class homes on both sides of the Atlantic (as with a Ledigenheim in general and a Ledigenheim Volksküche specifically), this positioning of a Volksküche as an institutional space points to two related trends—cooperation within and rationalization of the kitchen. Cooperative housekeeping experiments—pooling the resources and labor of separate households in the interests of decreasing waste and drudgery—commonly focused on the kitchen (see Chapter 4). Like the public kitchens and libraries of a reform Ledigenheim, cooperative housekeeping effectively "expanded the meaning of 'family' and 'household' from private homes to the public community," and the proponents of both used language associated with the world of business and technology to do so.[129] This is to say, they carefully positioned both interventions as rational and professional solutions to a particular problem, or set of problems. What had always been a concern of individual women, the feeding of one's family, was now a matter for expert professionals, both male and female—as would come to even greater expression in the Weimar era.

In keeping with this level of official oversight, including the rationalization of its spaces, authorities also carefully planned the meals to maximize health benefits. Although the records of what was provided to diners in the Ledigenheim on the Weberplatz are not available, an idea of what was served to these individuals can be ascertained by examining the offerings of the *Volkskaffee* and *Speisehallengesellschaft* of Berlin, whose four dining halls, built in 1907, provided a changing menu representative of Volksküchen located in Ledigenheime.[130] The meals ranged from fish with potatoes to green peas with sausage, potatoes with minced meat to cabbage with pork, red cabbage with potatoes to white cheese with potatoes.[131] While these were perhaps not the most appetizing options, including a starch, vegetable, and protein for *nearly every* meal meant these meals contrasted with the lighter meals offered by coffee halls[132] and, more significantly, the soup-based offerings of charities.[133] If a piece of bread and a bowl of soup was a marker of want, meat signified these meals read befit a higher class of patron.

Offering inexpensive and (by early twentieth-century German standards) healthy meals to residents and the general public kept the larger labor force healthy and—alongside the libraries and architectural style of such buildings—educated their palettes and wallets by providing a well-balanced and frugal example of what to eat. The meals countered problematic working-class habits, from "wasting" money on bread and potatoes, instead of "preparing wholesome meals," to drinking weak coffee or alcohol instead of milk.[134] The emphasis on healthy and balanced meals was in keeping with similar efforts to improve the dining habits of the working classes in America and Britain. It made Ledigenheime, including their Volksküchen, players in the transnational Progressive reform movement most commonly identified with women reformers such as Jane Addams (Chicago) and Alice Salomon (Berlin), who are often used as evidence of educated women moving into the public sphere.[135] Levying maternalist discourse about a woman's natural role as nurturer to forge new roles for themselves and others in "social and health services, education, and municipal welfare administration,"[136] Addams and Salomon were able to effect change by mining and pulling from an *existing* network of reformers and their organizations on both sides of the Atlantic.

In the case of designing public kitchens and educating the eating habits of the lower classes, this transnational exchange of ideas is similarly centered on the efforts of educated women and dates to the 1870s, when the American

Melusina Fay Peirce visited Lina Morgenstern's Berlin Volksküchen.[137] Later disciples of Peirce, Ellen H. Richards, and Mary Hinman Abel—feminists, campaigners for kitchen-less houses, and creators of the "scientific" Rumford Kitchen displayed at the Chicago World's Fair of 1893—claimed that their innovations derived from a knowledge of public kitchens, particularly the Volksküchen of Berlin, which, as we have seen, were almost always a central component of a Ledigenheim.[138]

Interestingly, Volksküchen included in Ledigenheime seem to have been far more successful—given that they were, in part, included to help support the operating costs of a Ledigenheim—than any of the American public kitchens appearing contemporaneously. These ranged from Abel and Richards' Rumford Kitchen and New England Kitchens, whose "American" dishes, from boiled hominy to Indian pudding,[139] were decidedly unappealing to the immigrant populations they sought to serve,[140] and to the Coffee House of Chicago's famed Hull House,[141] which was frequented by women and children, as well as male settlement workers, but remained markedly unpopular with most local men.[142]

Temperance Reform

Unlike the provision of "wholesome" food, alcohol in a Ledigenheim was a somewhat more contentious issue. Drink was not necessarily a problem in and of itself, but *where* it was typically consumed (the pub [*Kneipe*] or tavern [*Wirtshaus*]) and *what* was being consumed (hard liquor, often schnapps) was.[143] What drove reformers to advocate for controls on the provision and consumption of alcohol was the fear that men who had the potential to rise into the middle class would, if faced with the tavern and its dangerous offerings, either slide into total dissipation or come into contact with "uncontrollable influences," guiding them into the arms of the Social Democrats.[144]

The need to offer an alternative to the tavern and pub—a space within which young men felt free to gather, socialize, eat, and drink—drove reformers to carefully consider both the culture of these spaces and, more importantly, what, if any, alcoholic beverages were on offer. While the middle classes, even sympathetic figures like the Socialist Karl Kautsky, commonly assumed that lower classes were "awash in Schnapps,"[145] the majority of these men had a more nuanced relationship to drinking, and made the distinction between the consumption of hard liquor and drinking beer. This means that a man interviewed in Adolf Levenstein's 1912 survey of "workers" (broadly construed) was able to make the following (rather contradictory) statement: "I am a natural anti-alcohol advocate. I only drink beer. The Schnapps boycott makes me happy."[146] With the idea that beer did not qualify as "alcohol" to the majority of their constituents, the supporters of most reform Ledigenheime realized that restricting beer would probably backfire, and took the middle ground, typically offering beer, but always supplementing it with other beverages, from lemonade to coffee.[147]

Most significantly, and in keeping with Ledigenheime supported by Catholics and employers, the managers of reform Ledigenheim dining halls (even when not specifically designated as Volksküchen) did not require patrons to purchase alcohol with one's meal in order to receive a discounted rate on a meal, a common practice in pubs and taverns referred to as *Trinkzwang*.[148] Considering that rates on meals were already low in a Ledigenheim, there were no discounts on food to speak of, but more importantly, encouraging alcohol consumption, even if it was "just" beer, would have undermined the socially elevating purpose of the Ledigenheim.[149] Above all, reformers sought to underscore how these spaces differed from the traditional working-class *Wirtshaus* or *Kneipe*, which was frequented by the majority of lower-middle-class and working-class young men, and where political activism and the consumption of alcohol went largely unregulated.

Yet, the dining spaces of a reform Ledigenheim could not read as overly restrictive—certainly not infantilizing—as this would potentially drive patrons to precisely the places reformers feared.[150] These dining halls were thus intended to mediate young men's relationships to alcohol consumption, to carve out a middle ground between common working-class practices and spaces and what was acceptable to the educated middle classes. It is this temperate, rather than extreme and exclusionary, view of alcohol that helped to ensure the popularity of reform Ledigenheime dining halls by the turn of the century, as well as the building type as a whole.

National Health and Aesthetic Reform

While the inclusion of spaces serving residents and the general public, including the "fairer sex," were to have a softening and elevating effect on non-middle-class masculinity, the exterior style and decorative program of the building multiplied this effect. The supporters of reform Ledigenheime

Figure 3.9 Galluswarte Ledigenheim, Frankfurt am Main (1894).
Source: *Schalfstellenwesen und Ledigenheime*, 51.

stressed that their buildings were not to appear stark and bare, which would have provoked a comparison with the spare and barrack-like structures built by industry, but that their relative massiveness could be mitigated by tasteful decoration lending the buildings a less institutional and more domestic appearance. Considering that these homes were intended to train residents for domestic life and reformers of all stripes believed the domestic was an antidote for societal defects and a means to bridge class animosity, this was of the utmost importance.[151]

For example, the mansard roof of the Frankfurt Ledigenheim (1894) helped to deemphasize the height of the building, while also providing a "cozy" impression (Figure 3.9). The gables, executed in the style of "old-Frankfurt," helped the building blend with its surroundings, particularly historic domestic architecture.[152] Only a few years later, however, a reform organization would not have been singled out for praise if it supported the construction of a Ledigenheim, the only aesthetic value of which was that it appeared to be a "cozy" home, rather than a barrack. While buildings constructed after the turn of the century retained a domestic appearance, they commonly utilized the *Biedermeier revival* style.[153] As discussed in Chapters 1 and 2, the Biedermeier revival drew from the vernacular architectural traditions of Germany *c.* 1800 as popularized by groups associated with the *Bund Heimatschuz*, and recalled homes favored by the urban bourgeoisie around the turn of the *nineteenth* century. Placed in the express service of artisans (Chapter 1) and bellicose nationalism (Chapter 2) alike, the many advocates of Biedermeier revival positioned this modernized neoclassical style as nearly always applicable and desirable. Certainly, the style recalled the age of Goethe and Schiller, complementing the "classics" on offer in a reform Ledigenheim library, but more importantly, it firmly aligned the building type with certain members of the design reform community, who believed that particular styles had profound educational potential—not only for artisans (see Chapter 1) but also for the average German.

The reform Ledigenheim located on the Dankelmannstrasse in Berlin-Charlottenburg (1906) provides a perfect illustration of the Biedermeier revival, in regard to the relatively modest materials used (glazed brick with sandstone and terracotta accents), the limited and softly pastel color palette (brown, cream, and white), an overall symmetry,[154] and neoclassical symmetry and detailing—from the application of dormers and a pediment to delicately carved fabric swags, rose garlands, and stylized placards (Figures 3.10a, b). The latter hung

Figure 3.10a, b Dankelmannstrasse 46–47 Ledigenheim, Berlin-Charlottenburg (1908). Primary facade and "Abendgäste" detail.
Source: Author's photograph.

from stone ribbons and were emblazoned with mandate of this Ledigenheim (and the aim of all others), "Daily Work and Evening Guests."

Similarly, the Kaiser Wilhelm Ledigenheim, constructed on the Weberplatz in Essen (1912/13), was characterized by a contemporary architectural periodical as "an artful grouping enabled by the simple and sober handling of the contours . . . throughout a sober and self-reliant delivery of the heritage of the time of circa 1800 . . . of the good old building tradition" (Figure 3.11).[155] More specifically, this meant that masses were grouped in "proper" relation to one another, facades were "restful," and the hipped roof worked well with the rest of the composition.[156] While the solidity of the building was enlivened with gables, passages, arcades, and forecourts, it nevertheless presented a "functional and unified" whole.[157] In short, the building was restful and yet lively, exhibiting variety and unity. Yet, the Weberplatz Ledigenheim not only was cited as a model building for the reasons enumerated earlier but also, due to the employment of "the good old building tradition," was given credit for both the aesthetic and the *social* regeneration of square.[158]

So why was the Biedermeier revival held up for praise and given significant powers by those who favored its employment? According to its proponents, the

Figure 3.11 Kaiser Wilhelm Ledigenheim on the Weberplatz, Essen (1912–13). Primary facade.
Source: Wasmuths Monatsheft für Baukunst 2 (1915/16): 69.

Biedermeier revival was simple and unpretentious style of building, an alternative to the architectural bombast and faux-grandiosity that marked much of the official and domestic architecture of both the *Gründerzeit* and the *Wilhelmine* eras, the exemplar of which was the pseudo-baroque Reichstag building finished in 1894 by Paul Wallot in Berlin. While social and aesthetic reformers construed the latter as a symbol of Germany's moral and cultural decline, the Biedermeier revival was thought to intrinsically connote honesty and morality due to its clarity of form and its vernacular roots, as well as the fact that these roots lay in the last era where "good taste" was exercised before it was "corrupted" in the course of the nineteenth century.[159] These connotations appealed to reformers who felt that the built environment could elevate and train the tastes of the population, even mold moral character. The style was also appealing as its *middle-class* roots and relatively modest appearance were deemed appropriate to the class of individual to be housed within, the "day workers and evening guests" whom reformers sought to imbue with middle-class values and mores. It was both elevated and modest, patrician and of the German people (*Volk*).[160]

One only need remember the language used to describe the Ledigenheim on the Weberplatz in Essen, the Biedermeier revival building credited with raising the tenor of the entire square. In particular, one word stands out, "Sachlich."[161] This is a word somewhat difficult to directly translate into English, but refers to designs that were sober and dignified in their restraint, meaning that they avoided superfluous ornament, instead relying on "purity" of form and material. *Sachlich* designs were steeped in a knowledge of local materials and German building traditions, while they also embraced modern needs. Tradition-conscious and forward looking, they were simple and functional, pragmatic, and objective.[162]

Importantly, *Sachlichkeit* (Sachlich-ness) was consistently employed as an ideal to strive for by members of the Werkbund, from 1907 the leading national association of artists, architects, designers, and industrialists, and whose goal was to modernize German design culture. While the relationship between the Werkbund and German design culture is discussed in greater depth in Chapter 1, Joseph Lux, founder of the aesthetic reform journal *Hohe Warte* and leading Werkbund member, noted that one particular style—the Biedermeier revival—"astonishes us... because of the *Sachlichkeit* of its forms."[163] *Sachlichkeit* and the associated Biedermeier revival were thus positioned as the balm to heal German design culture, providing it with roots in the great architectural and design traditions of the *German* past while carefully moving it forward into the modern age.

More specifically, when constructed in the *Sachlich* Biedermeier revival style, a reform Ledigenheim provided visual access to a style deemed aesthetically desirable and *appropriate* to the class of (German) individuals it was to serve, those drawn from the bedrock of the nation, the *Mittelstand*. In their use of a style referencing a less fractious time, and one that was to serve as an impetus to a new German golden age, the supporters of reform Ledigenheime underscored their residents' rootedness and potential to rise, rather than their fragile position as atomized individuals. To a greater extent than the artisan-residents of Catholic Ledigenheime, and certainly far more than the working-class denizens of industrial Ledigenheime, the residents of municipally supported Ledigenheime were positioned as *partners* of the *Bildungsbürgertum*—with the ultimate aim of regenerating the taste of the nation.

Bedroom and the Sliding Scale of Privilege

While reformers emphasized the power communal spaces and even the style chosen for a home's facade had in the molding of character and bourgeois habits, private spaces—namely, bedrooms—were always central to reformist discourse, with the single bedroom symbolizing both the agency and individuality of the resident. However, just as public dining rooms and libraries were included in reform Ledigenheime not only because community interaction was thought to have a positive effect on the residents (and vice versa) but also due to economic considerations, financial constraints meant that most Ledigenheime employed well-appointed single rooms, but mediated this ideal by also providing other bedrooms of varying sizes and price points. The result was that the private spaces of the Ledigenheim actually underscored the slight economic and class differences of the residents, differences that the communal spaces of these buildings and the discourse surrounding the building type attempted to paper over. Residents would have been patently aware that a man residing in a single bedroom was most likely drawn from the lower middle class and was the economic superior of a (generally younger) man sharing a bedroom with several other individuals.

The distinction between different classes of bedroom and resident was particularly evident in early reform Ledigenheime, such as the Galluswarte building in Frankfurt am Main (1894), which featured four double rooms, as well as individual sleeping compartments measuring 1.5 meters by 2.5 meters and constructed of thin wooden partition walls.[164] While one could consider an individual sleeping compartment as more private, and thus possibly more appealing than a shared room, the language used to describe these two options indicates that the former was far less desirable. The residents of double bedrooms resided in a "home-like fashion,"[165] whereas the sleeping compartments' main selling point was their affordability.[166] One would think that they were also more private (and quiet) than a shared room. Instead, each compartment shared a window with its neighbor, the thin partition walls were hardly a barrier to noise, none of the chambers were electrified (as double rooms were), and worst of all, residents rarely had access to the same compartment from day to day—an aspect of unregulated lodging reformers found appalling. The final indication that these rooms were less desirable—or at least that the residents were undeserving of the same level of trust as the residents of (more desirable) double rooms—was that the apartment of the house inspector was located directly across from the sleeping compartments.[167]

In fact, the employment of sleeping compartments was more in keeping with British practice than German efforts. In particular, German reformers took note of the English Rowton Houses, which were built beginning in 1892 in London and Birmingham (Figures 3.12a, b).[168] Initially, the economic success of this British precedent allowed German reformers to claim that mass housing for single people—when properly administered and practically built—was a wise financial investment by reformers and municipalities alike. Certainly, the costs associated with the "Kabinensystem" were lower at the outset than other forms of construction, which made this option appealing.[169] However, although ostensibly less expensive to build, sleeping compartments actually carried higher economic risk than the construction of permanently walled rooms, as they could not be as easily converted into another building type, should a Ledigenheim fail.[170] They were also problematic from the standpoint of physicians, for unenclosed rooms more easily facilitated the spread of communicable diseases. As such, homes utilizing sleeping compartments often contained designated sick rooms and some larger homes even had a doctor on-site.[171]

Ultimately, though, what doomed the widespread employment of sleeping compartments in reform Ledigenheime was that reformers deemed them *inappropriate* to the class of residents they sought to serve. German reformers believed that Rowton Houses served the lowest strata of British society, men who were "work shy" and "out of work" (*Arbeitsscheuen* and *Arbeitslosen*), conflating them with the patrons of the so-called common lodging house, which did serve the dregs of the British working class. For reformers whose ultimate

Figure 3.12a, b Rowton House in Newington Butts, London (1890s). View of primary facade and a sleeping cubicle.
Source: Schlafstellenwesen und Ledigenheime, 100, 108.

goal remained the cultivation of bourgeois propriety among men with the potential to rise into the lower middle class, even the middle class, bedrooms needed to function as a restful place to relax and cultivate a resident's interests—ideally, advance his *Bildung*—not simply provide a place to sleep for the night. Consequently, German reformers qualified their praise for what they termed "the English model,"[172] even though Milanese and Viennese authorities also constructed homes with basic sleeping compartments, or *Kabinen* (Figure 3.13). These "barrack-like" models were simply a useful starting point, upon which

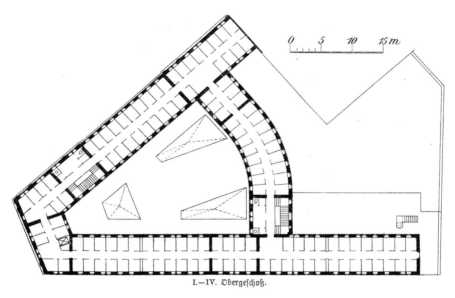

Figure 3.13 "Albergo Popolare," Milan (c. 1900). Plan of upper floors.
Source: *Schlafstellenwesen und Ledigenheime*, 113.

improvements suitable to German life and the German worker could be made.[173] After all, as social reformer, Werkbund member, and liberal nationalist politician Friedrich Naumann pointed out, the well-trained and disciplined German worker was already of a higher caliber than his competitors, an advantage that merely needed to be maintained and, ideally, furthered.[174] Although the nativist and nationalist underpinnings of this kind of rhetoric cannot be dismissed, particularly in light of rising political tensions between Germany and Great Britain, to advocate for a model that did not appear to aid ascent into the lower middle or middle class would have been to abandon one of the main tenants of the German reform project. In fact, it was to be "opposed on the grounds of social hygiene."[175] Instead, the ideal "German" solution was a room that could be closed off from the rest of the Ledigenheim to create "a homey, even ever so small space of one's own."[176]

Like the Catholic homes that preceded them, a single room was the preferred means to create an atmosphere both "German" and "homey." *Unlike* their Catholic brethren, however, secular reformers deemed a double or triple room acceptable if a single room was not economically feasible.[177] Secular reformers were apparently untroubled by the specter of homosexual activity in double rooms, deeming any solidly constructed room preferable to the sleeping compartment, provided that these rooms were complemented by a number of other spaces for education and entertainment. For example, the bedrooms of the Stuttgart Ledigenheim (1890) were evenly split between "well-furnished" singles and doubles, which contemporaries—at least in 1892—considered more than acceptable (Figures 3.14a, b).[178] Double rooms typically contained not only two individual beds (quite an improvement for one used to sharing a *Schlafstelle*) but also included individual wardrobes that could be locked, as well as a shared washing table and a table with drawers for storage. In the single rooms, the furnishings were the same, except that a sofa replaced the second bed.[179] Yet, while double and triple rooms were certainly acceptable, reformers constantly strove to tilt the balance toward the single room, efforts that seem to have borne

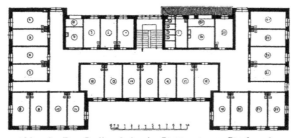

(a) Abb. 78. Das Ledigenheim in Stuttgart. 1. Stockwerk.
1—27 Wohnräume, *a* u. *a*₁ Veranden, *b* u. *b*₁ Putzräume, *c* Aborte.

Figure 3.14a, b Villa Strasse Ledigenheim, Stuttgart (1910). Plan of the first floor and view of the primary facade.
Source: Weyls' Handbuch der Hygiene (Leipzig: Barth, 1918), 351–2.

fruit by the close of the first decade of the twentieth century with the Düsseldorf Ledigenheim (1910/11) and the Dankelmannstrasse Ledigenheim (1908, Berlin-Charlottenburg) (Figure 3.15). The former offered four different lodging options, with its 139 single rooms far outnumbering 28 doubles, 16 triples, and one 14-man sleeping hall,[180] while the Dankelmannstrasse building featured 285 single rooms out of a total of 309.[181]

Would this division of have and have-nots represented by the single room not have been problematic? Ultimately, it seems that a number of rooms at varying levels of privacy and price points were intended not only to accommodate men of varied financial means but also gave the less affluent—literally right down the hall or stairwell—something to work for. The price distinction between lodging in a sleeping hall at 9 marks a month or renting a triple at 11 marks in the Düsseldorf Ledigenheim was not so great as to seem impossible to surmount with hard work.[182] While a single room at 15 marks a month might have seemed an impossibility, the staggering of quality and price within a single building at least gave those residing in less salubrious surroundings the impression that upward mobility within the home (and within society) was at least possible.[183]

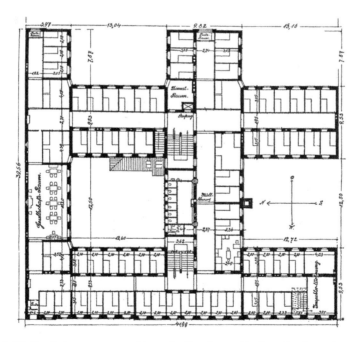

Figure 3.15 Dankelmannstrasse 46–47 Ledigenheim, Berlin-Charlottenburg (1908). Plan of the first upper floor.

Source: Weyls' Handbuch der Hygiene (Leipzig: Barth, 1918), 355.

Yet, it was not simply the status conveyed or level of privacy conferred that made a private or semiprivate space in a Ledigenheim appealing—one's bedroom, his "*own* four walls,"[184] complete with appropriate furnishings and decorations, was what made a Ledigenheim a home, not simply a *Schlafstelle*.[185] Even the smallest and simplest space could be transformed into a home, provided it was "well decorated and furnished."[186] Yet, decorations and furnishings need not be costly, for even small touches, such as the motifs painted on the bedroom doors and wardrobes of the Dankelmannstrasse Ledigenheim,[187] aided the creation of what a contemporary reformer termed a "clean and sound home."[188]

While reform Ledigenheime disallowed the bringing of personal furniture on hygienic grounds—wooden furniture coming from a tenement was viewed as an incubator of vermin—rather than the aesthetic reasons given by the supporters of Catholic homes,[189] supporters were very specific in prescribing the type and quality of the furnishings to be provided to *their* residents. For example, the 285 single rooms of the Dankelmannstrasse Ledigenheim in Berlin-Charlottenburg (1908) featured a "good" mattress, a table and two chairs, a wardrobe stand with washbasin and washing pitcher, bed linens, and a woolen coverlet (see Figure 3.1).[190] Similarly, a single bedroom in the Kaiser Wilhelm Ledigenheim on the Weberplatz in Essen circa 1913 included a white enameled metal bedstead with linens and pillow, a large wooden wardrobe, a set of hooks on the wall, and a table covered with a tablecloth.[191]

In fact, the furnishings provided to the residents of both buildings were on par with what was typically provided to a *Zimmermieter*, rather than a *Schlafgänger*, who rarely would have been offered his own bed, much less his own "good" mattress.[192] Indicating some parity in the treatment of Ledigenheim residents and even more affluent single men, the number and type of furnishings in the decidedly more modest surroundings of a Ledigenheim bedroom are nearly identical to those prescribed for a well-to-do single man at an interiors exhibition held in Würzburg in 1911. In 1912 the architectural journal *Architektonische Rundschau* featured a two-room dwelling that consisted of a small living room and bedroom and was specifically designed for a single man (Figures 3.16a, b). While slightly larger in square footage, the only additions to what would typically feature in a reform Ledigenheim bedroom included an occasional table (with chessboard), several chairs, and two small glass-fronted display cases. Instead, class difference manifested in detailing of the space, such as the quality of the furnishings (cherry wood), the soft green, blue, and grey paint on the walls, and the carpeted floors.[193]

Making the Municipality a Home 169

Figure 3.16a, b Model bedroom and living room for a single person, exhibited at the *Ausstellung bemalter Wohnräme*, Würzburg (1911).
Source: *Architektonische Rundschau* 28, no. 10 (1912): table 89.

Even more importantly—and *unlike* the residents of any other Ledigenheim variant—the residents of reform Ledigenheime were actively encouraged to *customize* their rooms with pictures, flowers, and even potted plants.[194] Essentially, they were to curate their surroundings, carefully choosing decorative elements much as the diligent housewife would. Taking into account nineteenth- and early twentieth-century conceptions of womanhood, which not only considered the domestic sphere as woman's "natural setting" but also invested them with the responsibility for running—and for our purposes—arranging the domestic sphere,[195] curating domestic space placed single men in a feminine role—one that was invested with great moral importance. If the "right" decorative choices could cultivate certain desired behaviors and create the perfect setting for family life, thoughtfully chosen pictures, even a potted palm, could constitute the ideal environment for a young man who aspired to a well-lived bourgeois life.

While a bedroom could never function as the primary space where one performed one's identity to others—it was certainly not a space where one entertained, as with a middle-class parlor—it was a place where a resident could express his identity to himself.[196] This is to say, a reform Ledigenheim resident was encouraged to modify his space, not simply dwell in it. Most important, contemporaries posited that this distinction between *Raumbenutzung* (use of a space) and *Raumbeherrschung* (control of a space) was precisely what distinguished a dangerous Schlafgänger from a respectable Zimmermieter.[197] An individual's single status was no longer problematic when he was accorded the ability to control and modify his space, even in the smallest of ways—this level of agency was a marker of middle-class identity. It also speaks to an intensification of mass consumer culture by the first decade of the twentieth century and a culture that regarded both improper and insufficient materialism a danger to the capitalist order.[198] Proper consumption—careful and measured engagement with consumer culture—was what marked an individual as the right sort of bourgeois (or potentially bourgeois). Like the "city recruits" of "uncertain [social] standing" Paul Groth has written about in his work on single occupancy hotels in the United States, the residents of reform Ledigenheime similarly sought to at least approximate the markers of middle-class respectability by engaging in consumerism to transform their rooms into homes.[199]

Beyond distinguishing the ideal resident from the lower classes, this encouragement to customize and curate one's own space in Ledigenheime for men also speaks to a sharp distinction between these buildings and those for female contemporaries. As I discuss in Chapter 4 in greater depth, the proponents of Ledigenheime for women (just as those for men) noted that a well-appointed Ledigenheim interior helped to create a "home-like" space keeping residents from a "nomadic life."[200] However, while decorating one's *own* space was encouraged for male residents, it was actively discouraged in homes for all but the most well-educated and affluent women, indicating that the discomfort with consumerism reformers espoused was highly gendered.

Contemporary supporters of Ledigenheime housing for women even stated that the pleasant spaces *already* provided—both public and private—would help curb residents' innate impulse to purchase "pretty things," including, but not limited to, decorations and furnishings.[201] Thus, men could play the role of decorator, but due to their natural sobriety and rational nature, they would not be as easily lured by frivolous items—certainly they would not squander all their earnings on them—as their female counterparts. Guided by the well-appointed and yet sober surroundings of the Ledigenheim, even if left to their own devices, the residents' rooms would be marked by decorations bespeaking comfort, but of the correct type and quantity. This is to say, *this* consumerism did not necessarily indicate weakness or effeminacy, nor did it mark the consumer as lower class.

What was considered bric-a-brac when purchased and displayed by women or the lower classes was recast as expressing the comforts of home when purchased by a man attempting to educate and improve himself, to perform the bourgeois identity he desired. No longer a danger to German culture and proof of a "nineteenth-century mindset," tasteful male domestic consumption was repositioned as a kind of anti-consumerism.[202] At the very least, this was a refashioned consumerism that had nothing to do with the vagueries of fashion and the latter's connection to women. It was "productive," rather than wasteful and corruptive, measured, rather than indicating (feminine) excess.[203] In short, residents were positioned as the (male) "designers" of their space, rather than (female) "decorators."[204] Additionally, while men could play a "feminine" role, they themselves would not become *overly* feminized (though the unbecoming uber-masculine edges of working-class life might well be polished off), and their rooms would not become feminine spaces. Residents were encouraged to play the role of both husband and wife—served and servant—appointed their own moral guardian in this (albeit very small) domestic sphere.

Ultimately, the majority of reformers realized that both privacy and the small comforts provided within individual rooms could play as large a role as the inclusion of communal spaces in attracting and retaining residents. The success of a reform Ledigenheim was not only the result of the competitive pricing of a variety of rooms at different price points, communal facilities, and a pleasant exterior, but also that it welcomed residents with a profusion of "cozy details" that lent the Ledigenheim a domestic appearance and feeling.[205] While a reform Ledigenheim could not quite replicate the warmth of a well-appointed (bourgeois) familial home, it could come close, and as regards hygienic and technological measures, it was a vast improvement over the typical lower-middle-class or working-class dwelling (and even some middle-class dwellings). From the beginning of the period of their construction, reform Ledigenheime surrounded residents with the most modern and advanced technology, ranging from electric light to central heat,[206] elements that were relatively rare in middle-class homes, much less working-class ones.

Numerous other services and spaces also aided the interests of hygiene and were improvements over what the residents would have had access to outside of a Ledigenheim, and were decidedly lacking in a *Schlafstelle*.[207] Personal hygiene was attended to through the ample provision of sinks, footbaths, and toilet facilities, which were generally located on every floor (though sinks were sometimes provided in individual rooms too), as well as showers and tubs commonly located in the basement of the building.[208] Residents often also had access to "free" linen service (i.e., it was included in their rent), which not only provided bed linens but also washed and changed said linens every week.[209] They could typically even have their clothing laundered and boots cleaned on-site for a nominal fee (*c.* 20 pfennig per week), though specific spaces to air clothing and clean boots were usually provided.[210] In fact, the housekeeping that a wife, mother, maiden aunt, or sister traditionally would have provided (or arranged for a servant to do on her behalf) was rationalized and commodified in a Ledigenheim. Residents were consumers, who, with their newfound purchasing power, could buy that which had traditionally been the (unwaged) domain of the diligent housewife.[211]

The degree to which reform Ledigenheime came to be associated with technological and hygienic advancements is well illustrated by the role the Dankelmannstrasse Ledigenheim of Berlin-Charlottenburg played at the Hygienic Exhibition of Dresden in 1911, a venue where reformers working through numerous avenues came together to discuss solutions to the problematic state of housing and hygiene in Germany.[212] Only three years after its completion, the Dankelmannstrasse building was featured as a model to emulate, not only for other reform Ledigenheime but for reformed housing in general. Supporters noted that advances in technology were easily and readily applied to this building type,[213] and positioned it as the ideal venue within which to experiment—research that would bear fruit on a mass scale under the Social Democrats in the 1920s.

This continual emphasis on the most modern technological and hygienic surroundings also makes sense considering the increased risk of communicable disease outbreaks with large numbers of men living in close proximity to one another. Just as importantly, it also speaks to the need to differentiate the Ledigenheim from the physically *and* morally unhealthy surroundings of a *Schlafstelle*. Physical cleanliness was a signifier of both middle-class status and moral rectitude,[214] and as such, the supporters of reform Ledigenheime were keen to highlight elements enabling it. Ledigenheime were to be clean and neat, aping the well-run bourgeois home, even without the requisite housewife.

Similarly, every image published of the residents shows cleanly attired, freshly shaven, and well-scrubbed young men engaged in healthful and morally unambiguous, even "feminine," poses and pursuits. With the exception of images of Volksküchen, which featured groups of men both sitting and standing—albeit always calmly—most images of Ledigenheime featured men sitting quietly by themselves, even if in a group setting. Simply resting, or deeply engaged in activities such as reading and drawing, individuals rarely even look directly at the imagined viewer of the photograph (Figures 3.17, 3.18,

Figure 3.17 Waldenserstrasse 31 Ledigenheim, Berlin (1914). View of the roof garden. *Source:* Julius Schnaubert, *Ledigenheime für Berlin* (Charlottenburg: Lehsten, 1918), 18, 25–7.

Figure 3.18 Dankelmannstrasse 46–47 Ledigenheim, Berlin-Charlottenburg (1908). View of the *Gesellschafts-raum* (community room).
Source: *50 Jahre Volkswohnheim Gemeinnützige Aktien-Gesellschaft Berlin-Charlottenburg* (Basel: Länderdienst Verlag, 1955), 42.

see also 3.1, 3.2).[215] This level of quietude and self-containment, accompanied by the indirect gazes of the men, stands in stark opposition to popular perceptions and imagery of working-class men, which painted them as alternately lazy and rabble-rousing, aggressive in manner and gaze, and often in threatening groups. Additionally, residents were shown undertaking leisure activities that could be read not only as furthering their *Bildung* but also as "feminine." Certainly, alongside needlepoint and piano playing, drawing and reading were acceptable pastimes for well-brought-up young women. However, that which could be read as feminine was disciplined and made unproblematic in the way a resident's decorating of his bedroom was—by imagining *what* a resident was reading (the classics, rather than a novel or *Schundliteratur*) and that his drawing or painting was undertaken in the service of his education, rather than in a dilettantish fashion. As will be discussed further in Chapter 4, even the exterior style of most reform Ledigenheime—the Biedermeier revival—balanced "masculine" rectilinear neoclassical forms with "feminine" delicate detailing. Ultimately, one can consider the Ledigenheim—at least in its ideal formulation—as playing the role of a properly bourgeois mother *and* father, from the patriarchal emphasis on rule following and education, to "maternal" physical comforts and moral surroundings.

The Ultimate Success of the Reform Ledigenheim

Reform Ledigenheime were situated by advocates as a highly rational and logical response to overcrowding and the evils of unregulated lodging but, more importantly, were positioned as the solution to the "Social Question," particularly as it pertained to the *Mittelstand*. Attributed great powers of transformation and entrusted with the ultimate goal of raising lower-middle-class or skilled working-class men into the lower fringes of the middle class for the benefit of all society,[216] supporters of secular Ledigenheime considered their intervention to be superior to similar buildings erected by employers and Catholic organizations. It certainly was highly popular with the sort of young men reformers it sought to house and were intended to aid, as illustrated by the example of the Düsseldorf Ledigenheim (1910/11), which housed the majority of its 233 residents for an extended period of time—years, not weeks or months (Figure 3.19).[217] This was a remarkable feat when one considers that the majority of residents were between twenty and thirty years of age, with a significant number falling under twenty years of age, precisely when single men tended to be the most transient.[218]

Figure 3.19 Eisenstrasse Ledigenheim, Düsseldorf (1910/11). Primary facade.
Source: Weyls' Handbuch der Hygiene (Leipzig: Barth, 1918), 358.

Certainly, the vitriol of an attack a leading newspaper for landlords mounted against the Dankelmannstrasse Ledigenheim (1908) indicates something of the potential they saw for such homes and the danger they posed to their livelihoods. Characterizing the Ledigenheim as a "failure" despite the efforts of a Herr Stadtrat Sampter, the acting *Dezernent für Wohnungspflege* (Housing Councilor), who "threw his loving arms around this institution," they assured readers that despite the low prices and stylish interiors of the Ledigenheim, the "marriage-hungry" single women of Berlin had nothing to fear from its construction.[219] Reminding him of the military and its restrictions on his freedom, these "barracks" for single men would certainly not enthrall residents to the extent that they would abjure eventual marriage and family. He would only live there as long as he must, and certainly not for a long time.[220] Yet, reform Ledigenheime were *never* intended to warehouse young men in perpetuity. Although the skeptics of the Deutsche Hausbesitzer Zeitung feared otherwise, they were always intended as means to their residents' sociocultural advancement and, more importantly, their eventual departure.

Success stories such as the Düsseldorf or Dankelmannstrasse buildings do not tell the whole story though. While many found a "home" in reform Ledigenheime, not all those who sought residency could be served, nor could a few hundred buildings significantly stem the tide of substandard lodgings. Even under the most optimal of circumstances, a single building type could not possibly remake, regenerate, and reform all of society, or even a particular demographic.

The Ledigenheim also had competition by the turn of the century. Existing somewhere between a settlement house and a Ledigenheim, the end of the nineteenth century saw the emergence of the *Volkshaus* (sometimes referred to as a *Gewerkschaftshaus* or *Volksheim*), a Socialist "house of the people," the first of which was built in Dresden in 1888.[221] Usually concentrated in highly industrialized regions, such as the Ruhr, parts of Saxony, and around Frankfurt am Main—where the industrial labor force had long been highly organized,[222] a Volkshaus (somewhat unsurprisingly) contained assembly rooms, union offices, and the offices of the Social Democratic Party,[223] but also typically included spaces for "educational, cultural and leisure activities . . . [they] contained libraries, and [they] organized musical events, concerts, theatre and play readings."[224] Positioned by supporters as a healthy alternative to a pub or tavern, the reading and social rooms of the seven Volkshäuser of the Dresden *Verein Volkswohl* were light and bright, and patrons neither had to put up with the smoke or beer splashed floors of a pub, nor the pressure to purchase alcoholic drinks.[225] Coming out of organized labor's roots in the artisan estate and the tradition of the "tramping" skilled artisan, these homes also often included rooms one could rent.[226]

Regardless of their Social Democratic emphasis and the fact that Volkshäuser were not intended to primarily function as housing, it is clear that they were markedly similar to Ledigenheime in what they *provided* to patrons (comfortable spaces and restful activities). The supporters of Ledigenheime and Volkshäuser even employed nearly identical language as to their intentions, with Ledigenheim apologists writing of the power of their buildings to build bridges among social classes,[227] and the proponents of Volkshäuser stressing that they sought to "overcome all class pride and class hate."[228] Yet, if the bourgeois supporters of Ledigenheime claimed to be building bridges, they built them in a manner that reflected and promoted their own priorities and interests. The residents of Ledigenheime were to be remade into a faint facsimile of educated middle-class tastes and proclivities, enabling them to identify with those above them in station, rather than those below. While working-class, even lower-middle-class, culture was purposefully culled from Ledigenheime, the supporters of Volkshäuser—despite public claims that they were concerned for the welfare of *all* social classes—primarily sought to support and instill a sense of community among their members, drawing from whatever influences they deemed useful.[229]

Tellingly, despite the inclusion of spaces that read as nearly identical to those of Ledigenheime, the style employed for Volkshäuser differed greatly from place to place, even from building to building. Unlike the prototypical Biedermeier-inspired turn-of-the-century Ledigenheim, there was no single identifiable Volkshaus "style" or "type."[230] While turn-of-the-century Ledigenheime visually reflected their close ties with bourgeois reform efforts, including the reform of aesthetics, Volkshäuser appropriated certain aspects of bourgeois hegemonic culture and discarded others. Ledigenheime were safely "tasteful," whereas the supporters of Volkshäuser employed and combined architecture styles on their own terms, sometimes "counter(ing) the visual splendor produced by (mid-century) bourgeois capital" with splendid forms of their own,[231] much to the chagrin of aesthetic reformers who mocked a decidedly overwrought Volkshaus in Hamburg (1906) as a representation of "un-culture" (*Unkultur*).[232]

Yet, despite the far different ends their supporters sought, many contemporaries saw both building types as addressing similar needs, evidenced by the fact that a number of prominent architects who built Ledigenheime also supported the construction of Volksheime. For example, Theodor Fischer, who would build the only Ledigenheim remaining in operation today (1925, located on the Bergmannstrasse in Munich) (see Figure **5.1**), wrote as early as 1907 that he sought to create a new symbol of societal togetherness (*Gemeinschaft*) through the form of the Volkshaus, terming this his "Volkshaus-wish" (*Volkshauswunsch*).[233] Noted Ledigenheim architects Peter Behrens and Bruno Taut also built Volkshäuser, the former in 1900 and the latter as late as 1918, and saw these activities as two sides of the same coin.[234] The Volkshaus took an even more prominent position in architectural and utopian thought during the First World War and at the advent of the Weimar era. Repositioned as people's temples within the new communities imagined by members of the Glass Chain during the war,[235] these "cathedrals of the future" were further evoked in the immediate postwar era—most notably by Lyonel Feininger's Expressionist frontispiece to the *Bauhaus Manifesto* of 1919.

However, utopian Volkshäuser and the Ledigenheime they stood in competition with were soon eclipsed by a project of great physical scale and symbolic meaning—rationalized *Siedlungen*, or integrative housing settlements. Largely constructed between 1924 and 1933, most notably in Berlin and Frankfurt am Main under the supervision of Martin Wagner and Ernst May, these Weimar-era municipal housing efforts drove the production of collective housing for families to a level unseen before the 1920s, dwarfing the physical scale of Ledigenheime. While the largest prewar municipal Ledigenheime may have housed several hundred men at a time, which was then replicated by dozens of homes throughout the German Reich, the famed *Hufeisensiedlung* (Horseshoe Settlement) in Berlin-Britz, constructed between 1925 and 1933 under the watchful eye of architect Bruno Taut, planner Martin Wagner, and landscape designer Leberecht Migge, contained no less than 1,285 apartments and 679 row houses alongside communal facilities.[236] Yet, while other prewar initiatives have been excavated as precedents for Weimar Siedlungen—for example, the relationship of the Garden City movement to the provision and organization of green space in a settlement such as Taut's—I argue that municipal Ledigenheime provide another link to the genesis of Weimar-era settlements, even as their construction began to slow and they were rarely included as components of completed *Siedlungen*.

Unlike other forms of single-sex mass housing elsewhere—such as rooming houses, the YMCA, even Salvation Army homes in the United States—where locations in central business districts "kept an independent low-paid work force available to downtown industries . . . [and helped them] forge personal independence and a subculture *separate* from the city's family zones,"[237] municipal Ledigenheime only sought to separate the lodger from the familial apartment, *not* from residential or mixed-use neighborhoods. In fact, the typical reform

Ledigenheim was so highly integrated within the urban fabric that a casual observer would not have been able to distinguish this form of mass housing for single people from the surrounding housing stock. With the inclusion of public libraries and public kitchens, this meant that they came to play a role as a center of public life, bridging the gap between the private home and public sphere to

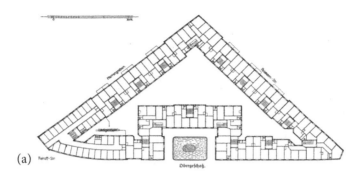

Figure 3.20a, b, c Rehoffstrasse and Herrengraben Ledigenheim, Hamburg (1910). Plan of the complex built by the *Bau Verein zu Hamburg, Aktiengesellschaft*; exterior view of the complex; photograph of the Volksküche.

Source: *Hamburg und Seine Bauten I* (Hamburg: Boysen and Maasch Verlag, 1914), 585–6, 588.

Figure 3.20a, b, c (Continued)

better support the social aspirations and physical health of both residents and local families.

By the first decade of the twentieth century, such Ledigenheime increasingly served as lynchpins in even more ambitious building projects employing *new* urban forms not only to serve but also to house *both* singles and local families. The Ledigenheim of *Bau Verein zu Hamburg, Aktiengesellschaft* (1910), located at the intersection of the Rehoffstrasse and the Herrengraben in Hamburg, formed one corner of a larger housing development featuring familial apartments intended for lower-middle-class members of a nonprofit building society, the *Bau Verein zu Hamburg* (Figs. 3.20a, b, c).[238] Not only did the Ledigenheim contain a Volksküche for residents, building society members, and the surrounding community, but in the manner of planners like Unwin and Stübben (and as popularized by Messel, Gessner, Möhring, and Eberstadt in Berlin),[239] the complex also formed an early version of the Superblock (termed *Blockrandbebauung*)—like the Ledigenheim, yet another answer to the Mietskaserne. This meant that *shared* green space in the middle of the triangularly shaped lot was fully enclosed by a perimeter block, a continuous wall of Ledigenheim and reformed tenement following existing street lines. With *Blockrandbebauung*, the well-defined street face still read as

Figure 3.21 Dankelmannstrasse 46–47 Ledigenheim (for men), Berlin-Charlottenburg (1908). Passage through the Ledigenheim to the local school (*Gemeindeschule*).
Source: Author's photograph.

urban and public, though the light-filled and green communal space within was semiprivate—a grander scale of the public-private divide playing out within the walls of other Ledigenheime, as well as within the Ledigenheim of the *Bau Verein zu Hamburg*.

Because they were often constructed on land owned by the municipality—which was sold outright or leased to the organization building the Ledigenheim for free or at reduced rates—the positioning of municipal Ledigenheime near additional resources for the general public was not uncommon. The Dankelmannstrasse building abutted a public boy's primary school (a passage to the school cut through the southern side of the Ledigenheim) (Figure 3.21, see also Figure 3.4a, b), and the Ledigenheim erected by the *Verein für das Wohl der arbeitenden Klassen* in Stuttgart (1910) was located on a plot of land along the Neckar River in front of a foundlings' home (*Säuglingsheim*), as well as a public bathing facility erected by the nonprofit *Stuttgarter Badegesellschaft*.[240] However, while the positioning and role of the municipal Ledigenheim of Berlin-Weissensee (designed 1911/completed 1914) recall these (slightly) earlier buildings, its supporters took a different approach, expanding many of the spaces and program of a typical Ledigenheim outward to form a "campus" of *Wohlfahrtseinrichtungen* (Figures 3.22a, b, c).

Christened the *Kommunalen Zentrum*, or "communal center," the complex featured a public bathing facility, a public gymnasium to which an open square for gymnastics was attached, a garden "laid out in the English style" surrounding a reservoir, a restaurant with attached beer garden, and a high school (*Ober-Realschule*), as well as a pump station and firehouse. The eastern

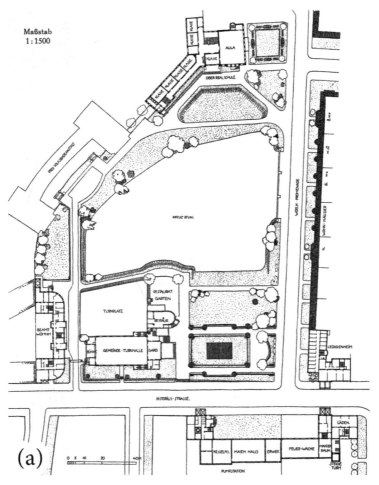

Figure 3.22a, b, c Kommunalen Zentrum Ledigenheim, Berlin-Weissensee (1911–14). Plan of the settlement (note the apartment houses along the Woelk-Promenade terminating in the Ledigenheim at the corner of the Woelk-Promenade and Pistorius Strasse); detail of the facade of the Ledigenheim; pamphlet celebrating the opening of the Ledigenheim in 1914.

Source: Moderne Bauformen (1915): 214–18.

Making the Municipality a Home 183

Figure 3.22a, b, c (Continued)

edge of the *Kommunalen Zentrum* was defined by an apartment block housing families, the southern end of which terminated in a Ledigenheim housing thirty-three men and thirteen *women* that also featured a dining hall, health insurance fund office, and retail space rented to a bookseller.[241] Certainly, the mixing of genders in one home—albeit with separate entrances and internally unconnected wings—was unconventional in a Ledigenheim, though the creation of communal facilities embedded in and connected to each other by *shared* green space pointed even more firmly to the future. While a member of the community could hardly wander into the typical prewar Ledigenheim Volksküche or Volksbibliothek by accident, as many were located off inner courtyards only accessible through passages in the street facade and signage was not always provided, the Weissensee complex facilitated interactions between single residents, families, and even visitors that felt more spontaneous and less mitigated by placing all the facilities previously available *within* a Ledigenheim more firmly in the *public* realm, or at least a miniaturized and sanitized version of it. If the danger of the city lay in its illegibility and uncontrollability, the *Kommunalen Zentrum* organized and clarified the components of an ideal urban life—minus workplaces—arranging buildings, paths, streets, and green spaces to carefully calibrate the relationship between the public and private realms, even grouping semipublic spaces for the use of all in public parkland at the center of the complex. Open space replaced the courtyards and passages of earlier Ledigenheime, ensuring oversight *and* building community, just as earlier Ledigenheime had done *within* their walls.

One year after the Weissensee Ledigenheim was opened to the public, Bruno Taut designed a Ledigenheim for the Garden City Falkenberg in Berlin-Grünau (1914, unbuilt).[242] Primarily intended to house wounded and disabled veterans, the Ledigenheim featured individual rooms grouped around an arcaded central courtyard, ample workshop space for residents, and a U-shaped restaurant for the use of both residents and the general public. Yet, while family housing was located largely to the south of the Ledigenheim and the restaurant was positioned on the north side, no direct access was provided through the building to the restaurant—unlike in Weissensee, the Falkenberg Ledigenheim remained largely self-contained. While the invalid status of many of its residents likely influenced this closed-off design, Taut took the opposite course for the next Ledigenheim he designed. In Lindenhof (Berlin, 1919), Taut designed the Ledigenheim before the rest of the settlement, using the building to clarify the ideal relationship between a Ledigenheim and the surrounding community (Figure 3.23).[243] Here, Taut moderated the somewhat isolated position of the Ledigenheim, located on the northeastern corner of

Making the Municipality a Home

Figure 3.23 Siedlung Lindenhof Ledigenheim, Berlin-Schöneberg (1919). View of the Ledigenheim from the street outside the settlement.
Source: Albert Gut, *Der Wohnungsbau in Deutschland nach dem Weltkriege* (Munich: Bruckmann, 1928), 567.

Figure 3.24 Siedlung Lindenhof Ledigenheim, Berlin-Schöneberg (1919). View of the Ledigenheim from inside the settlement.
Source: Albert Gut, *Der Wohnungsbau in Deutschland nach dem Weltkriege* (Munich: Bruckmann, 1928), 567.

the settlement by reimagining it as a gatehouse—complete with towers and turrets—through which *all* residents and visitors approaching the complex from the north and northeast passed. He positioned the wings of the building to curve around the plaza directly outside of the settlement, as if protectively embracing and guarding residents and visitors, while funneling them toward the passage at the center of the building. This passage not only provided access to a grocer and restaurant within the building but also led to the rest of the complex—directly on axis with a monumental fountain and central *allée* of terraced family housing (Figure 3.24). While the outward facing facade of the Ledigenheim approximated a fortress, albeit a playful version of one, Taut utilized a simplified version of the Biedermeier revival on the side facing the settlement, mitigating the massiveness of the building and underscoring its connection to Lindenhof's familial housing. With Lindenhof, Taut took the role of the "reform" Ledigenheim as a resource for the surrounding community to a symbolic level. A pragmatic version of his utopian city crown designs, Lindenhof was unfortunately the last of Taut's settlements featuring Ledigenheime—later designs never fulfilled such early promise, at least not for single individuals.

Yet, municipal Ledigenheime had effectively paved the way for Weimar-era Siedlungen, not only in privileging hygienic, well-ordered housing for those who could never have afforded quality surroundings otherwise but also by blurring the lines between the public and private realms and disentangling housing from the twin evils of land speculation and unscrupulous landlords. With both the reform Ledigenheim and the Weimar Siedlung, the municipality had become, at least to a certain extent, the landlord. More significantly, the project of the Ledigenheim provided a useful testing ground for reformers and their allies in government—a place of experimentation that helped to spur the interwar expansion of numerous reinforcing and complimentary social welfare programs and policies, which were recast, not as aid but as the prerogative of all citizens. Ironically, however, even as the events of 1933 and the nightmare years to follow put lie to such hopes, the Siedlung—not the Ledigenheim—was positioned as the kernel from which a new society might develop. As will be further disentangled in the Conclusion, the hardworking and respectable German family of limited means—not the single individual—was the seat of regenerative potential.

Yet, unlike Weimar Siedlungen, Ledigenheime were never charged with such massive responsibility. The latter were not symbols of the new order, nor a means of creating a new society, a political necessity in a new Germany whose government promised every citizen decent housing and which was struggling to find its feet in the wake of a war that had seemingly obliterated all that came before. Instead, these homes were always a means to negotiate modernity, to *manage* the detrimental effects of rapid industrialization and urbanization without entirely calling into question the capitalist order that had enabled such expansion. By promulgating a vision of personal agency and community in a society where self-determination and support were increasingly rare, Ledigenheime provided an appealing answer to the *Social Question*—a means to stem the tide, rather than sweep away the world that called them into being.

Notes

1 *Schlafstellenwesen und Ledigenheime: Vorbericht und Verhandlungen der 13. Konferenz der Zentralstelle für Arbeiter-Wohlfahrtseinrichtungen am 9. Und 10. Mai in Leipzig.* (Schriften der Zentralstelle für Arbeiter-Wohlfahrtseinrichtungen (No. 26)) (Berlin: Carl Henmanns Verlag, 1904).

2 The moderators of the conference were drawn from all over the Germany Reich, and held very different official job titles, such as *Beigeordneter* Dr. Wiedfeldt from Essen, *Oberregierungsrat* Falch of Stuttgart, a representative from the Protestant *Innere Mission*, Secretary Dr. Salzgeber of the Berlin Catholic *Charitas Verband*, and the *Baumeister* Berndt of Bochum, who spoke from the standpoint of his employer, the Bochumer Verein—of the ten discussants, seven held PhDs or medical degrees and none were women (*Schlafstellenwesen und Ledigenheime*, ii).

3 *Der Arbeiterfreund* (1904): 215.

4 Johannes Altenrath, *Das Schlafstellenwesen und seine Reform: Statistik, Schlafstellenaufsicht, Ledigenheime* (Rechts und Staatswissenschaft Fakultät Dissertation, Universität Halle, 1916), 1–2.

5 Otto von Leixner, *Soziale Briefe aus Berlin: 1888–1891* (Berlin: Friedrich Pfeilstücker, 1891), 125.

6 These included publications by the *Deutscher Verein für öffentliche Gesundheitspflege* and writers such as Gustav Schmoller in his article "Ein Mahnruf in der Wohnungsfrage," (*Jahrbuch für Gesetzgebung, Verwaltung und Volkswirtschaft im Deutschen Reich* 11 (1887): 425–48, cited in Brian Ladd, *Urban Planning and Civic Order in Germany* (Cambridge: Harvard University Press, 1990), 143–4).

7 The year 1904 can be considered a high point in reformist activity, for according to Kevin Repp, a purge of Social Democratic moderates from the Social Democratic press in 1905 "contributed to [an] ebb in reformist momentum mid-decade" (*Reformers, Critics, and the Paths of German Modernity* (Cambridge: Harvard University Press, 2000), 225).

8 Andrew Lees, *Sin, Cities, and Social Reform in Imperial Germany* (Ann Arbor: University of Michigan Press, 2002), 43, 244.

9 Lees, 386.

10 British Board of Trade, xii.

11 J. F. Geist and K. Kürvers, eds., *Das Berliner Mietshaus, 1862–1945* (Munich: Prestel, 1980), 305.

12 Mike Hepworth, "Privacy, Security and Respectability: The Ideal Victorian Home," in *Housing and Dwelling*, ed. Barbara Miller Lane (London: Routledge, 2007), 151.

13 A. Kelly, ed., *The German Worker: Working Class Autobiographies from the Age of Industrialization* (Berkeley: University of California Press, 1987), 4.
14 Ladd, 84–5.
15 Ladd, 141.
16 As an illustration of these connections, the opening of a Catholic Ledigenheim in Cologne in 1893 (the Hermann-Joseph Haus) was not only attended and led by the Suffragan Bishop, a Dr. Fischer, but also the mayor of Cologne, who came as a representative of the *Stadtverwaltung*, and a record of the proceedings featured in the *Arbeiterwohl*, a periodical supported by major Rhine-Ruhr industrialists (*Arbeiterwohl* (1893): 56).
17 In Germany, the origin of the Verein Volkswohl of Dresden (Organization for the Welfare of the People of Dresden) is a good illustration of the intersections of various reform organizations, as well as the reformers populating their ranks. The Verein Volkswohl began life in 1880 as the Deutscher Verein für Armenpflege und Wohltätigkeit (German Organization for the Care of the Poor and Charity), though it quickly joined forces with another social reform organization in 1883, the Deutscher Verein gegen den Missbrauch geistiger Getränke (German Organization against the Abuse of Alcohol) (*Der Arbeiterfreund* 51 (1913): 393). Renamed the Verein Volkswohl, it aimed "to care for the welfare of all social classes and also to support and instill a sense of community in its members" (393).
18 Ladd, 30.
19 Altenrath, 101.
20 Repp, 26.
21 Standish Meacham, *Toynbee Hall and Social Reform: 1880–1014* (New Haven: Yale University Press, 1987), 2. Of course, none of these groups can be considered monolithic. Aside from blurring the vast distinctions between urban and rural people, as well small townsmen, such broad categories cannot accurately capture regional discrepancies (Mack Walker, *German Home Towns: Community, State, and General Estate, 1648–1871* (Ithaca: Cornell University Press, 1971), 110–11).
22 Eve Rosenhaft and W. R. Lee, "State and Society in Modern Germany—Beamtenstaat, Klassenstaat, Wohlfahrststaat," in *The State and Social Change in Germany, 1880–1980*, ed. W. R. Lee and Eve Rosenhaft (Providence: Berg, 1990), 10, 26.
23 Ladd, 25 and Dawson, 64.
24 Ladd, 84.
25 Dawson, 35.
26 Dawson, 35.
27 Ladd, 32.
28 Repp, 137.
29 Dawson, 76–8.

30 Werner Sombart, "Wir müden Seelen," *Morgen* 1, no. 7 (October 4, 1907): 514, cited in Repp, 213; Daphne Spain, *How Women Saved the City* (Minneapolis: University of Minnesota Press, 2001); Marta Gutman, *A City for Children* (Chicago: University of Chicago Press, 2014). American women tended to play a greater role in the creation of such spaces than German women did.

31 L. Abrahms, *Workers' Culture in Imperial Germany: Rheinland and Westphalia* (London: Routledge, 1992), 55, 66.

32 Wiedfeldt, *Schlafstellenwesen und Ledigenheime*, 124; Spiegel, *Ledigenheime: Referat für den Verein fuer Sozialpolitik*, 415.

33 Irina Winter, *Georg Benjamin: Arzt und Kommunist* (Berlin: Verlag Volk und Gesundheit, 1962), 29, 31.

34 Spiegel, 416.

35 Wiedfeldt, 125–8. One could start to turn large profit of nearly 100 marks with three *Schlafgänger* per room, and 182 marks for five *Schlafgänger*, as opposed to only 35 marks for two *Schlafgänger*, and a loss of 9 marks with only one *Schlafgänger*.

36 Richard Calwer, *Das Kost und Logiswesen in Handwerk* (Berlin: Verlag d. Generalkomm. d. Gewerkschaften Deutschlands, 1908).

37 Calwer, 16–17. For similar standards, see: *Das Schlafstellenwesen in Posen: Vortrag, gehalten im Verein zur Fürsorge fuer Kranke Arbeiter in Posen* (February 1, 1906), 4).

38 Calwer, 19, see also: *Das Schlafstellenwesen in Posen*, 4.

39 Calwer, 24.

40 Calwer, 35–51.

41 Ladd, 171.

42 Dawson, 184.

43 Dawson, 180–4.

44 Horsfall, 46. This proposed bill was published by both the *Kölnische Zeitung* and the *Zeitschrift für Wohnungswesen*, in addition to Horsfall, an English observer of German housing reform efforts.

45 Anthony Bullock and James Read, *The Movement for Housing Reform in Germany and France, 1840–1914* (Cambridge: Cambridge University Press, 1985), 264). As late as March 1914 no systematic system of house inspection existed in Prussia (Dawson, 183).

46 Ladd, 176.

47 Ladd, 147.

48 Spiegel, *Ledigenheime, Referat für Verein für Sozialpolitik*, 424; *Förderung der Gemeinnuezigen Bautätigkeit durch die Gemeinden* (1901), 213; *Neue Untersuchungen über die Wohnungsfrage* (1901), 213.

49 Madge C. Jenison, "The Tenements of Berlin," *Harper's Monthly Magazine* (February 1, 1909), 367–8.

50 William Harbutt Dawson, *Municipal Life and Government in Germany* (New York: Longmans, Green and Co., 1914), 177.
51 Horsfall, 93.
52 *Soziale Praxis* 39 (1903): 1048.
53 *Schlafstellen und Ledigenheime*, 194.
54 Altenrath, *Staatswirtschaftliche Dissertation*, 142.
55 *Soziale Praxis* 39 (1903): 1048.
56 R. J. Radomski, *Über Fürsorge für Ledige Arbeiter in Posen* (Posen: W. Decker und Co., 1911), 5.
57 Radomski, 5.
58 "Münchner Wohnungskommission diskutiert Bau eines Ledigenheims" Stadtarchiv München, Wohnungsamt 26 (5. Sitzung der Wohnungskommission der Stadt München am 11.Dez. 1908), cited in *Wohnalltag in Deutschland*, ed. H. J. Teuteberg and C. Wishcermann (Münster: Coppenrath, 1985), 337.
59 Gerhard Ute, "Die Radikalen im Kampf um Recht und gegen doppelte Moral," in *Unerhört: die Geschichte der Deutschen Frauenbewegugn* (Hamburg: Rohwolt Taschenbuch Verlag, 1990), 218.
60 *Der Arbeiterfreund* 47 (1907): 369. Minna Cauer of Berlin and Ernst Kahn of Frankfurt aired such views at the Fourth General Congress of the *Verband fortschrittlicher Frauenvereine.*
61 *Wohnalltag in Deutschland*, 337.
62 Altenrath, 143–4.
63 "Münchner Wohnungskommission diskutiert Bau eines Ledigenheims" Stadtarchiv München, Wohnungsamt 26 (5. Sitzung der Wohnungskommission der Stadt München am 11. Dez. 1908), cited in *Wohnalltag in Deutschland*, 337. Emphasis mine.
64 *Reichsarbeitsblatt* (1913): 440.
65 Dawson, 76–8.
66 Radomski, 5.
67 Adam, "Philanthropy and the Shaping of Social Distinctions," 61.
68 Paul Boyer, *Urban Masses and Moral Order in America, 1820–1920* (Cambridge, Harvard University Press, 1978), 97.
69 Meacham, 114.
70 Boyer, 119.
71 Altenrath, 109.
72 Dawson, 264–6, 271, 301.
73 Dawson, 271. For a fuller discussion of the class status of the intended beneficiaries of late nineteenth-century British and German social insurance systems, see Dietrich Milles, "Industrial Hygiene: A State Obligation? Industrial Pathology as a Problem in German Social Policy," in *The State and Social Change in Germany, 1880–1980*, ed. W. R. Lee and Eve Rosenhaft (Providence: Berg, 1990), 178.

74 Dawson, 301; see also: Altenrath, 112.
75 Rudolf Walter, *Archiv der Freistudenten-Bewegung: Die Studentenheimfrage* (Leipzig: Demme, 1909).
76 Regarding middle-class fears of "luxury," see Warren G. Breckman, "Disciplining Consumption: The Debate about Luxury in Wilhelmine Germany, 1890–1914," *Journal of Social History* 24, no. 3 (Spring 1991): 485–505.
77 Repp, 258.
78 Levenstein's survey reported that 33.8 percent of workers read *Schundliteratur* in 1911 (*Die Arbeiterfrage: mit besonderer berücksichtigung der sozialpsychologischen seite des modernen grossbetriebes und der psycho-physischen einwirkung auf der arbeiter* (München: Ernst Reinhardt, 1912), 392).
79 Gideon Reuveni, *Reading Germany: Literature and Consumer Culture in Germany before 1933* (New York: Berghahn Books, 2006), 61.
80 Reuveni, 13.
81 Derek Linton, *Who Has the Youth Has the Future* (Cambridge: Cambridge University Press, 1991), 206.
82 *Rundschau: Monatschrift für Jünglingspflege* (1911), 78. Emphasis mine.
83 Richard J. Evans. *Proletarians and Politics: Socialism, Protest and the Working Class in Germany before the First World War* (New York: St. Martin's Press, 1990), 97, 141.
84 Evans, 141.
85 Oberregierungsrath Falch, "Schlafstellenwesen und Ledigenheime vom Stadtpunkte der Inneren Mission der evangelischen Kirche (Versammlungsbericht)," in *Schlafstellenwesen und Ledigenheime* (Berlin: Carl Henmanns Verlag, 1904), 153.
86 Supporters—in this case supporters of the Stuttgart reform Ledigenheim—constantly stressed that these residences for single craftsmen and workers needed to be both "good" and "inexpensive" (*Deutsche Bauzeitung* (November 5, 1892): 546).
87 *Der Arbeiterfreund* 51 (1913): 395.
88 *Schlafstellenwesen und Ledigenheime*, 136.
89 Public baths (*Volksbäder*), especially bathing pools, were rapidly gaining popularity among municipalities (and even industrialists) as a way to keep the population healthy, particularly from 1880 (Adna Ferrin Weber, *The Growth of Cities in the Nineteenth Century* (Ithaca: Cornell, 1899), 353).
Ledigenheime *never* featured bathing pools, though by the 1880s they always included disinfection facilities and showers, and to a lesser extent, bathtubs (*Soziale Praxis* 11, no. 37 [1903]: 998).
90 An *Arbeitsamt* was particularly geared toward keeping the working-class population from "wandering" (*Arbeiterwohl* 21 (901): 323). Like the Ledigenheime they were often allied with, these organizations were purportedly "disinterested and impartial" (*Der Arbeiterfreund* 48 (1910): 176–84).

91 *Schlafstellenwesen und Ledigenheime*, 143.
92 *Schlafstellenwesen und Ledigenheime*, 51–3.
93 *Arbeiterfreund* (1912): 460.
94 Reuveni, 174.
95 Reuveni, 175.
96 This is borne out by the fact that a least one Ledigenheim (in Stuttgart, dating to 1890) included a private reading rooms for the sole use of residents and a Volksbibliothek open to both residents and the general public (Theodor Weyl and August Gärtner, eds., *Weyls Handbuch der Hygiene* (Leipzig: Barth, 1912), 352/124).
97 Men born in late 1880s averaged 5'4 in height (Sophia Twarog, "Heights and Living Standards in Germany," in *Health and Welfare during Industrialization*, ed. Richard Steckel and Roderick Floud (Chicago: University of Chicago Press, 1997), 294).
98 *Schlafstellenwesen und Ledigenheime*, 511.
99 Wiedfeldt, 108.
100 Evans, 15.
101 Evans, 15.
102 With the exception of those working night shifts, residents entering the Ledigenheim outside of 5:00 a.m. to midnight were fined 10 pfennig, payable to the night porter (Dix, 356/128); see also Ralf Zünder, *Vom Ledigenheim zum Studentenwohnheim* (Berlin: Studentenwerk, 1990), 45.
103 In 1913 the administration of the Dankelmannstrasse building directly accused the political journal *Vorwärts* (the organ of the Social Democratic Movement) of provocative activities, even making threats (Zünder, 40).
104 Reuveni, 157–75; on the American context, see Abigail A. Van Slyck, "The Lady and the Library Loafer," *Winterthur Portfolio* 31, no. 4 (Winter, 1996): 239.
105 Van Slyck, 239.
106 Winter, 31.
107 Hepworth, 153.
108 Josh Tosh, "New Men? The Bourgeois Cult of Home," *History Today* 46, no. 12 (December 1996): 4.
109 Tosh, 4.
110 von Leixner, 69–70.
111 von Leixner, 62.
112 von Leixner, 71.
113 von Leixner, 63–4.
114 von Leixner, 63–6.
115 Frevert, 131–47.
116 *Rundschau* 2, no. 9 (1911): 266.
117 Winter, 39–40.

118 Lina Morgenstern, "Die Volksküchen in Berlin," *Die Gartenlaube* 27 (1866): 431; "The People's Kitchens in Vienna," *The Nineteenth Century* 36 (1894): 744; Lina Morgenstern, *Berliner Volksküchen* (Berlin: Otto Loewenstein, 1870).
119 Frank Carpenter, "The Berlin Poor," *LA Times*, December 4, 1892, 9.
120 *Schlafstellenwesen und Ledigenheime*, 51–3.
121 Essen Stadtarchiv, Hausakten Signatur 45-18015.
122 Essen Stadtarchiv, Hausakten Signatur 45-18015. In regard to terminology employed, the basement kitchen below the *Wirtschaftslokal* was termed a *Volksküche*, so it appears in this case that these terms are fairly interchangeable (*Reichsarbeitsblatt* 11, no. 6 (June 23, 1913).
123 *Weyls*, 151/379.
124 For a specific example, see the 1911 rules governing the operation of the Verein Ledigenheim e.V. of Berlin (Generalakten, Landesarchiv Berlin, B Rep. 042, Nr. 26245, item no. 3).
125 Essen Stadtarchiv, Hausakten Signatur 45-18015.
126 "Konzessions-Urkunde für den Schankbetrieb" (Essen Stadtarchiv, Hausakten Signatur 45–18015).
127 Essen Stadtarchiv, Hausakten Signatur 45-18015. The application was filed in October of 1913, and soon after an *Erlaubnischein* (# B 834) was granted to the governing body of the Ledigenheim from the *Städtische Verwaltung*.
128 In the first decade of the twentieth century, half of the dwellings in Berlin consisted only of a single room and a Wohnküche, and over 4,000 dwellings consisted simply of a kitchen space (Dawson, 164).
129 Suzanne Spencer-Wood, "The World Their Household," in *Housing and Dwelling*, ed. Barbara Miller Lane (London: Routledge, 2007), 164.
130 *Weyls*, 151/379.
131 *Weyls*, 283/55, see also "The People's Kitchens in Vienna," 749–52).
132 Coffee houses or *Kaffeehäuser/Kaffeestuben* (sometimes even *Kakaostuben*), such as that of Lübeck (1889), served coffee, milk, buttermilk, soup (with bread included), rolls and pastries, sausages and other meat (*Weyls*, 380/152).
133 In the Berlin Asyl on the Fröbelstrasse in Berlin-Prenzlauerberg dinner consisted of 200 grams of bread and 1 liter of warm soup, which was served at 8:00 p.m. (*Concordia* [1911]: 28).
134 Ute Frevert, "The Civilizing Tendency of Hygiene: Working Class Women under Medical Control in Imperial Germany," in *German Women in the Nineteenth Century: A Social History*, ed. John C. Fout (New York: Holmes and Meier, 1984), 324.
135 Kathryn Kish Sklar, Anja Schüler, and Susan Strasser, *Social Justice Feminists in the United States and Germany: A Dialogue in Documents, 1885–1933* (Ithaca: Cornell University Press, 1998).
136 Repp, 109.

137 Dolores Hayden, *The Grand Domestic Revolution* (Cambridge: MIT Press, 1981), 82–3. Correspondingly, Morgenstern was interested in the lives and activities of female American reformers, writing about figures like Lucretia Mott and Harriet Beecher Stowe in her 1888–91 publication, *Die Frauen des neunzehnten Jahrhunderts (Women of the Nineteenth Century)* (Kish Sklar, 23).

138 Caroline Hunt, *The Life of Ellen H. Richards* (Boston: Whitcomb and Barrows, 1912), 221; Hayden, 155–7. See also Ellen H. Richards, *The Rumford Kitchen Leaflets* (Boston: Rockwell and Churchill Press, 1899).

139 Hayden, 157.

140 Hayden, 159.

141 This space was derived from the Rumford Kitchen exhibited at the 1893 Chicago World's Fair (Hayden, 151).

142 Helen Lefkowitz Horowitz, "Hull House as Women's Space," *Chicago History* 12, no. 4 (Winter 1983): 47–8, 53. Because it was a complex largely devised and peopled by women—despite the presence of male children visitors and some male settlement workers—scholars have argued that Hull House was a space gendered female, which may have been off-putting to local men.

143 Wine drinking was not associated with the working classes, though drinking brandy, schnapps, and beer was (Elaine Glovka Spencer, "Policing Popular Amusements in German Cities: The Case of the Prussian Rhine Province, 1815–1914," *Journal of Urban History* 16 [1990]: 375).

144 *Der Arbeiterfreund* 46 Jahrgang (1906): 8; *Arbeiterwohl* (1893): 55.

145 Even Karl Kautsky, editor of *Die Neue Zeit*, the Socialist organ, saw the Lumpenproletariat as "awash in Schnapps," as compared to the beer-drinking socialist (James S. Roberts, *Drink, Temperance and the Working Class in Nineteenth-Century Germany* [Boston: Allen and Unwin, 1984], 87).

146 Levenstein, 249.

147 For example, the Stuttgart Ledigenheim (1890) offered beer and coffee (*Weyls*, 352/124).

148 *Reichsarbeitsblatt* 11, no. 6 (June 23, 1913).

149 *Die Bauwelt* no. 19 (1911): 25.

150 *Reichsarbeitsblatt* (1913): 440.

151 I have translated "Heilmittel" as antidote, "Mängel" as defects, and "Klassenhass" as class animosity (Albert Weiss, "Die Garten-Wohnstadt Margarethenhöhe bei Essen," *Gartenstadt: Mitteilungen der Deutschen Gartenstadtgesellschaft* 7, no. 10 [1913]: 208).

152 Spetzler, 309.

153 Of the twenty-two reform Ledigenheim published on between 1890 and 1914, well over half utilized a style that referenced the early nineteenth-century *Biedermeier* period and its associated style.

154 Generalakten, Landesarchiv Berlin, B Rep. 042, Nr. 26245, item no. 3; *Zentralblatt der Bauverwaltung* 17 [1925]: 203).
155 *Wasmuths* (1915): 64.
156 *Wasmuths* (1915): 64.
157 *Wasmuths* (1915): 64.
158 Essen Stadtarchiv 155 229, Akten betreffend Evang. Ledigenheim Weberplatz.
159 See Paul Mebes' *Um 1800: Architektur und Handwerk im Letzten Jahrhundert ihrer Traditionellen Entwicklung* (Munich, 1920) and Paul Schultze-Naumburg's *Kulturarbeiten* series (1901–17) and *Die Entstellung unseres Landes* (Munich, 1907/08).
160 Otto Voepel, "Untersuchungen über den Charakter der Gebäude: Eine vorschollene Äesthetic der Baukunst aus dem Jahre 1788," *Architektonische Rundschau* 28, no. 10 (1912): 37–40.
161 *Wasmuths* (1915): 64.
162 For a fuller discussion of Sachlichkeit in German design culture, see the work of John Maciuika, *Before the Bauhaus* (Cambridge: Cambridge University Press, 2005), 64–89.
163 "Monumentale Wirtshäuser," *Deutsche Bauhütte* 11, no. 35 (1907): 285, cited in Mark Jarzombek, "Joseph August Lux: Werkbund Promoter, Historian of Lost Modernity," *JSAH* 63, no. 2 (June 2004): 209.
164 *Bautechnische Zeitschrift* 19 (1904): 308.
165 *Bautechnische Zeitschift* 19 (1904): 309.
166 Single compartments were located on the second floor, while four double rooms were on the third floor. Rents ranged from 1.50–1.80 marks a week for a second-floor sleeping compartment to 2.10 marks for double rooms on the third floor (*Bautechnische Zeitschift* 19 [1904]: 309).
167 *Bautechnische Zeitschift* 19 (1904): 309.
168 *Schlafstellenwesen und Ledigenheime*, 183; Winter, 42–3.
169 Radomski, 7.
170 *Schlafstellenwesen und Ledigenheime*, 183; Essen Stadtarchiv 155 229, Akten betreffend Evang. Ledigenheim Weberplatz.
171 Winter, 41, 43.
172 Winter, 183.
173 Winter, 32.
174 Stanford Anderson, "Peter Behrens, Friedrich Naumann, and the Werkbund: Ideology in Industriekultur," in *The Architecture of Politics: 1910–1940* (Miami Beach: Wolfsonian, 1995), 20.
175 Winter, 33.
176 Winter, 33.
177 Schweitzer, 112.
178 *Deutsche Bauzeitung* 26, no. 89 (November 5, 1892): 546.

179 *Deutsche Bauzeitung* 26, no. 89 (November 5, 1892): 546; *Schlafstellenwesen und Ledigenheime*, 45.
180 *Zeitschrift für Wohnungswesen* (1912): 96.
181 Besides the 285 single rooms, the Danklemannstrasse building included twelve double rooms and twelve triple rooms. Rent varied from 10 to 15 marks a month dependent upon whether the room was a single, double, or triple room (Generalakten, Landesarchiv Berlin, B Rep. 042, Nr. 26245, item no. 3).
182 *Zeitschrift für Wohnungswesen* (1912): 96; *Reichsarbeitsblatt* 11 (1913).
183 Room size, placement, and privacy indicated one's current place in the hierarchy, or to use the words of Michel Foucault, his rank, the most important element in discipline (Foucault, *Discipline and Punish*, 145).
184 Altenrath, 100. Emphasis mine.
185 Arthur Dix, "Ledigenheime," in *Conrads Jahrbücher für Nationalökonimie und Statistik* (III Folge, Bd. XXV, Jena: Gustav Fischer Verlag, 1903), 494, 510.
186 *Rheinische Blätter für Wohnungswesen und Bauberatung* 12 (1916): 40–43; *Zeitschrift für Wohnungswesen* (1912): 96. For a criticism of overly small rooms, see Klara Trost, *Ledigen-Heime für weibliche Erwerbstätige ; Eine Forderung aus d. Kriegswirtschaft mit Grundrißbeispielen* [Hannover: Deutsche Bauhütte, 1918], 12).
187 Generalakten, Landesarchiv Berlin, B Rep. 042, Nr. 26245, item no. 3.
188 Altenrath, 116–17.
189 For a discussion of unhygienic wooden furniture in the American context, see Lizabeth A. Cohen, "Embellishing a Life of Labor: An Interpretation of the Material Culture of American Working Class Homes, 1885–1915," in *Common Places: Readings in American Vernacular* Architecture, ed. Dell Upton, and John Michael Vlach (Athens, GA: University of Georgia Press, 1986), 261–80; B. L. Holden, "Tenement Furnishings," *House Beautiful* 7 (April 1900), 307–13.
190 Generalakten, Landesarchiv Berlin, B Rep. 042, Nr. 26245, item no. 3.
191 *Rheinische Blätter für Wohnungswesen und Bauberatung* 12 (1916): 40–3; *Zeitschrift für Wohnungswesen* (1912): 96.
192 K. F. Arnold, *Das Miethwesen in München* (München, 1879), s. 166f.
193 *Architektonische Rundschau* 28, no. 10 (1912), table 89.
194 Altenrath, 116–17; Dix, 494, 510.
195 Regarding a nineteenth-century woman's physical and moral responsibility for the arrangement and running of the familial home and relevant literature, see footnote 38 of the Introduction.
196 A transient, single, young man of modest means would have had little opportunity to obtain many possessions. The establishment of the marital home was traditionally associated with the accumulation of possessions. Again, see Cohen, 261–80; Holden, 307–13.
197 Altenrath, 28.

198 *Living Downtown: The History of Residential Hotels in the United States* (Berkeley: University of California Press, 1994), 222–6.

199 As characterized by Paul Groth, single occupancy hotel residents at the turn of the century "often held strong family values but were living outside of a family; they were capable of being well dressed but only in one or two outfits; they aspired to material comfort but had access to very little of it; they aimed for economic security but lived with uncertain incomes" ("YMCAs and Other Organization Boarding Houses," in *Housing and Dwelling*, ed. Barbara Miller Lane [London: Routledge, 2007], 114).

200 Mathilde Kirchner, "Das neuerbaute Arbeiterinnenheim in Berlin," *Westermanns Monatsheft: Illustrierte Deutsche Zeitschrift für das Geistige Leben der Gegenwart* (54 no. 107 (October–December 1909), 391).

201 Kirchner, 392.

202 For a good discussion of the symbolism and disparagement of bric-a-brac extending into the 1930s—particularly the gendered dimensions of this discourse—see Esra Akcan's work on Bruno Taut and other members of German architectural culture working in exile (*Architecture in Translation* [Durham: Duke University Press, 2012], 180–1).

203 Breckman, 492.
Breckman speaks to the distinction Wilhelmine cultural critics made between productive rather than unproductive consumption (490), as well as the association of consumerist excess (especially luxury) with women (488, 492).

204 For further discussion of the distinction between a designer and the decorator in modernist discourse, see Peter McNeil, "Designing Women: Gender, Sexuality and the Interior Decorator," *Art History* 17, no. 4 (1994): 631–57; Bobbye Tigerman, "'I am not a Decorator': Florence Knoll, the Knoll Planning Unit and the Making of the Modern Office," *Journal of Design History* 20 (2007): 61–74.

205 Arthur Dix, "Ledigenheime," in *Conrads Jahrbücher für Nationalökonomie und Statistik* (III Folge, Bd. XXV, Jena: Gustav Fischer Verlag, 1903), 494, 510.

206 In 1910 only a small percentage of Berliners had access to electric light (Arthur Dix, "Ledigenheime" in *Conrads Jahrbücher für Nationalökonomie und Statistik* [III Folge, Bd. XXV (Jena: Gustav Fischer Verlag, 1903)], 510).

207 Dix, 494, 510.

208 *Deutsche Bauzeitung* (November 5, 1892), 546; *Zeitschrift für Wohnungswesen* (1912): 96.

209 *Deutsche Bauzeitung* (November 5, 1892): 546; *Schlafstellenwesen und Ledigenheime*, 45; *Haus für Ledige Männer*, 33.

210 *Deutsche Bauzeitung* (November 5, 1892), 546; *Zeitschrift für Wohnungswesen* (1912): 94; *Schlafstellenwesen und Ledigenheime* (1904), 45, 182–4; Dix, 494.

211 See Chapter 4 for a fuller discussion.

212 Generalakten, Landesarchiv Berlin, B Rep. 042, Nr. 26245, item no. 3.
213 Changes to the hygienic surroundings typically occurred when new building materials intended to create a more hygienic environment had become available or inexpensive enough to employ. For example, instead of the bare pine floors of earlier Ledigenheime, linoleum was employed in the Düsseldorf Ledigenheim to facilitate easier cleaning (*Zeitschrift für Wohnungswesen* [1912]: 94).
214 See John Potvin, "Hot by Design: The Secret Life of a Turkish Bath in Victorian London," in *Craft, Space and Interior Design*, ed. Sandra Alfoldy and Janice Helland (Burlington: Ashgate, 2008), 11–25.
215 For representative images, see *Rheinische Blätter für Wohnungswesen und Bauberatung* 12 (1916): 40–3; *Zeitschrift für Wohnungswesen* (1912): 96.
216 *Schlafstellenwesen und Ledigenheime*, 5.
217 *Zeitschrift für Wohnungswesen* (1910/11): 93.
218 *Reichsarbeitsblatt* 11, no. 6 (June 23, 1913).
219 I have translated Fehlschlag as "failure," though it really translates better to the American idiom "a hit and a miss." "Marriage hungry single women of Berlin" is slightly crueler in the original wording, "Heiratslustigen Damenwelt." ("Die 'Junggesellen-Kaserne' ein Fehlschlag" *Deutsche Hausbesitzer-Zeitung* 15, no. 42 [1908]: 4f., cited in *Wohnalltag in Deutschland*, 336–7.)
220 *Wohnalltag in Deutschland*, 336–7.
221 Andrew Lees, *Cities, Sin, and Social Reform in Imperial Germany* (Ann Arbor: University of Michigan Press, 2002), 264.
222 Anke Hoffsten, "The 'Volkshaus' (worker's assembly hall) in Germany between 1890 and 1933: Architectural Aspects of a Building Type of the Early Phase of Modernity," *International Journal of Heritage Studies* 19, no. 5 (2013): 476.
223 Holger Gorr, "Volkshäuser (houses of the people) in Germany: A Historical Overview from 1900 until Today," *International Journal of Heritage Studies* 19, no. 5 (2013): 459.
224 Gorr, 459.
225 *Der Arbeiterfreund* 53 (1913): 47.
226 Gorr, 460; Hoffsten, 476.
227 *Reichsarbeitsblatt* (1913): 440.
228 *Der Arbeiterfreund* 53 (1913): 395.
229 *Der Arbeiterfreund* 53 (1913): 44.
230 Hoffsten, 476.
231 Hoffsten, 477.
232 Hoffsten, 478. By contrast, leading Social Democrat August Bebel termed the Hamburg Volkshaus a "spiritual armour smithy" (477).
233 Kristiana Hartmann, *Deutsche Gartenstadtbewegung: Kulturpolitik und Gesellschaftsreform* (Munich: Heinz Moos, 1976), 29.
234 Hartmann, 39.

235 For a concise treatment of Glass Chain, see Barbara Miller Lane, "Modern Architecture and Politics in Germany," in *Housing and Dwelling*, ed. Barbara Miller Lane (London: Routledge, 2007), 26.
236 Annemarie Jaeggi, "Hufeisensiedlung Britz: Planungs- und Baugeschichte," in *Siedlungen der zwanziger Jahre – heute*, ed. Norbert Huse (Berlin, 1984), 111–36.
237 Groth, "YMCAs and Other Organization Boarding Houses," 115.
238 *Hamburg und seine Bauten: under Berücksichtigung der Nachbarstädte Altona und Wandsbek 1914* (Hamburg: Boysen und Maasch, 1914), 583, 586.
239 Jean-Francois Lejeune, "From Hellerau to the Bauhaus: Memory and Modernity of the German Garden City," *The New City* 3 (Fall 1996): 64; Wolfgang Sonne, *Dwelling in the Metropolis: Reformed Urban Blocks* (Glasgow: University of Glasgow and RIBA, 2005), 3.
240 *Bauwelt* 19 (1913): 26.
241 *Moderne Bauformen* 2 (1915): 214; *Berliner Architekturwelt* 13 (1911): 337; *Berlin und Seine Bauten* (Berlin: Ernst und Sohn, 2003), 333; *Weyls*, 359; *Reichs-Arbeitsblatt* 11, no. 6 (June 23, 1913); Winter, 34, 36.
242 Lejeune, 61; Marcus Eisen, *Vom Ledigenheim zum Boardinghaus* (Berlin: Gebr. Mann Verlag, 2012), 78–87.
243 Albert Gut, *Der Wohungsbau in Deutschland nach dem Weltkrieg* (München: F. Bruckmann, 1928), 567; Bruno Taut, "Ein Ledigenheim in Schöneberg," *Stadtbaukunst Alter und Neuer Zeit* 1 (1920): 136–9; "Ein Ledigenheim," *Bauwelt* 14 (1922): 241–3; Eisen, 103–7, 112–14.

4

The Woman Question and the Housing Question

Single women were both invisible and hyper-visible in Germany at the turn of the century. The single person was by default a man, and yet the unmarried woman (*alleinstehende Frau*) was a popular signifier of modernity—at once a victim and a heroine of the modern age—one literally "standing alone" (*alleinstehend*) in society through no fault of her own. Although demographic studies have disproven the notion of an increase in the overall number of single women in late nineteenth- and early twentieth-century Germany,[1] as Stallybrass and White have claimed, "what is socially peripheral is so frequently symbolically central."[2] It did not matter that the proportion of unmarried women in the population had hardly changed over the course of the nineteenth century. As was the case with her American counterpart, the "woman adrift," the very existence of such a woman was code for a growing discomfort with a rapidly changing society and economy.[3]

Late nineteenth-century German commentators of every political persuasion agreed that unmarried women—whose numbers *appeared* to be rising—were remaining single through no fault of their own. After all, who would choose such a fate? Instead, blame was primarily laid at the feet of a changing economy, one which no longer required the household labor of older sisters and maiden aunts, and provided single men with the option to marry later, if at all. Unmarried middle-class women, and to a lesser extent lower-middle-class women, had become what contemporaries termed "surplus women," whose lives would increasingly be played out in public realm, as working-class women's lives already did. Displaced from the traditional domestic realm, these women faced a world where it was largely dishonorable for a respectable woman to work outside of the home and live on her own.[4]

It was dishonorable because nineteenth-century conceptions of respectable womanhood positioned women and men as having different innate interests and aptitudes, all of which had spatial implications. What has been termed the "ideology of separate spheres" aligned men with the public sphere of politics and business due to their purported propensity for action and rational thought. A woman's innate piety, refinement, passivity, and closeness to nature meant that she was more suited to nurturing children and family life and, by extension, was most comfortable in the domestic realm, even though this was not absolute. In particular, middle-class women were active consumers of what a modern city had to offer, from public transport and libraries to theaters and museums. The management of a household meant that the respectable woman needed to venture into new department stores. Due to her claim to moral authority, she was also well suited to philanthropic spaces where she might aid the less fortunate. Relatedly, even though it was more tightly associated with women (and children), the married man spent a great deal of time in the domestic realm, with special rooms marked out either as shared space or his domain.

What was problematic—even unnatural—in the unmarried woman was that she was increasingly working for wages outside of the home—most likely out of necessity, and possibly because she enjoyed her work. This was wholly unbecoming in a fully domesticated middle-class or lower-middle-class woman, even when the work in question could be construed as maternal. Additionally, a single working woman's movement into the public world of business and commerce was not tempered by her daily return to the family home. The purported existence of unmarried "surplus" women working outside of the home was an economic *and* a moral question, and became a critical device for criticizing the status quo.[5]

On the far left, Karl Marx and Friedrich Engels maintained that the single woman's displacement from the middle-class family of her birth was an example of the bourgeois family's eventual dissolution and the revolution to come.[6] Taking his lead from Marx and Engels' *Communist Manifesto* (1848), August Bebel, cofounder of the German Social Democratic Party (SPD), built upon the notion that the surplus woman was resultant to the advance of capitalism in his *Woman and Socialism* (1879). Similarly, Clara Zetkin, leading Marxist theorist and member of the SPD, gave numerous speeches to colleagues at party congresses on the relationship of surplus women to the capitalist economy, calling for the formation of a supportive milieu that she believed would better enable such women to "combat a patriarchal world that had long silenced their voices through dependency and exclusion from public life."[7]

Moderate feminist reformers, from Helene Lange and Gertrud Bäumer to Alice Salomon, also seized upon the single woman as a means to advocate for better educational opportunities for women, lest a woman meet the dire fate of being both unmarried and without the means to support herself. As the mid-nineteenth-century German educator Betty Gleim warned, a woman educated only to be a wife and mother, should she not marry was "the most useless, most miserable, and most unfortunate of creatures... created for a purpose (she) can never fulfill... for which alone (she has) been prepared for so long."[8]

Addressing the morally unacceptable, outmoded and old-fashioned, or simply unaffordable housing options of a modern single woman such as through the creation of gender-specific purpose-built mass housing was yet another means to grapple with the problematic aspects of industrial capitalism without entirely subverting the status quo. Providing women left without domestic sanctuary a morally uncompromised space where they were not objects, nor property, and where they could find community, the Ledigenheim building type was a practical means to mitigate the difficult situation facing these individuals—ultimately helping to establish the conceptual category of the single, respectable, working woman (Figure 4.1).

Figure 4.1 Alt Moabit 38 Ledigenheim, Berlin (1908), detail of primary facade in 2008.
Source: Author's photograph.

In many ways, the lives of the women who resided in such homes were far more open than those of most women regardless of their class, not only because of their employment outside of the home but also because of the socially progressive nature of the Ledigenheim institutional type. The Ledigenheim was a third space, somewhere between the masculine and feminine, the public and private, both confirming and challenging traditional gender roles for single women at the turn of the century. The highly differentiated and integrated spaces of the buildings provided residents with a safe and secure space from which to navigate the public world. It supported their efforts to build community with other working women and allowed them to maintain their respectability.

Though still acceptable to bourgeois mores by adhering in the main to a traditional value system; called "homes," rather than institutions (Heim translates to home in German), and never signaling *overt* rebellion from social convention; Ledigenheime for women also challenged traditional gender roles by often mirroring the style and internal organization of buildings for men, breaking forever from the restrictive model of the convent or cloister and, most importantly, largely freeing residents from the burden of housework. In providing a morally unproblematic housing option for single women working outside of the home and enabling the cultivation of a more public life, the Ledigenheim was a powerful answer to at least *part* of the "woman question" (*Frauenfrage*), which asked what role women—single or married, young or old—could play in the social, political, and economic life of Germany, and modernity itself.[9]

The Housing Question

The initial concern of reformers supporting the creation of Ledigenheime for women was the provision of appropriate housing to those unmarried women who could not otherwise afford lodgings commensurate with their social station. These women were increasingly visible within the growing and changing German economy as factory workers, clerks, teachers, social workers, nurses, and doctors.[10] While teaching, nursing, and social work were occupations strongly associated with women, even clerking, previously a means to economic and social advancement for young men of middling means, had become feminized (and proletarianized) by the beginning of the twentieth century.[11] In the 1880s, there had been a few thousand female clerks, by the First World War, 25 percent of clerks in Germany were women.[12] Significantly, many of these new or newly feminized positions required women to relocate from their hometowns,[13] and generally only paid one-half of the wages a man in a similar position might receive.[14] In 1906, August Bebel, the cofounder of the Social Democratic Party in Germany, cited the findings of an 1893 investigation, revealing that 70 percent of working women in Mannheim factories earned "veritable starvation wages" of between 6 and 19 marks a week.[15] Although Bebel was reporting on the dire situation facing working-class women, this disparity in pay existed across the board, from factory workers to white-collar workers, and even to professional women. Poor wages determined that women had fewer housing options than their male counterparts, even as housing for single men was similarly problematic.

Certainly, *Pensionen*, or family homes providing lodgers with separate quarters and meals, existed, but these were relatively expensive and were generally geared toward housing single middle-class men (*Zimmerherrn*),[16] making them not only an impossibility for lower-class men but also a poor choice for a single woman living far from home. The next possibility was a furnished room *without* board, an option that required residents to obtain meals in a restaurant or *Gasthaus*—hardly conducive to a woman's supposed desire to create a comfortable and cozy home for herself. An even less desirable solution was the much-maligned *Schlafstelle* (a bed for rent), as recounted below by Minna Wettstein-Adelt in 1893—a solution that often ended "tragically."[17]

> *The first Schlafstelle was located on the ground floor of a small half-collapsed hut that was soon-to-be condemned; the cellar-like room had a stone floor and untreated walls. A spider web hung over the center of the (relatively-speaking) decent bed and on the wall a great grey spider glared at me. . . . It was not the worst option, as there were no other lodgers, the five children appeared nice and well-mannered, and the father and mother made a good (albeit very depressed) impression. . . . The second Schalfstelle was in every way the opposite to the first. It was located on the fourth floor of a fearsome Mietskaserne (rental barracks/ tenement); out of every room I passed on the floor resounded the cries of children and the shrieking voices of women.*[18]

Contemporaries readily admitted that for a woman, obtaining good private lodgings required a combination of "optimism, specific knowledge (of the world), a certain reputation, and not least of all, luck."[19]

The social reform journal *Soziale Praxis* went so far as to make the argument that all purpose-built housing for women was untenable and that money would be better spent in the construction of *Arbeiterinnen-Klubs* (clubs for working women), or *Tagesheime* and *Abendheime* (day and evening homes/clubs),[20] as had been popularized by moderate social reformers like Alice Salomon.[21] Such buildings focused on providing healthy food and elevating popular taste and education, rather than providing housing.[22] The freestanding single-family home was dismissed as an economic impossibility for single women (and single men) of all classes.

Further complicating their situation, women generally spent more time at home than their male counterparts, much to the irritation of landlords.[23] Rather than being seen as a manifestation of poverty—if a young woman was forced to spend the bulk of her wages on her lodgings, this left little money for leisure activities that took place outside of her residence—this was attributed to a woman's supposed love of home (*Heimliebe*). Women's innate inclination toward domesticity was accepted as fact from reactionary groups to radical Social Democratic circles.[24] As the moderate feminist activist Wilhelmine Mohr claimed, a woman's "love of home" never wavered, regardless of how different her life was from the traditional role of housewife and mother.[25] Even the model female tenant was purportedly less lucrative and more demanding of her landlord than her male counterpart, a set of circumstances that circumscribed the housing options of the educated single woman, and certainly her poorly paid and less-educated sister.

The only *affordable and respectable* housing options for an unmarried German woman before the advent of the Ledigenheim, regardless of education or social status, were charitable *Stiftungen*, which were usually run by a religious organization,[26] and short-lived non-confessional experiments like the ladies' homes of Berlin (*Damenheime*), of which there were only three in 1911.[27] Governed by rigorous rules and placed great emphasis on self-improvement,[28] both alienated potential residents and ran the risk of "turn(ing) people who are capable of helping themselves into charity cases."[29] Decried as "insufficient on numerous levels," and characterized as "nasty barracks, (with) tight cells, bad air circulation, insufficient heating, (and) little cleanliness," some Stiftungen even required that residents vacate the premises on Sundays from 10 to 10, as homeless shelters typically required.[30] If these "homes" were to be utilized at all, reformers noted that they were only of use to *young* workers *searching* for work, not those in permanent employment.[31]

The denominational focus of charitable religious institutions was also problematic. Reformers of varying degrees of sociopolitical radicalism saw this as harmful and backward looking, from moderates Lina Morgenstern and Minna Cauer to leftist radicals Lily Braun and Clara Zetkin.[32] Most importantly, Stiftungen had historically served aged women, hardly conducive to a woman who was a participant in society, and certainly not middle-class professional women as a class.[33] This explains why the vast majority of Ledigenheime for women were founded on a nondenominational basis and why their supporters actively turned away from older models.

Reformers also considered current laws and regulations governing the housing of single women to outdated and ineffective. Unconcerned that they were buttressing what some might see as an undesirable lifestyle, moderate activists positioned their work as "founded firmly on the ground of reality, rather than floundering around in the realm of possibility," just as the supporters of Ledigenheime for single men situated the building type as a logical and rational solution to a set of complex social problems.[34] In fact, Wilhelmine Mohr, writing in the left-leaning publication *Die Hilfe*, mentioned specific Ledigenheime for men as the precedent for women's Ledigenheime: namely, the Dankelmannstrasse building in Berlin-Charlottenburg and the Konkordia-Haus in Hamburg (Figures 4.2a, b).[35]

Rather than positioning unmarried women as delicate creatures in their bid to construct Ledigenheime, reformers generally appealed to a sense of class consciousness or solidarity, highlighting the fact that a subset of those in need, the single educated and professional German woman, was drawn from the same social class as the reformers coming to her aid.[36] For example, Hauptmann a. D. W. von Kalckstein of Bremen, a participant in the 1904 *Schlafstellenwesen und Ledigenheime* conference in Leipzig, noted the difficulty skilled and ladylike single women had in finding suitable housing,[37] but also stressed the commonalities between these women and the middle-class (male) conference participants, noting that they were all "workers" in a loose sense of the word.[38] Implicit in these statements is the fact that these reformers realized that the status quo was untenable, and that *certain* "surplus women," particularly those working in feminized professions from clerking to social work, did have a place in the larger economic development of Germany. They took the situation of middle-class and lower-class women working outside of the home as a given.

By the turn of the century, freeing the single woman from the constraints of the nuclear family and her marginal position in it while simultaneously enabling a more public life—changes made more possible by the production and availability of purpose-built *quality* housing—had become an international phenomenon discussed with great intensity not only in Germany but also in Great Britain and the United States. The construction of Ledigenheime was thus related to and supported by international social experiments (undergirded by new educational opportunities) where moderate women, and single women in particular, took a leading role. With their purportedly innate maternal tendencies,

Figure 4.2a, b Dankelmannstrasse 46–47 Ledigenheim (for men), Berlin-Charlottenburg (1908). Primary façade and detail.
Source: Zentralblatt der Bauverwaltung 31 (1911): 635; author's photograph.

women—even childless single women—had the ability to bring a "special cultural contribution" to a public world that had long been shaped by men and male values.[39] This expanded version of motherhood, a "spiritual motherhood" (*geistige Mütterlichkeit*), rather than physical motherhood, manifested itself in what scholars have termed "municipal housekeeping," including, but not limited to, the construction of settlement houses, free kindergartens, public kitchens, and public libraries by individuals and philanthropic voluntary organizations.[40] In fact, both public kitchens and public libraries were often central components of Ledigenheime for women. These Ledigenheime were thus the architectural equivalent of a conventional gender ideology that enabled women to enter the public sphere as nature's housekeepers.

Despite this careful positioning, the construction of Ledigenheime for all segments and subsets of the single female population in Germany remained problematic, despite the fact that as late as 1912 half of German women over eighteen years of age were unmarried, and most of these individuals were working outside of the home.[41] This reticence to support the construction of homes for single women in employment cannot simply be attributed conservatives who were horrified by the mere fact of any woman working outside of the home (married or single), nor the far left's contention that these homes would not improve single women's material or emotional lives.[42]

From the beginning, reform efforts had concentrated on the housing of single men, not women in permanent employment, with the housing of single women only gaining traction after a number of municipally backed Ledigenheime for men had been constructed. Exacerbating the problem, women were *perceived* to lodge as single individuals for a very limited period before marriage. This led reformers to view the housing of single women as less pressing than that of their unmarried male counterparts, most of whom married at a slightly later age than their female counterparts, and whose need for quality housing was assumed to intensify with the founding of a family. This helps to explain the dual emphasis on the housing of single young men and the housing of families by German reformers, often to the detriment of single women, particularly those women who remained single—a bias problematizing the task of the architectural historian. Not only were fewer buildings for women constructed, but when they were, they were not covered in the popular or architectural press to the degree men's homes were. In particular, adequate visuals pertaining to homes for women are few and far between. However, this does not mean that evidence does not exist, but rather that the architectural historian must carefully pick out representative examples where the visuals do exist and heavily supplement the visual evidence by turning to written accounts of what these buildings "looked" like. The proof of the single woman's problematic economic and social status ultimately lies not only in what her contemporaries did report regarding her plight but also in the (lack of) coverage given to the homes built to save her from this marginal existence.

General Characteristics

Ledigenheime for single women, as for single men, were not *homes* in the conventional sense. Ledigenheime serving women were hybrids of the public and private realms, meaning that they often included dining halls and libraries open to and primarily serving the general public in order to defray costs. For example, the *Lehrerinnenheim* (Ledigenheim for teachers) in Berlin-Pankow contained fifty one- to three-room residences, each with its own kitchen, and also a *Speisewirtschaft* (restaurant) open to residents and the community at large (Figures 4.3a, b). Similarly, the *Arbeiterinnenheim* (Ledigenheim for lower-middle-class women) of Berlin-Moabit not only housed sixty-six residents, thirty-seven of them in single bedrooms, but also provided the community and residents with the use of a *Kaffeestube* (a coffee shop), dining hall, and a reading room, although the use of the latter was restricted to women (Figures 4.4a, b). A Ledigenheim was both a focal point in the larger community and a place where residents existed well outside of contemporary conventions that impacted men, but more deeply circumscribed most women's interactions with the greater world. Supporters of Ledigenheime for women insisted upon several requirements that indicate the relative freedom residents enjoyed. There was to be no hint of the "convent or the cloister," for as reported earlier, reformers found this older model of housing single women profoundly unsuitable to working women. Instead of restrictive rules, the buildings were to feel "home-like," with carefully chosen furnishings and decorations.[43] The only nod to the *Stiftung* was a modern and secular version of the Mother Superior, the directress (*Leiterin*)—ideally an "intelligent and warmhearted" woman who understood the "requirements and proclivities typical of her residents."[44] Playing a role akin to that of the director of a women's college, as it had recently been constructed in Britain and the United States, her presence would ensure ladylike behavior.[45]

However, as will be examined in greater depth later, elements that constituted a home were not consistent across class lines, indicating that the Ledigenheim, although a socially progressive institution, was a marker of the sharp divisions

Figure 4.3a, b Lehrerinnenheim, Berlin-Pankow (1909). Exterior and dining hall.
Source: *Wasmuths Monatsheft für Baukunst* (1915/16): 136; *Mitteilungen des Rheinischen Vereins für Kleinwohnungswesen* 8 (1915/16): 48.

Figure 4.4a, b Alt Moabit 38 Ledigenheim, Berlin (1908). Elevation of the street façade and detail of the primary entrance. Note that the entrance to the *Kaffeestube* is located directly to the right of the primary entrance.

Source: Der Baumeister 7, no. 8 (1909): 86.

between social classes in Wilhelmine Germany. Despite the use of the word "worker" in their speeches, reformers never suggested that the treatment of middle-class women ought to be consistent with that of their working-class sisters. Certainly, it was taken for granted in Imperial Germany that middle-class women should not be housed with women of a lower social class, and that each class of single female worker deserved her own type of Ledigenheim.[46]

As will be discussed, class specificity was shown not only by the relative elegance of the furnishings and decorations provided in specific Ledigenheime but also by the greater number of differentiated spaces provided for the middle-class resident as opposed to her less-affluent sister.[47] I will first investigate Ledigenheime housing skilled working-class and lower-middle-class women, and then those of their more educated, genteel, and affluent counterparts—women who best symbolized the plight of the "surplus woman" in middle-class eyes.

Ledigenheime for Skilled Working-Class and Lower Middle-Class Women

Lower-middle-class and skilled working-class women, often employed in the service sector as bookkeepers, telephone operators, seamstresses, and saleswomen,[48] typically earned roughly half of what an unskilled male laborer earned,[49] severely limiting their housing options. While a single woman engaged in a profession might not have been able to afford housing that suited her sensibilities, that which was substandard in her eyes was entirely out of reach for a single woman of lower socioeconomic standing, who typically resided on the fringes of the housing market. To such a woman, the option of a Ledigenheim meant that she would have sanitary living conditions, a bed of her own, access to healthful food in house, and a place to build community with women of similar social standing. Although Ledigenheime for skilled working-class and lower-middle-class women were referred to by contemporaries as *Arbeiterinnenheime*, or homes for working women, they were not and are not to be confused with the majority of housing built by employers for their unskilled female workforce, which were closer in conception to barracks than to Ledigenheime for women or men, and thus are not treated in this study.[50]

An early example of this new form of housing for women was the Stuttgart *Herberge für Fabrikarbeiterinnen*, or home for skilled female factory workers, built in 1874 by the *Verein zur Fürsorge für Fabrikarbeiterinnen*. Founded in 1868, this group was not linked to any particular employer but comparable to reform organizations supporting the construction of Ledigenheime for men (and the subject of Chapter 3).⁵¹ As with the latter, the supporters of the Stuttgart Herberge/Ledigenheim for women sought to provide residents with physically hygienic surroundings, morally uncompromising spaces, and community. Regarding hygiene, the Stuttgart Ledigenheim included bathroom facilities on each floor, and both the corridors from which a resident accessed her bedroom and the bedrooms themselves were brightly lit and well ventilated, for all contained at least one large window that could be opened (Figure 4.5).

As to the creation of community, the Stuttgart building included a (heated!) gathering hall. Intended for genteel recreational activities, ranging from choral classes and reading out loud to working on embroidery, this gathering hall bore much similarity to the assembly room provided in nearly every contemporaneous Ledigenheim constructed for men as, though the use of such a room—generally the largest space in the building—tended to be more heavily programmed, and was often reserved for lectures.⁵² Additionally, not one *Volksküche* (public kitchen), but two Volksküchen (plural)—one for men and one for the use of women and children—were

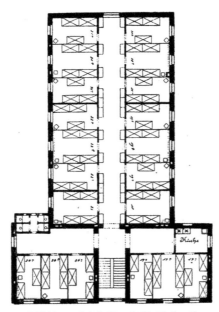

Schlafzimmer des I., II. und III. Stockwerks.

Figure 4.5 Herberge für Fabrikarbeiterinnen, Ludwigstrasse 15, Stuttgart (1874). Plan of first, second, and third floors. Note the WCs and small kitchen (*Küche*).
Source: Schlafstellenwesen und Ledigenheime, 73.

The Woman Question and the Housing Question 215

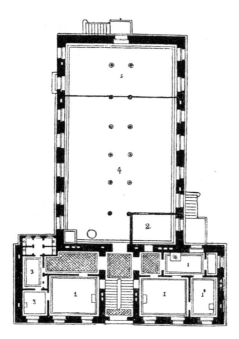

Figure 4.6 Herberge für Fabrikarbeiterinnen, Ludwigstrasse 15, Stuttgart (1874). Plan of basement. Note the two public kitchens (#1 is the Volksküche for men, #2 is the Volksküche for women and children).
Source: Schlafstellenwesen und Ledigenheime, 72.

included (Figure 4.6). The inclusion of an in-house dining option was intended to discourage residents from frequenting local coffeehouses and taverns in the evening, as reformers considered the "exchanges" that took place in such locales both inappropriate for and unappealing to "the delicately composed woman."[53] Interestingly, public kitchens—occasionally gender specific, though usually for the use of mixed company—were nearly always a feature of "reform" Ledigenheime for men and were similarly intended to entice residents to enter a semipublic realm while remaining in the building, indicating that this was not a gender-specific tactic. Even more importantly, considering that Ledigenheime for women of *every* social class contained spaces loosely approximating a restaurant, the latter was a place they *must* have frequented with some regularity, either out of need or inclination (despite reformers' claims that these places held no appeal for women). The inclusion of something akin to a tavern in the controlled environment and purportedly elevating surroundings of a Ledigenheim was what made the former more reputable. Ledigenheime thus enabled German women of the skilled working class and lower middle class, while remaining respectably "at home," to visit a traditionally masculine space merely by walking downstairs. This directed participation in the public realm—outside of their working lives—indicates that German women's interactions with the public sphere were more nuanced than has traditionally been thought.

Despite these programmatic similarities, a few significant differences marked early Ledigenheime for women from contemporaneous developments for men, some of which would remain leitmotifs throughout the development of the building type. Although obtaining meals within the aforementioned Volksküche for women was certainly an option for residents, small semiprivate kitchens were available for residents to use; one was located on each of the upper three floors in close proximity to the residents' bedrooms (see Figure 4.5). Additionally, the residents were required to clean the home on a regular basis. Significantly, cooking was not supported in any Ledigenheim housing men. The advocates of Ledigenheime for men only supported the construction of central kitchens with associated dining halls, rendering private cooking not only improbable but impossible. Nor was any male resident ever required to clean his place of residence, regardless of his social class.

Finally, the scale of Ledigenheime for women tended to be smaller, and thus less noticeable in the urban fabric, even as the buildings were made more visible to the public through the inclusion of public kitchens. For example, the Arbeiterinnenheim located on the Theresienstrasse in Munich, the construction of which was supported by the reform organization Frauenverein Arbeiterinnenheim in 1891, was typical of Ledigenheime for women in that could only house seventy residents, in contrast to contemporaneous Ledigenheime built for men by reform organizations, which often accommodated hundreds of men.[54] Even a larger home for women, such as the Stuttgart Herberge für Fabrikarbeiterinnen, only housed 150 residents in 60 bedrooms distributed over 3 upper floors.[55] Although one might be tempted to think this was due to the fact that there were fewer female workers in need of housing than male workers, this is not mentioned in any of the literature. Instead, the smaller scale of these buildings, facilitated by lower numbers of residents in each building, was thought to be necessary due to the supposed detrimental effects that larger buildings of greater heights had on the health of women.[56] Correspondingly, Ledigenheime for women tended to be smaller and more intimate. This relative intimacy was also thought to be intrinsically linked to the formation of a "home-like" atmosphere, particularly when coupled with an emphasis on elegant surroundings and exteriors reflecting the latest style.

This need to reference the domestic, to contextualize Ledigenheime as homes, rather than institutions, is significant. While it can be assumed, based on turn-of-the-century gender roles, that a German woman was possibly willing and certainly able to clean her home and to prepare small meals for herself, where a German man would not and could not cook for himself, requiring residents to cook and clean functioned as a kind of domestic training. While a Ledigenheim freed a resident from household drudgery to a certain degree, freeing her entirely might have encouraged her to forget her traditional role. Similarly, a smaller scale building helped to maintain the illusion that a Ledigenheim was not mass housing for unmarried women, but simply a larger version of a family home.

In fact, the supporters of Ledigenheime for women believed that a building which did not maintain an architectural and programmatic "façade of domestic normalcy" would be less appealing to the potential resident due to her abhorrence of the Stiftung and her love of home.[57] Recourse to the domestic could also help to forestall criticism from the general public. While not necessarily known of by the supporters of German Ledigenheime, early women's seminaries, most famously Mt. Holyoke in Massachusetts, commonly required that students help clean their residence, and the patrons of the first women's colleges in Britain carefully built smaller scale institutions. Both tactics were a means to allay fears that these institutions created undomestic women who were less likely to ultimately marry.[58] Considering how visible Ledigenheime for women (and men) were in the urban landscape of Germany—as opposed to early British and American women's seminaries and colleges, which were often placed in pastoral settings on the periphery of cities and towns—the need for such markers of domesticity was even more pressing.[59]

Later Ledigenheime for Skilled Working-Class and Lower-Middle-Class Women

Slightly later variants of reform Ledigenheime for skilled working-class and lower-middle-class women retained many of the components of earlier housing experiments for women, but in general presented a more elegant appearance, bringing them closer aesthetically to those built for their male counterparts. In particular, as exemplified by the Arbeiterinnenheim located at Alt Moabit 38 in Berlin (1909), these turn-of-the-century Ledigenheime had much in common with the style of Catholic, municipal, or reform-society supported Ledigenheime for men,[60] indicating the level to which Ledigenheime in general had become associated with a particular architectural style, the *Biedermeier revival* (as discussed in previous chapters). Significantly, the use of the same style for men's and women's Ledigenheime stands in contrast to other notable models of gendered mass housing, such as contemporaneous Oxbridge dormitories. For example, residences for female students were not only scaled and massed differently from those of men, but early versions typically employed the Queen Anne, a nineteenth-century style of "decidedly middle-class origins" marked by "simple charm, picturesque variety and modified classicism," rather than mimic the Gothic precedent of the male dormitory.[61]

Although it was termed *Berliner Zopf* style by the author of the article in *Die Architektur des XX Jahrhunderts*, the Alt Moabit Ledigenheim was a variation of the Biedermeier revival, which, like the Queen Anne in Britain, was a flexible style that could read as both elevated and homey (Figure 4.7, see also Figures 4.4a, b).[62] The five-story facade of the Alt Moabit building, topped with a mansard roof, is a light-hearted and informal application of a simplified and vertically articulated neoclassical style. Decorative details and exterior treatments recall a late eighteenth- or early nineteenth-century urban residence, as owned by a prosperous burgher. While this popular turn-of-the-century style was employed in Ledigenheime for men as a means both to elevate their aesthetic

Figure 4.7 Alt Moabit 38 Ledigenheim, Berlin (1908). Primary facade in 2008. *Source:* Author's photograph.

taste to "timeless models" and to cultivate gentle and refined habits—softening the edges of working-class and lower-middle-class masculinity while remaining suitably masculine—it performed a similar balancing act for female residents. Feminine in its decorative detailing, the Biedermeier revival was drawn from an age associated with quiet domesticity rather than political tumult, while also recalling neoclassical rationality. The use of a restrained and measured style that still read as feminine, though not overly so, is also significant considering the two most common negative depictions of the (aging) single woman: the grim, joyless, and masculinized spinster, and the slightly ridiculous girl-woman, still beribboned and twittering despite her advancing age.[63] The Biedermeier revival referenced the domestic, and yet was not excessively feminine. Nor was it unbecomingly masculine. In short, it physically countered the charges commonly leveled at unmarried women, proactively deflecting criticism from the women housed within its walls.

Additionally linking this building to contemporaneous reform Ledigenheime for men (as well as earlier Ledigenheime for women and men), the building included a dining hall (*Speisesaal*) that could accommodate up to 150 visitors at one time, and a coffee house (*Kaffeestube*), both of which were open and readily accessible to members of the general public.[64] Entry to the coffee house, located a few feet to the right of the residents' primary entrance, was even advertised by signage carved into the facade, further underscoring the dual role the building played (see Figures 4.4a, b). In serving its residents and the surrounding community, the Ledigenheim blurred the lines between the public and the private realms, and did so to a greater degree than earlier buildings for women and contemporary buildings for men, even reform Ledigenheime serving lower-middle-class male residents.

The coffee house was easily accessible to the general public (and to residents returning from work) through an entrance fronting the street. Interior entrances to it and to the public dining hall were nearly as direct. Both the dining hall and coffee house were located off of an L-shaped hallway on the ground floor (Figures 4.8a, b). This hallway led from residents' primary entrance, past the main staircase at the front of the home, and terminated in a fountain mounted on the wall. If not arriving directly from her place of employment, but from her bedroom or the shared common spaces upstairs, a resident merely had to descend the front stairs, walk a few steps, and pass through a doorway to gain entry to the coffee house, with access to the dining hall directly to the left of the wall fountain.

By contrast, male residents' access to the "public" spaces of their Ledigenheime was sharply curtailed. In most cases, there was no direct internal access from the private or semiprivate spaces to the public spaces of the home. Male residents

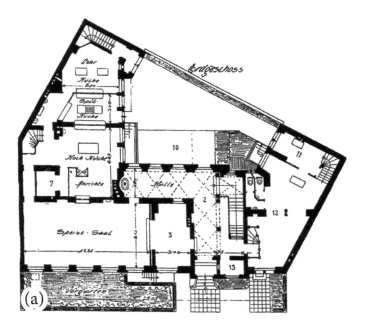

Figure 4.8a, b Alt Moabit 38 Ledigenheim, Berlin (1908). Plan of ground floor and photograph of the ground floor hallway and primary stairwell. On the plan, please note the locations of the dining hall (Speisesaal), reading room (#3), coffee shop (#12), directress' office (#13), and teaching kitchen (Lehrküche).

Source: Die Architektur des XX. Jahrhunderts 9, no. 3 (1909): 42–4; Der Baumeister 7, no. 8 (1909): 87

either had to actually go out onto the street in order to enter the public kitchen or public library or, as in the case of the Dankelmannstrasse building, enter into a small vestibule fronting the building and serving as the connector between the residence proper and the public kitchen (Figure 4.9 [also 3.4]). Such careful

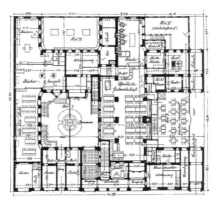

Figure 4.9 (also 3.4) Dankelmannstrasse 46–47 Ledigenheim (for men), Berlin-Charlottenburg (1908). Plan of the ground floor. Note the vestibule labelled Vorhalle.
Source: Weyls' Handbuch der Hygiene (Leipzig: Barth, 1918), 354.

calibration of single men's interactions with public space and the general public indicates middle-class reformers' fears that—despite their ministrations—residents were not yet domesticated, and thus could not be entirely trusted to behave in the prescribed way. Women, with their innate inclination to domesticity, posed far less of a threat.

This being said, a Ledigenheim for women such as Alt Moabit was not entirely open and accessible. The upper floors, which contained all the residents' bedrooms, were certainly off-limits to the general public, and the usage of another ostensibly public space was limited. The ground floor reading room was only open to women, not men nor children.[65] Denying men and children access certainly circumscribed the potential number of patrons, and limiting the use of the reading room to women without children in tow meant that visitors were most likely the residents themselves, other childless women, or women whose children were grown. Why limit access to the reading room when spaces associated with the consumption of food and drink were open, and the reading room directly abutted the dining hall with only a large sliding door dividing the two spaces? Considering the noise and mess that children (particularly small children) make, restricting their access makes sense if the goal was to cultivate a peaceful place where reading and (relatively) quiet conversation was the mandate. Although small communal parlors were located on the upper floors, there was no other gender-specific space where a resident might meet and socialize with nonresident female friends and acquaintances. Interestingly, this also means that there were no spaces apart from the public dining hall and coffee house where men and the female residents might spend time together. The supporters of Ledigenheime were not nearly as interested in facilitating the eventual marriage of a resident as were the boosters of other contemporaneous homes for young unmarried women, such as the YWCA, which purposefully provided ground-floor parlors where a resident might meet a potential beau in morally uncompromising and semiprivate circumstances.[66]

How enforceable was this gendered divide and how was order maintained in such a permeable building? The multiple interior and exterior entrances to Alt Moabit's public and semipublic spaces meant the directress, whose small office was positioned directly inside and to the right of the resident's primary entrance, could not monitor all the movements of the residents and guests (see Figure 4.8a). However, like contemporaneous Ledigeneheime for men, the directress did have a clear sightline to the staircase serving the upper floors, meaning that access from the ground floor to residents' bedrooms, common rooms, and bathroom facilities was placed under her watchful eye (a servant staircase running from the basement through to the upper floors was only accessible on the ground floor from a teaching kitchen at the rear of the scullery, and thus did not present a worry). On the upper floors, much like single men's homes (and the Stuttgart home for women), the resident's bedrooms were arranged along two corridors that intersected near the southwest side of the building, to the west of the main stairwell and the directress' living quarters opposite it. This enabled the directress and the residents to police behavior and to ensure that unwelcome visitors did not breach the line, or climb the staircase, running between the public and semipublic spaces of the ground floor and the semiprivate and private spaces above. The residents of Alt Moabit were clearly prepared to sublimate the privacy so valued in bourgeois circles to the need for a residence protecting their reputations.

The supporters of Alt Moabit further ensured proper behavior (or at least its appearance) through programming that taught residents both occupational skills *and* ladylike accomplishments, including, but not limited to, evening courses in tailoring, singing, gymnastics, stenography, German, and English in a small lecture room (*Vortragszimmer*) on the first floor (Figure 4.10, room labeled 17).[67] While teaching stenography and the fundamentals of German grammar seem especially well suited to women employed in white-collar jobs (clerking in particular), and fell well within the tradition of middle-class women's efforts to support lower-class women, other courses emphasized activities more suited to the comfortably situated daughters of the bourgeoisie. Singing and English lessons would not be of much help to a telephone operator in her day-to-day life, but as genteel activities associated with the middle-class domestic sphere, they might aid her in navigating slightly more elevated social circles. Far more programmatically complex than an earlier building like the Stuttgart Ledigenheim,

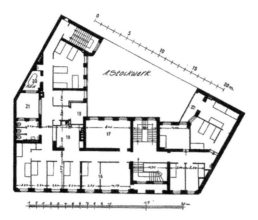

Figure 4.10 Alt Moabit 38 Ledigenheim, Berlin (1908). Plan of the first upper floor. Note the location of the Vortragszimmer (#17).
Source: *Die Architektur des XX. Jahrhunderts* 9, no. 3 (1909): 42–4.

which had seemed so progressive thirty-five years earlier with its "gathering space," Alt Moabit's programming balanced preparing residents for their very public working lives and the skills its middle-class supporters deemed necessary in a fully domesticated woman, just as the public kitchen was offset by the semiprivate kitchenettes on the first through third floors and a teaching kitchen.

The teaching kitchen (*Lehrküche*), attached to the rear of the scullery of the professional kitchen serving the dining hall, was a marker of both gender and class (see Figure 4.8a). Such spaces were never included in Ledigenheime for professional women, and certainly never in Ledigenheime for men. Highly rationalized and organized spaces, teaching kitchens have often been associated with the rise of home economics classes that reached their zenith under the auspices of the state and the League of German Women's Associations (*Bund Deutscher Frauenvereine*) in the Weimar Republic.[68] Such courses and model kitchens were geared toward instructing the working-class housewife (or future housewife) on how best to save labor and resources in what was usually a technologically up-to-date space, and have been read as a means to women's re-domestication by scholars like Susan Henderson and Sophie Hochhäusl.[69] Like these later teaching kitchens (and the noted Frankfurt kitchen designed by Margarethe Schütte-Lihotzky), the teaching kitchen of Alt Moabit was organized and managed by others, and should be read as a guarantee that the Ledigenheim was a transitional space, rather than a permanent home. The emphasis teaching kitchens placed on properly and economically preparing food means that the residents were being trained either for domestic service or for their future lives as housewives. The former is unlikely, considering that service was both more demanding and more poorly paid than the position a typical resident would already have held. The latter, despite having no parlor to properly entertain a suitor in, is more certain, although the Alt Moabit kitchen was far better appointed than any kitchen they would use as married women, at least until the 1920s.

Despite the inclusion of certain markers of domesticity, there was *some* parity in the treatment of female residents of Ledigenheime and their male counterparts. Like the Dankelmannstrasse Ledigenheim for men built several years earlier in neighboring Berlin-Charlottenburg, the Alt Moabit building provided "all modern conveniences in light, air circulation, and cleanliness,"[70] including central heat, as well as bathing and toilet facilities in close proximity to the bedrooms.[71] The majority of the bedrooms were single rooms (the ideal for any Ledigenheim according to housing reformers), with these thirty-seven (of forty-seven total) bedrooms measuring on average 8 square meters—each appointed with a window seat, roomy wardrobe, and large good bed.[72] In a nod to the resident's innate domestic tendencies, the single bedrooms in Alt Moabit were 3 meters larger than the single bedrooms in the Dankelmannstrasse building, a contemporaneous "model" Ledigenheim for men.

Additionally, *parlors* where the residents could socialize were provided on the second and third floors (Figure 4.11).[73] While the Dankelmannstrasse building provided a similarly scaled "men's lounge" (*Gesellschaftsraum*) equipped with five tables and twenty-five chairs on each of the four upper floors (see Figures 3.15, 3.18), such unprogrammed space—not a classroom or a reading room, simply a space to relax and converse—was rare in Ledigenheime built for men, and never occurred in those constructed for skilled working-class men by employers. In general, the supporters of Ledigenheime for men tightly controlled the leisure

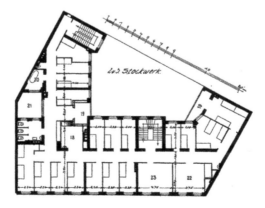

Figure 4.11 Alt Moabit 38 Ledigenheim, Berlin (1908). Plan of the second and third upper floors. Note the location of the kitchenette (#18).
Source: Die Architektur des XX. Jahrhunderts 9, no. 3 (1909): 42–4.

activities of the residents *and* programmed their contact with one another, even when they were "at home." The supporters of Ledigenheime for women had no such qualms, actively facilitating community through the inclusion of communal parlors, although the second-floor parlor in the Alt Moabit building was located directly next to the directress' lodgings. Communal space, which in a working-class tenement read as disordered and chaotic, was here a sign of bourgeois order. These parlors, even while shared with fellow residents, remained a link to and a tacit acknowledgment of the cult of domesticity.

Could the residents then treat their communal parlors as they might do a private parlor, that is to say, decorate the space to reflect their social standing and taste? They were given no such agency. Instead, the spaces of the Ledigenheime were carefully decorated to reflect the aesthetic conventions of the educated bourgeoisie, as filtered through the architect hired by Alt Moabit's boosters, *Baumeister* Heinrich Schweitzer. *Westermanns Monatsheft für Baukunst* noted that the interior was enlivened by artistic touches by *Baumeister* Schweitzer, which included different color schemes for each floor and coordinating fresh flowers in the hallways.[74] In fact, every space, from the private and communal rooms to the hallways, stairwells, and even the facade, was decorated to convey "quiet and cheeriness, freedom and beauty."[75]

This focus upon aesthetic matters by the supporters of Ledigenheime for women may appear peculiar until one considers that the provision of such pleasant surroundings was in fact a replacement for the restrictive rules of the cloister, as the refined and elegant decorations were considered by reformers to be central in retaining and controlling residents. Despite the relative permeability of these buildings, the well-appointed interior of a Ledigenheim would keep its residents from a "nomadic" life,[76] and the distractions of the city would be counteracted by "healthy rooms, good care, and cozy company."[77]

Pleasant surroundings were also intended to help young women to refine their taste and perhaps even curb impulses toward the purchase of frivolous items, cited by reformers as "pretty things, furnishings, clothing, and sweets," seeing that there would be no need to beautify their surroundings in an already elegant and prettily appointed space.[78] While middle-class reformers commonly positioned themselves as experts and arbiters of taste—the saviors of German culture writ large—this attempt to forestall problematic consumerism by women of lower-class origins reflects not only a decided lack of faith in the aesthetic proclivities of the lower classes in general but is also profoundly misogynistic. In Germany as elsewhere at the turn of the century, the decorative capabilities of lower-class women were held up for particular criticism. Derided for both their wastefulness and lack of sophistication, such women's efforts to aestheticize the domestic sphere served as cautionary tales of what *would* occur without expert guidance and support.[79] The not-so-subtle implication was that lower-class women ought to leave aesthetic matters to their betters, ideally professional architects and designers who were almost certainly male and middle class.

Yet, while the residents of Alt Moabit were discouraged from making their bedrooms or even their semiprivate parlors into expressions of their taste, and by extension, claim ownership of them, the middle-class female residents of Ledigenheime were actively encouraged to practice their domesticity by using *and* decorating private parlors. As discussed in Chapter 3, worries about consumption did not plague the supporters of Ledigenheime for skilled working-class and lower-middle-class men either, as evidenced by numerous and widely circulated images showing male residents relaxing in spaces that they had clearly decorated themselves (Figure 4.12, also 3.1). What constituted problematic taste in Wilhelmine Germany, as elsewhere, was tightly linked not only to class but to gender.

Figure 4.12 (also 3.1) Dankelmannstrasse 46–47 Ledigenheim (for men), Berlin-Charlottenburg (1908). Photograph of the "ideal" single room resident.
Source: *50 Jahre Volkswohnheim Gemeinnützige Aktien-Gesellschaft Berlin-Charlottenburg* (Basel: Länderdienst Verlag, 1955), 33.

Ledigenheime for Professional Women

To an even greater extent than those for skilled working-class and lower-middle-class women, Ledigenheime built for middle-class professional women at the close of the nineteenth and beginning of the twentieth century disprove conventional wisdom that a bourgeois woman's home, married or unmarried, was to be made within the setting of the nuclear family, from which she might venture out in a carefully calibrated engagement with public life, but to which she would always return.[80] Ledigenheime provided a home for unmarried women who did not desire to live an outdated and cloistered existence in a charitable Stiftung, or to reside as a poor relation in the home of her birth or with another relative; the figure of the "Alte Tante," or dependent maiden aunt, loomed large.

In general, these buildings housed women who had been brought up in a middle-class milieu, and were employed in professions or trades that had required them to obtain at least some, if not extensive, education and training for their positions. These women were not spinsters of the mid-nineteenth-century imagination, but "new women" engaged in numerous new (and often newly feminized) occupations, such as laboratory, hospital, and clinical assistants, chemists, librarians, artists, social workers, teachers, factory inspectors, superintendents of orphanages, nurses, police matrons, midwives, and school physicians, even architects and engineers.[81] In short, residents were members of the rising middle class by vocation and upbringing; yet, unlike most women of middle-class origins, they did not live in anything that approximated the *imagined* women's sphere so often written of in literature on bourgeois women (although to be fair, neither did bourgeois women).

These buildings for middle-class single women announced their presence in the urban landscape and their place as a part of an established building typology. Far larger in scale than those of her less-affluent sisters, a building such as the Pankow Lehrerinnenheim took up an entire city block. It was an unmissable statement of presence and permanence that aped both the scale and style of contemporary Ledigenheime for men. In fact, the exterior appearance of most Ledigenheime for middle-class women did not differ in any significant way from that of contemporaneous Ledigenheime for lower-middle-class or skilled working-class men. For example, the elegant baroque facade of the municipal Ledigenheim for women in Ulm recalled that of the Weberplatz Ledigenheim for men in Essen, as well as the Catholic Ledigenheim for men in Düsseldorf (Figures 4.13a [also 3.11], 4.13b). The Pankow Lehrerinnenheim loosely employed the Biedermeier-influenced decorative style common to

Figure 4.13a, (also 3.11) and 4.13b Kaiser Wilhelm Ledigenheim on the Weberplatz, Essen (1912–13) and the Ledigenheim for Women, Ulm (1907). View from the Weberplatz and Façade Elevation.

Source: *Wasmuths Monatsheft für Baukunst* 2 (1915/16): 69 (for Essen, left); *Zeitschrift für Wohnungswesen* 5, no. 24 (1907): 29 (for Ulm, right).

numerous Ledigenheime for men, from the Dankelmannstrasse Ledigenheim in Berlin-Charlottenburg to the Catholic Ledigenheime of Münster and Neuss, as well as the Catholic Breitestrasse building in central Cologne.[82] This is not particularly surprising, as Ledigenheime for lower-middle-class and skilled working-class women, with the marked exception of scale, had also employed a visual vocabulary akin to that of contemporaneous reform Ledigenheime built for men. Instead, the key differences between these buildings for professional women and other Ledigenheime for lower-class women (and men) were those not legible on the exteriors of the buildings.

Professional women, such as those who came to live in the Pankow Lehrerinnenheim, were able to advocate for themselves and their housing needs far more effectively than other Ledigenheim residents. While less empowered than the elite "club women" who constructed buildings like Berlin's famed Lyceum Club,[83] most of the future residents of the Pankow building were members of the Berlin Association of Female Elementary Teachers. These women had not only formed a housing cooperative, as was popular among (largely male) civil servants' groups but also purchased a plot of land and hired a prominent architect to design the building. The architect they chose, Paul Mebes, was not only noted for his work for the powerful Civil Servants' Housing Association of Berlin (Beamten- Wohnungs- Verein zu Berlin) but his recently published book, *Um 1800* (c. 1800), was lauded by the architectural profession and critically acclaimed in the popular press.[84] This degree of agency was hardly a reproducible paradigm across class lines. The lower-middle-class and skilled working-class women who lived in a building such as Alt Moabit had far less access to financial and social resources, and there is no record of the Alt Moabit residents having any voice in the planning or construction process of their residence. Such women were not allowed to build for themselves. Instead, they were positioned as the malleable beneficiaries of middle-class social reform efforts.

In fact, it was taken for granted in Imperial Germany that the single woman should be housed in a Ledigenheim specific to her social class, which seems illogical when one considers that housing *slightly* different social classes in a single Ledigenheim building was economically less risky. For this reason, Ledigenheime for men nearly always included rooms at slightly different price points, with the rent charged reflecting the level of privacy and amount of space provided. As an added bonus, the proponents of Ledigenheime for men believed that the possibility of upgrading one's room served as an enticement to hard work and the pursuit of education/training, akin to the "ladder principle" of room upgrades employed in the United States by the YMCA and YWCA, even the Salvation Army.[85] Instead, the basis for the segregation of social classes in Ledigenheime for women remained tied to the assumption that lower-class women needed to be "improved," while middle-class teachers and civil servants would not benefit from the ministrations of women drawn from their own social class.

Reformers also feared that a woman from a bourgeois background could potentially be "contaminated" by exposure to her less well-brought-up working-class sisters. By contrast, while the male resident of a Ledigenheim was purportedly under threat from the nefarious influences of the outside world, his fellow residents, even if drawn from a slightly lower social class, posed little danger to his moral rectitude. In the case of women, the concern stemmed from the belief that the moral standards of a lower-class woman were likely to be lower than those of a woman of middle-class upbringing, quite possibly due to the former's experience of unregulated lodging. In fact, the word "contamination" was commonly used to describe the moral danger an unregulated lodger posed to the eleven- or twelve-year-old daughter of a subletting family—though not to the family's eleven- or twelve-year-old son, indicating that it was a gender-specific term.[86] At the very least—and again, more worrying in a woman than a man—a woman of working-class background probably had a different conception of privacy due to close living quarters and was probably exposed to the expressions of human sexuality from earliest childhood.

Class specificity, to an exacting level that did not exist in Ledigenheime for men, was thus manifested in Ledigenheime serving middle-class professional women. This was not only exhibited in the relatively higher rents charged to residents but also through the amount of attention lavished on interior decorations thought to be in keeping with the residents' aesthetic sensibilities. Additionally, considering that privacy was a largely middle-class phenomenon, at least when compared to a working-class life, the female middle-class Ledigenheim resident was provided with a greater number of private and semiprivate spaces, which served as an indicator of her elevated social standing.[87]

A comparison of the principal gathering spaces of two contemporaneous Ledigenheime serves as an illustration of the level of decoration that was expected for and by middle-class residents, as opposed to lower-class residents. These functionally similar communal spaces were the most lavishly appointed spaces in the respective homes. Yet, the most cursory examination of the dining/gathering hall of the *Lehrerinnenheim* (home for teachers) on the Wisbyerstrasse in Berlin-Pankow (1909) with the gathering hall of the Mannheim-Walddorf *Arbeiterinnenheim* (home for working women—in this case, a Ledigenheim, of 1905) shows the elegantly appointed surroundings of the former to stand in stark contrast to the latter (Figures 4.3b, 4.14).[88] The Lehrerinnenheim's dining room was paneled in wood, and featured a wooden buffet, tables with floral arrangements and tablecloths. Sanitary, yet on-trend, *Jugendstil* designs were painted on the walls and a matching chandelier hung from the ceiling. By contrast, as disclosed by an article praising the building, the only embellishments in the hall of the Arbeiterinnenheim consisted of embossed detailing on the reinforced concrete arch dividing the hall; instead of an elegant chandelier, four bare bulbs hung from the ceiling.[89]

While it is tempting to read the sparse decoration of the Arbeiterinnenheim's primary social space as an illustration of Modernist tendencies—purposeful decorative restraint and an emphasis on volume as opposed to mass—such spare treatment was completely out of step with mainstream architectural trends in 1905, particularly as concerned the creation of middle-class and lower-middle-class domestic environments. Later Modernists may have fetishized spare interiors and bare walls, finding them not only suitable for factories but also

Figure 4.14 Arbeiterinnheim, Mannheim-Walddorf (*c.* 1905). Theater performance and concert hall.
Source: Baugewerkszeitung 39 (1907): 553.

desirable for domestic architecture, but here the extremely restrained interior of the Arbeiterinnenheim should be read as stark and bare—uncomfortably institutional, rather than home-like.

Instead, as discussed in Chapters 1 and 3, German architects, designers, and cultural critics in the first decade of the twentieth century idealized the creation of the total work of art, or *Gesamtkunswerk*, which was a room, or ideally, a building in which all the fixtures, fittings, furnishings, and art objects were designed to create a unified and livable environment. The idea of the Gesamtkunstwerk first gained traction in elite aesthetic reform circles in the last decade of the nineteenth century, particularly among admirers of the British Arts and Crafts movement and supporters of the many variants of Art Nouveau (including the *Jugendstil*, as featured in the Lehrerinnenheim dining hall). However, artists, designers, and manufacturers soon began to promote the notion of a carefully planned and unified living environment to the middle classes—such as Richard Riemerschmid's suites of factory produced furniture and fittings discussed in Chapter 1—even as the creation of these modest versions remained very much out of the reach of the working classes. Thus, it matters that the photograph of the dining room of the Lehrerinnenheim shows it to be a Jugendstil-inflected Gesamtkunstwerk, a space in keeping with current design trends and easily imagined full of residents, while the gathering hall of the Arbeiterinnenheim was photographed *entirely* bare of furnishings and decoration, emphasizing not its livability but its vastness. In this case, decoration, or the lack thereof, was a clear marker of class difference.

Nevertheless, while highly decorated in comparison with the Mannheim-Walddorf building, the Lehrerinnenheim in Pankow was not overly grand in comparison with some contemporary Berlin rental buildings serving the middle classes, complete with marble-floored entrance halls. This was a grandeur that Anna Schmidt, the author of an article in the *Mitteilungen des Rheinischen Vereins für Kleinwohnungswesen*, found unfitting. Instead, she advocated that the Lehrerinnenheim's "light, friendly, joyfully colored, and practical" entry hall serve as a model not only for other Ledigenheime but also for apartment buildings in general.[90]

The amount of privacy provided to residents also stood as a marker of difference between women from bourgeois backgrounds and residents largely drawn from the working class and lower middle class. Like Ledigenheime for less well-situated women, Ledigenheime for middle-class women generally contained both a central kitchen, where the majority of food was prepared by hired cooks and consumed in the in-house dining room, and small stoves or hotplates where individuals could cook small meals and brew tea or coffee.[91]

However, the application and form of these small kitchens differed depending upon whether the Ledigenheime in question was constructed for skilled working-class and lower-middle-class women, or for professionally employed middle-class women. For example, the Lehrerinnenheim in Pankow contained fifty one- to three-room residences, each with a private kitchen measuring 2.25 by 4 meters,[92] while Alt Moabit only provided a small semiprivate kitchen to be shared by the residents of each floor (Figure 4.15, compare to Figure 4.11). Even if employed for the same reason as the teaching kitchen and semiprivate kitchens of Alt Moabit—the continued domestication or re-domestication of the residents—the level of privacy provided to the residents of the Lehrerinnenheim, even in something as minor as the preparation of food, can be read as an expectation of daughters born of the middle class (even if their wages did not place them within the class into which they had been born).

The parlor was yet another marker of difference between middle-class female residents and lower-middle-class women (as well as between them and male Ledigenheim residents). Parlors or sitting rooms attached to private bedrooms never appeared in Ledigenheime for men, and never in those for lower-middle-class and working-class women, for whom communal rooms were evidently considered sufficient. The separate parlor was a clear marker of class that indicated the resident's respectability and upbringing, her acknowledgment of the middle-class cult of domesticity centered upon the parlor.[93] By contrast, undifferentiated space was seen as both dangerous and chaotic, associated with the overcrowded dwellings of the working classes, places where one or two rooms sufficed for all activities, and unappealingly not domestic.

Clearly reflecting the conventions regulating the layout of the bourgeois family home, with spaces for entertaining friends and acquaintances, and spaces where

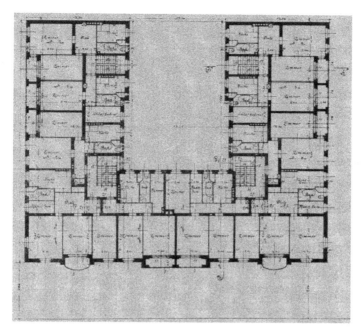

Figure 4.15 Lehrerinnenheim, Berlin-Pankow (1909). Plan of upper floors, and detail of a suite with a sleeping niche (Schlafkabinet), which also included a hall (Diele), living room (Zimmer), bathroom (Bad), and kitchen (Küche).
Source: Anna Schmidt, "Die Wohnungsfrage im Leben der Lehrerin und ihre Lösung" *Mitteilungen des Rheinischen Vereins für Kleinwohnungswesen* 8, no. 5 (May 1912): 47.

one rested and sought solitude, the Pankow Lehrerinnenheim provided forty-three of its forty-five residents with suites that not only contained a bedroom but also the aforementioned parlor and small kitchen, as well as a hall and bathroom (see Figure 4.15).[94] *All* of the suites included modern conveniences in regard to sanitation; each kitchen had its own window for ample light and air, as well as a cupboard, a built-in coal oven and two-burner gas cooker; bathrooms were equipped with a zinc bathtub and hot and cold faucets for running water; a loggia or balcony provided additional access to fresh air.[95] Yet, as in the typical bourgeois home, the overall number and type of differentiated spaces within each suite indicated fine distinctions between the social and economic status of the residents. Indicating a higher level of privilege among the body of residents, twelve of the forty-five suites included an extra room in addition to the requisite bedroom, parlor, hall, bathroom, and kitchen. Most significantly, this "extra" room was reserved for a servant, even though the majority of the residents' needs were taken care of communally, and it is highly unlikely that any of the residents could afford a servant. A room for a servant (*a Mädchenzimmer*) was superfluous—except as a symbol.[96]

As the residents were absolved from most—if not all—housekeeping drudgery, and there was ample space to pursue one's recreational activities in the elegantly appointed reading and writing rooms of the Lehrerinnenheim,[97] the inclusion of the individual parlor (and in twelve cases, the "servant's" room) betrays an interest in retaining socially significant spaces as an advertisement of the social standing of one's girlhood, even if only for purposes of making the residents feel nostalgically "at home." It allowed residents to perform the role they ought to have been playing, one that—considering that these homes were less transitional than homes for less-affluent and less-educated women—they would likely never fulfill in a traditional manner. The ladylike (nonproductive) activities that were facilitated by these spaces allowed residents to perform their middle-class identity, even as they were also used for professional activities like grading students' work. A resident might not be overseeing the cooking of an elaborate meal, but like her married middle-class peers, she could read a novel or work on her embroidery in peace and quiet. More importantly perhaps, a private parlor enabled the entertaining of friends in a space the resident had decorated to her taste.[98]

Unlike Ledigenheime serving women of lower socioeconomic status, here were no worries that the residents might squander their earnings on decorative trinkets or tasteless furniture. The decoration of a resident's parlor was explicitly cast as a positive, just as the personalization of a lower-middle-class male resident's bedroom had been. After all, these female residents had been trained in how best to decorate a room and care for these objects by their bourgeois mothers or, at the very least, by the domestic manuals that proliferated in the nineteenth and early twentieth century. The average resident and her mother would have been well educated by such manuals, with a typical German domestic manual dating to 1861 containing thirty-nine chapters, including subsections such as "Care of a Tablecloth" and "Remarks on Choosing Fabric/Material."[99] In fact, it does not appear that anyone had any concerns about the real or potential consumerism of the residents, as had plagued the supporters of the Alt Moabit building; private storage space in the basement and attic was provided to residents, enabling them to accumulate the trappings of middle-class domesticity without fear of an overstuffed and cluttered apartment.[100]

Yet, the separate small parlor or sitting room was not merely a socioeconomic marker associated with the female domain; it was also a way to defend the residents against charges of immorality. Contemporary discourse surrounding single women, and single professional women in particular, often associated single status with sexual deviance.[101] The entertaining of friends and associates in one's bedroom, a necessity if one could only afford a single room, opened the door to such charges.[102] The parlor not only signified one's connection to bourgeois convention but as the space where public and private realms met in carefully controlled way, it also provided a space for private entertaining that was not associated with bodily functions or sexuality in a way that the bedroom was. Even when the interests of space would have been better served by a single room with a daybed, the designers of the Pankow Lehrerinneheim included a two-by-four meter *Schlafkabinet* (sleeping cabinet) that served as a separate bedroom space.[103] The division of a small space into a parlor and a bedroom was means to manage sexual angst.

This interest in maintaining the *appearance* of propriety was perhaps even more pressing considering how private access to a resident's suite actually was. Instead of fronting long corridors like Ledigenheime for men or lower-class women, which could be readily monitored by a housekeeper or nosy fellow residents, the apartments of the Lehrerinnenheim were situated around semiprivate stairwells in groupings of three or four on each floor (see Figure 4.15). Why construct a system of access that not only provided less opportunity for monitoring or oversight but also was far more expensive than building one or two stairwells? Privacy, autonomy, and precedent provide the answer. Many dwellings in large Berlin apartment houses were accessed from semiprivate stairwells, and the "well system," where only two doors and a stairwell stood between the public and private realms, was similarly used in Oxbridge dormitories for men in order to provide the residents with greater autonomy (though less apt here, it was also intended to forestall horseplay in dormitory corridors).[104] While Paul Mebes, designing the Lehrerinnenheim in concert with its future residents, may not have been familiar with Oxbridge dormitories, he was certainly familiar with Berlin apartment buildings. It made sense to refer to an established type associated with domestic life if a Ledigenheim was a "home," rather than an institution.

However, it would be a mistake to conclude that all Ledigenheime for middle-class women provided the residents with private parlors (or such private entrances). The municipal Weissensee Ledigenheim, located in a northeastern suburb of Berlin, did not provide residents with private sitting rooms, and as such it was clearly expected that residents were solely to use the communal spaces. Yet, the Weissensee Ledigenheim was an outlier, rather than the rule, for as discussed in Chapter 3, it housed both men and women, albeit in different sections of the building. Most Ledigenheime for bourgeois women struck a careful balance. In providing the single woman with a space facilitating an independent and public life, providing community without the cloister, and functioning as an advertisement for her very existence, such buildings can be seen as places of liberation. Yet, the appearance of propriety had to be maintained through the reintroduction of gender-specific spaces and associated practices. The importance of the parlor, contextualizing the Ledigenheim as a private home, and simultaneously coupled with semipublic spaces—from public kitchens to libraries—cannot be overstated; these spaces illustrate the balance between tradition and progressive, even radical, change in the lives of Ledigenheim residents and the single professional women who followed in their footsteps. It is toward radical change that we now turn.

Links to Radicalism

Despite the maintenance of class distinctions between single women working outside of the home, as well as measured and logical explanations regarding both the need for Ledigenheime for women and the ways these institutions ought to be organized, an underlying radical—even revolutionary—edge can be discerned. While Ledigenheime were never constructed to offer *direct* support for nascent feminist advances, and certainly not radical feminism, the emancipatory potential was there. Ledigenheime emerged contemporaneously not only with municipal housekeeping, which sent women out into the world as ersatz "mothers," but also with growing calls for a reorganization of the familial household to free women (and married women with children in particular) from the drudgery of housework, thus enabling them to pursue a more public life.

According to leading political and social radicals August Bebel, Peter Kropotkin, and Lily Braun, reformed housekeeping was "one of the foundations of (women's) liberation."[105] It was possibly even a means to the dissolution of the nuclear family, which leftist thinkers positioned as intrinsically tied to capitalism and the ultimate seat of reaction, a concern picked up in the conclusion to this work. In her writings, informed by Bebel's *Woman under Socialism*, the Social Democrat and feminist Lily Braun quoted the anarchist Kropotkin, who wrote that to "liberate women means not only to open the doors to the university, the court of law, and parliament for them; rather it means to free them from the cooking stove and washtub, it means creating institutions that will permit them to . . . participate in public life."[106] Braun in particular chafed at the difficulty most women in fulltime employment faced in balancing professional work with the running of a household, writing that "a painter cannot spend her time in the kitchen, a writer cannot jump up every moment to see whether the soup is boiling over."[107] She came to advocate for an architectural building type that could potentially mitigate the double burden many women shouldered, the housing cooperative or "kitchen-less home" (in German, the *Einküchenhaus*). In 1901 Braun described a housing cooperative as

> A housing complex enclosing a large and prettily laid out garden of about fifty or sixty apartments, none of which contains a kitchen. There is only a small gas cooker in a little room . . . there is a central kitchen on the ground floor which is equipped with all kinds of modern labor-saving devices . . . the management of the entire household is in the hands of an experienced housekeeper . . . meals are either taken in the common dining room or carried to all the floors . . .heat is provided to the apartments by a central heating system.[108]

In many ways, Ledigenheime for women were remarkably similar to Braun's housing cooperative. A brief comparison of Braun's specifications with the layout and spaces of the Alt Moabit Ledigenheim serves to illustrate the close relationship between the two structures—one imaginary and one real— from the central courtyard garden to the number of rooms/apartments, the provision of central heat, the centrally located kitchen and dining hall, and even the housekeeper-cum-directress, all of which were intended to free the residents from household drudgery. The only significant difference is that the residents of the housing cooperative would be able to use the kitchen for the preparation of meals, aiding and supporting one another, thus saving time and energy, whereas in Alt Moabit the women did not cook the main meals themselves. They were only allowed in the training kitchen or, alternately, could use the small cookers on each floor. Nevertheless, the cooperative bears far more similarity to Ledigenheime for women than those for men, which took the preparation of food entirely out of the hands of the residents.

In fact, *all* Ledigenheime constructed for lower-middle-class and middle-class women contained a central kitchen, where professional cooks prepared meals for consumption in the in-house dining room, as well as small stoves or hotplates—either on a resident's hall or in her suite—where she could cook small meals or prepare snacks after hours.[109] Although Ledigenheime did not entirely free residents from the kitchen (if a small stove or hot plate counts as a kitchen), the shifting of a gender-specific burden such as cooking every meal from scratch (with a stove that needed continual tending) to the simple act of turning a dial to boil water for a cup of tea can hardly be discounted. The provision of the majority of her meals severed some of the traditional ties a woman had to her place of residence and freed her to pursue her profession, as well as leisure activities. This is particularly important when one considers that while housekeeping would have been a burden for a single woman of any social class, it would have felt particularly onerous to a woman from a bourgeois background. The middle-class residents of Ledigenheime could not afford to employ the cooks and maids they would have grown accustomed to in their girlhoods (despite the retention of spaces indicated for personal servants in the Lehrerinnenheim). Outside of a Ledigenheim these single women of middle-class origins would have been solely responsible for bearing the burden of cooking and housework, labor that lower-class women were certainly familiar with (though this hardly made it easier), and that their male counterparts would never stoop to undertake.[110]

While Lily Braun saw the housing cooperative as highly applicable to married women, and educated middle-class married women like herself in particular, rather than focusing on its usefulness for German working-class and/or single women in employment, she would have known of the existence of Ledigenheime for single working women. Whether she possibly considered these homes to be precedents for her own proposals, at least in that they lightened the burden of housekeeping for working women, she left unsaid. She was certainly cognizant of reformed housing serving single women *abroad*, citing English houses "in which single working women live and get fed in common" as evidence that her proposal for housing cooperatives was feasible.[111]

In fact, the idea of the household cooperative was popular in feminist circles on both sides of the Atlantic, and although—as with Braun—the focus *largely* remained on the role communal kitchens and cooperative housekeeping could play in the lives of middle-class housewives, their supporters were not blind to the possibilities such alternative living situations could bring single women. As early as 1868 in the United States, advocates posited that not only would such institutions solve the "servant problem," they would also enable "intelligent and ambitious young women of moderate means" to reenter the wider world as neither consumers nor servants, freeing them from being "burdens to society."[112] This view was seconded by British supporters, such as Walter Lionel George, who stated that "there is no reason why we should not eat in common as do millions every day in hotels, boarding houses, restaurants and cafes,"[113] and feminists like Clementina Black, who stressed that "a servant-less existence" would not only aid in quelling labor unrest[114] but also allow single and married women to enjoy social interaction on a regular basis.[115] American feminist and reformer

Charlotte Perkins Gilman, best known as the author of the semiautobiographical work, *The Yellow Wallpaper* (1892), also wrote extensively on the applicability of the household cooperative and kitchen-less house for both married and single women, and chose both fictional and nonfictional means to illustrate its potential.[116] Gilman claimed that her prescriptions would result in the following benefits for those who partook in such experiments: economic savings, increased health and efficiency, the ennobling of household work and workers (who would be paid a wage), decreased waste via group surveillance, and, most of all, freedom for women to work for wages outside of the home. Like Braun, Gilman saw the latter as central to women's physical and mental health—the primary means to women's liberation from nonvoluntary, alienating, and unspecialized domestic labor, as well as economic dependence on a man (through marriage or the family of her birth).

Yet, even as Braun, Gilman, and others leveraged maternalist discourse—relying on familiar tropes that situated domestic reform as naturally suited to women—and employed the (male) language of business and technology to position the household cooperative and kitchen-less house as rationalized, professionalized, and modern, such an expansion of the household from the private to the semipublic realm never gained the traction they hoped for. The cult of domesticity, which invested the private home with moral qualities and the labor done within its walls as an extension of a woman's love for her family, precluded *most* married women from joining a household cooperative. Yet, without such an intervention, freeing women from the majority of housework was not feasible or, at the very least, was extremely difficult to achieve for an *individual* household of modest means.

However, freeing women from the majority of housework was the central component of a Ledigenheim, where—provided other markers of domesticity remained—the removal of the private kitchen and the mitigation of household drudgery was largely accepted and taken as a rational solution to a pressing problem, rather than an attack on tradition and morality. This comparison indicates that reformed housing, in combination with professional work, was one of the most important elements in the relation of single women to the public sphere. Thus, the arrangement of space related to the preparation of food in Ledigenheime for skilled working-class, lower-middle-class, and middle-class women was not as conventional as it may appear, *even including* domestic markers such as the parlor, kitchenette, and teaching kitchen. Simply by enabling women to live "on their own" in a setting that was a combination of the public and private realms, but without the requirements of running a typical household, directing servants, or laboring herself, Ledigenheime were more progressive socially—even radical—than many of their (generally progressive) supporters believed.

Conclusion

Although the supporters of Ledigenheime for women generally construed them as nothing more than an economic and hygienic necessity, they formed an important basis for the transformation of German society. Significantly, the relative openness of female Ledigenheim residents' lives, an openness that the building type was instrumental in facilitating, stands in sharp contrast to the way in which nineteenth- and early twentieth-century women's interactions with the city have traditionally been considered by scholars, as well as by their contemporaries. Men were traditionally actors on the stage of the city, participants in civic life and masters of their fate, while women, particularly middle- or lower-middle-class women, were excluded from such interactions and encouraged to focus on domestic concerns, with the notable exception of municipal housekeeping (which was the domestic writ large). A respectable woman's natural state was that of marriage, her proper place was thought to be the home, and she was to have no ambition, nor profession. Of course, the fact that single women were supportive of, and integral to, the creation of Ledigenheime serving their own social and professional interests, as well as the interests of the surrounding community, belies such an assumption. In addition, the semipublic spaces of Ledigenheime, socially acceptable for women residents to visit, as well as easily accessible to all, indicate the growing parity between men and women in Wilhelmine Germany, despite other discrepancies.[117]

In short, these homes allowed women to take part in the larger world and the economic life of their country as never before and freed them from the familial home or specter of an unhappy marriage of convenience. Both agents of change and a reflection of mass societal changes, they not only facilitated the creation of communities of working women—places where single women could both form and confirm their new identities as public beings with fellow residents—but also functioned as a helpmeet, an ersatz servant or wife. In freeing residents from most domestic labor, a Ledigenheim maximized their time and energy. The building of Ledigenheime was a step toward making single working women happier, healthier, and fuller participants in the public and economic life of Wilhelmine Germany.

Yet, while serving as a platform for the emergence of the next generation of single women, the "liberated women" who left such a mark on Weimar Germany and have been written about extensively, the Ledigenheim disappeared as an architectural program during the course of the 1920s. As will be discussed in detail in the Conclusion to this work, more normative models prevailed, with the noted architect, communist, feminist (and designer of the famed Frankfurt kitchen) Grete Schütte-Lihotzky opposing "cooping women up together in a home," in favor of *Einliegerwohnungen*, or separate self-contained flats for single people located on the top floor of a block of flats for families.[118] Even an individual as astute as Schüttte-Lihotsky—herself a single professional woman for much of the 1920s—seems to have conflated the Ledigenheim with the hated *Stiftung*, forgetting (perhaps purposefully, considering their prewar bourgeois origins) the fuller lives facilitated by Ledigenheime, even the radical emancipatory potential these buildings once held. Ledigenheime for women anticipated the emergence of the much lauded and decried "new woman" of the 1920s, who was, ironically, less well housed.

Notes

1 Bärbel Kuhn, *Familienstand ledig: Ehelose Frauen und Männer im Bürgertum, 1850–1914* (Cologne: Böhlau, 2002), 39.

2 Peter Stallybrass and Allon White, *The Politics and Poetics of Transgression* (Ithaca: Cornell University Press, 1986), 5–6; quoted in Judith R. Walkowitz, *City of Dreadful Delight* (Chicago: University of Chicago Press, 1992), 20.

3 Regarding the American "woman adrift," see Daphne Spain, *How Women Saved the City* (Minneapolis: University of Minnesota Press, 2001), 43.

4 Regarding the "surplus woman" in German society, see Catherine Leota Dollard, *The Surplus Woman: Unmarried in Imperial Germany* (New York: Berghahn Books, 2009).

Concerning the disappearance of maiden aunts and unmarried daughters from middle-class American households, see Ruth Schwartz Cowen, "The 'Industrial Revolution' in the Home: Household Technology and Social Change in the 20th Century," *Technology and Culture* 17, no. 1 (Jan. 1976): 10–13.

5 Dollard, 123, 149.

6 Dollard, 166.

7 Karen Honeycut, "Clara Zetkin: A Socialist Approach to the Problem of Women's Oppression," in *European Women on the Left*, ed. Jane Slaughter and Robert Kern (Westport, CT: Greenwood Press, 1981), 38.
8 Bonnie Anderson and Judith P. Zinsser, *A History of their Own: Women in Europe*, vol. 2 (New York: Harper and Row, 1988), 159.
9 "die Frauenfrage," in *Brockhaus' Konversations-Lexikon* 14th edition, VII (Leipzig: Brockhaus, 1898), 235.
10 Wilhelmine Mohr, "Ledigenheime für Frauen," *Die Hilfe* 17, no. 47 (1911): 742.
11 Adams, 12.
12 Adams, 12.
13 Mohr, "Ledigenheime für Frauen," 741.
14 *Schlafstellenwesen und Ledigenheime: Vorbericht und Verhandlungen der 13. Konferenz der Zentralstelle für Arbeiter-Wohlfahrtseinrichtungen am 9. Und 10. Mai in Leipzig* (Schriften der Zentralstelle für Arbeiter-Wohlfahrtseinrichtungen 26 (Berlin: Carl Henmanns Verlag, 1904), 188.
15 August Bebel, *Woman and Socialism* (New York: Shocken, 1904), 174.
16 Klara Trost, *Ledigen-Heime für weibliche Erwerbstätige: Eine Forderung aus d. Kriegswirtschaft mit Grundrißbeispielen* (Hannover: Deutsche Bauhütte, 1918), 7.
17 Trost, 7; *Der Arbeiterfreund* (1909): 59, 77.
18 Minna Wettstein-Adelt, *3 ½ Months as a Female Factory Worker* (o.O., 1893), 62; quoted in Hans J. Teuteberg and Clemens Wischermann, *Wohnalltag in Deutschland, 1850–1914* (Münster: F. Coppenrath, 1985), 320–1.
19 Trost, 7; Mäthe Schivmachev, "Wie Wohnt die erwerbende Frau?" *Blätter für Volksgesundheitspflege* 11, no. 10 (1911): 230.
20 *Soziale Praxis* 12 (1903): 994.
21 These clubs only rarely included bedrooms (Despina Stratigakos, *A Woman's Berlin: Building the Modern City* [Minneapolis: University of Minnesota Press, 2008], 151).
22 *Soziale Praxis* 12 (1903): 994.
23 Schivmachev, 232; Käthe Schirmacher, "The Modern Woman's Rights Movement in Germany," (1912) in Magda Müller and Patricia A. Herminghouse, eds. *German Feminist Writings* (New York: Continuum, 2001), 136.
24 Roger Fletcher, ed., *Bernstein to Brandt: A Short History of German Social Democracy* (London: Edward Arnold, 1987), 134.
25 Mohr, "Ledigenheime für Frauen," 741.
26 Fanny Lewald, "Ninth Easter Letter for Women: Shelters for Working-Class Women," (1863) in *German Feminist Writings*, ed. Magda Mueller and Patricia A. Herminghouse (New York: Continuum, 2001), 79.
27 Stratigakos, 81.
28 Schivmachev, 230.

29 Lewald, 79.
30 Schivmachev, 230; *Der Arbeiterfreund* (1909): 77.
31 Mohr, "Ledigenheime für Frauen," 740.
32 Schivmachev, 235.
33 Mohr, "Ledigenheime für Frauen," 740.
34 E. G., "Frauen-Rundschau" *Schweizerische Lehrerinnenzietung* 11, no. 5 (1906-7).
35 Mohr, "Ledigenheime für Frauen," 742.
36 *Schlafstellenwesen und Ledigenheime*, 178-9.
37 *Schlafstellenwesen und Ledigenheime*, 178.
38 *Schlafstellenwesen und Ledigenheime*, 178-9.
39 Irene Stoehr, "Housework and Motherhood: Debates and Policies in the Women's Movement in Imperial Germany and the Weimar Republic," in *Maternity and Gender Policies*, ed. Gisela Bock and Pat Thane (London: Routledge, 1991), 222.
40 Stoehr, 222. On this phenomenon in the United States, see Marta Gutman, *A City for Children: Women, Architecture, and the Charitable Landscapes of Oakland, 1850-1950* (Chicago: University of Chicago Press, 2014) and Spain, *How Women Saved the City*. For the British context, see Martha Vicinus, *Independent Women: Work and Community for Single Women, 1850-1920* (Chicago: University of Chicago Press, 1985).
41 Käthe Schirmacher, "The Modern Women's Rights Movement in Germany," (1912) in *German Feminist Writings*, ed. Magda Mueller and Patricia A. Herminghouse (New York: Continuum, 2001), 133.
42 Martha Hoppe, "Heime für Textilarbeiterinnen," *Die Gleichheit* 20 (July 5, 1909): 308. The more damning charge here was that these homes were "in the interests of the capitalists," not residents.
43 Mohr, "Ledigenheime für Frauen," 743.
44 Mohr, "Ledigenheime für Frauen," 742.
45 Margaret Birney Vickery, *Buildings for Bluestockings: The Architecture and Social History of Women's Colleges in Late Victorian England* (Newark: University of Delaware Press, 1999), 6. See also Helen Lefkowitz Horowitz, *Alma Mater: Design and Experience in the Women's Colleges from Their Nineteenth Century Beginnings to the 1930s* (Amherst, MA: University of Massachusetts Press, 1993), 17, 37.
46 Mohr, *Die Hilfe*, 742.
47 Klara Trost, *Ledigen-Heime für weibliche Erwerbstätige; Eine Forderung aus d. Kriegswirtschaft mit Grundrißbeispielen* (Hannover: Deutsche Bauhütte, 1918), 9.
48 *Schlafstellenwesen und Ledigenheime*, 188.
49 Schivmachev, 230.
50 The housing of female domestic servants will also remain unaddressed, as women in domestic service generally lived with the families they served.
51 *Schlafstellenwesen und Ledigenheime*, 73-4.
52 Hoppe, 308.

53 Trost, 6.
54 *Schlafstellenwesen und Ledigenheime*, 86–94.
55 These rooms cost 2 marks per week for a double and 1 mark for a triple or quad (*Schlafstellenwesen und Ledigenheime*, 73–4).
56 *Deutsche Vierteljahrschrift für öffentliche Gesundheitspflege* 10 (1878): 260.
57 Vickery, xii.
58 Lefkowitz Horowitz, *Alma Mater*, 39; Vickery, 14.
59 Lefkowitz Horowitz, 32–3, 42; Vickery, 6, 43.
60 *Zeitschrift für Wohnungswesen* 2 (1905): 28–30.
61 Vickery, 54, 48.
62 *Die Architektur des XX Jahrhunderts* (1909): 42.
63 Dollard, 32.
64 Mathilde Kirschner, "Das neuerbaute Arbeiterinnenheim in Berlin," *Westermanns Monatsheft: Illustrierte Deutsche Zeitschrift fuer das Geistige Leben der Gegenwart* 54, no. 107 (October–December 1909): 392.
65 Kirschner, 392.
66 Spain, 25–43.
67 Kirschner, 392.
68 Susan R. Henderson, *Building Culture: Ernst May and the New Frankfurt Initiative, 1926–1931* (New York: Peter Lang, 2013), 149.
69 Susan R. Henderson, "A Revolution in the Woman's Sphere: Grete Lihotzky and the Frankfurt Kitchen," in *Architecture and Feminism*, ed. Debra Coleman, Elizabeth Danze, and Carol Henderson (New York: Princeton Architectural Press, 1996), 221–53; and Sophie Hochhäusl, "From Vienna to Frankfurt Inside Core-House Type 7: A History of Scarcity through the Modern Kitchen," *Architectural Histories* 1, no. 1 (October 2013): Art. 24.
70 Kirschner, 393.
71 *Die Architektur des XX Jahrhunderts* (1909): 43. Each upper floor contained three WCs and a single bathtub (in separate rooms).
72 Kirschner, 391.
73 Kirschner, 391. This room measured 4.75 by 3.9 meters.
74 Kirschner, 392.
75 Mohr, *Die Hilfe*, 742.
76 Kirschner, 391.
77 Trost, 10. This language is similar to that of YWCA boosters in the United States, who included "attractions for the pleasure loving girl" (Spain, 91).
78 Kirschner, 392.
79 Jennifer Jenkins, "The Kitsch Collections and the Spirit in the Furniture: Cultural Reform and National Culture in Germany," *Social History* 21, no. 2 (1996): 137. See also: Andreas Huyssen, "Mass Culture as Woman: Modernism's Other," in *After the Great Divide: Modernism, Mass Culture, Postmodernism* (Bloomington, 1986).

80 Many thanks to Abigail Van Slyck for helping me sharpen my thinking around the ideology of separate spheres.
81 Schirmacher, 134.
82 Anna Schmidt, "Die Wohnungsfrage im Leben der Lehrerin und ihre Lösung," *Mitteilungen des Rheinischen Vereins für Kleinwohnungswesen* 8, no. 5 (May 1912): 47; *Wasmuths* (1915/16): 113–42.
83 The women who built the Lyceum Club in Berlin were some of the most prominent figures in Wilhelmine Germany (male or female). Stratigakos, 17–52.
84 P. Heyer, "Lehrerinnenheim," *Monatsblatt für Berliner Lehrerinnen* 6, no. 1 (1910): 13; "Die Einweihung des Lehrerinnenheims," *Monatsblatt für Berliner Lehrerinnen* 6, no. 11 (1911): 216.
85 Spain, 139.
86 Otto von Leixner, *Soziale Briefe aus Berlin* (Berlin: Friedrich Pfeilstücker, 1891), 124.
87 Klara Trost, 9.
88 "Mädchenheim in Mannheim Walddorf," *Baugewerkszeitung* 39 (1907): 554.
89 "Mädchenheim in Mannheim Walddorf," *Baugewerkszeitung* 39 (1907): 554.
90 Schmidt, 47.
91 Of course, there were exceptions to this, such as the Ulm Ledigenheim for women (*Zeitschrift für Wohnungswesen* 2 [1905]: 31), and the Linden Arbeiterinnenheim (1910) (*Baugewerks-Zeitung* 43, no. 56 [July 15, 1911]: 396).
92 Schmidt, 47.
93 Lawrence Taylor has written of the nineteenth-century fixation on the "cult of domesticity and the belief in the power of rooms to produce and reproduce middle-class civility" ("Re-Entering the West Room: On the Power of Domestic Spaces," in *House Life: Space, Place and Family in Europe*, ed. Donna Birdwell-Pheasant and Denise Lawrence-Zuniga [New York: Berg, 1999], 228).
94 Schmidt, 48. Two of the "suites" contained a single room with attached kitchen, hall, and bathroom, while thirty-one contained two rooms, and twelve contained three rooms.
95 Schmidt, 47.
96 Schmidt, 48.
97 Schmidt, 48.
98 As Margaret Vickery reports on the life of female students at Girton College, Cambridge, private parlors allowed the resident to "enjoy for the first time the delights of hospitality in her very own domain . . . first opportunity of exercising her own taste" (36–7).
99 Anderson and Zinsser, 137.
100 Schmidt, 47.
101 As Judith Walkowitz has argued, concern over dangerous sexualities in the late nineteenth and early twentieth century had more to do with nonnormative

gendered behaviors, "work, lifestyle, self-display, non-familial attachments," than actual sexual activity (Walkowitz, 6).
102 Dollard, 59.
103 Schmidt, 48.
104 Vickery, 14.
105 Lily Braun, "Women's Work and Housekeeping," (1901) in *German Feminist Writings*, ed. Magda Müller and Patricia A. Herminghouse (New York: Continuum, 2001), 93.
106 Braun, 93.
107 Lily Braun, *Selected Writings on Feminism and Socialism: Lily Braun*, ed. and trans. Alfred Meyer (Bloomington, Indiana: Indiana University Press, 1987), 12.
108 Braun, "Women's Work and Housekeeping," 90.
109 Kirschner, 391.
110 The advocates of Ledigenheime for men only supported the construction of central kitchens and not additional small kitchenettes, rendering cooking done by male residents impossible. Similarly, female residents darned their own socks and mended their own clothing, unlike their male counterparts, who made use of on-site tailors (*Schlafstellenwesen und Ledigenheime*, 140; Hoppe, 308).
111 Braun, "Women's Work and Housekeeping," 91.
112 "Cooperative Housekeeping," *The Atlantic Monthly* 22, no. 133 (November 1868): 520.
113 Walter Lionel George, "The Home," in *Woman and Tomorrow* (London: H. Jenkins, 1913), 85.
114 Clementina Black, *A New Way of Housekeeping* (London: W. Collins Sons and Co. Ltd, 1890), 24. Servant-less here merely means that private households would not employ live-in help. Instead, cooks and maids would serve numerous families or individuals, enjoy regular hours, and be paid by the hour.
115 Black, 53.
116 Charlotte Perkins Gilman's nonfiction works include *Women and Economics* (1898); *The Home: Its Work and Influence* (1903); "The Passing of the Home in Great American Cities," *The Cosmopolitan* (December 1904): 137–47. Fictional works are not limited to, but include *What Diantha Did* (1909–10) and *Herland* (1915). For more on this phenomenon in the United States and its ties to feminism, particularly regarding Melusina Fay Pierce, Marie Stevens Howland, and Alice Constance Austin, see Dolores Hayden, *The Grand Domestic Revolution* (Cambridge: MIT Press, 1981) and "Two Utopian Feminists and Their Campaigns for Kitchenless Houses," *Signs* 4, no. 2 (Winter 1978): 274–90.
117 Sally Booth cites the fact that in places where "socially valued space (was) accessible to both men and women, there tend(s) to be more parity between the sexes" ("Reconstructing Sexual Geography," in *House Life: Space, Place and Family in Europe*, ed. Donna Birdwell-Pheasant and Denise Lawrence-Zuniga [New York: Berg, 1999], 140).
118 Henderson, *Building Culture*, 364–5.

Conclusion

Weimar Twilight and Continued Relevance

In summer 1920, the remaining residents of the Kaiser Wilhelm Ledigenheim published a circular begging former residents and community members to oppose the impending sale of their home to the city of Essen, which intended to convert the Ledigenheim on the Weberplatz into municipal office space. Their last ditch effort was for naught, and on August 15, 1920, the city purchased the Ledigenheim and everything in it—from kitchen equipment to beds. The residents of the Kaiser Wilhelm Ledigenheim mounted legal proceedings against the *Stadtverwaltung* of Essen in the fall of 1920, claiming that they had been told that only the first and second floors would be converted and begging to stay in the remaining rooms on the third and fourth floor, at least through the winter. At the same time, their brethren in Benrath, Frankfurt, and Berlin were facing similar fates.[1] By 1922, rising rents, cuts to utilities, and increasing unemployment among Ledigenheim residents from Hamburg to Danzig meant that the fate of most remaining homes hung in the balance.[2] What would have once been unimaginable was now a reality.

The Weberplatz Ledigenheim and many like it had been dramatically reconfigured during the First World War to meet the needs of the war economy. Social rooms and halls had been subdivided and filled with beds for munitions workers, while the two dining halls of the Weberplatz building served over 100,000 lunches and 65,000 dinners between November 1, 1914, and October 15, 1915. In spite of the usefulness of such buildings during the war, the German Empire's defeat in 1918, exacerbated by the loss or occupation of territories that had long been engines of economic growth, precipitated a profound economic collapse and total reordering of the social order.[3] Once again, single people were on the periphery. Like so many prewar initiatives in Germany and elsewhere—settlement houses, the YMCA, Volkshäuser—that either died out or continued through the interwar period with greatly transformed programming, the Ledigenheim was the residue of a vanished world.

Yet, the decline of this building type was not necessarily a foregone conclusion. Mass demobilization, growing unemployment, and a society that felt unrecognizable—buttressed by new laws guaranteeing *every* citizen the right to a sound dwelling—provided a context within which the needs of single people *could* have been carefully addressed. Proponents of Ledigenheime could have harnessed these new incentives to build upon an existing typology, just as the designers of German *Siedlungen* in the 1920s had, situating the Ledigenheim as a central component in the reimagination of both German housing and society.[4]

In fact, in specific locales and for a brief moment in time, it seemed as though this was precisely what would happen. Bruno Taut's Ledigenheim in the Lindenhof Siedlung (1919), as well as on the example of the Kommunalen Zentrum in Weissensee, seemed to point the way forward (see Figures 3.22a, b, c). So, too, did Theodor Fischer's Ledigenheim for men and women on Munich's Bergmannstrasse (1927), which while decidedly more spare and rectilinear on the exterior, was the stylistic and the programmatic child of Charlottenburg's Dankelmannstrasse building (Figures 5.1a, b).[5] Stylistically distinct from the former two, Hans Scharoun's Ledigenheim within the model settlement "Grüneiche," itself a component of the Werkbund's "Wohnung und Werkraum" exhibition outside of Breslau (1929), housed both singles and childless married couples (Figure 5.2). The building, while programmatically similar to prewar Ledigenheime in attempting to provide "urban nomads" a home and a role, utilized the visual language of the *Neues Bauen*.[6] The Ledigenheim, recently restored by the Polish authorities in what is now Wroclow, consists of three programmatically distinct wings pinwheeling out from a central core—all gleaming white facades, ribbon windows, and interconnected balconies mimicking the promenade of an ocean liner.

These Ledigenheime remained exceptions, however, rather than indications of a greater trend. Tellingly, the discourse surrounding them was largely restricted to architects and planners in dialogue with each other. Increased professionalization and governmentalization of reform initiatives as a whole (and housing reform specifically) meant that what had long been a strength of the Ledigenheim project—the ability of this common cause not only to bring together multiple stakeholders at different vantage points but even to pique the interest of the general public—no longer applied. More significantly, the same characteristics that had made Ledigenheime largely positive agents of change (with the exception of their industrial variants) eventually relegated the building type to obscurity. Such buildings had always contained within them the seeds of

Figure 5.1a, b Bergmannstrasse Ledigenheim, Munich (1927).
Source: Albert Gut, *Das Wohnungswesen der Stadt München* (Munich: Stadtrat München, 1928), 203 and Author's photograph.

Figure 5.2 Ledigenheim of the Werkbund Exhibition "Wohnung und Werkraum" (1929), Breslau (1929).
Source: Georg Münter, "Wohnung und Werkraum. Ein Versuch die Werkbund-Austellung in Breslau 1929 zu würdingen," *Wasmuths Monatshefte für Baukunst* 13, no. 11 (1929): 451.

their dissolution: namely, an emphasis on privacy (for those who had previously had little to none) and integration with the surrounding community.

In a leafy district on the western edge of Berlin-Charlottenburg, on the corner of Hebartstrasse and Dernburgstrasse, and overlooking a large park and enclosed pond, one can still see the former Ledigenheime for Female Postal Workers (*Ledigenheim der Postgehilfinnen*), also known as the Hedwig Rüdiger Häuser (Figure 5.3). Constructed between 1924 and 1925 by the architects Sucksdorf and Spalding, the complex of three, five-story brick buildings does not *seem* markedly different from prewar Ledigenheime for professional women. In keeping with precedents established by the Pankow Lehrerinnenheim, each resident was provided with a large sitting room opening out onto a private balcony, as well as a sleeping "niche" and cooking space (supplied with gas) connected to the sitting room—in other words, a small apartment suite.[7] Yet while earlier Ledigenheim for professional women supplemented these private rooms with semipublic and public spaces, the Hedwig Rüdiger Häuser contained no communal facilities at all—not even a dining hall or library. The only shared spaces were service spaces, such as hallways, entrances, and water closets, the latter of which were shared between just two residents.[8]

Four years later, the city of Frankfurt am Main and the Frankfurt Organization for Women's Dwellings (Frauenwohnungsverein) commissioned architect Dipl.-Ing. Bernhard Hermkes and Ferdinand Kramer to build two Ledigenheime "for women in professional employment" (*Ledigenheime für Berufstätige Frauen*) on the Adikesalle and Platenstrasse (Figure 5.4). They were visual markers of change and exemplars of Frankfurt's embrace of the *Neues Bauen* under planner

Figure 5.3 Hedwig Rüdiger Häuser, Berlin-Charlottenburg (1924–5).
Source: Author's photograph.

Figure 5.4 Adikesallee, Frankfurt am Main (1928). Garden view.
Source: Das Neue Frankfurt 4/5 (1930).

Ernst May—from their flat roofs and white (stucco covered brick) exteriors, all accented by shiny black metal trim-work, to the narrow buildings' east-west orientation, which facilitated cross breezes and even lighting.[9] The architectural journal *Bauwelt* lauded Hermkes and Kramer's efforts as both financial and aesthetic successes, the fruit of (new) rationalized planning and building methods.[10] What the *Bauwelt* article did not mention (though the *Zentralblatt* der Bauverwaltung article did) was that, while the Adikesallee building included 120 private bedrooms arranged around 43 living suites (each consisting of living room, small kitchen, and bathroom) to be shared by 2 to 4 individuals, the only fully communal space was a small theater complete with a grand piano.[11] All other planned communal elements, from a gymnasium to an electrically powered laundry, had been cut from the building budget due to unforeseen construction costs.[12] In an even greater departure from its prewar precedents, the Platenstrasse building contained *no* provisions for communal activities. The authorities had decided against including a communal kitchen and dining room because "women who worked in public all day and ate their lunches in cafeterias would make little use of collective spaces."[13] Platenstrasse residents did not even share interior hallway space with one another, as they were able to enter their residences from exterior hallways (*Laufgänge*) that ran along the entire facade of the building.[14]

Lest it seem that culling semipublic communal spaces—particularly those that had previously served to integrate the residents with the larger community—in favor of small private or semiprivate apartment units was a phenomenon that affected only the dwellings for single women, similar designs for single men began to appear in the waning years of the 1920s—Hans Schumacher and Erwin Gutkind's respective *Wohnhotels* (both unbuilt, 1929 and 1928), Franz Solomon's *Junggesellenhaus* (Berlin-Charlottenburg, 1929), Hans Scharoun's *Jungesellenhaus am Hohenzollenerdamm* (Berlin-Wilmersdorf, 1929/30), and Jakob Goettel's *Ledigenwohnungen* (Berlin-Mariendorf, Heimstatt settlement, 1929/30), among many others (Figure 5.5).[15] In Goettel's designs, each of the four buildings for single people contained eighteen self-sufficient units,

Figure 5.5 Ledigenwohnungen, Heimstatt Siedlung, Berlin-Mariendorf (1929/30). Streetview.

Source: "Ledigenwohnungen" *Der Neubau* 12, no. 6 (March 24, 1930): 103.

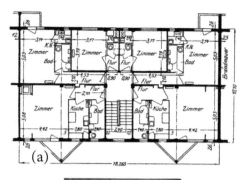

Figure 5.6a, b Ledigenwohnungen, Heimstatt Siedlung, Berlin-Mariendorf (1929/30). Apartment plans and interior view of an apartment.
Source: "Ledigenwohnungen" *Der Neubau* 12, no. 6 (March 24, 1930): 102.

complete with a combined living/sleeping room, cooking niche, entry hallway, and WC (Figures 5.6a, b). What they did not contain, despite their placement within a larger settlement housing families, were communal facilities for the use of the residents *or* the general public. There was no public kitchen, no laundry, and no bathhouse in any of the *Ledigenwohnungen*, as residents were expected to use the facilities in the nearby—and visually identical—*Zeilenbau* apartment blocks for families.[16] Similarly, Margarete Schütte-Lihotzky called for the visual and physical integration of housing for families with that of singles, using the term *Einliegerwohnung(en)* to refer to "gender neutral units" (essentially small apartments with no special services) she designed to be placed on the top floor of familial apartment blocks in Frankfurt. Ideally, this would both save costs and effect the de-marginalization of single residents.[17]

This scuttling of prewar language by Schütte-Lihotsky and Goettel (and others) was not only a means for their work to emerge from a sea of similar proposals[18] but also evidence of a need to distance their designs from prewar initiatives, not only visually but verbally. Such verbal acrobatics, when coupled with the stripping away of the communal spaces that had not only ensured the success of the building type but also supported nonnormative lifestyles, reveal an apparent discomfort with the Ledigenheim typology. Such buildings were both unacceptable holdovers from the Gründerzeit and Wilhelmine eras and a reminder of the scale of socio-architectural work remaining. As has been widely discussed, particularly in regard to interwar Germany, the Modernist interest in creating a socio-architectural tabula rasa often manifested in housing exhibiting a new visual language and in a location at a remove from the city, as well as the suppression of what largely middle-class municipal functionaries and designers deemed nonnormative family structures through the organization of public and private space. Indeed, the improvised and extended families typical of both the urban and rural laboring classes remained suspect in the Weimar era, as did the keeping of animals and other markers of agrarian society. With a few notable exceptions, Weimar-era housing developments were—in plan, if not in practice—cleansed of these indicators of disorder and backwardness. Likewise, while the lodger served as one of the *most* reviled and visible symbols of moral and social disorder before the war, Ledigenheime—or at least those recognizable as such—were an unpleasant reminder of both the old order and those individuals who continued to shirk their proper role in society.

Thus, the designs of Goettel and Schütte-Lihotzky were no longer monuments to *difference* (albeit ones intended to smooth residents' transitions into family and community life). Instead, elements originally used distinguish prewar Ledigenheim residents from *Schafgänger*—technological advancements and hygienic surroundings enabled by economies of scale, greater privacy, and the careful integration of residents with the community—had the opposite effect when taken to their extreme by Weimar-era architects. Ultimately, such modifications came at the expense of residents and the communities within which they lived.

While all prewar Ledigenheime for men *and* women (excepting industrial models) privileged privacy—in particular *Raumbeherrschung*, or the control of a space of one's own space—in an attempt to at least represent the status of a middle-class existence and to distinguish them from charitable housing initiatives and *Schlafstellen*, they never did so at the expense of internal or external community. If single rooms were not financially feasible, double or (as with Catholic homes) triple rooms were quickly substituted. Dining rooms, lecture halls, libraries, drafting rooms, club rooms, gymnasia, even bowling alleys were *never* sacrificed on the altar of cost savings. In fact, the integration of many of these communal spaces with and their use by the surrounding community were often precisely what made the construction of Ledigenheime financially feasible. Thus, "luxuries" such as single rooms and drafting halls were buttressed by multiuse spaces for multiple publics, with the cost savings incurred by these integrative services passed on to residents. Even when a Ledigenheim was placed in settlement like the Kommunalen Zentrum, community spaces outside the home (gymnasium, outdoor athletic grounds, and dining hall) were balanced by communal spaces within the home (dining hall and club room, even an employment agency) that could be used by residents of the Ledigenheim, the residents of the settlement, and even of the surrounding community of Berlin-Weissensee (see Figure 3.22a). With their use by the community ensured, the physical and visual integration of the Weissensee Ledigenheim with a larger block of familial apartments *should* not be read as similar to the integration of Goettel's *Ledigenwohnungen* nor Schütte-Lihotzky's *Einliegerwohnungen* within later settlements. The latter were so highly integrated *and* self-contained as to render their residents invisible.

The omission of precisely that which had always featured in prewar Ledigenheime—or, conversely, an emphasis on privacy and integration taken to an extreme—did not go unnoticed by contemporaries, particularly those standing outside of the architectural profession. As Susan Henderson notes, amid the fanfare surrounding the openings of the Adikesallee and Platenstrasse Ledigenheime, the Socialist newspaper *Volkstimme* gave its verdict. Not only was the Platenstrasse building unaffordable for most single working women, it did not include a reading room, a work room, or a communal kitchen—all of which they fully expected in a Ledigenheim.[19] In such Ledigenheime, as with Weimar-era settlements in general (and the private kitchen in particular), the opportunities presented by modern technology and an increasing fetishization of privacy also overrode the creation of community.[20]

For precisely whom, then, were the architects of late Weimar-era Ledigenheime designing? They claimed to be creating spaces that would serve the needs of lower-middle- and lower-class residents, but (as with many Siedlungen) these homes were often unsuited to residents' lived reality and were rarely within their financial reach. Displaying the same disingenuousness as those who decided to include a grand piano in the Adikesallee building while omitting laundry facilities, many designers apparently conflated the needs of residents (aspirational or not) with their own desires. Most telling of this mental slippage between designer and client are (among many similar designs) Walter Gropius's designs for a "Wohnhochhaus" (1931), Lily Reich's "Boardinghaus *Ledigenwohnung*" (1931), and Ludwig Mies van der Rohe's *Ledigenwohnung* (1931), which, though

Figure 5.7 Ledigenwohnung with vestibule, living room, and bath. Designed by Lily Reich for the exhibition, "Die Wohnung unserer Zeit" (Berlin, 1931).
Source: "'Die Wohnung unserer Zeit' auf der Deutschen Bauaustellung Berlin 1931," *Moderne Bauformen* 3, no. 7 (July 1931): 334.

ostensibly serving single people, were hardly targeted to former *Schlafgänger*, or even to *Zimmerherrn* (Figure 5.7). Instead, these were luxury apartments (at 68 square meters, Mies van der Rohe could have easily accommodated a family) coupled with sumptuously appointed communal spaces—elegant apartment hotels (or boarding palaces) for the 1 percent, not Ledigenheime. Despite the entreaties of noted urban planner Werner Hegemann that in 1930 "family togetherness and freedom, even the health of children, continues to be endangered by the presence of countless sub-letters and overnight lodgers . . . [a threat] even more dangerous than the war,"[21] Ledigenheime faded from the public consciousness—at least in Weimar Germany.

However, in the waning years of the 1920s, the Ledigenheim—identified with bourgeois reform and developed under a capitalist system in prewar Germany—reemerged as a means to challenge capitalism and, relatedly, traditional conceptions of family life in the east. Drawing on the ideas of Marx (filtered through Bebel and Braun), who posited the individual household as both a seat of reaction and site of misogyny, Communist thinkers and designers sought to reimagine not only traditional gender roles but the entire family unit. The bonds of family had to be loosened in order to create a highly socially conscious

Proletarian class that could undertake a distinctly Communist (or Soviet) way of life. Whereas prewar *Einküchenhäuser* sought to minimize a married woman's household labor (particularly cooking) in the interests of enabling a more public life, radical communists recast mother, father, and child as single individuals to be housed independently of one another.

As formulated by Czech Modernist and Marxist Karel Teige in his 1932 book, *The Minimum Dwelling*, the housing of the future (Communist) Czechoslovakia was an "abode purged of the family-based household: a personal sleeping cubicle for one adult individual."[22] The family dining room was to be abolished, as meals would be served and taken in a communal kitchen, and instead of relaxing in the bourgeois parlor (or its poorer imitations), Teige's ideal citizens would spend their nonworking hours in new centers of political and cultural life. Life was to be lived collectively.[23] Similarly, faced with the daunting task of remaking both Soviet citizens and their housing, and knowing that the simple miniaturization of the bourgeois household was neither desirable nor economical, El Lissitzky wrote in 1929 that the Soviet architect needed to create "a new standard of living . . . a new type of housing unit . . . not meant for unique individuals who stood in a state of conflict with one another, but for the masses."[24] Cooking would be "transposed from the individual kitchen into the communal culinary laboratory, the main meal into public eating halls" and individuals would be provided with *dwelling cells* of 6 to 7 feet square, which were to be used solely for sleeping and reading.[25] These cells would form the ideal basic unit of a new Soviet society and transform housing from a "collection of private apartments to a communal house."[26] In contrast to German architects, who increasingly designed self-contained apartments with or without collective facilities for single people, Communist architects called for including a single room buttressed by extensive collective facilities for every individual, regardless of age and marital status—a Ledigenheim for all, which they christened a housing commune, or *dom kommuna*. The most peripheral status was transformed into the most desirable, which (for a brief period) served as the cornerstone of avant-garde Soviet planning.

Of course, the architectural avant-garde in the USSR could hardly admit that the Ledigenheim was an (or even *the*) inspiration for new Soviet housing, as this would have undercut the radicalism of their entire endeavor. Communal housing based on the individual dwelling unit had to be perceived as an unmitigated and "uncontaminated" reflection of *Sovietness*, and could certainly not be linked to bourgeois housing reform efforts in Germany before the war. Both before the Bolshevik revolution and during the 1920s, however, strong intellectual ties had existed between German, Eastern European, and Russian architects and designers, including Hannes Meyer, who had worked for Krupp's housing department designing Ledigenheime among other buildings under the direction of Robert Schmohl during the First World War.[27] It is unlikely, therefore, that the Ledigenheim building type would have been entirely unknown to Soviet architects. While Meyer, who did move to the USSR following his tenure as director of the Bauhaus, remained mute on the subject of Ledigenheime, Teige provided an explicit link, not only by providing an image of a single "dwelling room" designed at the Bauhaus (under Meyer's tutelage) as a model for future dwelling cells within communal housing in Soviet Russia[28] but also by stating that he considered the prewar Ledigenheim to be an *embryonic* form of Soviet communal housing as it arose in the 1920s.[29]

Yet even after the 1928 founding of a research and design group—led by Moses Ginsburg, M. Barsch, A. Pasternak, G. Sum-Shchik, and V. Vladimirov—explicitly tasked with formulating prototype housing communes, the built reality failed to keep pace with radical proposals. Extreme housing pressures, coupled with Stalinist reaction, quickly curbed architectural experimentation so that most *dom kommuna*—including a 1929 proposal by Barsch and Vladimirov that would have housed 1,000 adults and 680 children—remained unbuilt.[30] Even when they were, they emerged in compromised form.[31] In the most famous (extant) *dom kommuna*, Moscow's Narkomfin building, designed by Ginsburg, I. Milinis, and S. Prokhorov between 1928 and 1929 for members of the People's Commissariat of Finance, only one-fifth of the dwelling models—so-called F units—were explicitly geared to the needs of an individual.[32] The four other dwelling units were conventional apartments, though the building did (initially) contain extensive communal facilities: a dining hall, central kitchen, laundry, gymnasium, library, roof garden, and day nursery.[33]

Hardly the prescription for a life to be lived collectively, the *dom kommuna* devolved into a combination of the traditional familial apartment and the *Einküchenhaus*—forming the kernel of what has been rebranded cohousing. While the feminist implications of cohousing (particularly as built in Scandinavia) are admirable, these homes remain (largely) geared to the needs of single parents or couples with children, not atomized individuals. In fact, the vast majority of contemporary discussions on the dearth of affordable and quality housing continue to center on the plight of the nuclear family with dependent children. This in spite of the fact that the single individual of limited means—from the rubble women (*Trümmerfrauen*) of the late 1940s and the guestworkers who enabled the "economic miracle" in 1950s and 1960s West Germany, to refugees and rootless youths—has made recurrent and troubling appearances throughout the twentieth and twenty-first centuries. While singles continue to serve as the locus of countless fears and anxieties, they also remain an afterthought, not the default from which designers work.

Today, the only housing types approximating Ledigenheim in terms of concept and purpose—namely, to create a home, as opposed to a barracks, that balances privacy with community and does not treat its residents as disposable—are dormitories (including Kolping's new homes) and assisted-living facilities (the modern day equivalent of the charitable Stiftung). Yet these are transitional spaces for those at the beginning and end of their productive lives. As such, they remain unsuitable for the majority of single people, particularly those who (by choice or involuntarily) remain single, desire community, and do not want (or cannot afford) to establish and maintain their own households. As news outlets report, even college-educated single workers in Silicon Valley are being priced out of renting their own apartments, much less purchasing a home.[34] Instead, they have turned to creating their own ad hoc versions of the Ledigenheime—banding together to rent spaces they could not have afforded on their own, even hiring in help with cooking and cleaning their individual and collective spaces. Yet such individuals are the present-day equivalent to the *Zimmerherr*, with most of their (far less affluent) contemporaries *Schlafgänger*.

What then was, is, and can be the legacy of the Ledigenheim? While it has many parallels within Euro-American nations, there were and are no duplicates for the Ledigenheim building type. Because the Ledigenheim was designed to be more than a transitional housing model to mitigate the most detrimental effects of rapid industrialization and urbanization, its emergence is indicative of the extent to which diverse individuals, private organizations, and governments could engage, and *can engage*, with the support and provision of housing to combat pressing social issues. Certainly, the seeds of the modern welfare state as it emerged in the Weimar Republic and expanded after the Second World War were sown through earlier initiatives like the Ledigenheim project. Most compellingly, while such a massive effort expended on behalf of a marginalized and demonized demographic may well feel foreign in today's divisive climate, it does provide proof that if it was once possible to balance social control with social mobility and to skillfully and successfully move between progressive and conservative positions in the interests of maintaining, or even building, a civil society.[35] It was the very everydayness and ordinariness of a Ledigenheim, set against the background of enormous socioeconomic pressures that makes the building type fascinating to study, and no more so than in light of recent housing crises and scholarly attempts to rethink how affordable housing can better support individuals, families, and communities. It is time to rewrite the rules of who deserves quality housing and of the shape this housing can take, to move beyond single-family homes and apartments, even "tiny houses" and cohousing, to consider every possible form and *all* demographics.

Notes

1 Essen Stadtarchiv, Hausakten Signatur 45-2329. See also Irina Winter, *Georg Benjamin: Arzt und Kommunist* (Berlin: Verlag Volk und Gesundheit, 1962), 45.
2 Winter, 54.
3 Essen Stadtarchiv, Hausakten Signatur 45-18015.
4 The designers of the German Siedlungen had capitalized on the expansive Weimar-era framework of rent controls, building-society subventions, minimum housing standards, and newly available public lands. They had also drawn on the work of prewar land and environmental reform groups like the German Garden City Association (DGG) (Barbara Miller Lane, "Modern Architecture and Politics in Germany, 1918–1945," in *Housing and Dwelling*, ed. Barbara Miller Lane (London: Routledge, 2007), 260.
5 "Ledigenheim München," *Die (Süddeutsche) Bauzeitung* 24 (1927): 228; "Das Neue Ledigenheim in München," *Der Baumeister* 25 (1927): 141–6; "Ledigenheim für Männer an der Bergmannstrasse," *Deutsche Bauzeitung* 62 (1928): 16; Winfried Nerdinger, *Theodor Fischer* (Berlin: Ernst und Sohn, 1988), 96–102; Markus Eisen, *Vom Ledigenheim zum Boardinghaus* (Berlin: Gebr. Mann, 2012), 197–219; Susan R. Henderson, *Building Culture: Ernst May and the New Frankfurt Initiative* (New York: Peter Lang, 2013), 363.
6 "Ledigenheim auf der Breslauer Ausstellung 'Wohnung und Werkraum' 1929," *Stein Holz Eisen* 2 (1930): 39–42; Hans Scharoun, *Bauten, Entwürfe, Texte, Schriftenreihe*, vol. 10, ed. P. Pfannkuch (Berlin: Akademie der Künste, 1993), 78; Ludwig Hilbersheimer, "'Wohnung und Werkraum' Austellung Breslau," *Die Form* 4 (1929): 451.
7 *Bauwelt* 16 (1925): 487.
8 *Bauwelt* 16 (1925): 487.
9 *Bauwelt* 16 (1925): 487.
10 *Bauwelt* 16 (1925): 487.
11 Susan R. Henderson, "Housing the Single Woman: The Frankfurt Experiment," *Journal of the Society of Architectural Historians* 68, no. 3 (2009): 366.
12 "Ledigenwohnungen in Frankfurt a. Main," *Zentralblatt der Bauverwaltung* 49, no. 12 (March 20, 1929): 184.

13 Henderson, *Building Culture*, 376.
14 *Deutsche Bauzeitung* 65 (1931), 498. This *Laubenganghaus* arrangement had a precedent in Wilhelm Riphahn's *Wohnheim für Ledige, Berufstätige Frauen* at Zollstockweg 13, constructed in 1929 in the Zollstock Siedlung (Werner Heinen and Anne-Marie Pfeffer, *Köln-Siedlungen* [Köln: Bachem, 1988], 222).
15 "Einzimmerwohnung für Kleinverdiener?" *Bauwelt* 27 (1928): 3–4; "Kritische Spaziergänge durch die Berliner Bauausstellung," *Deutsche Bauhütte* 35, no. 6 (August 5, 1931): 255–8; "'Die Wohnung unserer Zeit' auf der Deutschen Bauaustellung Berlin 1931," *Moderne Bauformen* 30 (1931): 329–47; *Der Neubau* 12, no. 6 (March 24, 1930): 100–3; Eisen, 307–21.
16 *Der Neubau* 12, no. 6 (March 24, 1930): 100–3.
17 Henderson, *Building Culture*, 364–5.
18 *Einliegerwohnung* is particularly inventive, taking as its base the word *Einlieger*, the term for a farm laborer who was housed in a single room within a farmer's larger dwelling (Henderson, *Building Culture*, 364–5).
19 Henderson, *Building Culture*, 380.
20 As Mary Nolan has noted, privacy and technological advances, both increasingly available to the masses, came at a steep price. In the 1920s, the rationalized apartment, and the electrified modern kitchen within it, was positioned as a helpmeet to the housewife, but at a cost to her agency within the space and the dissolution of informal networks of support outside it ("'Housework Made Easy': The Taylorized Housewife in Weimar Germany's Rationalized Economy," *Feminist Studies* 16, no. 3 (Autumn, 1990): 549–77).
21 *Das steinerne Berlin* (Berlin: Ullstein, 1930), 471.
22 Karl Teige, *The Minimum Dwelling* (Cambridge, MA: MIT Press, 2002), 365.
23 Teige, 365.
24 Barbara Kreis, "The Idea of the Dom Kommuna and the Dilemma of the Soviet Avant Garde" *Oppositions* 21 [Summer 1980]: 33). To this point, see also Milka Bliznakov, "Soviet Housing During the Experimental Years, 1918 to 1933," in *Russian Housing in the Modern Age: Design and Social History*, ed. William Craft Brumfield and Blair A. Ruble (Cambridge: Woodrow Wilson Center Press, 1993), 85–149; Caroline Humphrey, "Ideology in Infrastructure: Architecture and Soviet Imagination," *The Journal of the Royal Anthropological Institute* 11, no. 1 (March 2005): 39–58.
25 Kreis, 33.
26 Kreis, 33.
27 Roland Günter, *Der Deutsche Werkbund und seine Mitglieder* (Essen: Klartext, 2009), 91.
28 Teige, 259, 265–6.
29 Ibid., 213. Despite their resolve to dissolve the nuclear family and create a larger societal family, the Soviets never went so far as to build large sleeping halls, instead

relying on the successful model of single occupancy rooms combined with social gathering spaces.
30 Ibid., 355.
31 Norbert Schoenauer, "Early European Collective Habitation: From Utopian Ideal to Reality," in *New Housholds, New Housing*, ed. Karen Franck and Sherry Ahrentzen (New York: Van Nostrand Reinhold, 1989), 59–62; Freeman, 191–210.
32 Schoenauer, 60.
33 Schoenauer, 62.
34 Lauren Hepler, "Valley Building Boom Won't Fix Housing Crisis," *San Jose Business Journal* 32, no. 23 (August 2014): 6; Richard Scheinin, "Silicon Valley's Housing Affordability Crisis Worsens," *Oakland Tribune* (July 20, 2015).
35 I would like to thank one of my anonymous reviewers in helping me to better clarify this point, particularly the relevance of the Ledigenheim project to the current (relatively uncivil) sociopolitical climate.

Bibliography

50 Jahre Christlicher Verein Junger Männer zu Berlin: 1883-1933. Berlin: Christlicher Verein Junger Männer, 1933.

50 Jahre Volkswohnheim Gemeinnützige Aktien-Gesellschaft in Berlin-Charlottenburg. Basel: Länderdienst Verlag, 1955.

"100 Mill. Für Ausländerwohnheime." *Industriekurier unabhängige Zeitung für Politik, Wirtschaft u. Technik,* October 6, 1960.

Abrahms, L. *Workers' Culture in Imperial Germany: Rheinland and Westphalia.* London: Routledge, 1992.

Adam, Thomas. "Philanthropy and the Shaping of Social Distinctions in Nineteenth Century U.S., Canadian, and German Cities." In *Philanthropy, Patronage, and Civil Society: Experiences from Germany, Great Britain, and North America,* edited by Thomas Adam, 15-33. Bloomington: Indiana University Press, 2004.

Adam, Thomas. "Transatlantic Trading: The Transfer of Philanthropic Models Between European and North American Cities during the Nineteenth and Early Twentieth Centuries." *Journal of Urban History* 28, no. 3 (March 2002): 328-51.

Adams, Carole Elizabeth. *Women Clerks in Wilhelmine Germany: Issues of Class and Gender.* Cambridge: Cambridge University Press, 1988.

Akcan, Esra. *Architecture in Translation: Germany, Turkey, and the Modern House.* Durham: Duke University Press, 2012.

Allgemeine Rundschau: Wochenschrift für Politik u. Kultur. Munich: Verlag der Allgemeinen Rundschau, 1904-33.

Altenrath, Dr. "Hospize und Ledigenheime der katholischen Gesellenheime." *Concordia* 20, no. 18 (1911).

Altenrath, Johannes. *Das Schlafstellenwesen und seine Reform: Statistik, Schlafstellenaufsicht, Ledigenheime.* Rechts und Staatswissenschaft Fakultät Dissertation, Universität Halle, 1916.

Anderson, Bonnie S. and Judith P. Zinsser. *A History of their Own: Women in Europe (Volume II).* New York: Harper and Row, 1988.

Anderson, Stanford. "The Legacy of German Neoclassicism and Biedermeier: Behrens, Tessenow, Loos and Mies." *Assemblage* no. 15 (August 1991): 62-87.

Anderson, Stanford. "Peter Behrens, Friedrich Naumann, and the Werkbund." In *The Architecture of Politics: 1910-1940,* 8-21. Miami Beach: Wolfsonian, 1995.

Anderson, Stanford. *Peter Behrens and a New Architecture for the Twentieth Century.* Cambridge: MIT Press, 2000.

Andrews, Eulalie. "Apartments for Bachelor Girls." *House Beautiful* (November 1912): 168-70.

"The Apartment House." *The American Architect and Building News* (January 4, 1890): 3–5.

(der) Arbeiterfreund, Zeitschrift für die Arbeiterfrage. Organ des Centralvereins für das Wohl der Arbeitenden Klassen. Halle, 1863–1914.

Arbeitersiedlungen im 19. Jahrhundert: Historische Entwicklung, Bedeutung und aktuelles Erhaltungsintresse. Bochum: N. Brockmeyer, 1985.

(das) Arbeiterwohl, Organ des Verbandes katholischer Industrielle und Arbeiterfreunde. Cologne: Bachem, 1880–1914.

(der) Arbeitsnachweis in Deutschland: Zeitschrift des Verbands Deutscher Arbeitsnachweise, 1 (1913/14).

Architektonische Rundschau, 1885–1914/15.

(die) Architektur des XX Jahrhunderts: Zeitschrift für Moderne Baukunst. Berlin: Wasmuth, 1901–1914.

Arnold, K.F. *Das Mietswesen in München.* Munich, 1879.

"Ausbeutung und Philanthropie im Arbeiterinnenheim." *Gewerkschaftliche Rundschau für die Schweitz: Monatsschrift des Schweizerishen Gewerkschaftsbundes* 5, no. 2 (1913): unpaginated.

Avenarius, Ferdinand. *Der Kunstwart 15.2, 19.1 and 19.2 (April-September 1902, October 1905-September 1906)*. Munich: Georg D.W. Callwey.

Avenarius, Ferdinand, "Hausgruel." *Dürerbund. Flugschrift zur Ausdruckskultur* 44, no. 1 (November 1908): 369–81.

Bacmeister, W. *Louis Baare. Ein westfälischer Wirtschaftsführer aus der Bismarckzeit.* Essen, 1937.

Bade, K., ed. *Population, Labour and Migration in 19th and 20th Century Germany.* Leamington Spa: Berg, 1987.

Baer, C.H. *Kleinbauten und Siedlungen.* Stuttgart: Verlag von Julius Hoffmann, 1919.

Bajohr, Frank. *Zwischen Krupp und Kommune: Sozialdemokratie, Arbeiterschaft und Stadtverwaltung in Essen vor dem Ersten Weltkrieg.* Essen: Klartext, 1988.

Balducci, Temma and Heather Belnap Jensen, eds. *Women, Femininity and Public Space in European Visual Culture, 1789–1914.* Burlington: Ashgate, 2014.

Barkin, Kenneth T. "The Crisis of Modernity." In *Imagining German Culture, 1889–1910*, edited by Francoise Forster-Hahn, 19–35. Washington: National Gallery of Art, 1996.

Barnett, Henrietta. *Canon Barnett: His Life, Work, and Friends, Vol. 2.* London: John Murray, 1918.

Bauen in Bochum. Bochum: Schürmann und Klagges, 1986.

Baugewerks-Zeitung: Hauptorgan für das deutsche Baugewerbe. Berlin: Baugewerkszeitung, 1869–1934.

Bautechnische Zeitschrift. 1887–1909.

(die) Bauwelt: Zeitschrift für das gesamte Bauwesen. Berlin: Verlag Ullstein, 1910-.

Bebel, August. *Woman under Socialism.* Translated by Daniel de Leon. New York: Shocken, 1904.

Beck, O. "Förderung der gemeinnützigen Bautätigkeit durch die Gemeinden." *Neue Untersuchungen* 2 (1900): 172–272.

Bederman, Gail. *Manliness and Civilization: A Cultural History of Gender and Race in the United States, 1880–1917.* Chicago: University of Chicago, 1995.

Bellamy, Edward. *Looking Backward: 2007–1887.* Boston: St. Martin's Press, 1995.

Berghahn, Volker. *Imperial Germany, 1871–1914: Economy, Society, Culture and Politics.* Providence, RI: Berghahn Books, 1994.

Bericht über den Stand und die Verwaltung der Gemeindeangelegenheiten der Stadt Cöln in den Etatsjahren 1891-1900. Cöln: Statistisches Amt, from 1857–1928.

Berlin und Seine Bauten. Berlin: Ernst und Sohn, Verlag für Architektur und Technische Wissenschaften, 2003.

Berliner Architekturwelt: Zeitschrift für Baukunst, Malerei, Plastik und Kunstgewerbe der Gegenwart 21 (1910): 74, 306–7.

Berndt, Baumeister (Bochum). "Das Ledigenheim vom Stadtpunkte des Arbeitgebers, insbesondere das Ledigenheim des Bochumer Vereins für Bergbau und Gussstahl-Fabrikation (Versammlungsbericht)." In *Schlafstellenwesen und Ledigenheime*, 161–74. Berlin: Carl Henmanns Verlag, 1904.

Biecker, Johannes and Walter Buschmann. *Arbeitersiedlungen im 19. Jahrhundert: Historische Entwicklung, Bedeutung und aktuellles Erhaltungsintresse.* Bochum: N. Brockmeyer, 1985.

Biecker, Johannes and Walter Buschmann. *Bergbauarchitektur.* Bochum: N. Brockmeyer, 1986.

Black, Clementina. *A New Way of Housekeeping.* London: W. Collins Sons and Co. Ltd, 1890.

Blätter für Volksgesundheitspflege: Gemeinverständiche Zeitschrift, Organ des Deutschen Vereins für Volks-Hygiene. Berlin: Deutscher Verlag für Volkswohlfahrt, 1900–1933.

Blau, Eve. *The Architecture of Red Vienna 1919–1934.* Cambridge, MA: MIT Press, 1999.

Blau, Eve and Edward Kaufman, eds. *Architecture and Its Image.* Montreal: CCA, 1989.

Bliznakov, Milka. "Soviet Housing during the Experimental Years, 1918 to 1933." In *Russian Housing in the Modern Age: Design and Social History*, edited by William Craft Brumfield and Blair A. Ruble, 85–149. Cambridge: Woodrow Wilson Center Press, 1993.

Bochumer Verein, *Bericht über die Jubel-Feier des Bochumer Vereins.* Bochum, 1894.

Bode, Wilhelm von. "Vom Luxus." *Kunstwart: Rundschau über alle Gebiete des Schönen: Monatshefte für Kunst, Literatur, und Leben* 19, no. 2 (Heft 22) (1906): 493–503.

Bodien, E., ed. *Geschichte der gemeinnützigen Wohnungswirtschaft in Berlin.* Hamburg: Hammonia Verlag, 1957: 71–74.

Booth, Sally. "Reconstructing Sexual Geography." In *House Life: Space, Place and Family in Europe*, edited by Donna Birdwell-Pheasant and Denise Lawrence-Zuniga, 133–56. New York: Berg, 1999.

Bourdieu, Pierre. *Distinction: A Social Critique of the Judgement of Taste.* Cambridge: Harvard University Press, 1979.

Boyer, Paul. *Urban Masses and Moral Order in America, 1820–1920*. Cambridge: Harvard University Press, 1978.

Braun, Lily. *Die Frauenfrage*. Leipzig: Hirzel, 1901.

Braun, Lily. "Women's Work and Housekeeping" (1901). In *German Feminist Writings*, edited by Magda Müller and Patricia A. Herminghouse, 90–5. New York: Continuum, 2001.

Breckman, Warren G. "Disciplining Consumption: The Debate about Luxury in Wilhelmine Germany, 1890–1914." *Journal of Social History* 24, no. 4 (Spring 1991): 485–500.

British Board of Trade. *Cost of Living in German Towns*. London: H.M. Stationery Office, 1910.

Brueggemeier, L. Niethammer. "Schlafgänger, Schnappskasinos und schwerindustrielle Kolonie." In *Fabrik, Familie, Feierabend, Beitraege zur Sozialgeschichte des Alltags im Industriezeitalter*, edited by J. Reulecke and W. Weber, 153–74. Wuppertal: Hammer, 1978.

Bry, Gerhard. *Wages in Germany, 1871–1945*. Princeton, NJ: Princeton University Press, 1960.

Buder, Stanley. *Pullman: An Experiment in Industrial Order and Community Planning*. New York: Oxford, 1967.

Bullock, Nicholas and James Read. *The Movement for Housing Reform in Germany and France, 1840–1914*. Cambridge: Cambridge University Press, 1985.

Bürkle, J. Christoph. *Hans Scharoun*. Zürich: Artemis, 1993.

Butler, Judith. *Gender Trouble: Feminism and the Subversion of Identity*. New York: Routledge, 1990.

Cahn, Ernst. *Das Schlafstellenwesen in den deutschen Grossstädten und seine Reform*. Stuttgart, 1898.

Calwer, Richard. *Das Kost und Logiswesen in Handwerk: Ergebnisse einer von der Kommission zur Beseitigung des Kost- und Logiszwanges veranst. Erhebung*. Berlin: Verlag der Generalkommission den Gewerkschaften Deutschlands, 1908.

Campbell, Joan. *The German Werkbund: The Politics of Reform in the Applied Arts*. Princeton: Princeton University Press, 1978.

Carpenter, Frank. "The Berlin Poor." *LA Times*, December 4, 1892: 9.

Chickering, Roger. *We Men Who Feel Most German: A Cultural Study of the Pan German League*. Boston: George Allen and Unwin, 1984.

Chin, Rita. *The Guest Worker Question in Postwar Germany*. Cambridge: Cambridge University, 2007.

Chudacoff, Howard. *Age of the Bachelor: Creating an American Subculture*. Princeton, NJ: Princeton University Press, 1999.

Clelland, Doug, ed. *Berlin: an Architectural History*. New York: St. Martin's Press, 1983.

Cohen, Lizabeth A. "Embellishing a Life of Labor: An Interpretation of the Material Culture of American Working Class Homes, 1885–1915." In *Common Places: Readings in American Vernacular Architecture*, edited by Dell Upton and John Michael Vlach, 261–80. Athens, GA: University of Georgia Press, 1986.

Collins Cromley, Elizabeth. *Alone Together: A History of New York's Early Apartments.* Ithaca: Cornell University Press, 1990.
Collins Cromley, Elizabeth. "Alone Together." In *Housing and Dwelling,* edited by Barbara Miller Lane, 105–7. London: Routledge, 2007.
Concordia: Zeitschrift der Zentralstelle für Volkswohlfahrt. Berlin: Heymanns, 1901–20.
"Cooperative Home Builders in New York." *Cooperation* 12 (February 1926): 22–4.
"Cooperative Housekeeping." *The Atlantic Monthly* 22, no. 132 (November 1868): 513–24.
"Cooperative Housekeeping II." *The Atlantic Monthly* 22, no. 133 (December 1868): 682–97.
"Cooperative Housing De Luxe." *Cooperation* 12 (December 1926): 221–3.
Cowen, Ruth Schwartz. "The 'Industrial Revolution' in the Home." *Technology and Culture* 17, no. 1 (January 1976): 1–23.
Crawford, Margaret. *Building the Workingman's Paradise.* New York: Verso, 1995.
Crew, David Francis. *Town in the Ruhr. A Social History of Bochum, 1860–1914.* New York: Columbia University Press, 1979.
Däbritz, Walther. *Bochumer Verein für Bergbau und Gußstahlfabrikation in Bochum, 1842–1934: neun Jahrzehnte seiner Geschichte im Rahmen der Wirtschaft des Ruhrbezirks.* Düsseldorf: Verl. Stahleisen, 1934.
"Das neue Arbeiterinnenheim in Linden." *Baugewerks-Zeitung* 43, no. 56 (1911): 1–2.
"Das neue Ledigenheim der Postgehilfinnen." *Die Bauwelt* 21 (1925): 487–8.
Daunton, M.J., ed. *Housing the Workers: A Comparative History, 1850–1914.* Leicester: Leicester University Press, 1990.
Daunton, M.J. "Public Place and Private Space." In *Housing and Dwelling,* edited by Barbara Miller Lane, 128–32. London: Routledge, 2007.
Davis, Belinda. *Home Fires Burning.* Chapel Hill: UNC Press, 2000.
Dawson, William Harbutt. *Municipal Life and Government in Germany.* New York: Longmans, Green and Co., 1914.
Dees, Jesse Walter. *Flophouse: An Authentic Undercover Study of "Flophouses," "Cage Hotels," Including Missions, Shelters and Institutions Serving Unattached (Homeless) Men.* Francestown, NH: Marshall Jones Company, 1948.
Desai, A.V. *Real Wages in Germany, 1871–1913.* Oxford: Clarendon Press, 1968.
Deutsche Bauhütte, 1897–1942.
Deutsche Bauzeitung: Verban Deutscher Architekten und Ingenieur-Vereine (DBZ), Berlin, 1867–1940 (later *Deutsche Baukunst* and *Die Bauzeitung*).
Deutsche Vierteljahrschrift für öffenliche Gesundheitspflege (VfoeG), Braunschweig, 1869–1914.
Dix, Arthur. "Ledigenheime." In *Conrads Jahrbücher für Nationalökonimie und Statistik* 3, Vol. 25. Jena: Gustav Fischer Verlag, 1903: 489.
Dollard, Catherine Leota. *The Surplus Woman: Unmarried in Imperial Germany.* New York: Berghahn Books, 2009.

Ehmer, J. "Wohnen ohne eigene Wohnung." In *Wohnen im Wandel*, edited by L. Niethammer, 132–50. Wuppertal: Hammer, 1979.

"Die Einweihung des Lehrerinnenheims." *Monatsblatt für Berliner Lehrerinnen* 6, no. 11 (1911): 215–19.

"Einzimmerwohnung für Kleinverdiener?" *Bauwelt* 27 (1928): 3–4.

Eisen, Markus. *Vom Ledigenheim zum Boardinghouse: Bautypologie und Geselleschaftstheorie bis zum Ende der Weimarer Republic*. Munich: Gebr. Mann Verlag, 2012.

"Es geht nicht ohne Italianer." *Industriekurier unabhängige Zeitung für Politik, Wirtschaft u. Technik*, October 4, 1955, 3.

Escher, E. *Berlin und seine Umland*, vol. 47. Berlin: Einzelveröffentlichungen der Historischen Kommission zu Berlin, 1985.

Evans, Richard J. *Proletarians and Politics: Socialism, Protest and the Working Class in Germany before the First World War*. New York: St. Martin's Press, 1990.

Evans, Richard J. and W. R. Lee, eds. *The German Peasantry: Conflict and Community in Rural Society from the Eighteenth to the Twentieth Centuries*. New York: St. Martin's Press, 1986.

Fairbairn, Brett. "Self-Help and Philanthropy: The Emergence of Cooperatives in Britain, German, the United States, and Canada from the Mid-Nineteenth to Mid-Twentieth Century." In *Philanthropy, Patronage, and Civil Society: Experiences from Germany, Great Britain, and North America*, edited by Thomas Adam, 55–78. Bloomington: Indiana University Press, 2004.

Falch, Oberregierungsrat (Stuttgart). "Schlafstellenwesen und Ledigenheime vom Stadtpunkte der Inneren Mission der evangelischen Kirche (Versammlungsbericht)." In *Schlafstellenwesen und Ledigenheime*, 149–54. Berlin: Carl Henmanns Verlag, 1904.

Festing, Heinrich. *Adolph Kolping und sein Werk*. Freiburg: Herder, 1981.

Festschrift zum 100-jährigen Bestehen der Gerwerkschaft ver. Constantin der Grosse, Bochum. Essen, 1948.

Festschrift zum 100-jährigen Bestehen der Zechen Hannover und Hannibal. Bochum, 1947.

Festschrift zum Fünfzigjährigen Bestehen des Beamten-Wohnungs-Vereins zu Berlin. Berlin: Feese und Schulz, 1950.

Fichter, Joseph. *Roots of Change*. New York: Appleton, 1939.

Fletcher, Roger, ed. *Bernstein to Brandt: A Short History of German Social Democracy*. London: Edward Arnold, 1987.

Foucault, Michel. *Discipline and Punish: the Birth of the Prison*. Translated by Alan Sheridan. New York: Vintage Books, 1995.

Franck, Karen and Sherry Ahrentzen, eds. *New Households, New Housing*. New York: Van Nostrand Reinhold, 1989.

Frank, Hartmut. "A German Approach to the Question of European Architecture." *Rassegna* 20, no. 76 (1998): 72–87.

Die Frau: Monatschrift für das gesamte Frauenleven unserer Zeit, vols. 1–40 (1893–1933).

"Die Frauenfrage." In *Brockhaus' Konversations-Lexikon* VII, 14th edn, 235–7. Leipzig: Brockhaus, 1898.

Freeman, Joshua B. *Behemoth: A History of the Factory and the Making of the Modern World*. New York: Norton, 2018.

"Fremd- statt Gastarbeiter." *Handelsblatt: Deutsche Wirtschaftszeitung* 34 (February 16, 1967): 20.

Frevert, Ute. "The Civilizing Tendency of Hygiene: Working Class Women under Medical Control in Imperial Germany." In *German Women in the Nineteenth Century: A Social History*, edited by John C. Fout, 320–44. New York: Holmes and Meier, 1984.

Frevert, Ute. *Women in German History*. Oxford: Berg, 1989.

Fricke, Dieter. *Bismarcks Prätorianer: Die Berliner politische Politzei im Kampf gegen die deutsche Arbeiterbewegung*. Berlin, 1962.

Friedman, Alice T. "The Way You Do the Things You Do: Writing the History of Houses and Housing." *Journal of the Society of Architectural Historians* 58, no. 3 (1999): 406–13.

Friedrich Krupp, A.G. (Hrg.). *Kruppscher Wohnungsbau*. Hamburg, 1940.

Fried[rich] Krupp Aktiengesellschaft. Essen, 1928.

Fuchs, Georg. "Zur Weihe des Grundsteins: ein Festliches Spiel." *Deutsche Kunst und Dekoration* 6 (April–September 1900): 357–65.

Führer durch die Essener Wohnsiedlungen der Firma Krupp : Sommer 1930. Essen: Fried.-Krupp-Aktiengesellschaft, 1930.

Führer durch die Essener Wohnsiedlungen der Firma Krupp Körperschaft: Fried.-Krupp-Aktiengesellschaft. Essen: Graph. Anstalt der Fried. Krupp A.G., 1920.

Gamber, Wendy. *The Boardinghouse in Nineteenth-Century America*. Baltimore: Johns Hopkins University Press, 2007.

Geary, R. "Working Class Culture in Imperial Germany." In *From Bernstein to Brandt: A Short History of German Social Democracy*, edited by Roger Fletcher, 11–16. London: Edward Arnold, 1989.

Geist, J.F. and K. Kürvers eds. *Das Berliner Mietshaus, 1862–1945*. Munich: Prestel, 1980.

Gelsenkirchener Bergwerks-Aktien-Gesellschaft 1873-1913. Düsseldorf: A. Bagel, 1913.

George, Walter Lionel. "The Home." In *Woman and Tomorrow*, 57–94. London: H. Jenkins, 1913.

George, Walter Lionel. *Labour and Housing at Port Sunlight*. London: A. Rivers, 1909.

Gerhard, Ute. "Die Radikalen im Kampf um Recht und gegen doppelte Moral." In *Unerhört: die Geschichte der Deutschen Frauenbewegung*, 215–77. Hamburg: Rohwolt Taschenbuch Verlag, 1990.

Gilman, Charlotte Perkins. *The Home: Its Work and Influence*. Walnut Creek, CA: Altamira Press, 2002.

Gilman, Charlotte Perkins. "The Passing of the Home in Great American Cities." *The Cosmopolitan* 38, no. 2 (December 1904): 137–47.

Gilman, Charlotte Perkins. *What Diantha Did*. Durham, NC: Duke University Press, 2005.

Goldthammer, Dr. "Über die Kost und Logirhauser für die armen Volksklassen." *Vierteljahrschrift für gerechtliche Medizin und öffentliche Sanitätswesen (neue Folge)* 28 (1878): 296–333.

Gorr, Holger. "Volkshäuser (houses of the people) in Germany: A Historical Overview from 1900 until Today." *International Journal of Heritage Studies* 19, no. 5 (2013): 457–73.

Groth, Paul. *Living Downtown: The History of Residential Hotels in the United States*. Berkeley: University of California Press, 1994.

Groth, Paul. "Making New Connections in Vernacular Architecture." *Journal of the Society of Architectural Historians* 58, no. 3 (1999): 444–51.

Groth, Paul. "YMCAs and Other Organization Boarding Houses." In *Housing and Dwelling*, edited by. Barbara Miller Lane, 113–16. London: Routledge, 2007.

Gross, Michael. *The War against Catholicism: Liberalism and the Anti-Catholic Imagination in Nineteenth Century Germany*. Ann Arbor: University of Michigan Press, 2004.

Günter, Roland. *Der Deutsche Werkbund und seine Mitglieder*. Essen: Klartext, 2009.

Gustav-Wrathall, John Donald. *Take the Young Stranger by the Hand*. Chicago: University of Chicago, 1998.

Güttler, Peter and Sabine. *Zeitschriften-Bibliographie zur Architektur in Berlin von 1919 bis 1945*. Berlin: Gebr. Mann Verlag, 1986.

Gusstahlwerk Witten AG 1853–1954. Witten, 1954.

Gussstahlwerk Witten, Witten a/d. Ruhr. Barmen: Luhn, 1904.

Gut, Albert. *Der Wohungsbau in Deutschland nach dem Weltkrieg*. München: F. Bruckmann, 1928.

Gutman, Marta. *A City for Children: Women, Architecture, and the Charitable Landscapes of Oakland, 1850–1950*. Chicago: University of Chicago Press, 2014.

Gutschow, Kai. "Schultze-Naumburg's Heimatstil: A Nationalist Conflict of Tradition and Modernity." In *Traditional Dwellings and Settlements Working Papers Series*, vol. 36, edited by. Nezer Alsayyad, 1–44. Berkeley, CA: Center for Environmental Design Research, 1992.

Haase, Carl. *Die Archivalien zur Deutschen Geschichte*. Boppard am Rhein: Boldt Verlag, 1975.

Häder, Alexander and Ulrich Wuest. *Prenzlauer Berg: Besichtigung einer Legende*. Berlin: Ed. q, 1994.

Hänisch, W. "Was Lesen die Arbeiter?" *Die Neue Zeit* 18 (1900): 691–6.

Hagen, William W. *Germans, Poles and Jews: The Nationality Conflict in the Prussian East, 1772–1914*. Chicago: University of Chicago Press, 1980.

Hagspiel, Wolfram. *Der Kölner Architekt Wilhelm Riphahn. Sein Lebenswerk von 1913 bis 1945*. PhD Diss., University of Köln, 1982.

Hamburg und seine Bauten: under Berücksichtigung der Nachbarstädte Altona und Wandsbek 1914. Hamburg: Boysen und Maasch, 1914.

Hartmann, Kristiana. *Deutsche Gartenstadtbewegung. Kulturpolitik und Gesellschaftsreform*. Munich: Heinz Moos, 1976.

Haxhausen, Charles W and Heidrun Suhr. *Berlin: Culture and Metropolis*. Minneapolis: University of Minnesota Press, 1990.

Hayden, Dolores. "Catherine Beecher and the Politics of Housework." In *Women in American Architecture: A Historic and Contemporary Perspective*, edited by Susanna Torre, 40–9. New York: Whitney Library of Design, 1977.

Hayden, Dolores. *The Grand Domestic Revolution*. Cambridge, MA: MIT Press, 1982.

Hayden, Dolores. "Two Utopian Feminists and Their Campaigns for Kitchenless Homes." *Signs* 4, no. 2 (Winter 1978): 274–90.

Hays, Michael. "Tessenow's Architecture as National Allegory: Critique of Capitalism of Protofascism?" *Assemblage* 8 (1989): 1–22.

Hegemann, Werner. *Das steinerne Berlin*. Berlin: Ullstein, 1930.

"Heime für Textilarbeiterinnen." *Gleichheit* (1909): 308–10, 324–6.

Heinen, Werner and Anne-Marie Pfeffer. *Köln: Siedlungen 1888–1938*. Köln: Bachem, 1988.

Heinrichsbauer, A. *Harpener Bergbau AG 1856–1936*. Essen, 1936.

Heinrichsbauer, A. *Industrielle Siedlung im Ruhrgebiet*. Essen, 1936.

Helmigk, Hans Joachim. *Oberschlesische Landbaukunst um 1800*. Berlin: Verlag für Kunstwissenschaft, 1937.

Henderson, Susan R. *Building Culture: Ernst May and the New Frankfurt Initiative, 1926–1931*. New York: Peter Lang, 2013.

Henderson, Susan R. "Ernst May and the Campaign to Resettle the Countryside: Rural Housing in Silesia, 1919–1925." *Journal of the Society of Architectural Historians* 61, no. 2 (June 2002): 188–211.

Henderson, Susan R. "Housing the Single Woman: The Frankfurt Experiment." *Journal of the Society of Architectural Historians* 68, no. 3 (2009): 358–77.

Henderson, Susan R. "A Revolution in the Woman's Sphere: Grete Lihotzky and the Frankfurt Kitchen." In *Architecture and Feminism*, edited by Debra Coleman, Elizabeth Danze, and Carol Henderson, 221–53. New York: Princeton Architectural Press, 1996.

Henselmann, Hermann. *Hans Scharoun, Bauten in Berlin*. Berlin: Senatsverwaltung für Bau und Wohnungswesen, 1993.

Hepler, Lauren. "Valley Building Boom Won't Fix Housing Crisis." *San Jose Business Journal* 32, no. 23 (August 2014): 6.

Hepworth, Mike. "Privacy, Security and Respectability: the Ideal Victorian Home." In *Housing and Dwelling*, edited by Barbara Miller Lane, 150–4. London: Routledge, 2007.

Herbert, Ulrich. *A History of Foreign Labor in Germany, 1880–1980*. Ann Arbor: University of Michigan, 1990.

Heyer, P. "Lehrerinnenheim." *Monatsblatt für Berliner Lehrerinnen* 6, no. 1 (1910): 11–13.

Hickey, S.H.F. *Workers in Imperial Germany: The Miners in the Ruhr*. Oxford: Clarendon, 1985.

Hilbersheimer, Ludwig. "'Wohnung und Werkraum' Austellung Breslau." *Die Form* 4 (1929): 451.

Die Hilfe: Gotteshilfe, Selbsthilfe, Staatshilfe, Bruderhilfe, vols. 1–25 (1895–1919).

Hobsbawm, Eric. *The Age of Empire: 1875–1914*. New York: Pantheon Books, 1987.

Hochhäusl, Sophie. "From Vienna to Frankfurt Inside Core-House Type 7: A History of Scarcity through the Modern Kitchen." *Architectural Histories* 1, no. 1 (October 2013): Art. 24.

Hoffmeyer-Zlotnik, Jürgen. "Community Change and Invasion: The Case of Turkish Guest Workers." In *Spatial Disparities and Social Behavior*, edited by Jürgen Friedrichs, 114–26. Hamburg: Christians, 1982.

Hoffsten, Anke. "The 'Volkshaus' (worker's assembly hall) in Germany between 1890 and 1933: Architectural Aspects of a Building Type of the Early Phase of Modernity." *International Journal of Heritage Studies* 19, no. 5 (2013): 474–94.

Hohendahl, Peter U. "The Origins of Mass Culture: The Case of Imperial Germany 1871–1918." *New German Critique* 29 (1983): 1–2.

Holden, B.L. "Tenement Furnishings." *House Beautiful* 7 (April 1900): 301–13.

"Home for Educated Women Workers, Nutford House, Brown Street and Nutford Place, W." *The Building New and Engineering Journal* 109, no. 3166 (September 8, 1915).

Honeycut, Karen. "Clara Zetkin: A Socialist Approach to the Problem of Women's Oppression." In *European Women on the Left*, edited by Jane Slaughter and Robert Kern, 29–50. Westport, CT: Greenwood Press, 1981.

"Hopkinson House, Vauxhall Bridge Road." *The Building New and Engineering Journal* 89, no. 2659 (December 22, 1905): 865, 875.

Hoppe, Martha. "Heime für Textilarbeiterinnen." *Die Gleichheit* no. 20 (July 5, 1909): 308–10.

Hoppe, Martha. "Heime für Textilarbeiterinnen (Schluss)." *Die Gleichheit* no. 21 (July 19, 1909): 324–6.

Horowitz, Helen Lefkowitz. *Alma Mater: Design and Experience in the Women's Colleges from Their Nineteenth Century Beginnings to the 1930s*. Amherst, MA: University of Massachusetts Press, 1993.

Horowitz, Helen Lefkowitz. "Hull House as Women's Space." *Chicago History* 12, no. 4 (Winter 1983): 40–55.

Horsfall, T.C. *The Improvement of the Dwellings and Surroundings of the People: The Example of Germany*. Manchester: Manchester University Press, 1905.

Howard, Ebenezer. *Garden Cities of To-Morrow*. Cambridge: MIT Press, 1965.

Howe, Frederic C. *European Cities at Work*. New York: Charles Scribner's Sons, 1913.

Hull House Maps and Papers. New York: Thomas Y. Crowell and Co., 1895.

Humphrey, Caroline. "Ideology in Infrastructure: Architecture and Soviet Imagination." *The Journal of the Royal Anthropological Institute* 11, no. 1 (March 2005): 39–58.

Hunt, Caroline. *The Life of Ellen H. Richards*. Boston: Whitcomb and Barrows, 1912.

Hyde, Simon. "Roman Catholicism and the Prussian State." *Central European History* 24, no. 2 (1991): 95–121.

Jaeggi, Annemarie. "Hufeisensiedlung Britz: Planungs- und Baugeschichte." In *Siedlungen der zwanziger Jahre – heute*, edited by Norbert Huse, 111–36. Berlin, 1984.

Jahres-Bericht Verband Deutscher Bergarbeiter. Bochum: Hansmann, 1902–1910.

(Ein) Jahrhundert Heinrichshütte Hattingen, 1854–1954. Darmstadt, n.d.

James, Harold. "Municipal Finance in the Weimar Republic." In *The State and Social Change in Germany, 1880–1980*, edited by W.R. Lee and Eve Rosenhaft, 228–53. Providence: Berg, 1990.

Jarzombek, Mark. "The Discourses of a Bourgeois Utopia, 1904–1908, and the Founding of the Werkbund." In *Imagining Modern German Culture, 1889–1910*, edited by Francoise Forster-Hahn, 127–46. Washington: National Gallery of Art, 1996.

Jarzombek, Mark. "The Kunstgewerbe, the Werkbund, and the Aesthetics of Culture in the Wilhelmine Period." *The Journal of the Society of Architectural Historians* 53, no. 1 (March 1994): 7–19.

Jefferies, Matthew. *Politics and Culture in Wilhelmine Germany: The Case of Industrial Architecture*. Oxford: Berg, 1995.

Jenison, Madge C. "The Tenements of Berlin." *Harper's Monthly Magazine*, February 1, 1909.

Jenkins, Jennifer. "The Kitsch Collections and the Spirit in the Furniture: Cultural Reform and National Culture in Germany." *Social History* 21, no. 2 (May 1996): 123–41.

Jones, Peter Blundell. *Hans Scharoun*. London: Phaidon Press, 1995.

"Die 'Junggesellen-Kaserne' ein Fehlschlag." *Deutsche Hausbesitzer-Zeitung* 15, no. 42 (1908): 4. In *Wohnalltag in Deutschland*, edited by Teuteberg and Wischermann, 336–7. Münster: F. Coppenrath, 1985.

Junghanns, Kurt. *Bruno Taut*. Berlin: Henschelverlag Kunst und Gesellschaft, 1970.

"Das Kaiser-Wilhelm -Ledigenheim in Essen." *Rhein. Blatter f. Wohnungswesen: Bauberatung* 2: 40.

Kampffmeyer, Bernhard. "Die Gartenstadtbewegung in England." *Die Tat, Monatsschrift für die Zukunft deutscher Kultur, Herausgegeben Eugen Diederichs Verlag* 8 (1916/17): 105–20.

Keil, Wilhelm. *Erlebnisse eines Sozialdemokraten*. Stuttgart, 1947.

Kelly, Alfred. *The German Worker: Working Class Autobiographies from the Age of Industrialization*. Berkeley: University of California Press, 1987.

Keun, Irmgard. *The Artificial Silk Girl*. Munich: Ullstein Verlag, 1932.

Kierdorf, Alexander. *Köln: ein Architekturführer*. Berlin: Dietrich Reimer Verlag, 1999.

Kieren, Martin. *Hannes Meyer: Dokumente zur Frühzeit (1919–1927)*. Heiden: Niggli, 1990.

Kirschner, Mathilde. "Das neuerbaute Arbeiterinnenheim in Berlin." *Westermanns Monatsheft: Illustrierte Deutsche Zeitschrift für das Geistige Leben der Gegenwart* 54, no. 107 (October–December 1909): 391–3.

Klapheck, Richard. *Neue Baukunst in den Rheinlanden*. Düsseldorf, 1928.

Klapheck, Richard. *Siedlungswerk Krupp*. Berlin: Ernst Wasmuth Verlag, 1930.

Klass, Gert von. *Krupps: The Story of an Industrial Empire*. London: Sidgwick and Jackson, 1954.

Knipping, Jörgens Steppat. *Zehn Jahre Treuhandstelle für Bermannswohnstätten im rheinisch-westfälischen Steinkohlebezirk GmbH in Essen (Jubiläumsschrift)*. Essen, 1930.

Koch, Alexander. *Wohnen Heute und Morgen*. Stuttgart: Verlagsanstalt A. Koch, 1949.

Kolping, Adolf. *Der Gesellenverein: zur Beherzigung für Alle, die es mit dem wahren Volkswohl gut meinen*. Köln/Neuss: Schwann, 1849.

Kolpingwerk Deutschland. "Jugendwohnen in Köln-Mitte," 2018, accessed May 20, 2018. https://www.kolping-jugendwohnen.de/koeln-mitte

Kracht, Hans Joachim. "Adolf Kolping und die Gründung der ersten Gesellenvereine in Westfalen." In *Studia Westfalica*, 195–213. Münster: Verlag Aschendorff, 1973.

Kreis, Barbara. "The Idea of the Dom Kommuna and the Dilemma of the Soviet Avant Garde." *Oppositions* 21 (Summer 1980): 53–77.

"Kritische Spaziergänge durch die Berliner Bauausstellung." *Deutsche Bauhütte* 35, no. 6 (August 5, 1931): 255–8.

Krupp'sche Gusstahlfabrik. *Krupp 1812–1912*. Jena: Verlag Gustav Fischer, 1912.

Kruse, Reinhold. *111 Jahre Köln-Nippes*. Köln: Emons Verlag, 1999.

Kuhn, Bärbel. *Familienstand ledig: Ehelose Frauen und Männer im Bürgertum, 1850–1914*. Cologne: Böhlau, 2002.

Kuhn, Walter. *Siedlungsgeschichte Oberschlesiens*. Würzburg: Oberschlesischer Heimatverlag, 1954.

Kulczycki, John. *The Foreign Worker and the German Labor Movement*. Oxford: Berg, 1994.

Ladd, Brian. *Urban Planning and Civic Order in Germany, 1860–1914*. Cambridge, MA: Harvard University Press, 1990.

Lampugnani, Vittorio Magnano. "Modernism, Lifestyle Reforms, City and Nature Experiments in Urban Design in Berlin from 1900 to 1914." In *City of Architecture, Architecture of the City*, edited by Thorsten Sheer, Josef Paul Kleihues, and Paul Kahlfeldt, 29–38. Berlin: Nicolaische Verlagsbuchhandlung Beuermann GmbH, 2000.

Lander, H. Clapham. "Associated Homes: A Solution to the Servant Problem." *Garden Cities and Town Planning* (1911).

Landesdenkmalamt Berlin im Auftrag der Senatsverwaltung für Stadtentwicklung Berlin, eds. *Siedlungen der Berliner Moderne*. Berlin: Verlagshaus Braun, 2007.

Langewiesche, Dieter. "Für Volk und Vaterland." In *Kulturgut oder Körperkult?*, ed. Ommo Gruppe, 22–61. Tübingen: Attempto, 1990.
"Ein Ledigenheim." *Bauwelt* 14 (1922): 241–3.
"Die Ledigenheime." *Zeitschrift für Gewerbehygiene* 15, no. 15/16 (1908).
"Die (deutschen gemeinnützigen) Ledigenheime." *Reichsarbeitsblatt* 11, no. 6 (1913).
"Ledigenheime: aus dem Jahrbuch des Ostdeutschen Jünglingsbundes." *Rundschau* 2, no. 9 (1911).
"Ledigenheime der Strassburger gemeinnützigen Baugenossenschaft." *Concordia* 19, no. 8 (1912): 152.
"Ledigenheime und Landesversicherungsanstalten. Beitrag des Reichsversicherungsamtes." *Reichsarbeitsblatt* 12, no. 11: 926.
"Ledigenheim auf der Breslauer Ausstellung 'Wohnung und Werkraum' 1929," *Stein Holz Eisen* 2 (1930): 39–42.
"Ledigenheim für Männer an der Bergmannstrasse." *Deutsche Bauzeitung* 62 (1928): 16.
"Das Ledigenheim in Kiel." *Kommunale Praxis* 14, no. 30 (1914): 946.
"Ledigenheim München." *Die (Süddeutsche) Bauzeitung* 24 (1927): 228.
"Ledigenheim der Rochlingschen Eisen-und Stahlwerke in Volklingen." *Concordia* 10 (1909): 206–9.
"Das Ledigenheim in Stuttgart." *Zeitschrift für Wohnungswesen in Bayern* 5 (1909/10): 67–9.
"Ein Ledigenheim und Einküchenhaus im Norden Berlins." *Rheinische Blätter für Wohnungswesen und Bauberatung* 17 (1921): 57.
Lees, Andrew. *Cities, Sin, and Social Reform in Imperial Germany*. Ann Arbor: University of Michigan Press, 2002.
"Lehrerinnenheim in Pankow." *Wasmuths Monatsheft für Baukunst* (1915/1916): 133–42.
Leixner, Otto von. *Soziale Briefe aus Berlin*. Berlin: F. Pfeilstücker, 1894.
Lejeune, Jean-Francois. "From Hellerau to the Bauhaus." *The New City* 3 (Fall 1996): 51–68.
Levenstein, Adolf. *Die Arbeiterfrage: mit besonderer berücksichtigung der sozialpsychologischen seite des modernen grossbetriebes und der psycho-physischen einwirkung auf der arbeiter*. München: Ernst Reinhardt, 1912.
Lewald, Fanny. "Ninth Easter Letter for Women: Shelters for Working-Class Women." (1863) In *German Feminist Writings*, edited by Magda Müller and Patricia A. Herminghouse, 76–9. New York: Continuum, 2001.
Lewis, Michael J. *The Politics of the German Gothic Revival*. Cambridge: MIT Press, 1993.
Leyden, Friedrich. *Gross-Berlin, Geographie der Weltstadt*. Berlin: Gebr. Mann Verlag, 1995.
Lidtke, Vernon L. *The Alternative Culture: Socialist Labor in Imperial Germany*. New York: Oxford University Press, 1985.
Lihotzky, Grete. "Rationalization in the Household." (1927) In *German Feminist Writings*, edited by Magda Mueller and Patricia A. Herminghouse, 96–8. New York: Continuum, 2001.

Linazasoro, Jose-Ignacio. "Ornament and Classical Order." *Architectural Design* 54, no. 5/6 (1984): 21–5.

Linton, Derek S. *Who Has the Youth, Has the Future: The Campaign to Save Young Workers in Imperial Germany*. Cambridge: Cambridge University Press, 1991.

Loewe, Ludwig. *Schlesische Holzbauten*. Düsseldorf: Werner Verlag, 1969.

Lotz, Dr. Wilhelm. *Wie Richte ich meine Wohnung ein?* Berlin: Verlag H. Reckendorf, 1930.

Lupkin, Paula. *Manhood Factories: YMCA Architecture and the Making of Modern Urban Culture*. Minneapolis: University of Minnesota Press, 2010.

Maciuika, John V. *Before the Bauhaus: Architecture, Politics, and the German State, 1890–1920*. Cambridge: Cambridge University Press, 2005.

"Mädchenheim in Mannheim-Walddorf." *Baugewerks-Zeitung* 39 (1907): 553–5.

Manchester, William. *The Arms of Krupp*. New York: Little, Brown, and Co., 1968.

Marhoffer, Laurie. *Sex and the Weimar Republic: German Homosexual Emancipation*. Toronto: University of Toronto, 2015.

Maynes, Mary Jo. *Taking the Hard Road: Life Course in French and German Workers' Autobiographies in the Era of Industrialization*. Chapel Hill: University of North Carolina Press, 1995.

Mazon, Patricia. *Gender and the Modern Research University: The Admission of Women to German Higher Education, 1865–1914*. Palo Alto: Stanford University Press, 2003.

McCreary, E. "Social Welfare and Business: The Krupp Welfare Program, 1864–1914." *Business History Review* 42 (1968): 24–49.

McElligott, Anthony. *The German Urban Experience, 1900–1945*. London: Routledge, 2001.

McNeil, Peter. "Designing Women." *Art History* 17, no. 4 (1994): 631–57.

Meacham, Standish. *Toynbee Hall and Social Reform: 1880-1014*. New Haven: Yale University Press, 1987.

Meakin, Budgett. *Model Factories and Villages: Ideal Conditions of Labour and Housing*. Philadelphia: George W. Jacobs and Co., 1906.

Mebes, Paul. *Um 1800: Architecktur und Handwerk im Letzten Jahnhundert ihrer traditionellen Entwicklung*. München: F. Bruckmann A.G., 1920.

Meinhof, Ulrike Marie. "Kuli oder Kollege? Gastarbeiter in Deutschland." *Konkret* (November 1966): 22–7.

Meller, Helen. *European Cities: 1890–1930s: History, Culture and the Built Environment*. Chichester: John Wiley and Sons, 2001.

Meyer, Hannes. *Bauen und Gesellschaft-Schriften, Briefe, Projeckte*. Dresden, 1978.

Meyer, Hannes. *Hannes Meyer: Bauten, Projekte und Schriften*. New York: Architectural Book Pub. Co., 1965.

Michaelis, Kate. *Alfred Krupp: a Sketch of His Life and Work*. New York: T. Prosser, 1888.

Miller Lane, Barbara. *Architecture and Politics in Germany, 1918–1945*. Cambridge: Harvard University Press, 1968.

Miller Lane, Barbara. "Modern Architecture and Politics in Germany, 1918–1945." In *Housing and Dwelling*, edited by Barbara Miller Lane, 259–71. London: Routledge, 2007.

Miller Lane, Barbara. *National Romanticism and Modern Architecture in Germany and the Scandinavian Countries*. Cambridge: Cambridge University Press, 2000.

Miller, Susanne and Heinrich Potthoff. *A History of German Social Democracy*. New York: St. Martin's Press, 1986.

Milles, Dietrich. "Industrial Hygiene: A State Obligation? Industrial Pathology as a Problem in German Social Policy." In *The State and Social Change in Germany, 1880–1980*, edited by W.R. Lee and Eve Rosenhaft, 161–99. Providence: Berg, 1990.

Mitteilungen des Rheinischen Vereins für Kleinwohnungswesen. Düsseldorf: Rheinischer Verein für Kleinwohnungswesen, 1910–1915.

Mittelbach, Robert. *Amtliche Entfernungskarte der Kreise Bochum-Stadt u.– Land u. Witten: (Regierungsbezirk Arnsberg)*. Leipzig: Mittelbach, 1904.

Moderne Bauformen: Monatshefte für Architektur und Raumkunst. Stuttgart: Hoffmann, 1902–1944.

Moeller, Gisela. *Peter Behrens in Düsseldorf: die Jahre von 1903–1907*. Weinheim: VCH, 1991.

Mohr, Wilhelmine. "Ledigenheime für Frauen." *Die Hilfe* 17, no. 47 (1911): 740–2.

"More Cooperative Housing." *Cooperation* 14 (February 1928): 34–5.

Morgenstern, Lina. *Berliner Volksküchen*. Berlin: Otto Loewenstein, 1870.

Morgenstern, Lina. "Die Volksküchen in Berlin." *Die Gartenlaube* 27 (1866): 431.

Morris, Susannah. "Philanthropy in the Voluntary Housing Field in Nineteenth- and Early-Twentieth-Century London." In *Philanthropy, Patronage, and Civil Society: Experiences from Germany, Great Britain, and North America*, ed. Thomas Adam, 138–62. Bloomington: Indiana University Press, 2004.

Mueller, Magda and Patricia A. Herminghouse, eds. *German Feminist Writings*. New York: Continuum, 2001.

Müller-Wulckow, Walter. *Die Deutsche Wohnung der Gegenwart*. Königstein i. Taunus: Langewiesche, 1932.

Murphy, R.C. *Guestworkers in the German Reich. A Polish Community in Wilhelmian Germany*. New York: Columbia University Press, 1983.

Muthesius, Hermann. "Wo stehen Wir?" *Jahrbuch des deutschen Werkbundes* (Jena, 1912): 11–26.

Mrozowski, Stephan A., Grace H. Ziesing, and Mary C. Beaudry. *Living on the Boott: Historical Archaeology at the Boott Mills Boardinghouses, Lowell, Massachusetts*. Amherst, MA: University of Massachusetts Press, 1996.

Nerdinger, Winfried, et al. *Hannes Meyer, 1889–1954: Architekt, Urbanist, Lehrer*. Berlin: Ernst und Sohn Verlag, 1989.

Nerdinger, Winfried, et al. *Theodor Fischer*. Berlin: Ernst und Sohn, 1988.

"Das Neue Ledigenheim in München." *Der Baumeister* 25 (1927): 141–6.

Die Neue Rundschau, vols. 1–14 (1890–1904).

"The New Homes of New York: A Study of Flats." *Scribner's Monthly* 8, no. 1 (May 1874): 63–76.

Niethammer, Lutz. "Wie Wohnten die Arbeiter im Kaiserreich?" *Archiv für Sozialgeschichte* 16 (1979): 61–134.

Niess, W. "Von Arbeitervereinslokalen zu den Volkshäusern (1848–1933)." *Hessische Blätter für Volks-und Kulturforschung* 16 (1984): 141–56.

Nolan, Mary. "'Housework Made Easy': the Taylorized Housewife in Weimar Germany's Rationalized Economy." *Feminist Studies* 16, no. 3 (Autumn, 1990): 549–77.

"Nutford House, W." *The Builder* 110, no. 3822 (1916): 341.

Olsen, Donald J. "Inside the Dwelling: the Viennese Wohnung." In *Housing and Dwelling*, edited by Barbara Miller Lane, 117–19. London: Routledge, 2007.

Otto, Christian F. "Modern Environment and Historical Continuity: The Heimatschutz Discourse in Germany." *Art Journal* 43, no. 2 (1983): 148–57.

"PBS NewsHour for June 25, 2018." *PBS Newshour* (June 25, 2018).

Pearson, Lynn F. *The Architectural and Social History of Cooperative Living*. New York: St. Martin's Press, 1988.

"The People's Kitchens in Vienna." *The Nineteenth Century* 36 (July–December 1894): 744–53.

Pommer, Richard. "The Flat Roof: A Modernist Controversy in Germany." *Art Journal* 43, no. 2 (Summer, 1983): 158–69.

Poore, Carol. "In Darkest Europe and the Ways Out, 1890–1918." In *The Bonds of Labor: German Journeys to the Working World, 1890–1990*. Detroit: Wayne State University Press, 2000.

Popp, Adelheid. "Autobiography of a Working Woman." (1903) In *German Feminist Writings*, edited by Magda Mueller and Patricia A. Herminghouse, 84–6. New York: Continuum, 2001.

Posener, Julius. *Berlin auf dem Wege zu einer neuen Architektur, des Zeitalter Wilhelms II*. Münich: Prestel, 1979.

Potvin, John. "Hot by Design: The Secret Life of a Turkish Bath in Victorian London." In *Craft, Space and Interior Design*, edited by Sandra Alfoldy and Janice Helland, 11–25. Burlington: Ashgate, 2008.

Pounds, Norman John Greville. *The Ruhr: A Study in Historical and Economic Geography*. London: Faber and Faber, 1952.

Pounds, Norman John Greville. *The Upper Silesian Industrial Region*. Bloomington, Indiana: Indiana University, 1958.

Der Profanbau. Leipzig: Arnd, 1905–1922.

Purdom, C.B. *The Garden City*. London: Dent and Sons, 1913.

Raabe, Edmund. *Fünfundzwanzig Jahre im Gewerbeschuldienst: Rückblick auf d. Tätigkeit d. Herrn Reg.-u. Gewerbeschulrats Oskar Spetzler zu Posen*. Posen: Marzbach, 1904.

Radicke, Dieter. "Die Entwicklung des öffentlichen Personennahverkehrs in Berlin bis zur Gründung der BVG." In *Anlagen und Bauten für den Verkehr (1) Städtischer*

Nahverkehr, Berlin und seine Bauten (part 10, Vol. B), edited by K.K. Weber, Peter Güttler, and D. Ahmadi. Berlin, 1979.

Radomski, J. *Das Schlafstellenwesen in Posen*. Posen: W. Decker und Co., 1905.

Radomski, J. *Über Fürsorge für Ledige Arbeiter in Posen*. Posen: W. Decker und Co., 1911.

Radke, Johannes. *Der Neubau der Anstalt*. Düsseldorf: Bagel, 1915.

"Ein Raum, in dem zehn Männer auf Strohsäcken liegen können." *Die Welt*, 22 August, 1960.

Rave, Paul Ortwin, Irmgard Wirth, and Hinnerk Scheper. *(Die) Bauwerke und Kunstdenkmäler von Berlin: Teil 2: Stadt und Bezirk Charlottenburg*. Berlin: Gebr. Mann Verlag, 1961.

Rave, Rolf and Hans Joachim Knoefel. *Bauten seit 1900 in Berlin*. Berlin: Kiepert, 1968.

Reich, Emmi. *Der Wohnungsmarkt in Berlin von 1840-1910*. Munich and Leipzig, 1912.

(die) Reichsarbeitsblatt. Berlin: Stollberg, 1903-1927.

Reimann, George J. *Das Berliner Strassenbild des XVIII und XIX Jahrhunderts*. Berlin: Henschelverlag, 1954.

Repp, Kevin. *Reformers, Critics, and the Paths of German Modernity: Anti-Politics and the Search for Alternatives, 1890-1914*. Cambridge: Harvard University Press, 2000.

Reuveni, Gideon. *Reading Germany: Literature and Consumer Culture in Germany before 1933*. New York: Berghahn Books, 2006.

Richards, Ellen H. *The Rumford Kitchen Leaflets*. Boston: Rockwell and Churchill Press, 1899.

Roberts, James S. *Drink, Temperance and the Working Class in Nineteenth-Century Germany*. Boston: Allen and Unwin, 1984.

Rock, Cynthia. "Building the Women's Club in Nineteenth Century America." *Heresies* 3, no. 3 (1981): 87-90.

Rodgers, Daniel T. *Atlantic Crossings: Social Politics in a Progressive Age*. Cambridge: Harvard University Press, 1998.

Rollins, William H. *A Greener Vision of Home: Cultural Politics and Environmental Reform in the German Heimatschutz Movement, 1904-1918*. Ann Arbor: University of Michigan Press, 1997.

Rollins, William H. "Heimat, Modernity and Nation in the Early Heimatschutz Movement." In *Heimat, Nation, Fatherland: The German Sense of Belonging*, edited by Jost Hermand and James Steakley, 87-112. New York: Lang, 1996.

Rose, William John. *The Drama of Upper Silesia; A Regional Study*. Brattleboro, Vermont: Stephan Daye Press, 1935.

Rosenhaft, Eve and W.R. Lee. "State and Society in Modern Germany—Beamtenstaat, Klassenstaat, Wohlfahrststaat." In *The State and Social Change in Germany, 1880-1980*, edited by. W.R. Lee and Eve Rosenhaft, 1-33. Providence: Berg, 1990.

Ruhrländisches Bauwesen 1904-1925-Festschrift zum 25jährigen Bestehen des Ruhrländischen Architekten-und Ingenieurvereins in Essen. Essen, 1929.

"Saint George's House, LXXIL, Vincent Square." *The Building New and Engineering Journal* (August 18, 1905): 218.

Salomon, Alice. *Character Is Destiny: The Autobiography of Alice Salomon*. Edited and translated by Andrew Lees. Ann Arbor: University of Michigan Press, 2004.

Salzgeber, Charitas-Sekretär (Berlin). "Veranstaltungen der katholischen Charitas (Versammlungsbericht)." In *Schlafstellenwesen und Ledigenheime*, 155–60. Berlin: Carl Henmanns Verlag, 1904.

Samter, Hans. "Das Charlottenburger Ledigenheim." *Der Arbeiterfreund* 47 (1909): 20–5.

Sassin, Erin Eckhold. "Single Women, Public Space, and the German Ledigenheim." In *Women, Femininity, and Public Space in European Visual Culture, 1789–1914*, edited by Temma Balducchi and Heather Belnap Jensen, 257–74. Burlington, VT: Ashgate, 2014.

Sassin, Erin Eckhold. "The Visual Politics of Upper Silesian Settlements in World War One." In *Empires in World War One: Shifting Frontiers and Imperial Dynamics in a Global Conflict*, edited by Andrew Tait Jarboe and Richard S. Fogarty, 282–302. New York: I.B. Tauris, 2014.

Scharoun, Hans. *Bauten, Entwürfe, Texte, Schriftenreihe*, vol. 10. Edited by P. Pfannkuch. Berlin: Akademie der Künste, 1993.

Scheinin, Richard. "Silicon Valley's Housing Affordability Crisis Worsens." *Oakland Tribune* (July 20, 2015).

Schirmacher, Käthe. "The Modern Woman's Rights Movement in Germany." (1912) In *German Feminist Writings*, edited by Magda Mueller and Patricia A. Herminghouse, 132–6. New York: Continuum, 2001.

Schivmachev, Maethe. "Wie Wohnt die erwerbende Frau?" *Blätter für Volksgesundheitspflege* 11 no. 10 (1911): 230–3.

Schlafstellenwesen und Ledigenheime: Vorbericht und Verhandlungen der 13. Konferenz der Zentralstelle für Arbeiter-Wohlfahrtseinrichtungen am 9. Und 10. Mai in Leipzig. Schriften der Zentralstelle für Arbeiter-Wohlfahrtseinrichtungen (No. 26). Berlin: Carl Henmanns Verlag, 1904.

Schmidt, Anna. "Die Wohnungsfrage im Leben der Lehrerin und ihre Lösung" *Mitteilungen des Rheinischen Vereins für Kleinwohnungswesen* 8, no. 5 (May 1912): 45–50.

Schmidt, R. and J. Rings. *Wollen-Können*. Essen: Allgemeiner Bauverein Essen A.G. (Allbau), 1923.

Schmitt, Eduard. "Volksküchen und Speiseanstalten für Arbeiter; Volkskaffeehäuser." In *Handbuch der Architektur, Vierter Teil: Entwerfen, Anlage und Einrichtung der Gebäude: Erholungs-, Beherbergungs- und Vereinszwecke*, edited by Josef Durm, Hermann Ende, and Eduard Schmitt, 156–72. Stuttgart: Arnold Bergsträsser Verlagsbuchhandlung, 1904.

Schmolke, Michael. *Adolf Kolping als Publizist: ein Beitrag zur Publizistik und zur Verbandsgeschichte des deutschen Katholizismus im 19. Jahrhundert*. Münster: Verlag Regensburg, 1966.

Schnaubert, Julius. *Ledigenheime für Berlin*. Charlottenburg: Lehsten, 1918.
Schoenauer, Norbert. "Early European Collective Habitation: From Utopian Ideal to Reality." In *New Households, New Housing*, edited by Karen Franck and Sherry Ahrentzen, 47–70. New York: Van Nostrand Reinhold, 1989.
Schubert, Dirk. "Theodor Fritsch and the German (völkische) version of the Garden City." *Planning Perspectives* 19, no. 1 (2004): 3–35.
Schultze-Naumburg, Paul. "Biedermeierstil?" *Kunstwart* 19, no. 3: 130–7.
Schultze-Naumburg, Paul. *Die Entstellung Unseres Landes*. Munich: Hofbuchdruckerei Raftner und Callwen, 1907.
Schultze-Naumburg, Paul. *Kulturarbeiten: Vol. 3, Dörfer und Kolonien*. Munich: G.D.W. Callwey, 1908.
Schumacher, F. *Die Kleinwohnung*. Leipzig: Verlag von Quelle und Meyer, 1919.
Schuster, Franz. *Ein Möbelbuch*. Frankfurt: Englert und Schlosser, 1930.
Schwartz, Frederic. *The Werkbund: Design Theory and Mass Culture before the First World War*. New Haven: Yale University Press, 1996.
Schweitzer, Msgr. Dr. *Hospize und Ledigenheime der kath. Gesellenvereine*. M. Gladbach: Volksvereins Verlag, 1911.
Sklar, Kathryn Kish, Anja Schüler, and Susan Strasser, eds. *Social Justice Feminists in the United States and Germany: A Dialogue in Documents, 1885–1933*. Ithaca: Cornell University Press, 1998.
"Sloane Garden House." *Work and Leisure: the Englishwoman's Advertiser, Reporter and Gazette* 14, no. 4 (April 1889): 87–8.
Smith-Rosenberg, Carroll. "The Female World of Love and Ritual." In *Disorderly Conduct: Visions of Gender in Nineteenth-Century America*, 53–76. New York: Oxford, 1985.
Sonne, Wolfgang. *Dwelling in the Metropolis: Reformed Urban Blocks*. Glasgow: University of Glasgow, 2005.
Soziale Arbeit: 1842-1942 (Bochumer Verein für Gusstahlfabrikation AG Bochum. Bochum), 1942.
Soziale Praxis und Archiv für Volkswohlfahrt. Jena: Fischer, 1910–1927.
Soziale Praxis: Centralblatt für Sozialpolitk, vols. 8–13 (1899–1904).
Spain, Daphne. *How Women Saved the City*. Minneapolis: University of Minnesota Press, 2001.
Spector, Scott. *Prague Territories: National Conflict and Cultural Innovation in Franz Kafka's Fin de Siecle*. Berkeley: University of California Press, 2000.
Speidel, Manfred. *Bruno Taut: Natur und Fantasie: 1880–1938*. Berlin: Ernst und Sohn, 1995.
Spencer, Elaine Glovka. "Policing Popular Amusements in German Cities: The Case of the Prussian Rhine Province 1815–1914." *Journal of Urban History* 16 (1990): 366–85.
Spencer-Wood, Suzanne. "The World Their Household." In *Housing and Dwelling*, edited by Barbara Miller Lane, 163–77. London: Routledge, 2007.

Sperber, Jonathan. *Popular Catholicism in Nineteenth Century Germany*. Princeton: Princeton University Press, 1984.

Sperber, Jonathan. "The Shaping of Political Catholicism in the Ruhr Basin: 1848–1881." *Central European History* 16, no. 4 (December, 1983): 347–67.

Sperber, Jonathan. "The Transformation of Catholic Associations in the Northern Rhineland and Westphalia 1830–1879." *Journal of Social History* 15, no. 2 (Winter, 1981): 253–63.

Spiegel, W. "Ledigenheime." *Schriften des Vereins für Sozialpolitik* 128 (1908): 415.

Spitzer, Heinz. *Berlin, von 1650 bis 1900: Entwicklung der Stadt in historischen Plänen und Ansichten, mit Erläuterungen*. Berlin: Tourist Verlag, 1989.

Stadtbaukunst alter und neuer Zeit. Berlin: Pontos Verlag, 1920–1928.

Stallybrass, Peter and Allon White. *The Politics and Poetics of Transgression*. Ithaca: Cornell University Press, 1986.

Stankiewicz, Mary Ann. "Art at Hull House, 1889–1901." *Woman's Art Journal* 10, no. 1 (Spring-Summer 1989): 35–9.

Stark, Gary D. *Entrepeneurs of Ideology: Neoconservative Publishers in Germany, 1890–1933*. Chapel Hill: University of North Carolina Press, 1981.

Starr, Ellen Gates. "Art and Labor." In *Hull House Maps and Papers*, 165–82. New York: Thomas Y. Crowell and Co., 1895.

Statistisches Jahrbuch des deutschen Reiches. Berlin: v. Stilke und van Muyden, 1870–1932.

Statistishes Jahrbuch deutscher Städte. Jena: Fischer, 1890–1933.

Statistisches Jahrbuch der Stadt Berlin. Berlin: Stat. Amt der Stadt Berlin, 1878–1943.

Statistisches Jahrbuch für Preussen. Berlin: Landesamt, 1904–1934.

Steinhauer, G., ed. *Festschrift 50 Jahre Allgemeiner Bauverein Essen A.G.* Essen: Allgemeiner Bauverein Essen A.G. (Allbau), 1969.

Stoehr, Irene. "Housework and Motherhood: Debates and Policies in the Women's Movement in Imperial Germany and the Weimar Republic." In *Maternity and Gender Policies*, edited by Gisela Bock and Pat Thane, 213–32. London: Routledge, 1991.

Stratigakos, Despina. *A Woman's Berlin: Building the Modern City*. Minneapolis: University of Minnesota Press, 2008.

Tafuri, Manfredo. *Architecture and Utopia: Design and Capitalist Development*. Cambridge: MIT Press, 1976.

Die Tat. Jena, 1909–1914.

Taut, Bruno. "Ein Ledigenheim in Schöneberg." *Stadtbaukunst Alter und Neuer Zeit* 1 (1920): 136–9.

Taylor, Lawrence. "Re-Entering the West Room: On the Power of Domestic Spaces." In *House Life: Space, Place, and Family in Europe*, edited by Donna Birdwell-Pheasant and Denise Lawrence-Zuniga, 223–38. New York: Berg, 1999.

Taylor, Robert R. *Hohenzollern Berlin: Construction and Reconstruction*. Port Credit, ON, Canada: P.D. Meany Publishers, 1985.

Teige, Karel. *The Minimum Dwelling*. Translated by Eric Dluhosch. Cambridge, MA: MIT Press, 2002.

Terlinden, Ulla and Susanna von Oertzen. *Die Wohnungsfrage ist Frauensache!* Berlin: Reimar, 2006.

Teuteberg, H.J. and C. Wischermann, eds. *Wohnalltag in Deutschland, 1850–1914*. Münster: F. Coppenrath, 1985.

Tigerman, Bobbye. "I Am Not a Decorator." *Journal of Design History* 20 (2007): 61–74.

Tims, Richard W. *Germanizing Prussian Poland: The H-K-T Society and the Struggle for the Eastern Marches in the German Empire, 1894–1919*. New York: Columbia University Press, 1941.

Tipton, Frank B. *Regional Variations in the Economic Development of Germany during the Nineteenth Century*. Middletown, CT: Wesleyan University Press, 1976.

Tobin, Elizabeth H. "War and the Working Class: The Case of Düsseldorf 1914–1918." *Central European History* 18, no. 3/4 (1985): 257–98.

Tobin, Robert Deam. *Peripheral Desires: The German Discovery of Sex*. Philadelphia: UPenn, 2015.

Tooley, T. Hunt. *National Identity and Weimar Germany: Upper Silesia and the Eastern Border, 1918-1922*. Lincoln: University of Nebraska Press, 1997.

Tosh, Josh. "New Men? The Bourgeois Cult of Home." *History Today* 46, no. 12 (December 1996): 1–9.

Trost, Klara. *Ledigen-Heime für weibliche Erwerbstätige; Eine Forderung aus d. Kriegswirtschaft mit Grundrißbeispielen*. Hannover: Deutsche Bauhütte, 1918.

Twarog, Sophia. "Heights and Living Standards in Germany." In *Health and Welfare During Industrialization*, edited by Richard Steckel and Roderick Floud, 285–330. Chicago: University of Chicago Press, 1997.

Twose, George. "The Coffee House at Hull House." *House Beautiful* 7, no. 2 (January 1900): 107–9.

Uhlig, Guenter. *Kollektivmodell "Einkuechenhaus"-Wohnreform und Archtekturdebatte zwischen Frauenbewegung und Funktionalismus, 1900–1933*. Giessen, 1981.

Umbach, Maiken. "Memory and Historicism: Reading between the Lines of the Built Environment, Germany c. 1900." *Representations* 88 (2005): 26–54.

Umbach, Maiken. "The Vernacular International: Heimat, Modernism and the Global Market in Early Twentieth-Century Germany." *National Identities* 4, no. 1 (2002): 45–68.

Unseren Kriegsinvaliden Heim- und Werkstatt in Gartenstadt-Siedlungen (Denkschrift der Deutschen Gartenstadtgesellschaft). Leipzig: Renaissance Verlag, 1915.

Van Slyck, Abigail Ayres. "The Lady and the Library Loafer: Gender and Public Space in Victorian America." *Winterthur Portfolio* 31, no. 4 (Winter, 1996): 221–42.

Vickery, Margaret Birney. *Buildings for Bluestockings: The Architecture and Social History of Women's Colleges in Late Victorian England*. Newark: University of Delaware Press, 1999.

Vicinus, Martha. *Independent Women: Work and Community for Single Women, 1850–1920*. Chicago: University of Chicago Press, 1985.

Voepel, Otto. "Untersuchungen über den Charakter der Gebäude." *Architektonische Rundschau* 28, no. 10 (1912): 37–40.

Voigt, Paul. *Grundrente und Wohnungsfrage in Berlin und den Vororten*. Jena: G. Fischer, 1901.

Voigt, Wolfgang. "The Garden City as Eugenic Utopia." *Planning Perspectives* 4, no. 3 (1989): 295–312.

Vogts, Hans. *Kölner Bauliche Entwicklung, 1888–1927*. Köln: Architekten- und Ingenieurverein für den Niederrhein und Westfalen und Köln mit Unterstützung der Stadt Köln. Festgabe zum Deutschen Architekten- und Ingenieurtag, 1927.

Volkov, Shulamit. *The Rise of Popular Antimodernism in Germany: The Urban Master Artisans*. Princeton: Princeton University Press, 1978.

Wagner (Oberbuergermeister). *Die Tätigkeit der Stadt Ulm auf dem Gebiete der Wohnungsfürsorge für Arbeiter und Bedienstete*. Ulm: J. Ebner, 1903.

Walker, Mack. *German Home Towns: Community, State, and General Estate: 1648–1871*. Ithaca: Cornell University Press, 1971.

Walkowitz, Judith R. *City of Dreadful Delight*. Chicago: University of Chicago Press, 1992.

Walser-Smith, Helmut. *German Nationalism and Religious Conflict*. Princeton: Princeton University Press, 1995.

Walter, Rudolf. *Archiv der Freistudenten-Bewegung: Die Studentenheimfrage* (Heft 2). Leipzig: Demme, 1909.

Wandel, Arthur. "Über das Schlafstellenwesen und über Ledigenheime." *Deutsche Vierteljahrsschrift für Öffentliche Gesundheitspflege* 40, no. 30 (1908): 483.

Wasmuths Monatshefte für Baukunst. Berlin: Ernst Wasmuth, A.G., 1914–1932.

Wätzoldt, Stephan. *Bibliographie zur Architektur im 19. Jahrhundert: die Aufsätze in den deutschsprachigen Architekturzeitschriften, 1789–1918*. Nendeln, Liechtenstein: KTO Press, 1977.

Weber, A. F. *The Growth of Cities in the Nineteenth Century: A Study in Statistics* (1899). Ithaca: Cornell, reprinted 1965.

Weber, Alfred. *Über den Standort der Industrien*. Tübingen: Mohr, 1909.

Weiner, Deborah E.B. "Hull House and the Production of Women's Space in the Late Victorian City." *Critical Matrix* 11, no. 2 (June 1999): 87.

Weiss, Albert. *Können die in den grossstädtischen Wohnverhältnissen liegenden Mängel und Schäden behoben werden?* Berlin: Heymann, 1912.

Welter, Barbara. "The Cult of True Womanhood: 1820–1860." *American Quarterly* 18, no. 2 (Summer 1966): 151–74.

Wendschuh, Achim and Barbara Volkmann, eds. *Bruno Taut, 1880–1938*. Berlin: Akademie der Künste Ausstellung/Brüder Hartmann, 1980.

Werkszeitung/Ruhrstahl-Aktien-Gesellschaft, Henrichshütte Hattingen (Werks-Zeitung der Ruhrstahl-Aktien-Gesellschaft für die Werke Witten, Hattingen, Gelsenkirchen, Oberkassel, Annen, Brackwede). Düsseldorf, 1930–1934.

Werner, Georg. *Ein Kumpel*. Berlin: Die Knappshaft, 1930.

Westermanns Illustrierte Monatshefte. Braunschweig: Westermann, 1856–1906.
Westermanns Monatshefte. München: Magazinpr. Verlag, 1906–1987.
Weyl, Theodor and August Gärtner, eds. *Weyls Handbuch der Hygiene: Soziale Hygiene (Volksspeisung, Schulskinderspeisung, Notstandsspeisung, Massenspeisung; Obdachlosenasyle, Herbergen, Schlafhäuser, Ledigenheime, Volksküchen und Wärmehallen)* Leipzig: Barth, 1912/18.
Wiedenhöft, Ronald. *Berlin's Housing Revolution.* Ann Arbor: UMI, 1985.
Wiedfeldt, R. "Einleitendes Referat (Versammlungsbericht)." In *Schlafstellenwesen und Ledigenheime,* 120–48. Berlin: Carl Henmanns Verlag, 1904.
Wilson, H. F. "Toynbee Hall." *Cambridge Review* (February 18, 1885).
Winter, Irina. *Georg Benjamin: Arzt und Kommunist.* Berlin: Verlag Volk und Gesundheit, 1962.
"'Die Wohnung unserer Zeit' auf der Deutschen Bauaustellung Berlin 1931." *Moderne Bauformen* 30 (1931): 329–47.
Wolff, M. P. *Die Ernährung der arbeitenden Klassen: Ein Plan für Gründung öffentlicher Küchen.* Berlin: Verlag Julius Springer, 1885.
Wright, Gwendolyn. *Building the Dream: A Social History of Housing in America.* Cambridge, MA: MIT Press, 1995.
Wrigley, E.A. *Industrial Growth and Population Change: A Regional Study of the Coalfield Areas of North-West Europe in the Later 19th Century.* Cambridge: 1962.
Zeitung des Vereins Deutscher Eisenbahnverwaltungen. Berlin: Springer, 1861–1932.
Zeitschrift für Baukunde. Munich: Ackermann, 1878–84.
Zeitschrift für Bauwesen. Berlin, 1851–1931.
Zeitschrift für Wohnungswesen (ZfW). Berlin, 1902–1940.
Zentralblatt der Bauwervaltung. Berlin, 1881–1931.
Zimm, Alfred. *Die Entwicklung des Industriestandortes Berlin: Tendenzen der geographischen Lokalisation bei den Berliner Industriezweigen von überörtlicher Bedeutung sowie die Territoriale Stadtentwicklung bis 1945.* (Ost) Berlin: Deutscher Verlag der Wissenschaft, 1959.
Zimmermann, Claudia. *Die Siedlung Lindenhof als Impuls für Sozialen Siedlungsbau in Berlin.* PhD diss., Free University Berlin, 1992.
Zimmermann, Susan, ed. *Urban Space and Identity in the European City 1890–1930s.* Budapest: Central European University, 1995.
Zünder, Ralf. *Vom Ledigenheim zum Studentenwohnheim.* Berlin: Studentenwerk, 1990.

Archives

Berlin Staatsarchiv
Eichborndamm 115-121, 13403 Berlin
Canadian Centre for Architecture

1920 Rue Baile, Montreal, QC H3H 2S6
Essen Stadtarchiv
Steeler Strasse 29, 45127 Essen
Frankfurt am Main Stadtarchiv (Institut für Stadtgeschichte)
Karmeliterkloster, Münzgasse 9, 60311 Frankfurt am Main
Historisches Archiv der Stadt Köln
Severinstrasse 222-228, 50676 Köln
Rheinisch Westfälisches Wirtschaftsarchiv Köln
Unter Sachsenhausen 10-26, 50667 Köln

Index

Abel, Mary Hinman 156
Abendheime 205
Adam, Thomas 104
Addams, Jane 155
agricultural workers 82–3
Altenhof estate 100
Alt Moabit Ledigenheim 218–24
American YMCA 20 n.40, 27
apprentices 68–70, 82–3
Arbeiterfreund 86
Arbeiterinnenheime 210, 213
Arbeiterinnen-Klubs 205
Arbeiterkaserne 84
Arbeiterwohl 86
Arbeitsamt 191 n.90
Arts and Crafts movement 24
Aschaffenburg Ledigenheim 75 n.121
Association of Progressive Women's
    Organizations 138

Barnett, Sylvan 139
barracks 84–8, 92–3
    Arbeiterkaserne (military barracks for
        workers) 84
    Mietskaserne (rental barracks) 3,
        63, 93
    Schlafbaracken (sleeping barracks) 84
    for single men 176
Barrett, Henrietta 8
Bauakademie 56
Bäumer, Gertude 133, 202
Bebel, August 202, 205
Bederman, Gail 9
beer 156–7
Behrens, Peter 59–61
Bellamy, Edward 101
Bentham, Jeremy 90
Bergmannstrasse Ledigenheim 249
Bethune, George W. 139
Biedermeier
    revival 57–9
    villa 102–3, 108

Bildung 7–8, 39
Bildungsbürger 132
Bildungsbürgertum 104, 132
Blaise Hamlet 100
Blockrandbebauung 180
Bochum city 87
Bochumer Verien 86–8
Boehmert, Victor 133
bourgeois life 45
bourgeois reform 8–9, 214
Bournville 100
Brace, Charles Loring 139
British Rowton Houses 91, 163–5
Brüggemeier, Franz-Josef 82
Buckingham, James Silk 101
Bund Heimatschutz 102–3
Butler, Judith 9

Cadbury, George 100–1
Calwer, Richard 134–5
"Catholic-Christian" home 36
Catholicism 32, 34–6
Catholic Ledigenheime 13–14, 27–8,
    31–40, 43–62, 69–70, 73 n.50,
    138, 148, 162, 188 n.16, 228
    aesthetics 61–9
    bedrooms 52–4, 61–9
    Church 32–3
    circulation within 50–4
    Cologne 47–8
    control 50–4
    dining halls 39–46
    emergence of 31
    freedom 50–4
    German Gothic revival in 54–61
    gymnasia 48–9
    ideal residents 31–2
    during Kulturkampf 35–6
    libraries and reading rooms 45
    movement 33
    rooms, types of 39–45
    spaces, multitude of 39–50

St. Antoniushaus 39–43
  state 33–9
  style, symbolism of 54–61
  Catholics 34
  Church 32–3
Coffee houses 193 n.132
Cologne Troubles (*Kölner Wirren*) 30
community (*Gemeinschaft*) 9–10
company towns 82–4
  and Ledigenheime 92–7
corporate advertising, Ledigenheime as 97–105
Czechoslovakia 257

Damaschke, Adolf 9
Dankelmannstrasse Ledigenheim 145–8, 158–60, 167–8, 172–4, 176, 226
Darmstadt colony 1
Dawson, William Harbutt 64, 136
Der Eigene 53
Deutsche Kunst und Dekoration (Fuchs) 1
Deutscher Verein für öffentliche Gesundheitspflege 132–3
Deutscher Werkbund 18 n.26, 59
Diederichs, Eugen 57
die Meistersinger von Nürnberg (Wagner) 56
Dioezesanpräsis 29
docile bodies 10
Dollard, Catherine 12
dormitories 89
Düsseldorf Ledigenheim 143–5, 167, 175

Einliegerwohnung(en) 253, 255, 261 n.18
Engels, Friedrich 202
era of reform, in Germany 129–30
Evangelische Arbeiterverein 153

Feininger, Lyonel 69–70, 178
Fischer, Theodor 79 n.211
Foucault, Michel 97
four-in-block family housing 92
Foxconn City 118
Frankfurt Ledigenheim 145, 158
Fuchs, Georg 1, 24, 59
Fürstengrube Ledigenheim 111–16
Fürstliche Plessische Bergwerkdirektion 111–16

Galluswarte building 162–3
garden cities 84, 101, 103
Garden City Association 101
Gemeinschaft und Gesellschaft (Tönnies) 9
Generalpräsis 29
George, Henry 101
German artisan 69–70
German farmhouse 102–3
German Garden City Association 101
Germany's Central Organization for Workers' Welfare, conference of 127–9
Gesamtkunstwerk 56
Gewerbe-Schulen 68
Gleim, Betty 203
Görres, Joseph 31
Gothic architecture 55–61
guestworkers, living conditions of 81–2, 117
Gutman, Marta 8, 133

"half-open" family structure 82
Hall, Toynbee 8, 139
Handwerker-Schulen 68
Handwerkerstand (artisan estate) 24–5
Hansastädte 77 n.165
Hedwig Rüdiger Häuser 250–1
Hegemann, Werner 256
Heimat 4
Heimatstil 114
Henderson, Susan 7
Herr-im-Haus 83, 104
Hirschfeld, Magnus 53
homosexuality 53–4
Hospize und Ledigenheime der kath (Schweitzer) 61
housing 16; *see also* Ledigenheime
  four-in-block family 92
  reform of
    aesthetic 157–62
    bedroom 162–74
    consciousness raising to action 135–8
    dietary 149–56
    era of 129–30
    expansion (1890s) 131–4
    impulse (beginnings) 130–1
    libraries 141–9
    national health 157–62

Index

poverty and   134–5
privilege, sliding scale of   162–74
residents and   138–41
sociological reports   134–5
success of   175–86
surveys   134–5
temperance   156–7
in Weimar Republic   18 n.22, 130–4
Howard, Ebenezer   101
Hufeisensiedlung (Horseshoe
   Settlement)   178
Hull House   156

industrialization, effects of   1–4, 29, 54,
   82, 130, 186, 259
industrial (proto-) Ledigenheime   83–6,
   88–9, 92, 140

Jahn, Friedrich Ludwig   48–9
Jenison, Madge   136
Jenkins, Jennifer   64
journeymen artisans   82–3

Kaiser Wilhelm Ledigenheim   148–9,
   152, 160–1, 247
Kautsky, Karl   142, 156
Kertbeny, Karl Maria   53
Kolping, Adolph   23–71
   Ledigenheim and   26–8
   Verband katholischer Gesellenvereine
      and   28–31
Kolpinghaus Düsseldorf   37–8
Kolping Jugendwohnen GmbH   71–2
Kolping Youth Home of Central
   Cologne   23
Kommunalen Zentrum
   Ledigenheim   182–4
Kronenberg "colony"   94
Kropotkin, Peter   101
Krupp, Friedrich Alfred   53, 94, 100
Kulczycki, John   3, 83
Kulturkampf   30
Kunstgewerbeschulen   68

Lange, Helene   202
Larsson, Carl   100
Ledigenheime   4–7, 18 n.21, 204
   as architectural/social project
      14–15
   building typology   15

Catholic   13–14, 27–8, 31–40, 43–62,
   69–70, 138, 148, 162, 228
   and company town   92–7
   as corporate advertising   97–105
   Dankelmannstrasse   145–8, 159–60,
      167–8, 172–4, 176, 226
   decline of   15–16
   Düsseldorf   143–5, 167, 175
   Frankfurt   145, 158
   of Fürstengrube   111–16
   gender identities, formation of   9
   importance   4–7
   industrial (proto-)   83–6, 88–9, 92,
      140
   Kaiser Wilhelm   148–9, 152, 160–1,
      247
   for men   10–11, 14, 170–1, 207, 209,
      214–19, 223–35, 246 n.110
   Neuss   40–2
   Pallenberg   105–10
   programming   7
   public *vs.* private   9
   reform
      aesthetic   157–62
      bedroom   162–74
      consciousness raising to action
         135–8
      dietary   149–56
      era of   129–30
      expansion (1890s)   131–4
      impulse (beginnings)   130–1
      libraries   141–9
      for lower-middle-class women
         217–26
      national health   157–62
      poverty and   134–5
      privilege, sliding scale of   162–74
      residents and   138–41
      for skilled working-class
         women   217–26
      sociological reports   134–5
      success of   175–86
      surveys   134–5
      temperance   156–7
   roots of   81–2
   safe harbor   26–8
   for single/unmarried women   12–14,
      204, 240–1
      general characteristics   210–13
      lower-middle-class   213–26

professionals   227–36
purpose of   204–10
radicalism, links to   236–40
reform   217–26
skilled working-class   213–26
spaces   7
Stahlhausen   86–93, 95–7
Stuttgart   166
as transformative places   7
variants   13–14
Weberplatz   152–5, 160–1, 168, 227–8, 247
working-class and   9
Ledigenwohnungen   252–3
Lehrerinnenheim   210
Lendersche Haus   28, 73 n.44
Levenstein, Adolf   157
Lever, William   100, 101
libraries, Ledigenheim   141–9
lodgers   3–4, 17 n.8
problem   4
unmarried   4
Logierhäuser   84
Lumpenproletariet   31

Maciuika, John   68
Malpricht, Alfred   111
Manchester, William   117
Mannheim, municipality of   136
Marx, Karl   202
Mazon, Patricia   12
Mebes, Paul   57
Menagen   84
Meyer, Hannes   258
Meyershof of Berlin-Wedding   130–1
Mietskaserne (rental barracks)   3, 63, 93
Migge, Leberecht   178
Milchversorgung   137
Minimum Dwelling, The (Teige)   257
Mittelstand (middle estate)   2, 25, 47, 65, 139–40, 162, 175
Morgenstern, Lina   151, 156
Morris, William   24
municipalities   129, 132–3, 136
municipal socialism   129–30
Muthesius, Hermann   78 n.201, 79 n.211

Nash, John   100
Naumann, Friedrich   165
Neues Bauen   18, 248

Neuss Ledigenheim   40–2
New England Kitchens   156
new woman   241
New York apartment building   19 n.34
Nolan, Mary   261 n.20

Olmstead, Frederick Law   101
Olsen, Donald   25
organic community   103

Pallenberg, Jacob   105
Pallenbergheime (Pallenberg's homes)   105–10
Pankow Lehrerinnenheim   210, 227–35, 250
Panopticon   90
Paul, Bruno   65
Peirce, Melusina Fay   156
Pensionen (family homes)   205
Popular Catholicism   30
Port Sunlight   100
Präsis   29
preindustrial artisan estate   24–5
professional women   227–36
Protestants   34
Prussia   2, 24–6, 30, 82–3, 130, 135–6
public baths (*Volksbäder*)   145, 191 n.89
public doss-house   140
Pullman, George   93–4, 101
Pullman Palace Car Company   93–4

Queen Anne style   58

redemptive spaces   8, 133
reform Ledigenheime
aesthetic   157–62
bedroom   162–74
consciousness raising to action   135–8
dietary   149–56
era of   129–30
expansion (1890s)   131–4
impulse (beginnings)   130–1
libraries   141–9
for lower-middle-class women   217–26
national health   157–62
poverty and   134–5
privilege, sliding scale of   162–74
residents and   138–41

for skilled working-class women 217–26
sociological reports 134–5
success of 175–86
surveys 134–5
temperance 156–7
Reichensperger, August 56
Reichensperger, Brothers 31
rental barracks (*Mietskaserne*) 3, 63, 93
Rhineland 29, 56
Richards, Ellen H. 156
Riehl, Wilhelm 4
Riemerschmid, Richard 65
Ruhr valley 29, 87
Rumford Kitchen 156
Ruskin, John 24

Said, Edward 115
St. Antoniushaus Catholic Ledigenheime 39–43
St. Antoniushaus of Cologne 41, 69
Salomon, Alice 155, 202–3, 205
Salt, Titus 100–1
Saltaire 100
Sampter, Herr Stadtrat 176
Schankkonzession 153
Schlafbaracken 84
Schlafgänger 127–8
Schlafhäuser 84–5
Schlafstelle 128
Schlafstellenwesen 25, 98, 127, 143, 164–5, 207, 214–15
Schmidt, Karl 65
Schmohl, Robert 100
Schultze-Naumburg, Paul 102–3, 114
Schütte-Lihotzky, Grete 241
Schweitzer, Msgr. 61
sexual immorality 83
Siedlung (settlement) 15, 178, 184–6
single men 1, 7, 112, 168
  artisan estate 28
  barracks for 176
  controlling of 88–92
  in feminine role 170
  housing (see Ledigenheim)
  unregulated lodgings of 127
single women 201–4
  displacement 202

Ledigenheime for 204, 240–1
  general characteristics 210–13
  lower-middle-class 213–26
  professionals 227–36
  purpose of 204–10
  radicalism, links to 236–40
  reform 217–26
  skilled working-class 213–26
  nineteenth-century 201–2
Smith, Helmut Walser 35–6
Social Catholicism 31
Social Democracy 32–3, 87
social insurance programs 129
society (*Gesellschaft*) 9–10
Sombart, Werner 133, 141
Soziale Briefe aus Berlin (von Leixner) 150
Spain, Daphne 8, 133
Spector, Scott 115
Speisehallengesellschaft 153
Speisewirtschaft 210
Spetzler's system 90–1
Stahlhausen 86–93, 95–7
Stallybrass, Peter 201
Stubenälteste 90
Stuttgart Ledigenheim 166
surplus women 201–2, 207

Tafuri, Manfredo 117
Tagesheime 205
Taut, Bruno 178
Teige, Karel 257
Tessenow, Heinrich 65
To-morrow: A Path to Real Reform (Howard) 101
Tönnies, Ferdinand 9
Tosh, Josh 27–8
Treitschke, Heinrich 33
Trinkzwang 157
true womanhood, cult of 19–20 n.34

unmarried lodgers 4, 14–15
unregulated lodgings 3, 15, 25–6, 149, 163
  diseases associated with 134
  evils of 138, 175
  illegitimate births and 53
  illicit liaisons and 53
  problems 127–8, 134–5
  of single people 127

Upper Silesian village models   114
urbanization   4, 29, 54, 82, 130, 186, 259

Verband katholischer Gesellenvereine
   23, 28–31, 41, 61, 70
Verband katholischer Industriellen und Arbeiterfreunde   86
Verein Volkswohl of Dresden   188 n.17
Verein zur Verbesserung der Arbeiterwohnungen (Organization for the Betterment of Workers' Housing)   82
Volkshäuser   5, 176–8
Volksküchen   43–4, 145, 149–57, 173, 179–80, 184, 214–16
von Bismarck, Otto   26, 30
von Goethe, Johann Wolfgang   24
von Kleist-Retzow, Hans   34
von Leixner, Otto   150–1
von Sybel, Heinrich   33

Wagner, Martin   178
Wagner, Richard   56
Wallot, Paul   161
warm kitchen   140
Weberplatz Ledigenheim   152–5, 160–1, 168, 227–8, 247
Weimar Republic, housing in   18 n.22
Wettstein-Adelt, Minna   205
White, Allon   201
Wiedfeldt, R.   116, 137
Wiener Café   150–1
"wild" lodging   25
Wirtschaftlokal; see Volksküche

Woman and Socialism (Bebel)   202
women
   clubs for   205–6
   educational opportunities for   203
   household, management of   202
   Ledigenheime for   204, 240–1
      general characteristics   210–13
      lower-middle-class   213–26
      professionals   227–36
      purpose of   204–10
      radicalism, links to   236–40
      reform   217–26
      skilled working-class   213–26
   nineteenth-century   201–2
   professional   227–36
   surplus   201–2, 207
   working-class   201–10, 213–26
working-class
   housing   3, 130–4 (*see also* reform Ledigenheime)
   Ledigenheime and   9, 130–1 (*see also* Ledigenheime)
   life   2–3, 131
   mothers   3
   women   9, 201–10, 213–26

YMCA buildings for American manhood   20 n.40

Zentral-Dombauverein   31
Zentralstelle   127
Zetkin, Clara   142, 202
Zimmerherrn   92, 205
Zimmerherr/Zimmermieter   127
"Zur Weihe des Grundsteins" (Fuchs)   1